Praise for *Trump and Political Philosophy*

"Bringing the wisdom contained within the history of political philosophy to bear on the shocking events of the past few years, these essays give us what we need most of all: illumination in place of obfuscation."
—Damon Linker, *Senior Correspondent, The Week*

"Anyone who believes that philosophy has the ability and responsibility to reflect upon the concerns of the present will find these volumes utterly compelling."
—Jeffrey Bernstein, *Professor, Philosophy, College of the Holy Cross, USA*

"Certainly we have had a plethora of books speaking about the rise of Trump... but there is nothing from this timeless perspective."
—Bryan Paul-Frost, *Associate Professor, Political Science, The University of Louisiana at Lafayette, USA*

D1601093

Marc Benjamin Sable
Angel Jaramillo Torres
Editors

Trump and Political Philosophy

Patriotism, Cosmopolitanism, and Civic Virtue

Editors
Marc Benjamin Sable
Universidad Iberoamericana
Mexico City, Mexico
Universidad de las Americas
Mexico City, Mexico

Angel Jaramillo Torres
National Autonomous University
of Mexico
Ciudad de México, Distrito Federal
Mexico

ISBN 978-3-030-08990-0   ISBN 978-3-319-74427-8   (eBook)
https://doi.org/10.1007/978-3-319-74427-8

Cover illustration: Donald Trump © Lorie Shaull The Noun Project
Cover Design by Fatima Jamadar

This Palgrave Macmillan imprint is published by the registered company Springer International Publishing AG part of Springer Nature.
The registered company address is: Gewerbestrasse 11, 6330 Cham, Switzerland

To our parents,
Socorro Torres Garduño and Angel Jaramillo Mendoza
and
Twyla Silverstein Sable and Robert Gerald Sable,
to whom we each owe so much.

PREFACE

To edit a volume compiling essays on the hypothetical opinions of classical and modern philosophers on the 45th Presidency of the United States is undoubtedly a challenge.

The predicament is compounded by the inescapable fact that Donald Trump is unlikely to be interested in philosophy. According to his own public testimonies, his favorite books are the Bible and *The Art of the Deal*—not necessarily in that order. But perhaps this book will find a place on the bookshelves of citizens interested in the fate of American democracy, and more generally the world they are living in as the twentieth-first century approaches its third decade.

Following a venerable tradition, we have divided this volume into three parts: Classical Political Thought, Modern and Liberal Thought, and Continental Perspectives.[1] We believe that the quarrel between ancient and moderns can help us to better understand the themes of patriotism, cosmopolitanism and civic virtue—themes critical for the America which has witnessed the rise of Trump. Political philosophy is, among other things, a meditation about the nature of justice and the character of citizens, both universally and in the particular case.

It should be noted that this book has a companion volume, *Trump and Political Philosophy: Leadership, Statesmanship and Tyranny*, and the project was original intended as a single volume. If the reader finds some great thinker or political stance lacking here, we hope that they will look there for insights.

This collection is undoubtedly diverse, not only in terms of the thinkers with whom our contributors engage, but in their politics. We have included authors who believe, explicitly or implicitly, that Donald Trump lacks the moral, political, and technical capacities to govern the United States. But we have decided to give voice as well to those who are optimistic about Trump and believe that he deserves a chance to demonstrate that he can deliver the goods.

Our decision is likely not to garner much assent from either side of the political spectrum, but since this book is written from the point of view of philosophy, we think that dogmatism is the most perfidious of intellectual vices. All in all, we subscribe to the Socratic injunction that one is an educated person to the extent one knows one's ignorance. Moreover, it is our conviction that the strengthening of the public sphere needs an open and non-dogmatic discussion of ideas about what Trump's surprising electoral victory means. If, as several of contributors point out, the dangers of the present political landscape stem from our inability to rationally discuss the great issues of our time—since we are more comfortable arguing with the like-minded—we hope that to foster a dialog across political divides that can improve the quality of American democracy.

Of course, this book cannot provide all the insights of the philosophers might bring to bear on contemporary politics, or even just Trump, even taken together with its companion volume. But like the proverbial exiled poet, we have launched this book like a bottle thrown into the sea. We hope some fishermen in search of human messages will take it up and read it. Perhaps it can help them to find their bearings amidst a troubled moment in the American political landscape.

NOTE

1. The term "liberal" is not used here in the typical contemporary American political sense, i.e., in opposition to postwar conservatism. We use the term "liberal" to refer to all those political philosophies and ideologies which place an emphasis of formal, legal freedom, and the constitutional orders which support it. Our use of the term does not entail any particular stance as to the proper role of government in regulation of business, about which our contributors disagree, i.e., some of them are liberal, some conservative, and some radical in the conventional terminology of American politics. Depending on context, "neoliberal" might refer to a general acceptance of free markets, which has dominated thinking worldwide since the 1980s, or it might refer to the specific position represented by the Clintons' reformist politics within the broad parameters of contemporary corporate capitalism.

ACKNOWLEDGMENTS

A project like this—which we count as including its sister volume, *Trump and Political Philosophy: Leadership, Statesmanship and Tyranny*—necessarily generates different sorts of debts than a work consisting of a single argument authored by a single scholar. These are the debts of friendship, in the broad sense of the Greek word, philia. We are indebted in three ways: institutionally, professionally and personally.

First, we thank the organizations which facilitated this project: The Northeastern Political Science Association (NPSA), where we organized the first "Trump in the Face of Political Philosophy" panels that took place three days after the 2016 presidential election. We thank the NPSA also for the two roundtables based on essays in this book, one year later, and, more generally, as a forum where we met many of the contributors. The Association for Core Texts and Courses was also an excellent venue, where in the spring of 2017 we met a number of the contributors to this volume, who have quickly become friends.

In addition, Angel Jaramillo was able to work on this project thanks to a postdoctoral fellowship provided by CONACYT (Mexico's equivalent of the National Science Foundation.) He was able to work on this project as part of a postdoctoral position at the Coordinación de Estudios de Posgrado at UNAM. He wishes thus to thank the coordinator in the area of philosophy at that time, Leticia Flores Farfán.

Second, there are also numerous individuals who facilitated this project, by helping to foster the conversation that we hope these two books constitute. We owe particular thanks to Nathan Tarcov of the University of Chicago, Richard Velkley of Tulane University, Joshua Parens of the

University of Dallas, William Kristol of the Weekly Standard, and Jeffrey Bernstein of the College of the Holy Cross. Although none contributed essays, each made suggestions for inclusions in the volume and generously put us in contact with scholars who did participate. Three others who did contribute essays—Catherine Zuckert, Susan Shell and Gladden Pappin—also helped us to identify scholars whose essays likewise grace this volume.

Above all, this project would have been impossible without the scholars who wrote essays for this book, and its sister volume. We believe their essays exhibit not only a very high quality of scholarship, but also a seriousness about politics. More prosaically, they were patient with two editors who learned "on the job" how to manage an intellectual project with thirty-seven contributors. Moreover, they were fine colleagues, responding to comments on drafts and providing materials in a prompt fashion. We thank them all.

We are, of course, grateful to the staff at Palgrave Macmillan, especially Michelle Chen and John Stegner who helped these novice co-editors through the process of turning a collection of essays into a finished manuscript. We are also highly appreciative of the Palgrave team for the striking cover designs. A thanks is also due to Chris Robinson, no longer at Palgrave, who first suggested that we turn two academic conference panels into a book-length project.

Finally, we wish to thank our teachers. In the case of Marc Sable, these include, especially, Amy Kass, David Greenstone, Susanne Rudolph, David Smigelskis and William Sewell, Jr. In the case of Angel Jaramillo, these include particularly, Rafael Segovia, James Miller, Heinrich Meier and Christopher Hitchens. Like the vast majority of human beings, our first teachers were our parents. We thank them, for helping us to become the people we are, and for their support, both emotional and material, which has enabled us both to become scholars and to bring this project to completion.

CONTENTS

LIST OF CONTRIBUTORS

Faisal Baluch is Assistant Professor of Political Science at the College of the Holy Cross. He received his Ph.D. in political theory from the University of Notre Dame with a dissertation on Machiavelli. At the University of Notre Dame he was a Loescher Teaching Fellow and an editorial intern at the *Review of Politics*. Faisal is a broadly trained political theorist with a particular interest in ancient, early modern and contemporary political thought. He has published on Arendt and Heidegger, and is currently working on a book-length study of Machiavelli's *Florentine Histories*. He has taught a number of courses at the University of Notre Dame and the College of the Holy Cross, including introduction to political theory, politics and literature, and a course on the Arab Spring.

Robert J. Burton is a Ph.D. student in Political Science at the University of Notre Dame. Within the fields of political and legal theory, his research focuses on the relationship between religion, law, and liberalism. He also conducts research in American political thought, particularly the American Founding. He received his M.A. in Political Science from the University of Notre Dame and a B.A. in English Literature and Politics from Southern Virginia University. Mr. Burton currently serves as an editorial intern at *American Political Thought*.

Christopher A. Colmo is Professor of Political Science and former chair of the Department of Political Science at Dominican University, where he teaches courses on philosophy of law, Gandhi and the Western classics, Latin American political thought, women in political philosophy and contemporary political thought. In 2015–2016 he was the President's Distinguished Service Professor at Dominican University. He is the author of *Breaking with Athens: Alfarabi as Founder* and has published in the Review of Politics and the American Political Science Review

Maira Colín García is a scholar and writer based in Mexico City. She has won several prizes for her writing, including the XVIII Timón de Oro Literary Contest for Prose and Poetry, the 2014 José Revueltas National Prize for Political Essays, and the 2017 Bartolomé Delgado de León National Prize for Poetry. She has published several books of children's literature and short stories, and collaborated in more than half a dozen anthologies. She was a fellow of the Fund for Culture and the Arts in the novel genre in Mexico. *Emergency Exit* (La Cifra Editorial, 2016) was her first novel. She is currently a doctoral student in Modern Literature at the Universidad Iberoamericana in Mexico City. She has participated in national and international conferences, in which she has presented her doctoral research, which includes authors such as Gilles Deleuze and Judith Butler. She currently works on the concepts of body, identity, community, and posthumanism.

Zachary K. German is Assistant Professor in the School of Civic and Economic Thought and Leadership at Arizona State University, where he teaches American political thought and constitutionalism. He received his Ph.D. in Political Science from the University of Notre Dame, specializing in Constitutional Studies and Political Theory. His research includes work on American political thought, constitutional interpretation, statesmanship, religion and politics, politics and culture, Montesquieu, and Tocqueville. His current book project compares the thought of Montesquieu, the Federalists, and the Anti-Federalists, concerning the relationship between institutional design, the character of a people, and social and cultural factors.

Aaron Harper is Assistant Professor of Philosophy at West Liberty University. He has published on Nietzsche in *The Journal of Nietzsche Studies* and *The Journal of Value Inquiry*. His other research interests include ethics, political and legal theory, ancient philosophy, and philosophy of sport.

Carson Holloway is a professor of political science at the University of Nebraska at Omaha and a visiting scholar at the Heritage Foundation's B. Kenneth Simon Center for Principles and Politics. His books include

All Shook Up: Music, Passion, and Politics, The Right Darwin: Evolution, Religion, and the Future of Democracy, and *The Way of Life: John Paul II and the Challenge of Liberal Modernity*. His most recent book is a study of American political thought: *Hamilton versus Jefferson in the Washington Administration: Completing the Founding or Betraying the Founding?* (Cambridge University Press, 2015). He has been a Visiting Fellow in Princeton University's James Madison Program in American Ideals and Institutions and a Visiting Fellow in American Political Thought at the Heritage Foundation. His scholarly articles have appeared in the *Review of Politics, Interpretation: A Journal of Political Philosophy*, and *Perspectives on Political Science*, and he has written more popular articles for *First Things, Public Discourse, National Review*, and *The Federalist*.

Douglas Jarvis currently teaches Canadian Politics at Lakehead University. He has also taught history of modern political philosophy at Carleton University. His current research interests are comparative North American studies in political thought, constitutional development, and literary culture. He has published in the *American Review of Canadian Studies* on the inter-relationship between antebellum Southern political thought and Canadian constitutional development. His doctoral thesis, which was completed at Carleton University, was entitled *The Family and the Western Political Order*. This dissertation explored the anthropological relationship between family structure transitions and political organization of the Western nation-state. During his dissertation, he published in the *Journal of Family History* on the relevance of Aristotle and Hegel in determining the core differences between traditional agrarian families and modern nuclear families in defining political citizenship. He is a recipient of the Rt. Hon. Lester B. Pearson Award of Excellence in Canadian Studies.

Julius Krein is the editor of *American Affairs*, a journal of public policy and political thought, and a consultant to institutional investors. He is a graduate of Harvard College.

Douglas Kries is Professor of Philosophy at Gonzaga University where he teaches political philosophy and ethics. He is the author of *The Problem of Natural Law* (Lexington Books, 2007). He has published essays on Aristotle, Augustine, Aquinas and Tocqueville, among others. He has a particular interest in civil religion. He is the co-editor and co-translator (with Ernest Fortin and Michael Tkacz) of *Augustine: Political Writings*

(Hackett Publishing, 1994). With Joshua Parens and Joseph Macfarland, he received an National Endowment for the Humanities grant to conduct a 2014 Summer Institute for College and University Teachers at Gonzaga, titled "Medieval Political Philosophy: Islamic, Jewish, and Christian."

Claudia Leeb is Assistant Professor in political theory at Washington State University. She is the author of *The Politics of Repressed Guilt: The Tragedy of Austrian Silence* (2018), *Power and Feminist Agency in Capitalism: Toward a New Theory of the Political Subject* (2017), *Working-Class Women in Elite Academia: A Philosophical Inquiry* (2004), and *Die Zerstörung des Mythos von der Friedfertigen Frau* (1998). Her works have been published in *Political Theory*, *Theory & Event*, *Perspectives on Politics*, *Contemporary Political Theory*, *Constellations*, *Social Philosophy Today*, *The Good Society*, *Philosophy & Social Criticism* and *Radical Philosophy Review*. She has also contributed several book chapters to anthologies on early Frankfurt School critical theory.

Marc Benjamin Sable taught political science at Bethany College in West Virginia for ten years; since 2016 he has taught at Universidad de las Américas and Universidad Iberoamericana in Mexico City. He earned his Ph.D. from the University of Chicago in 1997 with specializations in comparative politics, American politics, and political theory. He was a 1993–94 Fulbright grantee in Cairo, Egypt, and a 2014 NEH Summer Institute Participant. His research has focused on Abraham Lincoln, American political thought, and Aristotle, and is currently in the final stages of a book manuscript entitled, "Lincoln's Virtues and Aristotle's Ethics." He has served at the Northeastern Political Science Association, as section coordinator for Continental Political Thought and Modern Political Thought and on the General Council. In 2016–2017 he was Visiting Researcher at the Institute for Philosophical Research of the National Autonomous University of Mexico, where he prepared a translation and analytic essay on Carlos Sigüenza y Góngora's *Theater of Political Virtues*.

Adam Adatto Sandel is Lecturer on Social Studies at Harvard University. A graduate of Harvard College with a D.Phil. from Oxford University, he is the author of *The Place of Prejudice: A Case for Reasoning within the World*, published by Harvard University Press.

Eric Schaaf is Assistant Professor of Philosophy at Lincoln College. His interests center on Nietzsche, Rousseau and moral psychology. He received his Ph.D. from the University of Illinois at Urbana-Champaign and has taught at Illinois State University.

Susan Meld Shell is Professor, and currently Chair, of Political Science at Boston College. She is the author of *Kant and the Limits of Autonomy* (Harvard University Press, 2009), *The Embodiment of Reason: Kant on Spirit, Generation and Community* (University of Chicago Press, 1996), *The Rights of Reason: A Study of Kant's Philosophy and Politics* (University of Toronto Press, 1980). She is also the co-editor (with Robert Faulkner) of *America at Risk. Threats to Liberal Self-Government in an Age of Uncertainty* (University of Michigan Press, 2009) She has also written on Rousseau, German Idealism, and selected areas of public policy. She has been a Visiting Professor at Harvard University, and received fellowships from The National Endowment for the Humanities, The American Council of Learned Societies, The Bradley Foundation, the Deutsche Akademische Austauschdienst and the Radcliffe Institute.

Mark Shiffman is Chair of the Department of Humanities at Villanova University, specializing in philosophy, political theory and classical studies. He has published articles on such authors as Plato, Aristotle, Virgil and Plutarch, and he is the translator of Aristotle's *De Anima* (Hackett). He received his B.A. from St. John's College (Annapolis) and his M.A. and Ph.D. from the University of Chicago's Committee on Social Thought, and has taught at the University of Chicago, University of Pennsylvania, Brooklyn College and the University of Notre Dame. He serves on the editorial board of *Communio: International Catholic Review*, and has published in journals such as *Perspectives on Political Science*, *Polis*, and *First Things*.

Cole Simmons is an advanced doctoral candidate at the University of Dallas. His dissertation is on Locke's *A Letter Concerning Toleration*. He is currently working on a chapter examining the role of gratitude in American constitutionalism and an article on the origin of Socrates' marriage to Xanthippe. He has held fellowships with the Ernest L. Fortin and Donald Rumsfeld foundations.

Kevin Slack is Assistant Professor of Politics at Hillsdale College. He has published articles on Benjamin Franklin in *American Political Thought*, the *New England Quarterly* and *Pennsylvania Magazine of History and*

Biography. His book, *Benjamin Franklin, Natural Right, and the Art of Virtue*, was published by the University of Rochester Press in 2017. He also has published articles, and is completing a book manuscript, on post-1960s progressivism.

Angel Jaramillo Torres is currently Postdoctoral Fellow at Universidad Nacional Autónoma de México (UNAM). He has been a journalist, essayist, editor, speechwriter, public servant, consultant and academic. He holds a B.A. in International Relations for El Colegio de México, an M.A. and Ph.D. in Political Science for The New School for Social Research in New York, and was a DAAD fellow at the Ludwig-Maximilians-Universität München. He has taught at CUNY (York College and City College) and UNAM. He has worked for the Mexican government as foreign policy analyst and speechwriter. His journalistic pieces have appeared in several outlets in Spanish and English. He is the author of *Leo Strauss on Nietzsche's Thrasymachean-Dionysian Socrates: Philosophy, Politics, Science, and Religion in the Modern Age* (2017).

Ericka Tucker is Assistant Professor of Philosophy at Marquette University in Milwaukee, Wisconsin. Her work focuses on the concept of power in early modern political thought and contemporary social, legal and political philosophy. She is particularly interested in the relation between developments in the science and philosophy of mind and social and political questions. She is the author of several articles on Spinoza, Hobbes and political philosophy and is working on a book manuscript entitled: *Absolute Democracy: Spinoza's Theory of Power.*

Jean M. Yarbrough is Professor of Government and Gary M. Pendy, Sr. Professor of Social Sciences, with teaching responsibilities in political philosophy and American Political Thought. She has twice received fellowships from the National Endowment for the Humanities, first in 1983–84, when she was named a Bicentennial Fellow and again in 2005–2006, under a "We the People" initiative. She is the author of *American Virtues: Thomas Jefferson on the Character of a Free People* (Kansas, 1998) and more recently, has edited *The Essential Jefferson* (Hackett, 2006).

Catherine Zuckert is Nancy Reeves Dreux Professor of Political Science at the University of Notre Dame and currently serves as Editor-in-Chief of *The Review of Politics*. Her book *Natural Right and the American Imagination: Political Philosophy in Novel Form* won the Professional and Scholarly Publishing Award for the best book written in philosophy and religion by the American Association of Publishers in 1990. *Understanding the Political Spirit: From Socrates to Nietzsche*, edited by Zuckert, received a Choice award as one of the best books published in political theory in 1989. *Plato's Philosophers: The Coherence of Dialogues* received the R. Hawkins Award for the Best Scholarly Book Published in 2009 (in any or all fields). It also received an award for "Excellence in the Humanities", the Best Book Published in Philosophy, and Outstanding Academic Title, *Choice*, 2009. Her most recent book is *Machiavelli's Politics* (University of Chicago Press, May 2017).

Michael P. Zuckert is the Nancy R. Dreux Professor of Political Science at the University of Notre Dame. He works in the two fields of Political Theory and Constitutional Studies, in both of which he has published extensively. He has published *Natural Rights and the New Republicanism*, *The Natural Rights Republic*, *Launching Liberalism*, and (with Catherine Zuckert) *The Truth About Leo Strauss* and *Leo Strauss and the Problem of Political Philosophy*, in addition to many articles. He has also edited (with Derek Webb) *The Antifederal Writings of the Melancton Smith Circle*. He is currently completing *Natural Rights and the New Constitutionalism*, a study of American constitutionalism in theoretical context.

CHAPTER 1

Patriotism, Cosmopolitanism and Civic Virtue: Trumpians and Trumpism

Marc Benjamin Sable and Angel Jaramillo Torres

This volume gathers together a set of essays which, like its companion volume, *Trump and Political Philosophy: Leadership, Statesmanship and Tyranny*, seeks to make sense of contemporary politics through the works of many of the greatest political thinkers. Although the essays here are arranged chronologically and grouped by time period, it may be approached thematically. The purpose of this introduction is to explain how the reader may do just that.

This collection focuses on the socio-political context surrounding Trump, rather than on the man and his tactics. Principally, its questions revolve around the relationship between national interest and universal moral norms, their relationship to the character of good citizens, and the actual quality of citizenship in the United States today. By patriotism, we understand devotion to one's country; in modernity this means devotion to a nation-state. By cosmopolitanism, we refer to a commitment to universal norms which

M. B. Sable (✉)
Universidad Iberoamericana, Mexico City, Mexico

Universidad de las Americas, Mexico City, Mexico

A. J. Torres
Universidad Nacional Autónoma de México, Ciudad de México, México

© The Author(s) 2018
M. B. Sable, A. J. Torres (eds.), *Trump and Political Philosophy*,
https://doi.org/10.1007/978-3-319-74427-8_1

1

transcend national allegiance and entail a willingness to subordinate devotion to one's own to those norms. And by civic virtue, we refer to the qualities needed by citizens to sustain the polity, whether these are grounded in universal norms or specific commitments to their particular communities. Thus it can be argued that civic virtue is the term which mediates patriotism and cosmopolitanism, defining their normative and practical limits.

Prominent in this volume are three contemporary questions: Why did (some) voters support Trump? Is there a Trumpian ideology, and if so, what is it? And how do the motivations of Trump supporters connect with the values implicit in the Trump agenda? In short, our contributors seek to understand what makes a Trumpian, what "Trumpism" is, and why Trumpians support Trumpism. Underlying these concerns are themes which literally define the volume: What does patriotism mean in a globalized world? To what extent does Trump's rise force us to question the relationship between one's own and the universal values? And finally, what kind of people supported Trump—does their support indicate civic health or political decay?

Underlying the essays in this volume is the assumption that the values Trump represents are at best implicit. During the campaign this was reflected in the commonplace that one should take Trump seriously, but not literally. Certainly Trump and his "movement" cry out for explication, by both defenders and critics—as indicated by debates about the importance to his campaign of working class resentment, political correctness, racism and foreign policy (including free trade). Our contributors take this interpretive task a step farther, connecting explanations of Trumpism to debates about the ends of the state and interpretations of Trumpians in terms of human nature.

The essays approach these questions from two broad perspectives. On the one side are analyses of the rise of Trump, which posit essentially rational motivations and account for Trump's support as a reasonable response to threats to the American way, however conceived. These chapters explain support for Trump by articulating something we might call "Trumpism." On the other side are contributors who provide interpretations of Trump supporters which explain their support in terms of subrational features, broadly conceived, with reference to their passions, their presumptions or the features of democratic discourse itself. These chapters are essentially interpretations of "Trumpians," i.e., those who support Trump's policies, either particularly or generally, and hope for the success of his administration.

Naturally, many accounts here combine features of both. These emphasize the elements of political culture and institutional features which facilitate or impede rational deliberation by the people, an issue most salient to those who oppose Trump either due to his character or his politics.

A RATIONALIZED TRUMPISM

In the first category—interpretations which account for Trump's rise by means of a rationalized Trumpism—we can include the essays by Carson Holloway, Douglas Kries, Kevin Slack, Cole Simmons, Jean Yarbrough, and Julius Krein and Adam Adatto Sandel. Each of these essays, either directly or indirectly, explains Trump's support as a defense of values central to the political thought of the thinkers examined, be it Aristotle, St. Thomas Aquinas, Thomas Hobbes, John Locke, Alexis de Tocqueville or G.F.W. Hegel. Although these essays are not necessarily unalloyed in their defense of "Trumpism," they tend to put the best face on Trumpian politics and to see Trump supporters in a positive light. "Trumpians" are seen as citizens with fundamentally rational motives for supporting the man.

Given that Aristotle was the founder of political science, it is appropriate that Carson Holloway shows how Aristotelian political science can be applied to contemporary U.S. politics. Holloway deploys the framework of the *Politics*, and in particular its analysis of factional conflict, to explain Trump's surprising electoral victory. Central to this analysis are disagreements between the many and the few over the nature of justice. For Holloway, Trump's rhetoric is an explicit appeal to the many, identified as "the people—or at least to the sense of an electorally decisive part of the people," and, in particular as the white working class. As he presents Aristotle's teaching in *Politics* Book V, factions form because groups of citizens disagree on the meaning of justice, specifically, what constitutes the equality that should define fair treatment, above all with respect to the goods of honor and wealth. Trump's populism is thus a successful appeal to the many, who demand that the few give their concerns equal weight. For Holloway, the core of Trump's appeal was giving voice to a demand for economic security and linking this demand to issues of trade and immigration. Although the demand was in the first instance for a fair share of economic goods, Holloway points out that having this demand recognized was also a call for respect by the white working class. Reasonable resentment by the many is thus seen as the root of Trump's surprising electoral victory. However, a caveat is in order. Although Aristotle's political science is rooted in the idea of justice, the very term faction is critical—as in the famous definition offered by Madison in *Federalist* No. 10. Like Madison, Aristotle held that no one section of the body politic has a complete or true conception of justice. Thus, while Holloway does not state so explicitly, Trump's appeal cannot be based on justice per se.

Aristotle's notion of natural right was elaborated and given more definite content in St. Thomas Aquinas' idea of natural law, which is at the center of Douglas Kries' chapter on "Thomism and Trumpism." Kries offers a Thomistic analysis of Trump's supporters in two ways: first, by providing an interpretation of how Trump's program might plausibly accord with the teaching of Thomas; second, by showing how Thomas might explain the personal appeal of Trump to decent citizens. In the first part of his essay, Kries argues that one could see economic nationalism, "America First," and fears about immigration as expressing a positive attachment to one's own *patria*, rather than as hatred of the other. This patriotism, which he argues typifies many Trump supporters, especially in less globalized places, is in accord with Thomistic teaching, because while natural law defines the universal moral standard in the concrete instance these standards are rightly informed by myriad local conditions. In the second part of his essay, Kries argues that while opposition to a neglect of the local explains rejection of Clinton, Trump was preferred over his Republican primary opponents on the basis of personality traits that might seem to fit Thomistic notions of virtue. Thus, Thomas considered courage and prudence essential virtues for political leadership, and Trump's supporters saw fortitude in his combativeness and prudence in his business success. Admitting that Trump exhibits little in the way of temperance, magnanimity or the theological virtues, Kries concludes that we ought not seek to identify Thomistic political principles too closely with Trump's electoral success.

Perhaps no thinker differed more in temperament and foundational principles from St. Thomas Aquinas than Thomas Hobbes. Kevin Slack's chapter suggests that the egoistic motivations that define human nature, for Hobbes, can be used to explain the rise of Trump. In good Hobbesian fashion, Slack proceeds deductively. He lays out Hobbes' conception of the fundamental human drives—security, prosperity, and honor—and shows how, for Hobbes, the state arises to guarantee physical safety and security of property, then distributes honors to secure the state. Whenever any state fails to effect these guarantees, human beings feel thrown back into natural anarchy, the war of all against all. Slack argues that in our contemporary, globalized world, many Americans feel that these basic needs have not been met. Specifically, Trump's campaign relied on fears for physical safety, due to violent crime and political violence, and fears of downward economic mobility, attributed to free trade and competition from cheaper immigrant labor. Moreover, elementary problems, such as maintaining infrastructure, are neglected. Under such conditions, he argues people naturally desire a new sovereign, and since Slack's Hobbes is a classical liberal, this desire is rightly expressed in the ballot box. This analysis draws heavily on Parts I and II of *Leviathan,* but Slack adds one other dimension to his interpretation of contemporary politics, placing considerable emphasis on the less familiar Part IV, "Of the Kingdom of Darkness." In that section of *Leviathan,* Hobbes explains the obstacles to a true knowledge of political affairs, or why the body politic becomes diseased. Hobbes cites three sources: theologians, lawyers and philosophers, each of whom holds power over the people, achieving authority through the use of superstition. Slack identifies these superstitions in today's world with the growth of bureaucracy—which empowers lawyers through excessive, arbitrary and arcane regulations—and the pieties of political correctness, which in the media and the contemporary university he believes stifle rational discussion. He concludes with Hobbesian warnings to both political parties that political success depends on results and realism— that Republicans must deliver widely distributed economic growth and forego imperialism, while Democrats must be wary of excessive bureaucracy and the loss of national sovereignty.

The next great English political thinker after Hobbes is certainly John Locke. Cole Simmons' essay explores two themes within Locke's philosophy: political economy and prudence. By examining writings besides his most famous work, the *Second Treatise on Government,* Simmons offers both a subtle reading of both Locke's political thought and a guardedly conservative interpretation of Trump, because his Locke offers both comfort and criticism to Trumpian politics. He addresses two dimensions of the "Make America Great Again program": protectionism (with a sidebar on the welfare state and business regulation) and immigration. Locke's principles of political economy agree with the laissez-faire dimension of Trump's platform. At the same time, Locke's political economy is inconsistent with Trump's protectionism, and generally with his anti-immigration stance, although Locke would not necessarily criticize Trump's concerns about foreign allegiance as exhibited in the so-called Muslim ban.

In "Tocqueville's Great Party Politics and the Election of Donald Trump," Jean Yarbrough takes her bearings from Tocqueville's chief work on America's political, social, and spiritual condition: *Democracy in America.* At the start of her essay, she notes the ways in which Tocqueville would have been appalled at Trump's vulgarity and baseness, but the rest of her essay lays out the many ways in which Tocqueville would have agreed with Trump's political platform. She argues that Tocqueville held that a nation needs to cultivate its own particular identity, and thus that the United States should do so, while at the same time welcoming those who are willing and capable of being part of the American project. She then discusses Tocqueville's admiration for American townships and their role in nurturing the capacity for self-government, which she contrasts with the unaccountability of the federal bureaucracy. According to Yarbrough, Trump is attempting to undercut the pernicious growth of the administrative state. She argues that the Progressive era and the New Deal, embracing ideas from Hegel, transformed American government so that it now resembles the European welfare state. This development, Yarbrough argues, has undercut American freedom. Finally, she maintains that Tocqueville would have supported Trump's call for restoring American power and prestige, for greatness is a national project.

In "Uncivil Society: Hegel, Kojève and the Crisis of Political Legitimacy," Sandel and Krein challenge Fukuyama's rendition of Kojève's notion of the end of history. They argue that, far from completing Hegel's odyssey toward absolute freedom, modern society might be moving away from Hegel's vision of a well-ordered modern society. Drawing on his notion of modern ethical life (*Sittlichkeit*), as laid out in his *Philosophy of Right*, the authors argue convincingly that the realms of family and the state have been captured by the realm of civil society. They identify civil society with market capitalism, and identify various examples that support their main assertion. For Sandel and Krein, modern populism—and especially its American variant, the rise of Trump—is a reaction to the conquest of the state and family by civil society, in the form of capitalism. Taking their bearings from Kojève's analysis of authority, the authors suggest that modern society is in crisis because the authority of the father has been practically eliminated, giving rise to the authority of the judge, which is a bourgeois kind of authority. According to the authors, the genius of Trump was that he, perhaps instinctively, understood that a return of the authority of the father was desired by a sizeable part of the American electorate.

PSYCHOLOGIES OF TRUMPIANS

The second category of essays interprets support for Trump as a response to less than fully rational motives. These include the essays by Ericka Tucker, Aaron Harper and Eric Schaaf, Claudia Leeb, and Maira Colín Garcia. These essays use a variety of frameworks—derived from Spinoza,

Nietzsche, the Frankfurt School, and Jacques Deleuze, respectively—to characterize the limits of human reason in politics and how these limits explain support for Trump. On the left there were two main explanations for Trump's surprising electoral victory: working class resentment or enduring white racism, particularly among the less educated and those in rural areas. These essays strive to go beyond that dichotomy, examining questions of identity and the passions. While their assessments of Trump supporters are not wholly negative—indeed these authors often express sympathy for the economic distress which informed the Trump protest vote—they certainly take a critical perspective on Trumpian politics, both in their readings of Trumpian ideology and in the deep motivations of Trumpians.

Ericka Tucker's essay uses Spinoza's political theory to try to understand the relationship between American politics and the passions in the age of Trump. Drawing on Spinoza's analysis of human emotions in his *Ethics*, Tucker's dissection of hope, anger and hatred is well suited to describe the relationship between the multitude and the government in present-day America. Tucker argues that Obama's "audacity of hope" politics was not successful, thus leading to sentiments of resentment and indignation from a large number of American citizens. She hastens to add, however, that, for Spinoza, indignation and hatred diminish the power of a community. While indignation can be useful at times, Trump's politics of hatred and indignation is not a solution to the political problem besetting America today. Tucker offers an alternative—a solution inspired by Spinoza's endorsement of liberal democracy: escaping the politics of hatred entails strengthening American communities and increasing political participation.

Like Spinoza, Friedrich Nietzsche, the great philosopher of postmodernity, emphasized the role of affect in the construction of knowledge. Harper and Schaaf creatively employ three concepts developed by Nietzsche to explain Trump's appeal to his voters: power, resentment, and self-preservation. The authors of this essay take their bearings from Nietzsche's moral psychology. Drawing on Bernard Reginster's interpretation of the will to power, they conclude that many of Trump's behavioral traits are not intended to use power to overcome of resistance. Harper and Schaaf supplement their argument by "appealing to Nietzsche's treatment of the master and slave types." They see Trump following the patterns of the morality of the slave rather than the morality of the master. They argue that, for Nietzsche, the slave, "is not honest with himself; he is poisoned by resentment, cannot forget his enemies, and constructs an imaginary revenge on these enemies." Trump's psychological and behavioral characteristics fit this description, argue Harper and Schaaf. They distinguish this mentality from Nietzsche's idea of *ressentiment*, which they do not think explains well the Trump phenomenon. Still they find a striking similarity between Trump's and Nietzsche's characterization of priests. Like the tyrant described in Plato's *Republic*, both are of privileged birth but "have more in common with the slaves than the masters," i.e., they are slaves to base passions. The same can be said about the 45th President. Finally, they argue that Trump's voters saw in him a manner to preserve themselves as what they are.

In, "A Festival for Frustrated Egos," Claudia Leeb offers an interpretation of the rise of Trump from a critical theory perspective. She notes that the early Frankfurt School—which comprises thinkers such as Adorno, Horkheimer, and Marcuse—"drew on a combination of Freud and Marx to grasp the rise of fascism in Europe and the proto-fascist elements in the United States." Unlike other less careful analysts of the American political scene, Leeb does not commit the blunder of mistaking Trumpism for real fascism. However, she is keenly aware of the fact that a populist movement of the kind Trump triggered can become fascistic in nature. Drawing chiefly on Freudian psychoanalytical categories, Leeb argues that subrational mechanisms explain the appeal of Trump and ultimately his victory in the 2016 Presidential elections. These mechanisms include "ego ideal replacement, idealization in narcissistic love, the liberation from repressions and frustrations, and the displacement of hatred onto vulnerable groups." She ends her essay hoping that Trump supporters might realize that Trump is not the answer to their frustrations, which are mainly caused by the existence of a capitalist economic system and the ideology that supports it.

Maira Colín García's essay employs the thought of the late twentieth century French philosopher, Gilles Deleuze, to interpret Trumpian politics as a struggle to define who counts in American politics. Viewed from the standpoint of Deleuze and his close collaborator, Félix Guattari, the Trump administration looks like an attempt to normalize white Americans, thus placing a wedge between those who belong to America and those who do not. She uses Deleuze's term, "faciality", for this strategy. According to Colín's interpretation, faciality is the process of homogenizing individuals who, at a deeper level, all have heterogeneous identities. Like Foucault, Deleuze is interested in how this process of normalization affects the body. Because the definition of the normal is another way to define the boundaries of community, Trump's characterizations of who real Americans are could thus be characterized (in Aristotelian language) as rhetoric about the nature of citizenship, i.e., as political in both form and substance. At the end of her essay, Colín offers a possible solution to this problem, drawing on Levinas' ethics of the recognition of the other.

CIVIC CULTURE AND POLITICAL INSTITUTIONS

The remainder of the essays presented here combine features of both perspectives, principally by discussing the ways that political institutions and culture affect the capacity of the people to select effective leaders, whether by influencing the content or the intensity of their passions. In this group we can place the essays by Shiffman on Plutarch, those by Catherine Zuckert and Faisal Baluch on Machiavelli, Susan Meld Shell on Immanuel Kant, Douglas Jarvis on Burke, Zachary German, Robert Burton and Michael Zuckert on the Founders, and Angel Jaramillo Torres's essay on the Kojève-Strauss debate.

In "Roman Parallels," Shiffman relies on the didactic biographies of Plutarch to compare America under Trump and Rome under the control of the party of the populares (from which derives the term "populism"). The analogy between the Roman and American republics was one that the founders of the United States certainly had in mind. Drawing on Plutarch's descriptions, Shiffman finds remarkable similarities. According to Shiffman, Trump was able to fill the gap left as the result of the eclipse of the equivalent of the Roman tribunes. Because the House of Representatives, as Shiffman argues, has never really fulfilled the role of serving the interest of the downtrodden, the media has stepped in and has historically taken the side of the underdog. But lately the media has traded in this role for participation in the neoliberal oligarchy's internecine wars. He argues that Trump, perhaps unwittingly, took advantage of this situation and filled the gap. Shiffman traces the long-term causes of Trump's rise to the economic consequences of the postwar era, "the American Century," and compares these to Rome's rise to dominance in the Mediterranean. After the Punic Wars destroyed Carthage, Rome's elites (the equestrians and the patricians) were the winners at the expense of "a distressed and proletarianized Roman and Italian people," triggering the rise of the Gracchi. Likewise, American prosperity after World War II consolidated the power of a few multinational corporations at the expense of the middle class, thereby creating the conditions for what Shiffman calls "a tribunician moment."

Trumpism is the new face of the Tribune who is supposed to watch out for the underdog. The risk here, he alerts us, is that the underdog will most likely present itself as a mob willing to countenance political violence, which would ultimately lead to the suicide of democracy.

Catherine Zuckert draws on another scholar of Roman history, Niccolò Machiavelli, to explain the extent to which the American polity has become corrupted. Zuckert argues that the main cause leading to Trump's victory in the 2016 presidential elections is the corruption the American people have undergone in the last several decades. She takes her understanding of corruption from the treatises and comedies of Machiavelli. Taking issue with some of the intellectuals associated with the *Claremont Review of Books*, she denies that the source of corruption is the elite's construction of an administrative state. Rather, she emphasizes as the chief reason for such corruption the rise of unaccountable political parties, which control the government and the elections, and their dependence upon wealthy donors. Her prescriptions entail a Machiavellian change in modes and orders at the institutional level as a way to thwart the process by which the people become corrupt. Such action need not appear as an all-out revolution. She argues that the way candidates are elected through primaries should be reformed to allow vigorous public deliberation and to take power away from extreme partisans. Her solution, which follows Machiavelli, would be to strengthen political leaders' accountability to the people, the lack of which has produced a disaffected electorate. Although she thinks that Trump is not completely different from recent presidents, she does provide an enumeration of ways in which he has violated traditional limits.

Faisal Baluch offers a contrasting and less sanguine application of Machiavelli to the current American predicament, focusing on the role of honor and wealth in commercial republics. According to Baluch, populism can be explained by two conditions. On one hand, economic inequality, turning a sound republic into a corrupt one, winds up generating the conditions for the rise of a leader or prince who promises to turn things around. On the other, populism is founded on the equality of personal behavior that renders the leader closer to the people. Baluch's close reading of Machiavelli focuses on the difference between ancient Rome and Renaissance Florence. While Rome reached a kind of social stability by dint of giving the plebeians political representation, Florence became easy prey for internecine civil wars between powerful families. In republican Rome, the acquisition of wealth was not regarded as a qualification for exerting power. In Florence, by contrast, both acquisitiveness and economic inequality led to corruption and violence. But Baluch points out that inequality alone is not the great danger to commercial republics such as the United States: He addresses as well the importance of "equality of spirit." He makes his point by discussing Machiavelli's treatment of the politics of founding versus maintaining republics. For Machiavelli, the founder of political regimes acts alone and distances himself from the people, while republics need the gap between rulers and ruled to close. Based on his discussion of Machiavelli, Baluch maintains that in America "increasing economic inequality combined with equality of spirit explains how an individual like Donald Trump can become the candidate of choice for the working class"· his supporters saw in him at once a billionaire who would use his shrewdness to rescue them from economic hardship and a man equal to them in his vulgar behavior and common tastes. To combine these two traits was Trump's stunning appeal. This confluence, Baluch implies, is inevitable in commercial republics.

By elaborating Kant's distinction between active and passive citizenship, Susan Meld Shell complicates the relationship between equality and democracy in order to shed light on the American predicament under Trump. She points out that "Lincoln remains the best weaver of our fundamental national narrative." This original narrative is based upon the idea that "all men are created equal," but it was attacked in the period between his death and the birth of the Civil Rights Movement, when it was reclaimed. Present-day America faces a problem that the ascendancy of Trump to the Presidency has brought to light—the existence of passive (and hence unequal) citizens. Shell finds in Kant a paradigm to show that the state and society as a whole ought to recognize that passive citizenship is perhaps an unavoidable feature of modern societies. She prescribes ways for the state to help passive citizens to strengthen their autonomy and became active citizens. While she recognizes Trump's vices and flaws, she offers a convincing explanation of his rise. Part of such an explanation has to do with the fact that he presented himself as a credible champion of passive citizens. Obviously, however, the ridicule he hurls on political opponents and common citizens shows that he strays far from the Kantian ethical ideal.

In "The Demagoguery of Trump Era Politics and Edmund Burke's Theory of a Generational Compact," Douglas Jarvis investigates how Burkean conservatism can help us to make sense of how the Trump campaign appealed to conservatives, despite its close relationship to "alt-right nihilism." For Jarvis, the "greatest cultural challenge of our time" is to address the problem of potential political violence "fueled through mob anger and exclusionary identity politics." Jarvis argues that the demagoguery of the Trump era is "linked to an emerging new form of conservatism." This new conservatism is at odds with the classical conservatism advanced by the Irish statesman and political theorist, Edmund Burke. Jarvis maintains that the "on-going decay of traditional values" is the cause of the current political turmoil in America. The remedy would be a return to the "foundational values of classical conservatism" as championed by Burke. Specifically, Jarvis sees both 1960s counter-culture and the alt-right as eroding the "Burkean generational compact." Representing the alt-right is Steve Bannon, whose documentary *Generation Zero* receives an outstanding analysis in this essay. More likely than not, Burke would have regarded Bannon as a kind of Jacobin in his destructive intentions. Positioned between the Scylla of the far left's political correctness and the Charybdis of the alt right's demagogy, Burke can help us re-establish the generational compact by teaching us that history is the preceptor of prudence and the idea that there is a "great primeval contract" to keep civilization in motion among across generations. According to Jarvis, Burke's classical conservatism exhibits a humility which moderates both policy ambitions and the treatment of political adversaries, through its call for the toleration of dissent.

German, Burton and Zuckert discuss the political development of the Electoral College, the Constitutional mechanism by which Americans select their chief executive. First they analyze the purposes of the framers of the Republic in designing this mechanism. They conceived an Electoral College that would "refine and enlarge the public views" so that, while guaranteeing a democratic election of the President, it would secure the selection of men "who possess most wisdom to discern, and most virtue to pursue, the common good of the society." For a variety of reasons the scheme changed as the power of parties increased. The authors argue that the filtering function of the Electoral College was then filled *de facto* by the national party conventions. However, according to the authors, fundamental changes took place "in the Progressive Era and were brought to fruition in the Reform Era of the 1970s." The Progressives claimed that the system was not democratic enough and sought to reform it so that open primaries would ultimately decide the outcome, instead of the party conventions. In the 1970s reformers then "institutionalized a direct, democratic nomination vote." The authors argue that this political history has to be studied so that statesmen of the present or the future can envision "republican remedies to counter dangers inherent in republican liberty," i.e., combine democratic accountability with a mechanism to ensure that qualified persons attain the highest office.

In "Nationalism, Universalism and Nihilism," Angel Jaramillo Torres argues, contrary to conventional opinion, "that in their debate on tyranny, Alexandre Kojève and Leo Strauss were only apparently at loggerheads." For Jaramillo, both were "Socratic philosophers" in the sense that they affirm a "vote of ignorance" about the most important issues, and in particular, they have allegiance to no particular regime. In the section devoted to Kojève, Jaramillo argues that the French philosopher was as open to the scenario that history has not ended as he was to the scenario in which history had ended. Jaramillo then analyzes what Kojève would have thought about Trump under both scenarios. He maintains that in his debate with Kojève, Strauss did not take the side of nationalism or patriotism in the modern fashion. Both the nation-state and the universal and homogeneous state are products of modern, technological civilization, and thus face the same problems. Jaramillo argues that Strauss viewed modernity from what he understood was the position of classical political philosophy, and thus would see Trump as having a tyrannical soul, as someone who is fundamentally dangerous to the American republic. Jaramillo ends his essay by suggesting that, despite his qualms about Trump as a person, Strauss might have agreed with national greatness as a political project.

EVALUATING TRUMPISM AND TRUMPIANS

Arguably more important than Trump himself for the future of the American republic—and for understanding democratic governance—is the question of why 46 percent of the voters choose Trump. One way to understand this issue is by focusing on the divide between strictly rational and largely subrational accounts of the decision to vote for Trump. As is clear from our essays here and in the companion volume, the editors are highly skeptical of Trump as a political leader and of the values that are implicit in his platform. We consider it our obligation to lay out the reasons for our skepticism, while acknowledging that many Trump supporters, both those who seek a rational Trumpism and a rational account of Trumpians, do so in good conscience and according to the best lights of their own reason.

As we see it, there are five primary, positive meanings assigned to Trumpism. First, some see Trumpism as an attempt to restore American democracy by destroying the power of an oppressive bureaucracy. Second, Trumpism could also be an attempt to restore the declining fortunes of the American working class. Third, Trumpism can be understood as a call to restore American prestige and power by shedding exploitative international obligations. A fourth is emphasis on civic virtue understood as love of one's own. Finally, it may be conceived as a struggle against the pernicious effect of political correctness. All five together can be seen as means to "Make America Great Again."

Trumpism versus the Administrative State

Of course contemporary American conservatism is defined by its aversion to taxes and government regulation of business. But what distinguishes the critics of the administrative state from generic anti-regulation conservatives is that they are opposed to bureaucratic regulation as such. Among the most passionate academic defenders of Trumpism are some with ties to the Claremont School. They claim that America has departed from its founding principles through the expansion of the administrative state, which they trace to the Progressive movement, and ultimately to Hegelian conceptions of the state.[1] (This point of view is here articulated most strongly in Jean Yarbrough's essay on Tocqueville.) They argue that the American welfare state and regulatory apparatus on big business (which are not usually distinguished) are staffed by unaccountable bureaucrats and thus undemocratic. There is no doubt that the Trump administration has undertaken a sweeping assault on government regulation of corporations.

We are dubious that former industrial workers in Pennsylvania, Ohio, Michigan and Wisconsin voted for Trump because they feared the growth of the administrative state. However, even if one concedes that criticism of the administrative state was the conscious motivation of Trump voters, this would only be a fully *rational* motivation if it were a correct—or at least plausible—interpretation of economic decline and diminished democratic accountability. The empirical question, we think, is easily dispatched. American economic decline, relative to the rest of the world, does not stem from overregulation. First, the U.S. economy is less regulated, and its taxes lower, than its OECD competitors. Second, some of the most innovative and growing sectors are the most regulated, e.g., pharmaceuticals. Third, one would be hard pressed to claim that growth in the technology sector has been hampered by government regulation: we need only mention Google, Apple, and Facebook. The greatest innovative wave in the last 30 years took place not in heavily regulated regimes in Europe, China or Russia, but in free-market America.

In political terms, one can certainly claim that at a certain point the extent of government economic regulation becomes so extensive that it is self-perpetuating. However, this road-to-serfdom sociology ignores the realities of the past forty years, in which we have seen state control of the economy diminish worldwide. This, after all, is the defining feature of economic globalization, at least since the advent of the Washington Consensus. The best proof is the privatization of state owned businesses, in Britain, Germany, Japan, Latin America and Eastern Europe, some dating back to the 1950s, although most since 1980. Likewise, in fiscal affairs, marginal income tax rates in the United States are dramatically lower than they were in the 1950s, being lowered in the early 1960s and again in the early 1980s. If there is a line at which regulation of the economy by democratic governments becomes a permanent feature, the United States has never even come close.

But the administrative state thesis is not mainly concerned with questions of cause and effect in the shadows of political sociology. The burden of their case is that government regulation by trained bureaucrats is, as such, an expression of a set of ideas which are inherently autocratic, collectivist and elitist. Although we agree that large governmental bureaucracies tend to be instruments of elites and can be autocratic, we deny that they are any more collectivist than any other form of government. We criticize the administrative state thesis using the thought of Max Weber, the great scholar of bureaucracy, who understood that bureaucratic rule is not a uniquely governmental problem: bureaucracies permeate all aspects of modern life, including the university, the military and especially economic organization. As Weber points out, modern capitalism has been intensely bureaucratic since the rise of the modern corporation. This flies in the face of the false depiction by conservatives (both Trumpian and not) of government as the sole enemy of freedom.[2] British socialism was not Bolshevism, and Pinochet's Chile was still a tyranny. Moreover, Weber also points out that the growth of bureaucratic organization is a consequence of its greater instrumental effectiveness, and thus a necessary feature of modern life. As believers in the value and possibility of human freedom, we (like Weber) fear that state ownership of the economy is dangerous in that it would eliminate the tensions between competing large bureaucratic organizations—e.g., the modern state and the corporation—and thus consolidate bureaucratic rule, eliminating the possibility of politics that derives from the tensions arising from countervailing powers.[3] That said, practically no one advocates state ownership of industry today. Rather, to turn Weber on his head, we see at least an equal danger coming from unchecked corporate power. As Adatto Sandel and Krein's essay on Hegel points out, if the sphere of the market is left unchecked, the interests and values of the spheres of family and state suffer. The demise of modern liberalism might not begin with a totalizing Hegelian vision of the state. We do not believe that America is on the verge of being trapped in a Weberian iron cage. Although government regulation in some areas may be excessive, the solution is not that America should strive to be a libertarian utopia where all relations among human beings are determined by the market. All in all, some mix of public administration and market forces is healthy. Reasonable people can disagree on precisely what that mix should be, as do the editors themselves.

Trumpism as Economic Populism

The claim that Trumpism is populism is a staple of both the more sophisticated journalistic analysis and several essays by our contributors, e.g., Holloway, Slack, Simmons and Shiffman (here), and by Pappin (in the other volume). Some of these authors merely argue that Trump presented himself as a popular tribune defending workers, but the political question is surely whether he actually *is* such a figure. We believe that Trump's economic program does not, in fact, represent a defense of the Trump swing voter's true interests. On the contrary, the preponderance of his program is not in any way protective of American workers as such. If there is an economic Trumpism, its main features are tax breaks to the wealthy and to corporations at the expense of the middle class, combined with the removal of checks to corporate power. At any rate, this trickle-down economics is not new, for it was fostered by conservative orthodoxy going back to the Reagan administration. Unlike Reagan, however, Trump seems to have outsourced his economic policy to that devotee of Ayn Rand, Republican Speaker of the House Paul Ryan. Finally, as Kevin Slack of Hillsdale College notes in his essay on Hobbes, the American government has over the past several decades failed even in mundane matters, such as maintaining infrastructure. And yet while Trump claimed to be "a builder," and that America needs renewed infrastructure investment, there has as yet been no push for an infrastructure bill.[4]

The obvious Trumpian response is: Trumpist economic populism is expressed in protectionism and restrictions on immigration. Although reasonable people can disagree about the costs and benefits of pre-Trump policies in these areas, characterizing Trumpism as a populism based solely on these two policies rests on a fallacy. There is no proof that foreign trade and competition from immigrant labor is the *main* cause of the decline of the American working class. We can disagree about the extent to which immigration and foreign trade have injured the American working class. We can argue over whether we need more advantageous policies on legal immigration and stricter enforcement against illegal immigration. Even if one concedes that these are serious issues, and that new policies are needed, these leave untouched other more fundamental causes of working class economic decline. Protectionism and immigration restriction could only constitute a true populism if they were together a more or less complete solution to the negative effects of economic globalization. But this is not the case. First, it is not reasonable to believe that free trade agreements are so grossly unfair to the United States, given that the United States has used its unique capacity as the largest economic and military power on the face of the earth to its advantage. Likewise, other factors at least substantially explain working class decline, such as technological innovation, which displaces workers, weak worker bargaining power due to the decline of labor unions, and tax policies which allow the wealthiest to pay less despite increased incomes under globalized capitalism. Finally, if the majority of competition by immigrants affects the lowest paid workers, as seems the case, then immigration only exacerbates declining wages by semi-skilled labor; it does not cause the problems facing the middle class. All of these are questions of prudence. As soon as we began to deliberate over the "*main* cause" of American working class decline we began to think prudentially, because we spoke of contingencies driven by multiple factors, which require judgment about their relative weight and likelihood.

Trumpism and the Decline of American Power and Prestige

When it comes to foreign policy, Trump's rhetoric takes its bearings from the idea that most of the nations of the world are taking advantage of the United States through the use of multilateral agreements and covenants that allegedly lack democratic legitimacy. One would seek in vain in Trump's speeches for a recognition that the international liberal order was essentially the creation of the United States. A case can be made (and has been) that the founders of such an order were not mainly motivated by some kind of disinterested love for humanity, but rather for the American national self-interest. We believe that the Bretton Woods system and other multilateral institutions such as NATO and the United Nations have certainly facilitated American hegemony in the world as well as American economic prosperity and national security. Although some or many features of the international economic and political order need to be reformed, Trump's sole focus on the balance sheet and the pecuniary motive is certainly short-sighted.

Finally, we note that Tony Schwartz, the ghostwriter of *The Art of the Deal*, famously said that in all his conversations with Trump the term "moral" never came up.[5] Although we may still be living in "a Machiavellian age," we are struck by the effect Trump's amorality could have in the international arena. Trump seems unable to distinguish between decent and indecent regimes. We see his inability to evaluate oppressive governments differently from liberal democracies as dangerous for both the world and America.

Civic Virtue, Love of One's Own and Love of the Good

At the heart of debates about Trumpism is the proper relationship between patriotism as love of one's own and some objective definition of the good which transcends the interests and ways of one's own people. We think that Trumpism gets this balance wrong both in universal terms and in specifically American terms.

Of course, Trumpism is sloganized as "Make America Great Again" (MAGA). One way to characterize this slogan is that America has become too cosmopolitan, that Republican and Democratic party elites—as well as a broad section of the Democratic Party base—have come to prefer global over national interests. We think this is a red herring. This is partly because, as we noted above, that love of one's own is natural and it is practiced as a matter of course by all nations of the world. Many supporters of Trump see him as a patriot *precisely because he is anti-cosmopolitan*. MAGA erases the difference between one's own and the good, the true and the beautiful. Rather than the narcissistic impulse of contemplating ourselves, which seems to be the moral motive behind MAGA, we think it would be better to call Americans to strive for more goodness, truth and beauty.

There is something inherently (and paradoxically) cosmopolitan about American nationality. The American idea has always been premised on universal principles, on what Lincoln called both America's "ancient faith" and "a proposition": that all men are created equal. With this in mind, he praised Henry Clay, who "loved his country partly because it was his own country, but mostly because it was a free country; and he burned with a zeal for its advancement, prosperity and glory, because he saw in such, the advancement, prosperity and glory, of human liberty, human right and human nature."[6] The United States since its inception has always in principle been open to the world: At least Jefferson's, Lincoln's, Roosevelt's and Reagan's America always saw itself as representing principles of universal validity, and in that sense, as a cosmopolitan project.

Moreover, we would remind our readers that the distinction between one's own and the objective good is an originary distinction of political philosophy. As Plato makes clear in Book I of the *Republic*, notions of justice based on the friend enemy distinction are logically inconsistent. If one takes as a first principle of action the division of the world into "one's own" and the other, and the corollary distinction between friends and enemies, one has at the outset abandoned philosophy. As Aristotle tells us, the love of truth is more sacred even than friendship.

In Douglas Kies's essay in this volume, he makes the valid point that love of one's own does not entail hatred or disrespect of the other. However, in their pride for their own history, language, mores and institutions, most people find it hard not to look down on others. Given that a defining feature of Trump's rhetoric is insulting others—particularly foreigners and those whose interpretation of America differs from his—at the heart of Trumpism is the privileging of the self-centered or parochial as a matter of principle.

Political Correctness

Supporters of Trump have argued that political correctness in America has gone berserk. To some extent, they have a point. University campuses, the mass media, and the bureaucracy have imposed in some quarters a code of language and behavior that may endanger the sphere of freedom by preemptively censoring debate. However, we do not see a better alternative in the creation of a new culture founded on the values of the bully. Trump repeatedly hurls insults at those who disagree with him. In domestic politics, we think he has been unable to succeed in his main plans because, as a law of human interaction, nobody trades good will for insults. In foreign affairs, Trump's boorish behavior abroad is certainly calculated to intimidate other leaders of the world, believing this might give him an edge over them in future deals. Thus, we wonder if the MAGA mentality requires sacrificing diplomacy for the politics of the bully. Between the Scylla of the imposition of new codes of language based on puritanism and the Charybdis of a rhetoric of resentment, practiced by Trump and his followers, we advocate fostering a culture of reasoned disagreement.

The rhetoric of MAGA and "America First," to the extent that it rests on the legitimate demands of American workers on the American government, is a truism. The question is not whether the U.S. government should negotiate trade agreements which are to the advantage of the U.S. worker, nor whether it should design immigration policies which support major classes of its native-born citizens. Rather, it is whether in fact those agreements and policies do the job, and how important a factor they are in causing or exacerbating the problems facing America's working class. "America First" is a phrase, fundamentally, which implies that previous policies have not merely failed, but that they have betrayed the Americans who have been the losers in globalization. It implies that others have put America second. It is thus a "suicidally apodictic" rhetoric, one designed to close off argument. "America First" thus obscures rather than enlightens. We hope this volume will contribute to the promotion of an enlightened use of public reason.

NOTES

1. They share criticism of the modern state with libertarians, who take their guidance from social choice theory and ultimately from the Austrian School of economics. See F.A. Hayek, *The Road to Serfdom: Text and Documents*, Definitive ed. (New York: University of Chicago Press, 2007).
2. One could argue that the prospect of bankruptcy provides an external check on corporate bureaucratic rule, but this happens extremely rarely to large corporations.
3. This is analogous to Leo Strauss's fear that a single world government would open the way for a more permanent tyranny than had ever existed before.
4. Of course, one could take this simply as evidence that Trump is not serious about policy in general, but that is largely a question of his character as a leader, which is discussed in the other volume.
5. "The word moral never came up during the 18 months that I spent with Donald Trump," Schwartz said. "That was not part of his vocabulary...The idea of moral equivalence, I guarantee you that that phrase is no more than a few days old in Donald Trump's brain." Joe DePaolo, "Art of the Deal

Writer Says Trump Will Resign Before Year's End: Reminds Me of 'Last Days of Nixon'," August 17, 2017. https://www.mediaite.com/online/art-of-the-deal-writer-says-trump-will-resign-before-years-end-reminds-me-of-last-days-of-nixon/. Accessed September 9, 2017.

6. Abraham Lincoln, *The Collected Works of Abraham Lincoln. 9 Volume Set*, ed. Roy Basler (New Brunswick, NJ: Rutgers University Press, 1953), II:126.

List of References

Hayek, F. A. 2007, *The Road to Serfdom: Text and Documents*. Definitive ed. Edited by Bruce Caldwell. Chicago: University of Chicago Press.

Lincoln, Abraham. 1953. *The Collected Works of Abraham Lincoln. 9 Volume Set*. Edited by Roy Basler. New Brunswick: Rutgers University Press.

Marini, John, and Ken Masugi, eds. 2005. *The Progressive Revolution in Politics and Political Science: Transforming the American Regime*. Lanham: Rowman & Littlefield Publishers.

Trump, Donald J., and Tony Schwartz. 2015. *Trump: The Art of the Deal*. Reprint ed. New York: Ballantine Books.

PART I

Classical Political Thought

CHAPTER 2

Aristotle's Account of Factional Conflict and the Rise of Donald Trump

Carson Holloway

The rise of Donald Trump to the presidency of the United States is a remarkable, and even mystifying, event. Before his campaign was launched, practically no one, even among the most expert political analysts, predicted the possibility of such a potent outsider campaign. And after his campaign was launched almost all of the experts predicted, right up to the end, that it would fail.

It was the experts, however, who failed to understand what was happening. This failure of contemporary political expertise invites us to look afield to other sources of wisdom. If we turn to Aristotle's *Politics*, and particularly Book V's treatment of the causes of factional conflict, we find an account of human nature and politics that is of enduring relevance—and that is in fact relevant even to present day presidential politics in the United States of America.

In many obvious ways, America is a vastly different kind of community from the ancient Greek *polis* that was the object of Aristotle's inquiry. Nevertheless, if we examine the 2016 presidential election in light of Aristotle's account of faction, we find that the basic facts of human nature have not

C. Holloway (✉)
University of Nebraska at Omaha, Omaha, NE, USA

The Heritage Foundation, Washington, DC, USA

© The Author(s) 2018
M. B. Sable, A. J. Torres (eds.), *Trump and Political Philosophy*,
https://doi.org/10.1007/978-3-319-74427-8_2

changed in any decisive way. Trump's rise was fueled by recognizable contemporary versions of the very resentments and grievances that Aristotle warned, more than two thousand years ago, cause conflict in a political community: a desire for justice understood as some kind of equality, expectations of prosperity and respectability and the anger that arises when those expectations are frustrated, the inclination of the rich to exploit the poor and of the poor to blame their troubles on the rich, and the rivalries and mutual suspicions between citizens of different ethnicities. By demonstrating the durability of this ancient account of political conflict, the rise of Trump reminds us of Aristotle's just claim to be the true founder of political science.

Inequality as a Cause of Factional Conflict

Aristotle's account of factional conflict may be divided into two parts. In the first part (Book V, chapters 2–4) he deals with the question "in a general way" or, as he says later, in a "simple sense" (1302a17, 1304b17).[1] Here Aristotle considers how the causes of faction operate in "all regimes universally" (1304b6). In the second part (Book V, chapters 5–7) he examines the ways in which faction tends to arise in specific regimes. Aristotle's discussion of the general causes of faction is in turn organized around three issues: first, the "condition" human beings "are in when they engage in factional conflict"; second, the things for the sake of which they pursue such conflict; and third, the "beginning points of political disturbances and factional conflicts among" citizens (1302a18–22).

Aristotle claims that the "condition" human beings are in when they engage in factional conflict has been "spoken of already" (1302a25). Here he refers back to chapter 1 of Book V, which in turn offers a recapitulation of one of the key themes of Book III: Aristotle's examination of the debate between democrats and oligarchs. According to Aristotle's famous theoretical account of politics, virtuous activity is the aim of political life, and therefore the capacity for virtue is the most compelling claim to rule. According to Aristotle's realistic assessment of political life as it ordinarily occurs, however, the virtuous are too few in number to press a claim to rule with any hope of success (1301a39). As a result, politics is usually a contest between the people and the wealthy, each claiming to deserve to rule on the basis of a certain conception of equality and justice.

The people think that because they are equal in one thing, freedom, they ought to be equal in political power. The wealthy think that because they are unequal in one thing, wealth, they ought to be unequal in political power. Aristotle claims that both sides grasp a part of the truth—that justice is proportional equality: equality for those who are equal and inequality for those who are unequal. They err, however, in thinking that the qualities they possess—freedom, wealth—are central to political life as it ought to be and therefore the true claim to rule. But since those who possess the truly relevant quality—virtue—are so rare, politics usually turns out to be a clash between democrats and oligarchs over the proper understanding of equality and inequality.

For Aristotle, then, the "condition" men are in when they engage in factional conflict is a state of dissatisfaction induced by their understanding of justice as equality. "Factional conflict is everywhere the result of inequality   in general it is equality they seek when they engage in factional conflict" (1301b26–29). This striving for equality is most obvious in the factional conflict carried on by the many or the people. They become factious when they believe that they are being held in an inferior position by the wealthy, and they then struggle to secure a measure of equality that they can regard as just. In contrast, the wealthy seem to engage in factional conflict for the sake of inequality: being superior in wealth, and believing wealth to be a just claim to rule, they seek superiority in political power. Nevertheless, even their efforts can be understood, on Aristotle's account, as aiming at a kind of equality, proportional equality: they want their political power to be equal to their wealth.

Thus far, the Trump phenomenon is perfectly intelligible in light of Aristotle's teaching. As a candidate, Trump appealed to—and successfully rode to the presidency—the kind of factious impulses to which the people or the many are ordinarily prone. Trump presented himself as a populist and was so understood by practically everybody, among both his supporters and his critics. He spoke to the sense of the people—or at least to the sense of an electorally decisive part of the people—that they had been held down, kept in an inferior position, and thus denied the equality to which they are entitled. Trump struck this note with his characteristic colorfulness in his acceptance speech at the Republican National Convention: "I have joined the political arena so that the powerful can no longer beat up on people that cannot defend themselves."[2] As the campaign continued, Trump stuck faithfully to this theme, although sometimes presenting it in more refined terms. In his campaign speech at Gettysburg, for example, Trump, echoing President Lincoln, presented his candidacy as an attempt to restore "government of, by, and for the people."[3] Trump again emphasized this theme at the beginning of his inaugural address, where he characterized his elevation to the presidency as not just a transfer of power "from one party to the other," but in fact as a transfer of power from "Washington, D.C." to "the American people."[4]

PROFIT, HONOR, AND FACTIONAL CONFLICT

While the preceding discussion of inequality as a source of faction is fine as far as it goes, it is too abstract to be completely satisfactory. It does not yet reveal the more concrete grievances that drive political discord. Aristotle, then, turns to these in the second part of his discussion of the "general" causes of factional conflict. Here, economic well-being and social status emerge as powerful drivers of faction. The "things over which" men engage in "factional conflict," Aristotle says, "are profit and honor and their opposites" (1302a33).

Here, once again, Aristotle offers a realistic qualification of his more lofty theoretical teaching. In the *Nicomachean Ethics,* Aristotle rejects wealth and honor as candidates for the supreme good toward which all our actions should be directed. Wealth is merely instrumental and not desired for its own sake. And even honor is desired only with a view to something more fundamental, since men want it in order to be reassured of their virtue, which implies that virtue is more truly choice-worthy than honor (1095b23–30, 1096a6–10). Nevertheless, Aristotle's account of faction reminds us that these incomplete goods are precisely the ones over which most political battles are in fact fought.

Once again, we can see that Donald Trump's candidacy both expressed and exploited the kind of factionalism that Aristotle describes. A prominent part of Trump's campaign was his appeal to the economic interest of the voters he was courting. Generally, his rhetoric addressed the concern of many voters that they had not profited from existing public policies, or, indeed, that those policies had been positively detrimental to their economic standing. Thus Trump emphasized the decline of household incomes since the year 2000[5] and contended that the jobs and "wealth of our middle class has been ripped away from their homes."[6]

Moreover, Trump's appeal to the sense of economic insecurity that generates factional conflict was sharpened, and probably made more effective, by the way he linked it to two of his signature campaign issues: trade and immigration. There is, after all, nothing striking or compelling about a presidential candidate who claims to represent the economic aspirations of the American middle class. All presidential candidates make that claim. Trump, however, was able to press this claim more convincingly by relating it to issues that had been largely ignored by other candidates. Trump's critique of free trade is without precedent in American presidential politics over the last twenty-five years. Since the presidency of Bill Clinton, the highest-ranking leaders of both political parties have cooperated in promoting agreements to foster international trade. Other Republican presidential candidates had raised concerns about illegal immigration, but with nothing like the stridency or persistence Trump demonstrated in talking about the issue. And, again, Trump used these issues to speak in concrete terms about the economic interests of voters. In his speech announcing his candidacy, he suggested that many Americans could not get jobs because, as a result of international trade, "China has our jobs and Mexico has our jobs."[7] Similarly, his speech to the Republican National Convention contended that "[d]ecades of record immigration have produced lower wages and higher unemployment for our citizens."[8]

By making such arguments, Trump showed that he had correctly discerned or intuited the concerns of an electorally significant set of voters. Political observers generally agree that a key element of Trump's political success was his appeal to white working class voters not ordinarily drawn to vote for Republican presidential candidates. This view appears to be confirmed by a study conducted by the Public Religion Research Institute, which found that Trump won sixty-four percent of the white working class vote. This same study found, in addition, that these voters felt the sense of economic insecurity that Aristotle teaches makes people ripe for factional conflict and to which Trump appealed in the campaign of 2016. According to the study, these white working class voters are characterized predominantly by a sense of the deterioration of their economic conditions and by skepticism about the American dream (the idea that one can get ahead through hard work).[9]

Furthermore, the voters on whom Trump relied tended to share the diagnosis of the causes of their economic ills that he put forward in promoting his distinctive issues. According to a study by the Voter Survey Group, "[v]oters who experienced increased or continued economic stress were inclined to become more negative about immigration," and those concerned about illegal immigration "were more likely to switch their support from President Obama to Trump."[10] Similarly, the aforementioned PRRI study found that sixty percent of white working class voters believe that "free trade agreements with other countries are mostly harmful because they send jobs overseas and drive down wages."[11]

This brings us to the second of the "things" over which Aristotle says human beings engage in factional conflict: honor and its opposite. As was noted earlier, Trump campaigned as a populist. His pitch was to the people or the many—which is, indeed, in general the only kind of electoral pitch that can work in a democracy. We might doubt whether such a campaign would have room for an appeal to honor or pride. Aristotle suggests in the *Nicomachean Ethics* that it is men of refinement and men of action—not men in general—who are inclined to view honor as the good (1095b23–24). Similarly, Aristotle holds in his account of faction that "the many strive more for profit than for honor" (1318b16–17). It does not follow, however, that the many are utterly unconcerned with honor and dishonor. Aristotle's latter statement, after all, tacitly admits that the many strive to some extent for honor, just not as much as they strive for profit. It is more likely, then, that they experience a kind of pride, but a rather modest version of it. As Aristotle suggests in his discussion of the condition men are in when they engage in factional conflict, the many do not seek superiority but equality. Accordingly, their concern with honor is primarily negative or defensive. They do not ask to be elevated or glorified, but they resist being humiliated or dishonored. They ask only that they be accorded a certain decent minimum of respect, and if that is denied them, they are prone to faction.

In his run for the presidency, Trump exploited this cause of faction as well. He spoke not only to the economic interests but also to the wounded pride of his voters. The two appeals fit together nicely. The country's ruling elites had not only neglected the people's interests, Trump suggested, but had by doing so treated the people as insignificant, their concerns as unworthy of consideration. Over and over again, Trump referred to his followers as America's "forgotten men and women." In his inaugural address he told his voters that, thanks to his victory, "everyone" was now "listening" to them: "You will never be ignored again."[12] Again, these kinds of appeals had real purchase with the voters on whom Trump had to rely to win the presidency. For example, during the Republican primaries, exit polls found that large numbers of Republican voters were not only dissatisfied but also felt angry at and betrayed by their own party's leaders. Not surprisingly, such voters were inclined to seek new leadership from someone who was not an established politician.[13]

There is perhaps one other way worth mentioning in which Trump appealed to some voters' feelings of resentment at being dishonored. Trump presented himself as a promiscuous critic of "political correctness" and as a fearless or heedless violator of its norms. His claims in this regard were indirectly supported even by his most dedicated critics: their condemnations of him for his intemperate remarks tended to confirm his reputation as being indifferent to the demands of politically

correct dialog. Whatever may be intended by those who support political correctness, one of its inevitable consequences is to disrespect or
dishonor certain Americans by teaching them that their opinions are
disreputable, that they should not be expressed, or, if expressed, should
only by ventured with great caution and self-doubt. That subset of voters who felt thus dishonored by the demands of political correctness
probably took a vicarious pleasure in Trump's willingness to flout it and
were likely, in consequence, more inclined to vote for him.

The Beginning Points of Faction: The Many Versus the Few

We now come to the third and final part of Aristotle's "general" account
of faction, his discussion of the "causes and beginning points of the
changes" that lead to factional conflict (1302a33) Several of these are
helpful in understanding the Trump phenomenon.[14]

Aristotle speaks of "preeminence" as a cause of faction. Here, he contends, faction arises because "a certain person or persons are greater in
power than accords with the city and the power of the governing body"
(1302b15–20). Something analogous to this may have been at work in
American politics in recent years. Aristotle apparently has in mind the rise
of some individual or group of sufficient power to challenge the actual
governing institutions. Thankfully, America has seen nothing like this.
Nevertheless, in a representative democracy such as ours, it is possible for
the great mass of ordinary citizens to regard themselves as the governing
body, not in the strict sense of actually wielding authority, but in the looser
sense that their preferences should decide the basic direction of national
policy. On this view, there might be room to worry that the extremely
wealthy have gained an influence over our actual governing institutions
that is incompatible with the real sovereignty of the people—again, their
ability to successfully translate their preferences into public policy through
elections. In fact, concerns such as this have been commonly voiced in
America over the last decade at least. Such concerns no doubt helped to
fuel the left wing populist candidacy of Bernie Sanders, and it is likely that
Trump's right wing populism benefitted from them as well. In fact, both
Sanders and Trump spoke as if they were fighting very wealthy elites that
use their wealth to control elected officials.

Aristotle also presents "arrogance and profit" as "fairly evident" causes of factional disturbances in a political community. In this case "profit" refers not, as it did earlier, to the factious element's desire for economic gain or fear of economic loss. It refers rather to their resentment of what they perceive to be the unjust gains of those who profit from holding public office. "For it is when those who are in office behave arrogantly and aggrandize themselves," Aristotle contends, "that [men] engage in factional conflict" (1302b5–10).

As a candidate for the presidency, Donald Trump was particularly vehement in exploiting this cause of faction. It was, indeed, the theme of his second most prominent campaign slogan. His most prominent slogan, of course, communicated a largely positive message, although one that also conveyed dissatisfaction with the current state of things: "Make America Great Again!" In a close second place, however, we find a more negative and harder hitting catchphrase, devised near the end of the general election campaign, "Drain the Swamp." Trump used this expression to channel his voters' resentment at what they believed to be the culture of self-dealing and corruption in the nation's capital. Trump was willing to spell this message out with a brutal clarity seldom seen in presidential politics. Thus, even in his inaugural address, an occasion usually dedicated largely to unifying rhetoric, Trump was willing to say the following: "For too long, a small group in our nation's Capital has reaped the rewards of government while the people have borne the cost. Washington flourished—but the people did not share in its wealth. Politicians prospered—but the jobs left, and the factories closed. The establishment protected itself, but not the citizens of our country."[15]

According to Aristotle, "contempt" for the rulers is another fruitful source of political discord. This force, too, played a role in Trump's rise to power, although it showed itself in our politics in a way that Aristotle's account does not explicitly anticipate. Aristotle says that contempt for the rulers arises in oligarchies "when those not sharing in the regime are a majority"—when, in other words, the people or the many realize that they outnumber their masters and therefore "suppose themselves superior" in real power. They may then try to overthrow the oligarchy. In democracies, he continues, faction arises from the contempt the "well off" have for the "disorder and anarchy" that arises from the poor quality of democratic government (1302b25–33). When the disorder becomes intolerable, the wealthy try to overthrow the democracy.

Aristotle's examples do not include popular contempt for a governing class that is viewed as ineffective and incompetent, although his general sketch of contempt does not exclude this possibility. At any rate, much of Trump's political rhetoric aimed to exploit and to foster a popular sense of contempt for those who have been entrusted with governing America in recent decades. Trump's presidential announcement speech sounded this theme, which would echo throughout the following sixteen months of his campaign: "we have no competence"; our "politicians are all talk, no action", the country has been poorly served by "stupid" politicians who "don't have a clue."[16] Expressions such as these were staples of Trump's many rallies from June of 2015 to November of 2016.

Many commentators have understandably criticized Trump for the incivility of these attacks. This point is well taken. Nevertheless, Aristotle's account reminds us that such attacks probably would not have been able to succeed in the absence of an already existing sense of contempt on the part of the voters to whom Trump was appealing. The white working class voters who proved so important to Trump's victory would have been primed for such contempt by the causes of faction discussed earlier. Moreover, many other voters would also have been susceptible to contempt for the established governing class by the prominent perceived failures of government over the last two administrations. The two biggest public policy initiatives of the last fifteen years are the war in Iraq and the Affordable Care Act. George W. Bush staked his presidency on the former, and Barack Obama staked his on the latter. By the time of the 2016 presidential campaign season, most Americans viewed the Iraq war as a failure,[17] and more Americans viewed the Affordable Care Act unfavorably than favorably.[18]

The Beginning Points of Faction: Conflict Among the Many

So far, our discussion has focused primarily on the kind of faction that arises between the many and the few. This is, indeed, the main theme of Aristotle's account, and it seems to be Donald Trump's key political tool in his quest for the presidency. One might wonder, however, whether there can be factional conflict among the many, and whether this, too, might have played a role in Trump's rise.

At first sight, Aristotle appears to dismiss this possibility, at least in regimes such as America's. As he opens his discussion of faction, in chapter 1 of Book V, he suggests that in democracies "there is only" factional conflict "against the oligarchy, there being none that arises among the people against itself that is worth mentioning" (1302a10–12). Other passages, however, hint at the possibility of faction among the people themselves. When Aristotle introduces his discussion of the "causes and beginning points" of faction, he lists among them mere "dissimilarity" among the citizens (1302b4). Later, when he speaks of differences of location as a possible source of factional conflict, he speaks as if human beings are in fact prone to fall into faction over almost anything; "for just as in war the crossing of ditches, even if they are very small, splits the ranks, so every difference, it appears, makes a factional split" (1303b12–15). This remark calls to mind a similar passage in James Madison's tenth *Federalist* essay: "So strong is this propensity of mankind to fall into mutual animosities, that where no substantial occasion presents itself, the most frivolous and fanciful distinctions have been sufficient to kindle their unfriendly passions and excite their most violent conflicts."[19]

These considerations remind us that differences of ethnicity, race, nationality, or language may turn out to be causes of faction in a political community. Aristotle makes this explicit by listing "[d]issimilarity of stock" as one of the causes and beginning points of factional conflict. This is a sobering thought for Americans, who take pride in thinking of their country as a multi-ethnic democracy that has welcomed immigrants from many different countries and cultures. Aristotle does not, however, suggest that such an aspiration is impossible. For Aristotle, no less than for the modern political thought on which the American regime is based, the interests and aspirations on which the political community is based are shared by human beings as such. It is therefore possible for those of different "stock" to live together harmoniously in the same community. Differences in stock, he says, are a source of factional conflict at first, but they may cease to be so once a "cooperative spirit develops. For just as a city does not arise from any chance multitude, so it does not arise in any chance period of time." Nevertheless, Aristotle follows up this reassurance with a long and cautionary list of political communities in which factional conflict arose when one people "admitted joint settlers or later settlers" of different stock (1303a25–1303b4).

Few would deny that factional conflict based on differences in what Aristotle calls "stock" played a role in Trump's candidacy. As noted earlier,

Trump made illegal immigration a central theme of his campaign. To a lesser but still significant extent he also raised concerns about legal immigration. For the most part, Trump framed his complaints in terms that did not appeal to questions of stock or ethnicity. Generally, he spoke of immigration as an economic and security issue. Nevertheless, it is widely known that most illegal immigration comes across America's southern border, and this fact would serve to remind voters of the ethnic component of the question: most illegal immigration involves Mexicans, as well as Central and South Americans who pass through Mexico in order to enter the United States. In addition, Trump's promise to build a wall on the southern border, and to make Mexico pay for it, served to remind voters of the ethnic aspect of the issue. Moreover, Trump generally painted the government of Mexico as encouraging illegal immigration, either out of hostility or indifference to American interests. This, too, made the question of stock a part of the debate over illegal immigration.

Finally, factional conflict based on differences of stock may have interacted with two other of Aristotle's beginning points of faction in order to influence American presidential politics in 2016. According to Aristotle, faction also arises from the "disproportional growth" of some part of the city (1302b34–35). Aristotle reminds us that each city is composed of various parts that exist in a kind of balance. Therefore, the growth of one part beyond its accustomed size can change the character of the community. Thus, for example, if many of the "notables" are, say, killed in a war, the city will necessarily lean more toward democracy. If, in contrast, economic changes render some citizens extremely wealthy, the city will lean more toward oligarchy.

Although most of Aristotle's discussion of the disproportionate growth of a part focuses on the difference between the people and the wealthy, he indicates that this factor could also operate on the basis of other factors, including ethnic identity. He lays down the following general principle that he says "should not be overlooked": those who cause power to be acquired by anyone, "whether private individuals, officers, tribes, or generally a part or multitude of any sort, give rise to factional conflict. For either those who envy their being honored initiate factional conflict or they themselves are unwilling to remain on an equal footing on account of their preeminence" (1304a33–38).

One can readily see how this cause of faction might be brought into play on the basis of "stock" in a multi-ethnic democracy with a significant amount of immigration. A multi-ethnic democracy will possess some distribution of electoral power among its various ethnicities. Unless it regulates immigration with a view to maintaining the existing proportions of various ethnic groups, immigration will tend to change the established balance of electoral power. If the change tends to increase the presence of some particular group, then some other group or groups within the community may well regard this as a kind of "disproportionate growth" of a part of the community—and, regarding this development as unwelcome, may engage in factional conflict because of it.

This, then, brings us to a final occasion of faction: fear. According to Aristotle, men "engage in factional conflict through fear, both when they have committed injustice and are frightened of paying the penalty, and when they are about to suffer injustice and wish to forestall it" (1302b21–24). When a political community has been dominated by citizens of a particular stock, they may fear the loss of their power through immigration of persons of a different stock. They might also regard such a loss of power as an injustice to themselves and engage in factional conflict in order to prevent it. After all, people who are accustomed to power tend to regard it as just that they should continue to hold that power. Moreover, of course, the declining stock would sense injustice if the change in the society's composition resulted to some extent from illegal immigration

This is not to say that there is any "just" claim of a particular ethnicity to rule in a particular community. Nor is there any abstract, metaphysically correct proportional relationship among ethnicities in light of which the growth of one group can be judged objectively "disproportionate." It is only to say, as Aristotle would warn us, that experience teaches that differences of ethnicity within a community are fraught with the possibility of faction, especially when there appears to be the prospect of some change in the power relations among the various ethnicities.

Once again, there is evidence that some of Donald Trump's voters were motivated by such considerations. Trump depended for his margin of electoral victory on support from working class white voters that exceeded the support usually won by a Republican candidate. The aforementioned Public Religion Research Institute study of these voters indicates that they fear "cultural displacement." Large majorities of them (more than sixty percent) believe that America is in danger of losing its culture and identity and that the American way of life needs to be protected from foreign influence. Indeed, here Trump benefited from this concern beyond the white working class. The PRRI study found that this worry was also held by a majority of all voters, although not as large a majority as among the white working class.[20]

FACTION IN DEMOCRACY AND OLIGARCHY

The second part of Aristotle's account of factional conflict examines how it operates in specific regimes. He begins with democracy. In democracies, he contends, factional conflict tends to arise "particularly on account of the wanton behavior of the popular leaders" toward the wealthy members of the community. Such leaders harass "those owning property" and "egg on the multitude publicly [against them]" (1304b20–25).

It is easy to apply this explanation to the Trump phenomenon. We live in a kind of democracy, so this is presumably the kind of faction we should expect to see. Moreover, there is plenty of evidence that Trump presented himself as the tribune of the people against the wealthy and overbearing. In Trump's speeches, he named specific companies that had moved production, and hence jobs, out of the country and condemned them for having done so. He continually promised that as president he would prevent such actions. More generally, he painted his opponent, Hillary Clinton, as a mere tool of Wall Street who supported policies that were bad for the middle class. In the passage quoted above, the term translated as "popular leaders" is in fact related to the Greek word demagogue. A common complaint about Trump is that he played the demagogue by stirring up the people against the country's economic and political elites, blaming the latter for the troubles of the former.

Aristotle's remarks about the causes of factional conflict in an oligarchy also seem relevant, however. According to Aristotle, one of the main causes of faction in an oligarchy is when the oligarchs "treat the multitude unjustly. Any leader is then adequate" as a popular weapon against the oligarchs, "particularly when the leader comes from the oligarchy itself" (1305a36–40). One could view the 2016 election as a contemporary enactment of what Aristotle describes here. Trump's followers view him not as an irresponsible demagogue but as a necessary tool in a struggle against the abuses of a wealthy and powerful elite that is hostile to their interests. One the one hand, one hesitates to refer to Trump as just "any leader." As the builder and ruler of a large business empire, he could present himself as a plausible president. On the other hand, he had never held public office and therefore had no particular claim on the people's confidence. To that extent one could understand Trump's voters as willing to turn to "any leader" precisely because they had been provoked by the unjust treatment of an oligarchic elite.

Moreover, Trump benefitted, as Aristotle's account suggests, from being himself a member of the oligarchy. Trump ran as a billionaire businessman who was giving up business in order to defend the working and middle classes. Such a play is effective because the people are particularly charmed by such a leader. They are gratified by his support, because they think that it independently confirms the justice of their complaints. After all, such a leader has not himself suffered from the abuses of the oligarchy, so presumably his judgment is not distorted by economic self-interest. In addition, the people may be inclined to believe that a member of the oligarchy will be an especially effective leader against the oligarchs. Who would know better what they have been up to and how to resist them? And in fact we find Trump making precisely these claims. He often condemned the "system" as corrupt and "rigged" against ordinary people, while reminding his listeners that nobody knows that system better than he, who operated so long within it.

Conclusion

Aristotle's account indicates that factional conflict is not only to be analyzed but also to be judged. Those who engage in factional conflict always claim to be seeking justice or resisting injustice. We are thus compelled to ask whether those claims are persuasive or not. Certainly, few Americans need to be encouraged to take up this task of judgment in the case of President Trump. Many think of his rise as a kind of injustice, many think of it as a necessary response to injustice, but few have no opinion at all.

As we have seen, it is possible to view Trump's rise as the result of a spirit of wanton demagogy, or, alternatively, to see it as the result of injustices perpetrated by the oligarchic few on America's working class. The former view is more immediately obvious, because we live in a democracy, where the wealthy presumably lack the power to oppress the people. Nevertheless, the latter interpretation cannot be ruled out. Aristotle himself reminds us that oligarchy can, in a sense, exist within a democracy. The oligarchic spirit persists even where the people rule. Aristotle says that in "democracies the notables engage in factional conflict because they share in equal things although they are not equal" (1303b5–6). That is, even in democracies the *oligoi* still want to be in control, and they exert themselves toward that end. It is therefore possible—especially in a large, wealthy, commercial republic such as the United States—that the wealthy will succeed to a considerable extent in promoting their interests at the expense of the many. Indeed, this concern has been heard from both the left and the right in American politics, long before Donald Trump appeared on the political scene.

We are left, then, with the question whether the factious impulses driving Trump's candidacy were justified or unjustified, whether Trump was stirring up groundless complaints or exploiting real ones. Although Aristotle's account of faction cannot answer that question for us, it can teach us something very important about the spirit in which that necessary inquiry should be pursued. Aristotle would have us think and act in a spirit of moderation. It might seem like a shirking of responsibility to say that there is blame on both sides, or that both sides have some legitimate claims to make. This is, however, precisely the conclusion that Aristotle's teaching suggests is the most likely and the most helpful.

For Aristotle, both the many and the few are animated by an imperfect, incomplete conception of justice. From the standpoint of pure theory it is certain that neither is in the right, and it is therefore likely that in practice there will be something to be said on behalf of, and against, both. According to his theoretical account, politics aims to foster virtue. According to Aristotle's practical account, however, political life is ordinarily a struggle, not for virtue, but for power, between the few who are wealthy and the many who are not. The most realistic solution to that struggle—the best practicable regime—does not seek virtue or perfect justice but instead a reasonable and stable accommodation between the demands of the few and the many. That solution requires a spirit of moderation and mutual forbearance.

Accordingly, Aristotle teaches that the best way to preserve a democracy or an oligarchy is for the democrats or oligarchs to resist acting on their most powerful political passions and instead to act in opposition to them. In a democracy, where the people have power over the rich, the people should not attack the rich but should strive to reassure them that their position will be respected and secure. In an oligarchy, where the rich rule, the rich should not seek to gain wealth at the expense of the many but should instead do everything they can to show their solicitude for the people's interests. This spirit of moderation is necessary to prevent the kind of factional conflict that might destroy the regime.

The same spirit of moderation is necessary to preserve a mixed regime, in which both the many and the wealthy have a share of power. If either side tries to press its claims too far, it will provoke a reaction from the other side, which may set off a round of factionalism that will destroy the regime. And, we may add, applying Aristotle's teaching to our own situation, such a spirit of moderation is also necessary for the American regime. It is not a mixed regime, because wealth as such has no claim to rule here. Nevertheless, it is a large commercial republic, the size and prosperity of which cannot help but produce a class of very wealthy people—an oligarchic class that will be able to wield political influence far beyond the weight of its mere numbers. The stability and prosperity of such a regime depends on the support of both the great body of the people and the country's "oligarchs." This in turn requires that neither party pursue its interests at the expense of the other. If an unusual degree of factional conflict emerges in such a society, Aristotle's teaching on political moderation would counsel the parties on both sides to ask themselves why they had imprudently contributed to it and what they might do to calm it. The same Aristotelian lesson in moderation also applies, moreover, to America as a multi-ethnic country. Mindful of the ever-present danger of ethnic conflict, Aristotle would admonish members of all ethnicities not to press or to seek political advantages over other groups.

Aristotle would advise Trump and his supporters to be wary of the dangers of falling into demagogy. At the same time, he would warn Trump's opponents of the dangers of provoking demagogy by insisting on policies that many of their fellow citizens might reasonably regard as harmful to their interests. This spirit of moderation is worth pursuing because our regime is worth preserving. Aristotle reminds us that "it is indeed possible for an oligarchy or a democracy to be in an adequate condition in spite of departing from the best arrangement" (1309b30–32). This is surely true as well about America's modern commercial republic.

NOTES

1. I rely on Carnes Lord's translation of Aristotle's *Politics* (Chicago: University of Chicago Press, 1984)
2. "Full Text: Donald Trump 2016 RNC draft speech transcript," *Politico*, July 21, 2016, http://www.politico.com/story/2016/07/full-transcript-donald-trump-nomination-acceptance-speech-at-rnc-225974
3. CNN, October 22, 2016, http://transcripts.cnn.com/TRANSCRIPTS/1610/22/cnr.03.html
4. Donald Trump, "Inaugural Address," January 20, 2017, https://www.whitehouse.gov/inaugural-address
5. Trump, RNC speech.

6. Trump, "Inaugural Address."
7. "Here's Donald Trump's Presidential Announcement Speech," *Time*, June 16, 2015, http://time.com/3923128/donald-trump-announcement-speech/
8. Trump, RNC speech.
9. Daniel Cox, Rachel Lienesch, and Robert Jones, "Beyond Economics: Fears of Cultural Displacement Pushed the White Working Class to Trump," Public Religion Research Institute, May 9, 2017, https://www.prri.org/research/white-working-class-attitudes-economy-trade-immigration-election-donald-trump/
10. Voter Study Group, June 13, 2017, https://www.voterstudygroup.org/newsroom/press-release june 13 2017
11. Cox, Lienesch, and Jones, "Beyond Economics."
12. Trump, "Inaugural Address."
13. Nick Gass, "Early Exit Polls Suggest GOP Voters Feel Betrayed by Establishment," *Politico*, March 15, 2016, http://www.politico.com/blogs/2016-gop-primary-live-updates-and-results/2016/03/primary-exit-polls-republicans-feel-betrayed-220796
14. I omit discussion of those that seemed to me not very relevant to the politics of the 2016 election: underestimation, location, neglect of small differences, and electioneering.
15. Trump, "Inaugural Address."
16. Trump, "Presidential Announcement Speech."
17. Bruce Drake, "More Americans Say U.S. Failed to Achieve Its Goals in Iraq," Pew Research Center, June 12, 2014, http://www.pewresearch.org/fact-tank/2014/06/12/more-americans-say-us-failed-to-achieve-its-goals-in-iraq/
18. "Kaiser Health's Tracking Poll: The Public's Views on the ACA," Henry J. Kaiser Family Foundation, August 11, 2017, http://www.kff.org/interactive/kaiser-health-tracking-poll-the-publics-views-on-the-aca/#?response=Favorable--Unfavorable&aRange=twoYear
19. Alexander Hamilton, James Madison, and John Jay, *The Federalist*, ed. Jacob E. Cooke (Middletown, Connecticut: Wesleyan University Press, 1961), 59.
20. Cox, Lienesch, and Jones, "Beyond Economics."

BIBLIOGRAPHY

Aristotle. 1984. *The Politics*. Trans. Carnes Lord. Chicago: University of Chicago Press.
Hamilton, Alexander, James Madison, and John Jay. 1961. In *The Federalist*, ed. Jacob E. Cooke. Middletown: Wesleyan University Press.

CHAPTER 3

Roman Parallels: Plutarch and the Trump Election

Mark Shiffman

The beginning of 2017 brought with it a widespread sense in America that the election of Donald Trump represented an "unprecedented" state of affairs for this country, giving rise in many variations to the question: "How could this happen?" Is there something about our country or its political system and operations that is not what we thought it was? In such a disorienting situation, it is a natural reflex to seek illuminating perspective by looking outside our own political history, to ask whether there are in fact precedents in the historical and political experience of other peoples.

In his June 14, 2017 column for the *New York Times*, Ross Douthat rightly observes: "The decadent years of the Roman Republic are as good a comparison point for our late-republican discontents as any in the history books."[1] Responding to controversy surrounding the decision by Shakespeare in the Park director Oskar Eustis, in his production of *Julius Caesar*, to give a Trump-like appearance to the Roman dictator, who is assassinated on stage, Douthat argues that "the problem with a Trumpified Caesar is that the conceit fails to illuminate our moment the way a good classical allusion should." Accordingly, Douthat goes on to consider the merits of other possible parallel figures from the end of the Republic.

M. Shiffman (✉)
Villanova University, Villanova, PA, USA

© The Author(s) 2018
M. B. Sable, A. J. Torres (eds.), *Trump and Political Philosophy*,
https://doi.org/10.1007/978-3-319-74427-8_3

43

This approach to illuminating political phenomena on the basis of analogies between both political actors and the historical and institutional contexts in which their actions take shape is simultaneously pioneered and mastered in Plutarch's *Lives* (themselves the primary source material for Shakespeare's Roman plays). The *Lives* examine the careers, characters and choices of Greek and Roman statesmen, in each instance placing a Greek in parallel to a Roman. In this way, Plutarch not only provides insight into the finer points of how his historical characters respond to opportunities, challenges and temptations, but also enables his readers to see how these characters are formed by and respond to the state of political order and disorder in which they act.[2]

According to the classical political thought of Plato and Aristotle by which Plutarch is guided, the form of the regime has a certain character that it communicates to its citizens. Thus, at the same time as Plutarch sharpens our eye for statesmen's characters through analogy and dis-analogy, he sharpens our eye for the "character" of the regimes themselves as well, and gives us the means to reflect on the relationships between the two kinds of character. This complex interplay of analogies between city and soul, city and city, and soul and soul trains the reader to recognize the ordering principles of practical reason (both ethical and political) as they come to light within the concrete contexts of particular choices made by acting statesmen.

Within this complex structure, one term of analogy remains constant: the city of Rome. Plutarch's Greeks belong to many different polities with diverse regimes: Athens, Sparta, Thebes, Corinth, Macedonia and its successor kingdoms. His figures are founders, lawgivers, orators, generals, republican statesmen and monarchs. The constant presence of Rome provides material for reflection on a republican civic regime that lasted in a relatively constant form over five centuries, while gradually giving way in the last two of those centuries to empire and the rule of one man. If Rome and the gradual erosion of its republican liberty do indeed provide one of the most illuminating analogies for the political condition of the United States in the twenty-first century, then we may reasonably hope to gain valuable insight through Plutarch's form of reflection by analogy.

REPUBLICAN FORMS

The comparison of the American republic to the Roman, mediated by Plutarch, was a commonplace in the founding era. Alexander Hamilton's choice of the nom de plume "Publius" offers a prime illustration. Plutarch's

Life of Publius Valerius Publicola is the only ancient treatment of the origins of the Roman republican order that accords central importance to Publius in the establishment of the new regime. While he is a significant supporting actor in the overthrow of the Tarquin dynasty, his indispensable role for Plutarch is that of stabilizer of the new order, through his patient and prudent political work of maintaining unity of purpose and harmony between the nobles (Patricians) and the common people (Plebeians).

A large part of Publius' achievement lies in establishing precedents of conduct for the office of consul, the newly instituted pair of annually elected executives that replaces the monarchy. Men of consular rank (the consuls and the ex-consuls who are admitted to the senate) must bear themselves and conduct their office with a dignity and propriety that does not, by highlighting the sense of superiority that inevitably accompanies it, provoke alienation and envy in the people.[3] In Plutarch's *Life* of Coriolanus, the office of the tribunes of the people, instituted in the second generation of the republic as a concession to popular discontents with senatorial policies, initially appears to many of the Patricians to introduce a source of disharmony between the two orders.[4] The turbulent partiality of the tribunes, however, has the constitutional effect of compelling the consuls to present themselves, by contrast, as statesmanlike republican representatives of the whole city rather than just the Patrician faction. The proud Patrician Coriolanus egregiously refuses to play this game, with instructive near-disastrous results.

With the institution of tribunes, the Roman constitutional order attained the character of a mixed regime such as Aristotle had argued would prove best and most stable. Indeed, on the basis of his familiarity with the Roman republic, the historian Polybius crafted a more systematic version of Aristotle's teaching, in the now familiar terms of "checks and balances."[5] The consular office gave a distinct and prominent place in the regime to capable men of good character. The senate embodied a class that was at once an oligarchy of wealth and a martial aristocracy. The tribuneship gave voice and prerogatives to the mostly poorer multitude. The argument of Polybius, echoed by Cicero, that Rome provided the best model so far for the mixed regime helps to further explain why Rome would hold the place it does in Plutarch's system of analogies.

One way the method of analogy aids in political analysis is by highlighting elements of political order present in one regime and missing in comparable regimes. In his *Defence of the Constitutions of Government of the United States of America*, John Adams makes extensive use of this method of analogy. Examining the typical structures of American state constitutions in the light of classical as well as modern republics and authors, in order to offer guidance for a federal constitution, Adams draws extensively on the analyses of Polybius, Cicero and Plutarch, contending that the "science of government has received very little improvement since the Greeks and Romans."[6] What improvement it has received lies primarily in the separation of powers and in the division of the legislative power into three branches (two houses plus an executive veto power)—improvements found especially in the British constitution.

Adams thus places equal emphasis on the modern separation of powers and the ancient balancing in the political regime of the different parts of the actual constitution of the polity: the one, the few and the many. He finds that America lacks any proper equivalent to the office of tribune. The British constitution provides for the role of the tribunes to some extent in the House of Commons, and Adams worries that America has failed to follow this model sufficiently and so risks becoming too oligarchic. He observes: "The only remedy is to throw the rich and the proud into one group, in a separate assembly, and there tie their hands; if you give them scope with the people at large or their representatives, they will destroy *all equality and liberty, with the consent and acclamations of the people themselves.* They will have much more power, mixed with the representatives, than separated from them."[7] While the House of Representatives was intended to serve as the more popular of the two assemblies, Adams' classically-inspired analysis suggests that it will fail in its role, leaving a dangerous gap in the order and balance of the regime.

The fact that many American newspapers adopted the title of *Tribune* suggests that they saw themselves as filling this gap, serving as the voice of the common people's concerns. Certainly it is part of the self-image of American journalism that it serves as an extra-constitutional check on the government and a guardian of democracy. All three of these phenomena— the absence of a tribunician office, the consequent tendency toward oligarchy, and the extra-constitutional self-casting of the media in this unoccupied role—together shed some light on the success of Donald Trump.

Whatever the actual or likely policy realities of a Trump presidency, the rhetoric of his campaign has been described as populist—a term itself derived from the Roman political faction of the *Populares*, galvanized by the tribunes Tiberius and Gaius Gracchus and brought to the summits of power by seven-time consul Gaius Marius and his nephew Julius Caesar. As we will see, Trump's appeal shares features with that of the Roman faction, including analogous historical enabling conditions. In the light of the Roman *constitutional* analogy, however, one institutional enabling condition for a populist presidency seems to be the absence of a tribunician office already structurally placed to take on that profile.

One example of rhetoric in the tribunician mold is the Trump campaign's response to Hillary Clinton's slogan "I'm with Her" by means of the counter-slogan "I'm with You." Not only does Trump's slogan suggest of itself the tribune-like elaboration in his convention speech—"I'm with you, the American people, I'm your voice"—but it also recasts Clinton's slogan as an emblem of the factional wagon-circling of a culturally dominant elite committed to identity politics. This deft rhetorical move appears to convict Clinton out of her own mouth of speaking for one of the two wings of "the establishment," which is to say, the currently regnant oligarchy.[8]

The key identifying feature of the new oligarchy is not so much wealth per se as the (significantly, if not strongly correlated) factor of success in higher education. Every senator in the 115th Congress has a four-year degree, as do 95% of members of the House of Representatives (compared to 75% and 56%, respectively, in the 79th Congress, and to around 33% of the current general population).[9] College degrees are increasingly important for earning potential and job security, and they are increasingly concentrated in the hands of the children of the college-educated.[10] Degree-earning Americans are the best prepared to benefit from globalization and the most likely to support it; college campuses tend to inculcate a combination of identity politics, political correctness and cultural relativism that reinforce a repudiation of national identity, easing the way for transnational workforce integration and "global citizenship." Students who are lukewarm about or opposed to identity politics and political correctness commonly end up as the neoliberals and libertarians who increasingly dominate the Republican Party. Higher education thus tends to produce ideological moralists—whether strident progressive "social justice warriors" or ruthless Randian competitive individualists—whose social liberalism is often at odds with the cruder moralism or moderate and conventional sense of decency of the less educated, and whose hopes are directed toward global and international business, finance and NGOs rather than invested in local and American concerns.

According to a study by Nate Silver, "it appears as though educational levels are the critical factor in predicting shifts in the vote between 2012 and 2016," with degree-holding voters supporting Clinton to a higher level even than Obama, and a trend of electoral gains by Trump among the less educated, largely regardless of wealth or occupation. Silver offers as one plausible and fairly common interpretation the following:

> Education levels may be a proxy for cultural hegemony. Academia, the news media and the arts and entertainment sectors are increasingly dominated by people with a liberal, multicultural worldview, and jobs in these sectors also almost always require college degrees. Trump's campaign may have represented a backlash against these cultural elites.[11]

While a backlash against liberal cultural hegemony was no doubt a significant factor in the election, it should not be viewed in isolation from the trend toward an oligarchy of the educated—or perhaps the large subset of the educated described as the "managerial elite."[12] Insofar as these media send a political message, it is generally directed against the other faction of the oligarchy. The concerns of the less educated (excepting the concerns imputed to favored minorities) are often treated with derision. Even if something like Fox News provides an alternative voice, it is one of partisan opposition rather than popular representation.

In other words, the popularity of Trump's contempt for elite cultural values generally, and the news media in particular, might be best understood politically in the light of the media's abandonment of the tribunician role in favor of serving as the organ of "culture-wars" shaped mainly by intra-oligarchic factional politics. Trump's irreverent dismissal of prestigious news organizations like CNN and *The New York Times* resonates with citizens who experience them as megaphones for the contempt felt for them and their concerns by the educated ruling class.[13]

In the imaginary senatorial debate over the prerogatives of the tribunes that Plutarch summarizes in *Coriolanus*, the more experienced senators try to convince the younger and more partisan Patricians that the office will be less dangerous than they fear, "since it was not contempt of the senate, but the impression of being contemned by it, which made them pretend to such a prerogative."[14] In most circumstances, the policies and initiatives pursued by an office with the function and the narrowly limited authority of the Roman tribunate would tend to be less important as substantive goals than as symbolic gestures that defuse popular resentment, both by providing a representative voice to the people and by compelling rulers to make arguments for their decisions in terms of the broader public good. If the American regime lacks an office that serves this function, and if the elite media have abandoned it to serve as an organ of the oligarchy's internecine warfare, it is less surprising that a man characterized by disregard for elite decorum, and by promoting shoddily-conceived policies that serve primarily as symbolic attacks on the globalizing agenda of the new oligarchy, should be elected to the office capable of most effectively channeling popular resentment of an establishment blithely contemptuous of the common people's lot.

ROME: FROM REPUBLIC TO EMPIRE

As previously noted, the rise of the *Populares* as a Roman political party began with Tiberius and Caius Gracchus, toward the end of the second century BC. Of the twenty-three Roman figures whom Plutarch chooses as subjects of his *Lives*, the Gracchi are the only two whose claim to fame rests on their exercise of the office of tribune, though that office had formed an integral part of the constitutional order for over three centuries. The historical circumstances in which the Gracchi acted, the measures they proposed to meet the needs of the time, and the bitter and violent factionalism that openly took hold of Roman politics as a result of their populist tactics and which finally drove the republic to self-destruction, make their terms as tribunes and the historical moment that fueled their popularity a crucial turning point in Roman political life.

If the implications of the Trump slogan "I'm with You" suggest a critique of the ethos of the establishment or ruling oligarchy and evoke the missing constitutional element of the tribune, Trump's more famous slogan, "Make America Great Again," clearly gestures toward a sense of historical circumstances that purportedly necessitate his disruption of the established ruling order. The slogan seems to evoke two forms of prior greatness, both the military preeminence and the economic vibrancy of the Cold War era and its immediate aftermath. The populist rhetoric of Tiberius Gracchus makes a similar appeal. Plutarch reports Tiberius' complaint on behalf of the common soldiers who fought to establish Roman greatness: "They were styled the masters of the world, but in the meantime had not one foot of ground which they could call their own."[15] The parallel complaints of Gracchus and Trump may thus be abstractly summarized: Citizens of modest means labored to attain a national greatness whose benefits in the end accrued not to them or their descendants but to a ruling oligarchy. Let us fill out the larger historical parallels in order to clarify the analogies and disanalogies.

By 270 BC, the city of Rome had consolidated rule of the Italian main-land. There is little indication that Rome had ambitions beyond Italian shores, but in 264 BC the Romans accepted a request for support from Italians in Sicily, threatened by the Greeks and Carthaginians who domi-nated much of the island. The decision to intervene would bring Rome into conflict above all with Carthage, the great military and commercial power that dominated the Mediterranean Sea, thus requiring Rome to rapidly develop its then negligible naval power. The consideration that, upon mastering Sicily, Carthage—which already commanded most of the northern coast of Africa, much of Spain, and the islands of Corsica and Sardinia—would pose a powerful threat to Italy seems to have motivated Rome to enter upon this momentous conflict.[16] When it razed the city of Carthage in 146 BC, Rome had eliminated the only major power limiting the expansion of its sway over the whole Mediterranean world.

The Punic Wars fought against Carthage occupy a place in Roman his-tory comparable to that of the Cold War in American history. The American intervention in Korea, like the Roman in Sicily, involved entan-glement in a foreign conflict to prevent the expansion of a rival power, opposition to which entailed in principle a worldwide struggle in which both great power status and continued existence seemed to be at stake. In both cases, development of commerce and success in war went hand in hand, especially through military contracts; but while the Romans sought to usurp the commercial network Carthage already enjoyed, the United States sought the global spread of liberal economic development in part as a strategic bulwark against Soviet expansion through fomenting Marxist revolution. Thus in the Roman case, the sense of united effort revolved around military service and was galvanized by the immediate threat to Rome's existence posed by Hannibal's invasion of Italy in 218 BC. In the American case, the pursuit of economic production and growth at home and abroad, along with accompanying liberties, formed a major element of the unity of purpose felt to animate the struggle, subtly bolstered by awareness of being the primary target of the Soviet nuclear arsenal. As Romans served together in the army and enjoyed the spoils of victory together, so American laborers and owners, in an economy of nationally-based industries expanding outward, worked out arrangements for mutual benefit, so that decades of growth in economic productivity also generated widespread middle-class affluence for workers.

Rome's victory in the Punic Wars brought unprecedented opportunity for accumulating wealth from commercial activity and exploitation of natural resources abroad. At the same time, the bulk of the soldiers who fought the empire-consolidating wars found themselves spending longer periods of time on distant campaigns—economically ruinous for an army drawn from a population of yeoman farmers. As these smallholders fell into debt, farmlands became increasingly concentrated in Patrician hands, creating massive estates producing profitable export crops and worked by foreign slaves made plentiful by military conquests.[17] Some of these estates also fell into the hands of the new commercial class of Equestrians enriched by the wars and looking for investments; but this class also profited from public contracts for production, supply and tax-collection, all activities beneath Patrician dignity. As Equestrians found their way into office and thus also the senate, they together with the Patricians formed a new ruling class: an oligarchy of wealthy families with many shared interests that increasingly drove foreign and domestic policy, and which was increasingly marked off by an expensive shared education in Greek language and literature that gradually became a key to greater fortune.[18]

Roman society was thus increasingly polarized into a magnificently wealthy class ruling a multicultural empire and a distressed and proletarianized Roman and Italian people who resented the share of wealth that had fallen to their superiors. In this situation, the tribunician office became ineffective in its role of channeling and defusing popular envy and resentment. "The tribunes, once the leaders of the plebs, though still elected by the plebeians, no longer played an important part in public life: they belonged themselves to the senatorial nobility ... and lost touch more and more with the masses."[19] In these circumstances, Tiberius Gracchus, himself a patrician and the son of a consul, recognized the necessity for a restoration of the tribunician office.

Tiberius saw for himself the desolation of the rural districts of Italy on his way to Spain to serve as an officer, and he experienced firsthand the diminished discipline and effectiveness of an army of soldiers demoralized by the dwindling of the yeoman class and spoiled by arrogance and venality.[20] When it fell to him to broker a treaty with the Spanish resistance forces from an inferior strategic position, his political reputation was damaged by the anger of Romans accustomed to victory and strength.[21] The historian Guglielmo Ferrero provides a trenchant summary of the state of affairs:

This strange situation, owing to which Rome found herself obliged to preserve and extend her empire with diminished forces, explains the unrest of public opinion, the panics to which it so often gave way, and its frequent outbursts of irritation.... It seemed that Rome would soon perish ... if something were not done to prevent the ruin of the lower and middle-class landowners, the reservoir of the soldiers who had conquered both Italy and the empire…. Up to this point everyone agreed. But, when it came to taking action, the vested interests took alarm and there were always … plausible reasons for putting aside any remedies that might be suggested…. Thus things went from bad to worse. All wise men agreed that it was necessary to curb the spirit of greed which now pervaded the mass of the people. But it was found that no plans or undertakings succeeded except those the effect of which was to intensify it.[22]

Tiberius was not the first or only statesman to see the problem, but he was the first to pursue the solution with unflinching zeal and determination.

The Romans already had a law limiting landed estates to a size smaller than those possessed by the great landlords. Tiberius, elected tribune in 133 BC, proposed legislation setting up a commission to enforce the law and to distribute excess land to Roman and Italian veterans, providing compensation without penalty to those previously in violation of the land law. Unable to oppose any sound argument to this legal and equitable proposal, "the moneyed men, and those of great estates, were exasperated, through their covetous feelings against the law itself, and against the law-giver, through anger and party-spirit."[23] When they resorted to obstructing a vote on the law by obtaining the cooperation of another tribune, Marcus Octavius, Tiberius "was driven to a course neither legal nor seemly, and proposed to deprive Octavius of his tribuneship, it being impossible for him in any other way to get the law brought to a vote."[24]

As Ferrero observes, the removal of a tribune per se was not unprecedented.

But Gracchus found a new justification for his action which gave it a revolutionary character. The duty of a tribune of the people, he said, is to defend the people. If he fails in this duty, the people who appoint him can deprive him of office. In other words, the tribunes' right of veto must no longer be used, as had often happened in recent times, in the service of the aristocracy and the party of the rich. This theory could not but meet with general acceptance at a time of popular commotion, and Octavius was deposed by a unanimous vote of the tribes.[25]

Having thus cleared the way by popular referendum, Tiberius passed his law. Securing its proper execution, however, involved him in further breaks with political precedent. To insure that his three-man commission would perform its work with integrity, he composed it of himself, his brother Gaius, and his father-in-law Appius Claudius; and when his tribuneship was about to expire with the work of the commission barely begun, he took the extraordinary and illegal step of putting himself forward for a second consecutive term rather than see his work come to nothing.[26] Because of his popularity, his opponents could not prevent his candidacy, and could only resort to inciting mob violence on election day, which resulted in Tiberius' death.[27]

Let us at this point consider the resemblances of the American situation to the Roman, and the appeal of Trump to that of Tiberius, before returning to consider the political legacy of the Gracchi and its possible twenty-first century implications.

ROME AND AMERICA

At the heart of America's Cold War greatness, cohering relatively seamlessly with its projection of military power and its championing of social and economic rights and freedoms, lay a steadily growing industrial economy far more productive than any rival, along with a policy of developing similar productive capacity in Europe and Japan and cultivating markets (and therefore a degree of economic development sufficient to generate purchasing power) around the world. As defender of the "free world," the pioneer of its economic development, and the source of experience and knowledge required to grow the corporations that were the key to extending the system and binding it together, America prospered as the center from which an increasingly global order of liberal economics and politics radiated. This prosperity made it possible—and the still-national basis of industrial labor markets made it necessary—for industry to accommodate the demands of unions that helped to spread this prosperity downward and to create a working- and middle-class with high standards of living and hopes for a higher one for its offspring.[28]

After the Cold War, this system that American productivity had built began to shift its center away from the United States. Corporations that had grown separately on the soil of many nations were increasingly consolidated into a small number of multinational corporations dominating each industry.[29] Strategies for increasing profit margins shifted to creating diversified multi-national supply chains, moving production to less developed countries with cheaper labor, and avoiding taxes and regulation by relocating both production sites and official headquarters. The planning, coordination, analysis, distribution and public and foreign relations involved in this new corporate model put a greater premium than ever on an educated and flexible managerial elite. With a significant number of these companies pioneered and still largely based in America, whose institutions of higher education prepare students tolerably well for adaptation in this corporate culture, the proportions of Americans in management has thinned at a much slower rate than those of laborers.

America is studded with towns large and small where factories central to their economic life closed in the 1990s and after—the US lost over 70,000 factories from 1996 to 2012—due largely to mergers, acquisitions and consolidations.[30] Their inhabitants are less than enthusiastic about political parties more determined to provide tax breaks enabling oligarchs to reap greater profits from investments in multinational corporations than to address the epidemic of opioid addiction, or more intent on granting anatomical males access to the locker rooms used by their daughters than on bringing economic hope and family stability to their despised and depressed communities. As the middle class rapidly vanishes, America becomes more polarized into credentialed oligarchic beneficiaries of a successful Cold War strategy, looking optimistically abroad, and a population of communities whose local and social landscape tells them that they won the war and lost the peace.[31] These conditions are ripe for tribunician politics, especially when the Democratic Party has largely abandoned the concerns of the working class, whom it had buoyed up in better times through its support for unions.[32] As Matthew Continetti puts it: "Elite consensus had become so petrified, the beneficiaries of globalization so powerful and entrenched, the institutions of the administrative state so disconnected from the sentiments of the people that only a brash tycoon with no political experience could break the deadlock."[33]

A Tribunician Moment

As the Gracchi illustrate, one characteristic of the politics of tribunician revival is the ability to justify the abandonment of political precedents as necessary to combat the death grip of the ruling elite. Emily Bazelon notes: "Trump's flouting of norms was the siren song of his candidacy, and it has become a defining feature of his presidency;" accordingly, "it's natural enough for his supporters to dismiss talk of 'norms' as the useless hand-wringing of a worse-than-useless establishment."[34] Plutarch observes that Gaius Gracchus, Tiberius' younger brother who revived his populist program, departed from precedent by turning toward the people when he made his tribunician addresses, rather than speaking toward the senate as representative of the people: "An insignificant movement and change of posture, yet it marked no small revolution in state affairs," as it signaled a popularly gratifying abandonment of the attempt to maintain a traditional constitutional order.[35]

The popular appeal of the Gracchi's departures from precedent (including their political reliance on the loyalty of family and close friends) arose from frustration with the inability of the constituted order to deal with the social problem of popular distress and polarization of wealth. The consequence, however, was to further cripple the ability of any political process to function effectively, resulting in ever more acrimonious partisan strife and the outbreak and perpetuation of political violence. Bazelon quotes to similar effect the observation of Harvard law professor Jack Goldsmith: "'I detest much of the president's norm-defying behavior, ... [but] I worry at least as much about norms related to our governance that have been breached and diminished *as a result of, or in response to, Trumpism* [and about the prospect of] a downward spiral of tit-for-tat violations' that undermines institutional legitimacy in general."[36] Trump's petulant defiance intensifies a trend toward political violence from devotees of both parties, whether from protestors, flash mobs, lone shooters, or the proliferating social-media culture-war rhetoric of death threats and sexual violence. It also, however, reveals a further cause of frustration and confusion: while late-republic political violence had the clarity of pitting a popular party against a ruling oligarchic order, American frustration is compounded of intra-oligarchic two-party hatred and ineffective popular resentment channeled through Trump, which he can do little to assuage and much to aggravate.

It is impossible to return to the unipolar world economic conditions for which Trump encourages nostalgia, but it would be a mistake to conclude that the nostalgia will therefore pass. Similar structural changes in Rome's relationship to its world made the Gracchi's program unfeasible, but it was still the platform of the *Populares* seventy years after the assassination of Tiberius.[37] The logic of popular resentment dictates that failure to restore the golden days will be attributed to the malicious self-interest of the oligarchs, further intensifying frustration and intractable anger. It is political folly to believe that those who suffer from economic arrangements are ever inclined to accept—least of all from those who prosper—the argument that such an outcome is the inevitable trajectory of progress.

It would also be a mistake to consider Trump, however peculiarly problematic an individual he may be, as simply a bad character who happens to have gained the presidency, and whose removal promises to put American politics back on whatever the political optimist considers its normal course. Cornelius Sulla, after defeating Gaius Marius and the *Populares*, in 81 BC rendered the tribunes ineffective by removing their power to initiate legislation and to veto acts of the senate.[38] The ultimate consequence was that the *Populares*, revived by Caesar, had no recourse but to elect Caesar to the highest office and allow him to remain there by abolishing the republican order. Trump may not be Caesar, but he may be the precursor to a Caesar, even more so to the extent that he himself is neutralized by establishment politicians.

Plutarch, imagining the state of mind of the Romans as their politics devolved into faction, violence and governmental paralysis, remarks that Rome was "carried about like a ship without a pilot to steer her; while all who had any wisdom could only be thankful if a course of such wild and stormy disorder and madness might end no worse than in a monarchy."[39] The combined popularity of Trump and Sanders, two tribunician candidates identifying real problems to which they promised solutions often exceeding the constitutional limits of presidential power, may indicate the stirrings of a monarchic mood impatient with the limiting formalities of republican government. When this mood appears to be unwittingly shared by fashionable voices of the elite—when for example James Fallows waxes enthusiastic in *The Atlantic* about Jill Lepore's *New Yorker* article suggesting that income inequality can only be remedied by decreasing the number of governmental "veto players" (a quantitative social-science term roughly equivalent to "checks and balances")—anxiety for the future of the republic seems warranted.[40]

NOTES

1. Ross Douthat, "The Trumpiest Roman of Them All," *New York Times*, June 14, 2017. https://www.nytimes.com/2017/06/14/opinion/the-trumpiest-roman-of-them-all.html?emc=eta1&_r=0.
2. For a brief introduction to the *Lives* as a form of political reflection, see Hugh Liebert, *Plutarch's Politics: Between City and Empire* (New York: Cambridge University Press, 2016), esp. 28–36.
3. Mark Shiffman, "Why Publius?" in *Promise and Peril: Republics and Republicanism in the History of Political Philosophy*, ed.Will R. Jordan (Macon: Mercer University Press, 2017).

4. Plutarch, "Coriolanus," in *Plutarch's Lives, Volume I* (New York: Modern Library, 2001), 302.

5. Polybius, *The Histories III, Books 5–8*, VI.11.11–18.8 (Cambridge: Loeb Classical Library, 2011), 329–347.

6. John Adams, *Defence*, Volume I, Chapter VIII, accessed August 4, 2017. http://oll.libertyfund.org/titles/adams-the-works-of-john-adams-vol-4.

7. Ibid., Volume I, Chapter VI (emphasis in original), accessed August 4, 2017. http://oll.libertyfund.org/titles/adams-the-works-of-john-adams-vol-4.

8. Though he scrupulously avoids the term, Martin Gilens shows (on the basis of extensive quantitative analysis) that government in the United States has become oligarchic in the classical sense. See Martin Gilens, *Affluence and Influence: Economic Inequality and Political Power in America* (Princeton: Princeton University Press, 2014).

9. "The Changing Face of Congress in 5 Charts," Pew Research Center, accessed August 3, 2017. http://www.pewresearch.org/fact-tank/2017/02/02/the-changing-face-of-congress-in-5-charts/.

10. "America's New Aristocracy," *The Economist*, accessed August 3, 2017. https://www.economist.com/news/leaders/21640331-importance-intellectual-capital-grows-privilege-has-become-increasingly.

11. Nate Silver, "Education, Not Income, Predicted Who Would Vote for Trump," November 2, 2016. http://fivethirtyeight.com/features/education-not-income-predicted-who-would-vote-for-trump/.

12. The phrase comes from James Burnham 1941 book, *The Managerial Revolution*. For an application of Brunham's analysis to contemporary developments, see Michael Lind, "The New Class War," *American Affairs* I.2 (Summer 2017), 19–44.

13. For a journalistic *mea culpa*, see Will Rahn, "The Unbearable Smugness of the Press," CBS News, accessed August 3, 2017. http://www.cbsnews.com/news/commentary-the-unbearable-smugness-of-the-press-presidential-election-2016/.

14. Plutarch, "Coriolanus," in *Plutarch's Lives, Volume I*, 305.

15. Plutarch, "Tiberius Gracchus," in *Plutarch's Lives, Volume II* (New York: Modern Library, 2001), 361.

16. See Polybius, *The Histories I, Books 1–2*, I.10.3-9 (Cambridge: Loeb Classical Library, 2010), 27–29.

17. Plutarch, "Tiberius Gracchus," 360.

18. Guglielmo Ferrero and Corrado Barbagallo, *A Short History of Rome: The Monarchy and the Republic* (New York: Capricorn Books, 1918), 244; Michael Rostovtzeff, *A History of the Ancient World, Volume II: Rome* (London: Oxford University Press, 1927), 101.

19. Rostovtzeff, *History*, 115.

20. Plutarch, "Tiberius Gracchus," 360.

21. Ibid., 359.
22. Ferrero and Barbagallo, *Short History*, 247–249.
23. Plutarch, "Tiberius Gracchus," 361.
24. Ibid., 363.
25. Ferrero and Barbagallo, *Short History*, 257. In the popular assembly, the Romans voted according to the tribes into which the citizens were divided, the majority vote within each tribe determining the vote for the tribe as a whole.
26. Plutarch, "Tiberius Gracchus," 364, 367.
27. Ibid., 369.
28. It is perhaps noteworthy that Trump, according to CNN polls, had 53% support among Americans over 45, which is to say those who came of age before the fall of the Berlin Wall ("How we voted—by age, education, race and sexual orientation," *USA Today*, November 9, 2016). http://college.usatoday.com/2016/11/09/how-we-voted-by-age-education-race-and-sexual-orientation/.
29. See Peter Nolan, *Capitalism and Freedom: The Contradictory Character of Globalisation* (London: Anthem Press, 2008), esp. 104–105.
30. The data, from the Bureau of Labor Statistics, is discussed by Jon Greenberg, "MSNBC's Ed Schultz: Trade deals closed 50,000 factories," PunditFact, April 23, 2015 http://www.politifact.com/punditfact/statements/2015/apr/23/ed-schultz/msnbcs-schultz-trade-deals-closed-50000-factories/.
31. On the decline of the American middle class and the new socioeconomic landscape, see Joel Kotkin, *The New Class Conflict* (Candor, NY: Telos Press, 2014).
32. For post-election critiques of the Democratic Party by Democrats, see Thomas Frank, "Donald Trump is moving to the White House, and liberals put him there," *The Guardian*, November 9, 2016; and Michael Reeb, "I'm a Lifelong Democrat. Here are 3 Reasons I Voted for Trump," *The Daily Signal*, January 3, 2017. https://www.theguardian.com/commentisfree/2016/nov/09/donald-trump-white-house-hillary-clinton-liberals. http://dailysignal.com/2017/01/03/im-a-lifelong-democrat-here-are-3-reasons-i-pulled-the-lever-for-trump/.
33. Matthew Continetti, "Trump's Brand is Crisis," *National Review*, May 13, 2017. http://www.nationalreview.com/article/447606/trumps-crises-endanger-republicans-policies-message.
34. Emily Bazelon, "Ground Rules," *The New York Times Magazine*, July 16, 2017, 10.
35. Plutarch, "Caius Gracchus," in *Plutarch's Lives, Volume II*, 374.
36. Emily Bazelon, "Ground Rules," 11 (emphasis in original).
37. Rostovtzeff, *History*, 115, 134; Ferrero and Barbagallo, *Short History*, 256–259.

38. Rostovtzeff, *History*, 125.
39. Plutarch, "Caesar," in *Plutarch's Lives, Volume II*, 218–219.
40. James Fallows, "Why Paralyzed Politics Are Making America More Unequal," *The Atlantic*, March 17, 2015. https://www.theatlantic.com/politics/archive/2015/03/the-under-appreciated-connection-between-political-dysfunction-and-growing-inequality/388054/. Jill Lepore, "Richer and Poorer," *The New Yorker*, March 16, 2015. http://www.newyorker.com/magazine/2015/03/16/richer-and-poorer.

BIBLIOGRAPHY

Adams, John. 2017. *A Defence of the Constitutions of Government of the United States of America*. Online Library of Liberty. http://oll.libertyfund.org/titles/adams-the-works-of-john-adams vol-4 Accessed 4 Aug.

Bazelon, Emily. 2017. Ground Rules, *The New York Times Magazine*, July 16.

Continetti, Matthew. 2017. Trump's Brand Is Crisis. *National Review*, May 13 http://www.nationalreview.com/article/447606/trumps-crises-endanger-republicans-policies-message

Douthat, Ross. 2017. The Trumpiest Roman of Them All. *New York Times*, June 14. https://www.nytimes.com/2017/06/14/opinion/the-trumpiest-roman-of-them-all.html

Economist. 2017. America's New Aristocracy. https://www.economist.com/news/leaders/21640331-importance-intellectual-capital-grows-privilege-has-become-increasingly. Accessed 3 Aug.

Fallows, James. 2015. Why Paralyzed Politics Are Making America More Unequal. *The Atlantic*, March 17. https://www.theatlantic.com/politics/archive/2015/03/the-under-appreciated-connection-between-political-dysfunction-and-growing-inequality/388054/

Ferrero, Guglielmo, and Corrado Barbagallo. 1918. *A Short History of Rome: The Monarchy and the Republic*. New York: Capricorn Books.

Frank, Thomas. 2016. Donald Trump Is Moving to the White House, and Liberals Put Him There. *The Guardian*, November 9. https://www.theguardian.com/commentisfree/2016/nov/09/donald-trump-white-house-hillary-clinton-liberals

Gilens, Martin. 2014. *Affluence and Influence: Economic Inequality and Political Power in America*. Princeton: Princeton University Press.

Greenberg, Jon. 2015. MSNBC's Ed Schultz: Trade Deals Closed 50,000 Factories. *PunditFact*, April 23. http://www.politifact.com/punditfact/statements/2015/apr/23/ed-schultz/msnbcs-schultz-trade-deals-closed-50000-factories/

Kotkin, Joel. 2014. *The New Class Conflict*. Candor: Telos Press.

Lepore, Jill. 2015. Richer and Poorer. *The New Yorker*, March 16. http://www.newyorker.com/magazine/2015/03/16/richer-and-poorer

Liebert, Hugh. 2016. *Plutarch's Politics: Between City and Empire*. New York: Cambridge University Press.

Lind, Michael. 2017. The New Class War. *American Affairs* I (2 Summer): 19–44.

Nolan, Peter. 2008. *Capitalism and Freedom: The Contradictory Character of Globalisation*. London: Anthem Press.

Pew Research Center. 2017. *The Changing Face of Congress in 5 Charts*. http://www.pewresearch.org/fact-tank/2017/02/02/the-changing-face-of-congress-in-5-charts/. Accessed 3 Aug.

Plutarch. 2001. *Plutarch's Lives, Volumes I and II*. New York: Modern Library.

Polybius. 2011. *The Histories III, Books 5–8* Cambridge: Loeb Classical Library.

Rahn, Will 2017 The Unbearable Smugness of the Press. *CBS News*, http://www.cbsnews.com/news/commentary-the-unbearable-smugness-of-the-press-presidential-election-2016/. Accessed 3 Aug.

Reeb, Michael. 2017. I'm a Lifelong Democrat. Here Are 3 Reasons I Voted for Trump. *The Daily Signal*, January 3. http://dailysignal.com/2017/01/03/im-a-lifelong-democrat-here-are-3-reasons-i-pulled-the-lever-for-trump/.

Rostovtzeff, Michael. 1927. *A History of the Ancient World, Volume II: Rome*. London: Oxford University Press.

Shiffman, Mark. 2017. Why Publius? In *Promise and Peril: Republics and Republicanism in the History of Political Philosophy*, ed. Will R. Jordan, 31–48. Macon: Mercer University Press.

Silver, Nate. 2016. *Education, Not Income, Predicted Who Would Vote for Trump*. November 2. http://fivethirtyeight.com/features/education-not-income-predicted-who-would-vote-for-trump/.

USA Today. 2016. How We Voted—by Age, Education, Race and Sexual Orientation. November 9. http://college.usatoday.com/2016/11/09/how-we-voted-by-age-education-race-and-sexual-orientation/.

CHAPTER 4

Thomism and Trumpism

Douglas Kries

The editors of this volume have asked that I consider the question of whether pre-modern political thinkers, and especially Thomas Aquinas, may in some way enable us better to understand the remarkable rise of Donald Trump to the presidency of the United States. There are at least two ways to think about this question. First, we can consider the program or set of dogmas or creed upon which Mr. Trump campaigned for office and consider whether there is anything in the teaching of Thomas that would explain why that program has resonated with a significant percentage of American citizens. Secondly, in addition to considering Trumpism as a set of ideas or a political platform attractive to many, we can consider whether there is anything in the political teachings of Thomas that would explain why a significant portion of American citizens have attached their sympathies to Mr. Trump personally. In other words, what qualities or characteristics does Mr. Trump possess that have caused some Americans to support him so enthusiastically, and can Thomas explain why the Trumpites are attracted to those qualities or characteristics? In neither case will I be considering the advantages or disadvantages of Mr. Trump's program or character; political programs can and must change depending upon the vicissitude of political circumstances, and I have no first-hand,

D. Kries (✉)
Gonzaga University, Spokane, WA, USA

© The Author(s) 2018
M. B. Sable, A. J. Torres (eds.), *Trump and Political Philosophy*,
https://doi.org/10.1007/978-3-319-74427-8_4

unfiltered knowledge of Mr. Trump's personal character. What I will try to do instead, then, is to consider how Thomas would explain the desires and longings within the souls of Mr. Trump's supporters—the Trumpites.

THOMAS AND THE LONGINGS OF THE TRUMPITES

Generally speaking, the people who elected Mr. Trump are not from large metropolitan areas; instead, they tend to live in smaller towns or rural areas. They tend to dislike "big" government, along with its big capitol, the "swamp." It seems that they usually know their neighbors, and understand their neighbors as being fellow citizens. They often exhibit an attachment to these citizens that cosmopolitan American urbanites find difficult to understand. It is a misunderstanding for the cosmopolitans simply to call Trump supporters "racist." As a rule, the Trumpites have nothing against Mexicans who live in Mexico, or Chinese who live in China, or Iranians who live in Iran—so long as they do not threaten "American citizens who live in America." The Trump supporters are motivated not so much by a hatred of "the other" as by a love of their own, and, yes, by their own they do mean those who belong to their communities, which often means their own ethnic and linguistic groups. It is the immigrant, and especially the immigrant who is not a citizen, and especially the immigrant who is not a citizen and who will not assimilate, that offends their sense of political community. The Trumpites are not much interested in amassing an empire; they generally ignore foreign affairs, at least to the extent that *homeland* security will permit foreign affairs to be ignored. "America First" means, to them, not that it is necessary for America to rule over all the others, so that they must all be under her thumb. Rather, "America First" means, for them, that America worries about herself and her problems, failures, and successes, and leaves the others to worry about their own problems, failures, and successes. Mr. Bannon, for one, has come to call the Trump program "economic nationalism," by which phrase he means that America must consider the economic situation of her own citizens before taking up the economic problems of other nations. The phrase "Make America Great Again" thus means, pragmatically, 'make America a place where American workers and the families they support can prosper as they once prospered,' or at least as they are thought once to have prospered.

Thomists recognize the political urges that give rise to such a political program immediately. They would say that they belong to all human beings; that is, it is a universal longing of human beings to belong to a particular political community of modest size. A misreading of Thomistic natural law theory might incline some to disagree on this point. That is, some readers of Thomas might want to interpret him as arguing that human beings all stand under an identical, universal law of nature, and that, therefore, Thomas is a cosmopolitan globalist. What such interpretations overlook, however, is that Thomas's brief comments on the natural law are followed immediately by more extensive comments on the human law, in which he makes clear that there are multiple ways that human laws can be framed and still not be inconsistent with natural law, and that even local human customs, followed for a long time, can eventually come to constitute human law. He puts the matter succinctly in the second article on human law: "The general principles of the natural law cannot be applied to all peoples in the same way because of the great variety of human affairs."[1] And so there are different positive laws for different peoples. In the end, there is different law for each community, and Thomas understands most human beings to be attached to local, immediate concerns rather than cosmopolitan ones. Natural law is all well and good, but in the concrete it serves only as a check on human laws and does not constitute anything like a complete political law unto itself.

If doubt remains in the minds of some regarding Thomas's non-cosmopolitanism, the point is made even more clearly by Thomas's teacher, Aristotle. The Stagirite's famous claim that human beings are by nature political means that human beings are by nature inclined to live in a *polis*, which is a city of bounded or limited size and extent. Human beings by nature form cities of a manageable size, wherein most people know one another or at least possess the possibility of knowing one another. Human beings are themselves bounded by space and time, so they can only know so many other human beings, at least in a profound way. The small city is therefore the political unit that corresponds best to the temporal and spatial nature of human beings. Another of Aristotle's "students," Alexander the Great, preferred political units of massive size—empires. Thomas agreed with Aristotle that a smaller size is superior, for human possibilities are bounded by space and time. The city or *polis* is best for human beings who would know about the souls of their fellow citizens and help them progress.

Some small part of the pre-modern "small is beautiful" political teaching was preserved in the United States through the system of federalism. In recent years, however, it has had less "traction." The nation, with its over 300 million citizens, may be too large for federalism to function well; more to the point, the position that touts "globalism" (an unnatural position in the Thomistic-Aristotelian view) has been waxing stronger during the Obama years. At present, it isn't very clear what citizenship means to us anymore. For myself, I know intellectually that there are United States citizens who reside, say, in Kentucky, but I have never been to the state of Kentucky, and indeed I do not even know anyone from there. What can citizenship possibly mean in such a context? Thomists know that human beings are apt to flourish in smaller, more intimate political situations, and it is in such a smaller political arrangement that citizenship will seem valuable to them. "Small is beautiful" is the more natural position, Thomists say, so they would not be surprised to see such longings emerge even though they must struggle against the power of globalism.

A similar point can be made if we consider the question of friendship, which comprises two whole books of the *Nicomachean Ethics* and is still present in the works of Thomas. In Aristotle's view, the best chance for knowing the soul of another will arise in political settings smaller even than the city. Because friendship demands even more time than citizenship, one will have far fewer friends than one has fellow citizens. Indeed, Aristotle thinks that about the most that one can hope for is a small circle of friends who know each other and who help each other make progress in living well. Ideally, they will be able to philosophize together, or at least to reflect daily on living well.

Another political unit smaller than the city is the family; Aristotle was clear that not only are human beings political animals, but also "coupling" animals. Family is more natural to human beings even than political life, at least in the sense that family arises first temporally and remains more urgent and necessary to human beings even than the city. In addition to their frustration at the debasement of American citizenship, some Trumpites are frustrated at the demise of the American family, and perhaps most immediately with the inability of young Americans to command the economic and moral resources to form families. They think that a human being ought to be able to earn enough through actual laboring to form a family and to raise children (in the *plural*). It isn't just "jobs" that Trumpists want, but jobs that pay enough so that family life can resume a position of *dignity*. And so Thomists who are listening to the souls of America ought to be able to understand the longings of the Trumpists on this point as well.

The text in Thomas where these feelings of attachment to one's own political community come most to the fore is in a part of the *Summa theologiae* that is not much emphasized today even among scholars of Thomas. It is found in the second part of the second part of *Summa theologiae*, among the questions that treat the virtue of justice. Justice is concerned with what is owed to whom, but in one of the questions, Thomas also notes that piety or *pietas* is often considered part of justice because it considers what is owed to God, parents, and country. Piety is not simply a matter of religion, as even the pagan philosopher Cicero recognized when he claimed (and Thomas cites him as an authority on the subject), "It is by piety that we do our duty towards our kindred and well-wishers of our country and render them faithful service." Going beyond the foundation laid down by Cicero, Thomas says that God is the first principle of our own individual being and government. Nevertheless, he adds,

> In the second place, the principles of our being and government are our parents and our country, that have given us birth and nourishment. Consequently man is debtor chiefly to his parents and his country, after God. Wherefore just as it belongs to religion to give worship to God, so does it belong to piety, in the second place, to give worship to one's parents and one's country.
>
> The worship due to our parents includes the worship given to all our kindred, since our kinsfolk are those who descend from the same parents.... The worship given to our country includes homage to all our fellow-citizens and to all the friends of our country. Therefore, piety extends chiefly to these.[2]

THOMAS AND TRUMPIAN VIRTUE

It seems, then, that Thomistic principles, if employed to consider the current situation of the United States, would not be surprised at the rise of something like Trumpism or "America first" or "economic nationalism"; at the very least, Thomistic principles seem to be consistent with such elements within Trumpism. The next question, however, is whether Thomistic principles can explain why the people who hold the sorts of views that Thomas would expect them to have about piety, love of their own country, an appreciation for the heritage and gifts of one's own country, and the economic well-being of their families and political communities, came to attach such political longings to Donald Trump. If one has such feelings within one's soul, why turn those feelings over to this particular individual? Given the cosmopolitanism or globalism especially associated with former president Obama, and given that such a perspective was inherited and reinforced by the career and candidacy of Secretary Clinton, it is obvious enough why Americans with the longings that Thomas would predict of them would prefer almost anyone to the cosmopolitan alternative. Thus, it is not surprising why they would vote for the alternative to the Obama-Clinton position, and consequently the test case cannot be the general election. The intriguing question concerns the nominating process for the Republican Party. There were a great many Republican candidates who spoke along the lines of Mr. Trump and who could, in the sense we are speaking of it here, be described broadly as harboring Thomistic principles in their hearts. What was it about Mr. Trump that led people to rally around him with such enthusiasm as compared with the other Republican candidates?

Thomas Aquinas was himself not well-versed in electioneering, and speaks directly about it not at all. In general, though, Thomas suggests that what matters most about a political leader are the characteristics possessed by the leader in his or her soul. He does not write much about the policies a leader should have—these are too changeable and vary dramatically according to the unique situations of time and place and circumstance. In addition, Thomas generally thinks that a lot of the success of a political leader has to do with factors that the leader cannot control anyway. So, in his view, the best strategy is to have a leader with the right soul, or who possesses the right characteristics. Such a person will have the best chance of governing in the best way because he or she will be able to find the best policies and be able to figure out how to promote them, whatever they may happen to be. What is needed is not in the first instance a plan or set of policies, but a person with a certain kind of character.

What are these characteristics of soul that we should hope for? For Thomas, they are twofold. First, there is a set of characteristics that were discussed by the ancients and that came to be known by Thomas's time as cardinal virtues. Plato treats these four characteristics in the *Republic*, but they are already well-known by the time the *Republic* was written. It seems, however, to have been Ambrose who first called them "cardinal" or "hinge" virtues. Thomas's mentor Aristotle added to this list of four virtues, but even in the *Nicomachean Ethics*, these four still receive the most attention. Courage and temperance are treated first, in Book 3. Courage is understood as controlling the primal fears of the soul, and especially fear of death; temperance as controlling the primal desires of the soul, and especially the desires for food, sex, and drink. Justice receives its own book in the *Ethics*, namely Book 5, as does prudence in Book 6. Second, even higher than these four virtues for Thomas is the threefold list of theological virtues inherited from St. Paul. Paul had said that the three most important qualities for a human being to possess were faith, hope, and charity, and that at the top of the list was charity.

In Thomas's view, *all* human beings would be well-advised to attempt to acquire all seven of these qualities, even though the acquisition of the last three depends largely upon the free disposition of God's grace. In discussing political leaders, however, Thomas is particularly aware that certain virtues are especially necessary; these virtues are courage and prudence. Thus, if Thomas's views are able to help us understand how the souls of many Americans became attached to the person of Donald Trump, what we would anticipate discovering is that many Americans find Mr. Trump to be particularly courageous and particularly prudent.

Let us begin with courage, since in the Aristotelian and Thomistic views, there is something especially basic or primordial about the need for courage among political leaders. Aristotle was clear that the best way to test courage was on the battlefield, where one risked one's own life, but Mr. Trump has no military experience. On the other hand, courage clearly has wider connotations than the feelings associated with the military battlefield, even if that is where courage is most on display. The courageous person is also not afraid to disagree, to butt heads, to fight with words when fighting with swords is not available, and Mr. Trump presented himself as more truculent than the other Republican candidates during the nominating process. He was not afraid to "mix it up" with the other candidates, and such an approach resonated with many Republican voters. A remark generally heard from the Trumpites was that the other Republicans had been sent to Washington, D.C., with certain marching orders, but they had not marched. They were afraid of what others would say about them, afraid to "shut down the government," afraid of what the voters would say at the next election, and in general afraid to change the situation. In speaking of courage in the *Ethics*, one surmises that Aristotle is alluding to Achilles; no one would think of Mr. Trump as being the modern Achilles, but he is viewed by some as being willing to fight. In short, he seems to possess a sort of political courage, or at least that is how he is perceived by many of the Trumpites.

Perhaps the moment where this attitude most came to the forefront for primary voters was during the few weeks leading up to the Florida primary.

Senator Rubio had emerged briefly as the leading alternative to Mr. Trump, but he was belittled by Trump, with the assistance of Governor Christie, and made to appear as too weak and unmanly to be acceptable. When Senator Rubio attempted to do some chest-thumping of his own, most observers thought it seemed forced or feigned, and Mr. Trump won the Florida primary and thereby pushed Rubio out of the race.

Of course, Thomas Aquinas was well aware of Aristotle's doctrine of the mean for moral virtue, according to which there are extremes with respect to feelings of fear as with all feelings. Thomas thus understood that not only cowardice but also recklessness is to be avoided, and that courage lay somewhere between the two. Mr. Trump's critics claim that he does not attain the mean but tends toward recklessness; the view of the Trumpites, of course, was that he was at least more courageous to the others and thus very much to be preferred.

The other virtue particularly prized in statesmen is prudence, which Aristotle had understood as an intellectual virtue through which one is able to secure the good and repel the bad for human beings. Securing the true good for oneself is prudent, but securing the good for one's family or one's city is even a greater display of prudence. The Trumpites did not use the word "prudent" much in speaking of their candidate, but they did cite his business acumen as an important qualification. Obviously, knowing how to secure the good for one's country is not the same as knowing how to secure success in business. Nevertheless, in the minds of many Americans, it has been quite some time since anyone has been able to bring about something good in politics at all.

Moreover, the sort of business acumen that Mr. Trump seems to be especially successful at is construction, and large building projects may be more closely related to prudence than many non-Trumpites understand. In constructing something like Trump Tower, one would have to work with city officials, labor unions, and bankers. One would have to watch a budget and meet payrolls. And one would have to, in the end, produce something that would be helpful to many different human beings who would work and visit such a structure. One would have to, in short, secure something good for a great many people. The sort of good the Trump business enterprises seek is not the political good in the highest sense, but businesses often do help a great many people in some lesser but still significant ways. Despite what is sometimes said by the cosmopolitans, businesses—at least the great ones—are about more than turning a profit. Perhaps it is an American weakness not to distinguish carefully between prudence proper and the sort of prudence necessary to run a great business enterprise or to oversee the construction of a great building, but in the mind of many Trump supporters at least, their candidate had demonstrated a quality of soul that would seem to resemble prudence. If nothing else, Mr. Trump was thus able to claim to possess an important quality that none of the other Republican candidates could claim to possess.

This argument about economic prudence came to the fore as the debate process was beginning for the Republican nomination. Mrs. Fiorina was herself an accomplished businesswoman, and she performed very well in the earliest debates, so much so that at one brief point it became an important question whether she or Mr. Trump were actually more successful at business. From the fact that the question came to the fore, one concludes that most Republican primary voters agreed that business acumen matters; the only question was who had more of it. At least in the minds of the Trump supporters, the argument was won by Mr. Trump, since he had built his own business and, despite periodic setbacks, was extremely successful in advancing it. Mrs. Fiorina, for all her qualities, had worked primarily for a company constructed by others, and was perceived not to be as successful at running it. The importance of economic prudence has been stressed by President Trump himself in recent months. Democrats have been complaining that wealthy businesspeople have been tapped to fill cabinet positions like Secretary of Treasury, which are concerned with economic matters. What they see as a bad thing, though, seems just the opposite to the new president, who thinks that business success is a necessary qualification for holding important economic positions. To be sure, being good at economics is not prudence in the complete sense of the term, and Aristotle and Thomas would be among the first to say so. But to the American mind, the two look a lot alike, and thus we are not surprised, and Thomas would not be surprised, to find that some voters find such a quality to be an important consideration in selecting a candidate.

There are, needless to say, a number of virtues that President Trump is perceived to be lacking. Since virtues belong to the soul, and since the soul is hard to observe, this author for one withholds judgment on what Mr. Trump's character is actually like. But even many of the Trumpites would admit that Mr. Trump has displayed, for example, a lack of temperance, at least in the past. It is said that he does not drink alcohol, but it is also said that he has indulged and overindulged a weakness for feminine beauty. It is a matter of record, moreover, that he has been married three times, although the current marriage is apparently solid. Moreover, there are the virtues that Aristotle discusses in Book 4 of the *Nicomachean Ethics*, the virtues that have to do with the giving and receiving of property and honor, as well as the social virtues. These virtues culminate in magnanimity, but Mr. Trump does not seem to match the description that Aristotle provides for the magnanimous man very closely. And then there are the three theological virtues that are, in the view of Thomas Aquinas, the most important virtues of all. In Thomas's view, these virtues are important and valuable even for kings and statesmen, whose job is to guide the souls of human beings into heaven. In the general election, neither Mr. Trump nor Secretary Clinton were perceived to possess great theological virtue. In the Republican primary, though, some candidates were viewed as possessing such virtues to a greater degree than others. Senator Cruz, for example, was especially viewed as a virtuous Christian by some, and Senator Cruz did do well in some states wherein Evangelical Christians comprise a large proportion of the Republican electorate. Mr. Trump made an awkward attempt to reach out to Evangelicals, and most of them voted for him in the general election; few of them, however, would think of Mr. Trump as possessing great theological virtue. Many of the Trumpites are Christians, but it seems unlikely that they are Trumpites *because* they are Christians.

All of these perceived lacunae in the list of virtues possessed by President Trump serve as evidence against identifying too closely the political principles of Thomas Aquinas and the astonishing rise of Donald Trump to the presidency. There are surely differences—and extensive ones—between Thomism and Trumpism. Still, Thomism offers a great many insights into the phenomenon of Trumpism and in the end may well explain it much better than the alternatives.

NOTES

1. *Summa theologiae*, Ia-IIae, q. 95, a. 2, reply to obj. 3.
2. *Summa theologiae*, IIa-IIae, q. 101, a. 1.

BIBLIOGRAPHY

Aristotle. 1932. *Politics*. Vol. XXI. Trans. H. Rackham. Cambridge, MA: Harvard University Press.

———. 1934. *Aristotle, XIX, Nicomachean Ethics (Loeb Classical Library)*. 2nd ed. Cambridge, MA: Harvard University Press.

Aquinas, Thomas. 1947. *Summa Theologica*. 3 Vols. Trans. Fathers of the English Dominican Province. New York: Benziger Bros., Inc.

PART II

Modern and Liberal Thought

CHAPTER 5

Trump as a Machiavellian Prince? Reflections on Corruption and American Constitutionalism

Catherine Zuckert

For the last two years pundits in the popular press have regularly asked whether Donald Trump is a Machiavellian "prince." Emphasizing his low regard for the truth, willingness to renegotiate deals rather than keep his word, and stated admiration for "tough guys" like Vladimir Putin and Rodrigo Duterte, some commentators have argued that he is.[1] However, noting that Trump has not managed always "to appear merciful, faithful, humane, honest, and religious," as Machiavelli recommends in *Prince* 17, or to secure his own place by using "cruelty" all at once to eliminate his competitors, others have concluded that the president has not been able to make himself either feared or loved.[2]

According to Machiavelli, however, political outcomes are not simply determined by the character or competence (virtue or *virtù*) of leaders.[3] Results of campaigns and policies are also shaped by circumstances or "the times" as well as the institutional and legal framework in which leaders operate. Indeed, *the* central point of Machiavelli's two most widely read treatises, *The Prince* and *Discourses on Livy,* could be said to be: don't rest

C. Zuckert (✉)
University of Notre Dame, Notre Dame, IN, USA

© The Author(s) 2018
M. B. Sable, A. J. Torres (eds.), *Trump and Political Philosophy,*
https://doi.org/10.1007/978-3-319-74427-8_5

73

your hopes for good government on the virtuous character of your leaders. Politically ambitious men are as self-regarding as ordinary citizens or subjects. Instead of trying to educate a political elite of "the best and the brightest" to govern others, you should learn from the example of Rome how to construct "new modes and orders." As sketched in his *Discourses*, these new modes and orders would, as James Madison famously stated in *Federalist* 51, make ambition counteract ambition so as to enable those who govern to control the governed without oppressing them. Rather than ask whether Trump has the qualities of a Machiavellian "prince," a few scholars have suggested, Machiavelli would advise Americans worried about the election of Trump as president to trust in the constitutional checks on the powers of the executive.[4] Unfortunately, students of the American constitutional order have been worrying for some time about the growth of "the imperial Presidency."[5] Since Machiavelli argues that political leaders always strive to secure themselves by increasing their resources, he would undoubtedly think such scholars are correct. But, if they are, America's problems do not lie in Trump or his election so much as in the failure of generations of American leaders to adapt the constitution to the radically changing circumstances of the modern world.

Since Trump did not win a majority of the popular vote, some have blamed the "outdated" constitutional provisions for an electoral college for producing an undemocratic outcome. But even in his most explicitly "republican" work, Machiavelli does not advocate a purely or simply democratic form of government. Although he argues that "the multitude is wiser and more constant than a prince" (*D* 1.58), he also suggests that the people make characteristic mistakes in electing leaders and directing public policy.[6] People generally prefer bold or spirited policies whose benefits are immediately evident to cautious policies whose beneficial results become evident only gradually after much time. The Roman people thus elected Varro consul, because he promised to rid them of the threat posed by Hannibal, as the delaying tactics employed by Fabius Maximus had not. But Varro's incompetence as a general and subsequent defeat at Cannae left Rome vulnerable to conquest. Only Hannibal's failure to take advantage of the opportunity saved the republic from destruction. Because decisions must ultimately be referred to the people in a republic, Machiavelli acknowledges, it is not possible to avoid such dangers entirely. Leaders who sincerely wish to work for the common good should nevertheless be aware of the problem and try to counteract it.

Because he saw that the preservation of republic government requires those who have held the highest offices not merely to cede them to their duly elected successors, but to serve under them (D 1.36, 3.47), Machiavelli would have congratulated the out-going President, Barack Obama, and the losing candidate, Hillary Clinton, for conceding rapidly and urging their followers not to contest the results of the election. For the same reason he would have found Donald Trump's threats not to do so worrisome.

Would Machiavelli think that the Trump election shows that the American constitutional order—not merely the laws, but the basic political organization of the people, the offices of government and the way they are selected—should be reformed? That would depend, Machiavelli suggests, on whether the American people have become corrupt.

Constitutions and laws are thought to derive much of their power from their longevity.[7] In Rome, Machiavelli observes in *Discourses* 1.18, "the order of the state was the authority of the people, of the Senate, of the tribunes, of the consuls; the mode of soliciting and creating the magistrates; and the mode of making the laws"; and "these orders varied hardly or not at all." However, he suggests, over time civilized peoples tend to become corrupt. Ironically, as a result of their becoming accustomed to obeying others, they lose the skills necessary to govern themselves. The Romans attempted to counteract various kinds of moral and political vices that gradually emerged in the republic—for example, adultery, excessive displays of wealth, and ambition—by passing new laws. But these laws were not effective, Machiavelli suggests, because the orders were not changed along with them.

Machiavelli gives his readers two examples of modes and orders that worked well so long as the Roman people were not corrupt, but that later had pernicious effects. The first concerns the character of the individuals elected to the highest offices. So long as the people were not corrupt, he observes, the Romans elected virtuous men who had demonstrated both their dedication to the republic and their ability. So no one put himself forward who was not virtuous lest he be shamed in public by not being selected. After the people became corrupt, however, they began to choose men who entertained them rather than those who know how to secure the safety of the republic and its people from foreign aggression. And becoming ever more corrupt, they stopped favoring those who pleased them and began electing those whose power they feared.

Similarly, Machiavelli argues, the law that enabled not merely any representative of the people, but any citizen to propose a measure and all citizens to discuss it, was good so long as the citizens were good. Everyone

was encouraged to put forward ideas about how the public could be benefitted, and the people were generally able to judge which would be best
after all options were heard. But after the citizens had become bad, this
seemingly free and egalitarian "order" had terrible effects, because only
the powerful dared propose laws. They sought not to preserve the freedom of all, but only to increase their own power; and others were afraid to
risk offending the powerful by speaking out against their proposals.

So, have the American people gradually become corrupt like the
Romans? In an interview with a *New York Times* reporter shortly before
the inauguration, the only Silicon Valley tycoon who publicly supported
the election of the president suggested that Trump appealed to the same
desire for entertainment while simultaneously arousing fear. "The election had an apocalyptic feel to it," Peter Thiel observed. "There was a
way in which Trump was funny, so you could be apocalyptic and funny
at the same time. It's a strange combination, but it's somehow very powerful psychologically."[8]

Other observers of the election noted the way in which Trump violated
all sorts of conventional norms, both political and moral. In the first
debate among the Republic candidates he made his lack of partisan loyalty
manifest by refusing to promise that he would support the party's choice.
This was not the only respect in which Trump showed a lack of faith.
Unlike his predecessors, Trump had no publicly declared religious affiliation nor had he been seen attending church. Although previous candidates and Presidents had been castigated for being divorced (Stevenson)
and extra-marital affairs (Gary Hart and Bill Clinton), evangelical
Christians voted overwhelmingly for the thrice-divorced man who
unabashedly treated women as sexual objects both in word and deed. Nor
did Trump voters seem to be concerned about potential conflicts of interest between the businessman's operations and his powers as President. It
had become customary for candidates for the U.S. presidency to release
their federal income tax returns and to promise to put all their assets in a
blind trust to avoid any such conflicts. Trump refused to do either, and his
supporters did not seem to care that he may not have contributed anything to supporting the government that made it possible for him to
become so wealthy (or to know how wealthy he actually was). Or that he
had obtained a somewhat questionable medical excuse from military service. Or that he had been embroiled in a series of law suits alleging breach
of contract and deceptive promises. A majority of white Christians voted
for him, at least because of his anti-abortion stance and promise to appoint

a similarly minded conservative judge to the Supreme Court. And despite evidence of Russian attempts not merely to tamper with an American election, but to swing it toward Trump, a majority of those in active military service voted for him as well.

But is the election of a man of questionable character to the highest office not by a majority, but with the support of a large number of voters sufficient to show that the American people as a whole have become corrupt and that the future of the republic is endangered? Could the Trump election not merely be an example of the way of which the public can be misled by the promises of an irresponsible candidate? They may have to suffer the effects, but under a republican government a leader who proves to be incompetent or corrupt leader can be voted out of office. Some observers have worried that Trump will use his power to begin a nuclear war that will destroy republic and its people. He might see fighting a war as a means of unifying his support at home. Machiavelli would remind his readers, however, that the defeat of Varro at Cannae threatened the complete destruction of Rome; and, more fundamentally, that no state should "ever believe that it can always adopt safe courses. ... For in the order of things it is found that one never seeks to avoid one inconvenience without running into another, but prudence consists in knowing how to recognize the qualities of inconveniences, and in picking the less bad as good" (*P* 21). Some people knowingly took a risk in voting for Trump, because they thought that there was no question that both Hillary and Bill Clinton were corrupt.[9] In other words, they did not vote for Trump so much as they voted against his competitors.[10]

Just as Machiavelli observed that the Roman people became corrupt gradually over time, so a small group of commentators in *The Claremont Review of Books* have argued that the American republic has gradually become corrupted in the decades following World War II. Writing under the pseudonym Publius Decius Mus, Michael Anton reminded his readers that "one of the *Journal of American Greatness's* deeper arguments was that only in a corrupt republic, in corrupt times, could a Trump rise."[11] Granting that "Trump is worse than imperfect," Anton assured his readers that electing Trump constituted their last chance of overturning the stupid immigration, economic and foreign policies that had disunited the country. Going even further in the same apocalyptic direction, in an article entitled, "After the Republic," Angelo M. Codevilla declared that it would not matter whether Hillary Clinton or Donald Trump was elected, because there are no longer any effective constitutional restraints on the exercise of power. Whether Democrats or Republicans are elected, "executive orders, phone calls, and the right judge mean a lot more than laws. Over the past-century, presidents have ruled not by enforcing laws but increasingly through agencies that write their own rules ... As for the Supreme Court, the American people have seen it invent rights where there were none—e.g., abortion—while trammeling ones that had been the republic's spine, such as the free exercise of religion and freedom of speech." However, although he observed that "two-thirds of Americans believe that elected and appointed officials ... are leading the country in the wrong direction: that they are corrupt, do more harm than good, make us poorer, get us into wars and lose them" and are thus attracted to an explicitly "anti-establishment" candidate, Codevilla did not think that there is a majority "ready to support a coherent imperial program to reverse the course of America's half-century." But like Mus and John Marini, author of a third article published in the CRB on "Donald Trump and the American Crisis," Codevilla did not blame a corrupt people. He blamed "the ruling class" which has instituted an "administrative state" based on expert knowledge in place of a republican political order.[12]

Machiavelli would agree that the fall of a republic should be attributed to failures of its ruling class. But he would not wholly accept the CRB's authors' understanding of political corruption or endorse their response. These authors emphasize the importance of preserving, if not reviving religious faith, conventional sexual mores, and virtue in the leaders. Although Machiavelli praises the way in which leaders of the Roman republic used religion to command and control their fellow citizens, he also shows that training and a proved record of success are more reliable.[13] In both his prose writings and comedies he shows the importance of retaining the appearance of conventional morality in marriages and of shared religious beliefs on the part of leaders, but he suggests that it is only the appearance that is required. He himself did not provide a model of either form of faith. In observing the effects of the corruption of the Roman people, Machiavelli explains not only that it occurred gradually, but also that it began after they won the Punic War and no longer felt themselves threatened by foreign aggression. Machiavelli's definition of a corrupt people is one that no longer recognizes the need to risk their own lives to defend the fatherland or to elect virtuous leaders. Unwilling to acknowledge that some people are more able than others, they are animated by envy and enjoy seeing their leaders' faults exposed in public. But without trusted and able leadership, such people also become increasingly subject to fear.

Later in the *Discourses* (3.1) Machiavelli argues that there are two ways of counteracting this tendency of peoples living in a republic to become corrupt. The first is to have the very existence of the republic and its people threatened by a foreign invasion. Under such circumstances people readily see the need to risk their own lives in defending it and to elevate individuals of demonstrated virtue and ability to lead them. However, this is obviously a very dangerous way of renewing republican institutions; provoking a foreign invasion can just as easily result in the destruction of the republic. So Machiavelli recommends a less risky alternative. To revive the fear that leads peoples form governments in the first place and makes people willing both to elevate virtuous citizens to positions of authority and obey their commands or laws, he argues that it is necessary to institute and enact "public executions" of outstanding citizens accused of trying to overthrow the republic every five to ten years. The examples of such "executions" he gives are of public trials of Roman leaders that did not in all cases lead to their conviction, much less death. He apparently thought that seeing prominent and powerful leaders subjected to such a trial would suffice to arouse the fear of punishment for less obvious failures to obey the law on the part of ordinary citizens by showing that no one was above or beyond its reach.

Article II, Section 4 of the U.S. Constitution might seem to institute such trials for American public officials, since it includes provisions for the removal from office of the president, vice president, and all civil officers of the United States on impeachment for, and conviction of, treason, bribery, or other high crimes and misdemeanors. But the rise of political parties shortly after the Founding destroyed the potential effect of this provision. Ambition can counteract ambition only when the interests of the man are linked to the powers of his office. And it has not proved to be in the political interest of many legislators to see a member of their own party removed from office. It is no accident that in more than two hundred years only two presidents have been impeached, and that none has been convicted.

Other scholars have pointed out that the rise of political parties also deprived the electoral college of its intended filtering function. Thinking that members of the public at large would not know the candidates, the founders sought to create a body that would be able to make an informed judgment of the candidates. But the political parties quickly acquired control not only of nominating candidates but also of selecting the official "electors" who would determine the outcome of the election.[14] These officials are now bound by state laws to follow the results of the popular election, and are not allowed to exercise their own, independent judgment.

However, as the Trump victory shows, major American political parties are no longer able to control their own nominations. Candidates are selected by a series of primary elections in which individuals able to form their own organizations and raise funds to support them compete for the support of a small plurality of the population that tends to be more ideologically extreme than the American people as a whole. There is no longer any intermediary body of individuals with more political experience and knowledge than the public at large that "vets" the individual candidates. Candidates are subject to ever more intrusive examination by the popular press, which becomes more concentrated as candidates are eliminated in a timed series of primary contests that begin in states with rather atypical electorates. But, as the Trump election has also made clear, the "mass media" is no longer trusted by many voters and increased use of "social media" has made the circulation of "fake" or false news more prevalent.[15] As Machiavelli saw in Rome, the corruption of the electoral process goes hand in hand with the corruption of public debate.

Unlike many contemporary commentators, Machiavelli would not consider the current division within the American electorate to be unusual—or undesirable. On the contrary, he observed, all political communities are divided between two "humors," that of "the great" who want to command and oppress and that of the people who do not want to be commanded or oppressed. These "humors" or dispositions do not represent natural differences or economic classes. Both arise from the fact that individual human beings are weak and feel the need to associate with others in order to secure their lives and property, but that once they feel relatively secure, they seek more property and more power to preserve what they have. So, Machiavelli observes (D 1.37), the Roman plebs first sought protection from oppression by the patricians by establishing the offices of the tribunes, but once they received such protection, the plebs then sought to share the offices or honors formerly held exclusively by the patricians, such as the consulate. The two "humors" do not constitute two groups that differ by nature, the great and the ordinary; on the contrary, everyone is always seeking to acquire more. Nor do the two humors correspond simply to economic classes or interests. As Machiavelli sees, the individuals who control the coercive force of government have the ability to seize what they desire and thus become wealthy. In established republics, such "great" individuals seek to acquire dominion by competing for the support of the people, who seek merely not to be oppressed. Forms of oppression differ, however. So in the U.S. we now see the leaders of the Republican

Party promising to relieve their followers of economic regulations they find costly and policies that force them to tolerate behavior that is contrary to their deeply held religious convictions as well as from various foreign threats. Democratic leaders, on the other hand, promise to provide governmental protection to groups that have experienced oppression in the form of discrimination on the basis of race and gender. In any free polity, Machiavelli sees, there will be differences of opinion and private interests. As a result, politics will be contentious. To suppress conflict would be to destroy liberty.[16] What is necessary is to devise and maintain laws and institutions, "modes and orders," that channel the conflict so that the contending groups check the excesses of the others—without, however, bringing government to a halt. (See *D* 1.50.)

Analyzing the ills of his own republic, in the *Florentine Histories* Machiavelli declares that "those who hope that a republic can be united are very much deceived." But he argues, "Some divisions are harmful to republics and some are helpful. Those are harmful that are accompanied by sects and partisans. Thus, since a founder of a republic cannot provide that there be no enmities in it, he has to provide at least that there not be sects." As in *D* 3.28 he observes that citizens acquire "reputations," i.e., offices and influence, in two ways: public or private. They acquire public recognition by winning a battle, executing a major policy initiated with care and prudence, or "advising the republic wisely and prosperously." But they acquire personal, partisan supporters "by benefiting this or that other citizen, defending him from the magistrates, helping him with money, getting him unmerited honors, and ingratiating themselves" with the people by sponsoring public celebrations and gifts.[17] Like a detective in a mystery story, Machiavelli thus suggests that in seeking the causes of dysfunctional divisions within a republic, one should "follow the money." In contemporary U.S. politics that would mean examining and finding ways to remedy the effect private wealth and donations now have on the self-nominations of candidates for high office to be determined by primary elections and the way Congressional rules have given political parties control over committee assignments and campaign funds so that it has become extremely dangerous for a legislator who wants to be re-elected to "cross over the aisle" and negotiate a compromise with the opposition. Control of both major parties has been placed increasingly in the hands of extreme partisans and ideologues. And each party is united primarily by its desire to block the initiatives of the other. No wonder there are so many negative ads and the level of animosity in public political discourse continues to increase.

Stasis at the national level has, moreover, descended into the states and localities. While the Democratic Party concentrated on winning national elections, Republicans organized to win control of the state governments whose legislatures determine the definitions of electoral districts. As a result, they have been able to design districts that, while not obviously gerrymandered, maximize the impact of their votes and dilute those of their competitors. Under these circumstances it will be difficult, if not impossible for a majority of American voters to express their dissatisfaction with the current Republican domination of all levels and branches of government at the next midterm election. It is not clear at this point whether the Democrats, who have tended to concentrate their efforts on the national government, will respond, as they should, by organizing and campaigning more vigorously in state and local elections.

Machiavelli's reflections on the problems inherent in republican government suggest, however, that reforming the nominating system so that it more clearly reflects the preferences of the electorate at the time of the election will not suffice to obtain better candidates or choices. It is important to design and maintain institutions that force candidates for high office to seek popular support. But, he recognizes, the people can be misled by candidates who make rash or unfulfillable promises. It seems, indeed, as if American politicians and commentators need to be reminded of the instability of politics in direct democracies. There is an important, indeed, essential role for experience and expertise—political as well as scientific. In selecting the last two U.S. Presidents, we have seen voters favor candidates who ran as outsiders and promised undefined "change." The election of Barack Obama was taken by many to signal the end of residual discrimination on the basis of race, but during his presidency that promise seemed to evaporate in the face of greater tensions between police and African-Americans. And his efforts to revive the economy, improve U.S. relations with Muslim nations, and provide universal healthcare all ran into such serious difficulties, that some of the same voters became disillusioned with him and his party. Although Trump appealed more to his supporters' fears than to their hopes, at the very beginning of his presidency he seems to have encountered many of the same difficulties in fulfilling his campaign promises. Both he and Obama entered office without much experience in Washington; and their failures have added to popular disillusionment with the institutions of American government. In order to obtain better and more effective government with popular consent, Machiavelli would urge more knowledgeable political elites to devise ways of taking better control of the process through which candidates are selected—not directly but indirectly, for example, by changing the number, order, and timing of primary elections held in the states.[18] The primary voters in Iowa and New Hampshire who, in effect, now determine the first cut in the selection of the candidates for president are not representative of the diverse American electorate. If the primaries were organized differently, e.g., by dividing the nation in fourths and staggering the elections, so that the candidates are winnowed earlier in the process, the media could report less on who's winning the "horse race," and provide more information about and analysis of the individuals competing. More reforms in campaign finance laws and the legislative process will be necessary, however, to reassure the public that special interests do not have the role in determining public policy that they currently appear to have. The demand for "transparency" in the legislative process as a means of curbing the influence of special interests has contributed to the stasis and so popular disillusionment with American public institutions by making it difficult, if not impossible for representatives to distance themselves from the particular interests of their districts and supporters enough to compromise with others in passing more generally beneficial laws.

But Machiavelli would also emphasize, such reforms fall very short of a "revolution" in the American constitutional order. They constitute the kind of "remedies" he argues that leaders of republican governments must constantly devise in order to adjust its laws and orders to changing circumstances, if those laws and orders are to be maintained.[19] Trump may have made demagogic appeals to some of his voters, but constitutional checks on executive power remain in place. He is commander-in-chief of the armed forces, but these forces are not private or partisan like the troops of the Roman leaders who overthrew that republic or the brown shirts who served Hitler. We have seen U.S. courts almost immediately slow, if not entirely block some of his first moves to control immigration. And even with his party controlling both houses of Congress, there is constant talk of impeachment. To be sure, Machiavelli warns, no one in politics should ever be complacent. People do not like to be constrained or taxed, but they need an effective government to protect their lives, liberties, and properties. If the government of the United States continues to be stymied by partisan stasis, demands for more serious, dangerous changes will increasingly become credible.

NOTES

1. For example, David Ignatius, "Donald Trump is the American Machiavelli," *Washington Post,* November 10, 2016, https://www.washingtonpost.com/opinions/donald-trump-is-the-american-machiavelli/2016/11/10/8ebfae16-a794-11e6-ba59-a7d93165c6d4_story.html?utm_term=.6f0d;   Andrew Sheng and Xiao Geng, "Donald Trump is the ultimate Machiavellian prince," *Financial Review,* December 21, 2016, http://www.afr.com/news/politics/world/donald-trump-is-the-ultimate-machiavellian-prince-20161220-gt-exc3; Jannik Skadhauge Sano, "Machiavelli, Trump, and success," April 18, 2017,   https://www.linkedin.com/pulse/machiavellianism-trump-succes-jannik-skadhauge-sano; Susan B. Glasser, "Machiavelli Would Approve," *Politico,* April 17, 2017, http://www.politico.eu/article/donald-trump-rus sia-foreign-policy-machiavelli-would-approve michael anton/.

2. For example, retracting his earlier opinion, David Ignatius, "Trump is not so Machiavellian after all," *Washington Post,* March 23, 2017, https://www.washingtonpost.com/opinions/trump-is-not-so-machiavellian-after-all/2017/03/23/01eb9516 0ffd 11c7 ab07-07d9f521f6b3_story.html?utm_term=.2f9490afe; Peter Sahlins, "Sincerely, Niccolo Machiavelli: An Open Letter to Donald Trump," *Berkeley Blog,* February 26, 2017, http://blogs.berkeley.edu/2017/02/26/sincerely-niccolo-machiavelli-an-open-letter-to-donald-trump-from-a-berkeley-freshman-published-in-salon-magazine/; Maurizio Viroli, "Machiavelli not in support of Donald Trump," *Princeton University Press Blog,* April 11, 2016, http://blog.press.princeton.edu/2016/08/11/maurizio-viroli-machiavelli-not-in-support-of-donald-trump/; Jack Butler, "4 Ways Donald Trump Doesn't Live up to Machiavelli," *The   Federalist*   (2016).   http://thefederalist.com/2016/01/22/4-ways-donald-trump-doesnt-live-up-to-machiavelli/; Steffen White, "Machiavelli's Verdict on Trump: He's No Prince," *Bureaucracy   Blog,*   March   27,   2017,   https://bureaucracybuster.com/2017/03/27/machiavellis-verdict-on-trump-hes-no-prince/;   Doyle McManus, "Trump is neither feared nor loved," *Los Angeles Times,* July 2, 2017,   http://www.latimes.com/opinion/op-ed/la-oe-mcmanus-trump-fear-love-20170702-story.html; "If Trump Has Read Machiavelli, It Doesn't Show," *The Heisenberg Blog,* July 7, 2017, https://seekingalpha.com/instablog/47439673-the-heisenberg/5008973-trump-read-machiavelli-doesn-t-show.

3. As David Wooten argues, "Introduction," *Niccolò Machiavelli "The Prince"* (Indianapolis: Hackett, 195), xxviii, by "prince" Machiavelli does not refer simply to a son who will inherit power from his father, the king. He begins *The Prince* by cataloging the many different ways a "prince" can acquire rule, not only by means of force but also with the support of his people.

4. Maurizio Viroli, *How To Choose a Leader* (Princeton: Princeton University Press, 2016); Robert Zaretsky, "The Hands of a Leader: Donald Trump and Niccolò Machiavelli," *Los Angeles Times Book Review, May 31, 2016*, https://lareviewofbooks.org/article/218473/.

5. Most recently, but before the election of Donald Trump, such concerns were expressed during the Obama administration by Bruce Ackerman, *The Decline and Fall of the American Republic* (Cambridge, MA: Belknap Press, 2013). However, as Eric A. Posner, "POTUS-phobia," *The New Republic,* December 23, 2010, points out in his review of Ackerman's book, Arthur Schlesinger warned about the development of an "imperial presidency" in the 1970's. Indeed, worries about a concentration of power not merely in the national government, as opposed to the states and localities, but specifically in the executive branch can be traced back to the founding era, in disagreements between the Federalists and Anti-federalists, Alexander Hamilton and Thomas Jefferson. To counteract the necessarily slow decision-making processes in deliberative bodies, Machiavelli himself argued for the utility of an office like the Roman dictatorship (*D* 1.34), which gave unlimited powers to an individual to deal with a specific emergency for a strictly limited period of times.

6. *D* 1.53. Quotations from Niccolò Machiavelli, *Discourses on Livy,* trans. Harvey C. Mansfield and Nathan Tarcov (Chicago: University of Chicago Press, 1996), 115.

7. See *Federalist* 49; Aristotle *Politics* 2.8.1268b4-1269a24.

8. Maureen Dowd, "Peter Thiel, Trump's Tech Pal, Explains Himself," *New York Times,* January 11, 2017, https://www.nytimes.com/2017/01/11/fashion/peter-thiel-donald-trump-silicon-valley-technology-gawker.html.

9. Amy Davidson, "Donald Trump's Stunning Win", *New Yorker,* November 9, 2016, http://www.newyorker.com/news/amy-davidson/trumps-stunning-win.

10. James G. Wiles, "Machiavelli's Advice for Mr. Trump—and Us," *American Thinker,* April 30, 2017, http://www.americanthinker.com/articles/2017/04/machiavellis_advice_for_mr_trump_and_us.html, argues that the question is whether the expanded welfare policies of the Obama administration have so corrupted the American people that they will not be able or willing to do without them. But are these the "people" who voted for Trump? If so, Machiavelli would see Obama and the Democratic Party as having sought partisans by handing out individual benefits. However, since the benefits were provided by law and not delivered directly or personally and public health is a public good, Machiavelli would not think that people who sought to retain goods they had obtained from their government through political action are corrupt. As he states in *P* 14, he thinks that it is very natural to desire to acquire, and those who do so successfully are praised. A corrupt people for Machiavelli are those that have lost the organizational and deliberative skills to rule themselves. (See *D* 1.16.)

11. Publius Decius Mus [Michael Anton], "The Flight 93 Election," http://
    www.claremont.org/crb/basicpage/the-flight-93-election/.   Michael
    Anton had been one of the founders of that on-line journal which was
    taken down almost as soon as it appeared. He has since become a national
    security advisor for the Trump administration, and the *Journal of American
    Greatness* has been replaced by a seemingly more respectable, evidently
    better funded journal entitled *American Affairs,* available both in print
    and on-line. Machiavelli would, no doubt, have been puzzled by Anton's
    choice of a pseudonym. In *D* 2.16 and 3.45 Machiavelli compares the
    intentional sacrifice of his life in battle to inspire courage in his troops first
    by Publius Decius Mus the elder and then by his son Publius Decius Mus
    unfavorably to the alternative policy adopted by their fellow consuls,
    Manlius Torquatus and Fabius Rullianus, who held part of their troops in
    reserve to attack and prevail over a tired enemy. In *D* 3.1 Machiavelli recognizes that extraordinarily self-sacrificing acts of leaders such as the Decii
    inspired good men to imitate them and made the wicked ashamed not to
    follow produced "almost the same effect" as laws and orders, i.e., that laws
    and orders are a more reliable way of preventing a people from becoming
    corrupt than inspiring examples of virtuous behavior.
12. John Marini, "Donald Trump and the American Crisis," *CRB Digital,* July
    22, 2016, http://www.claremont.org/crb/basicpage/donald-trump-and-
    the-american-crisis/.
13. *D* 1.15.
14. See James W. Ceaser, *Presidential Selection: Theory and Development*
    (Princeton: Princeton University Press, 1979), and the chapter by Robert
    Burton, Zachary German, and Michael Zuckert in this volume.
15. Hunt Alcott and Matthew Gentzkow, "Social Media and Fake News in the
    2016 Election," *Journal of Economic Perspectives* 31, No. 2 (Spring 2017):
    211–36.
16. Cf. *Federalist* 10.
17. Niccolò Machiavelli, *Florentine Histories,* trans. Laura F. Banfield and
    Harvey C. Mansfield (Princeton: Princeton University Press, 1988), 7.1,
    276–77.
18. See *D* 1.47-48. After the debacle of the McGovern election, the Democratic
    Party tried to do this by creating superdelegates. But it was unlikely that the
    nomination of Hillary Clinton would have been accepted as legitimate if she
    had not won a majority of the votes in the primary elections. Machiavelli
    suggests that elites should not merely select the candidates, but select them
    in such a way that the people will vote for the candidates selected.
19. *D* 1.49, 3.49.

BIBLIOGRAPHY

Ackerman, Bruce. 2013. *The Decline and Fall of the American Republic.* Cambridge, MA: Belknap Press.

Alcott, Hunt, and Matthew Gentzkow. 2017. Social Media and Fake News in the 2016 Election. *Journal of Economic Perspectives* 31 (2 Spring): 211–236.

Aristotle. 1959. *Politics.* Trans. H. Rackham. Cambridge, MA: Harvard University Press.

Ceaser, James W. 1979. *Presidential Selection: Theory and Development.* Princeton: Princeton University Press.

Hamilton, Alexander, James Madison, and John Jay. 2001. The Federalist. In *The Gideon Edition*, ed. George W. Careyand and James McClellan. Indianapolis: Liberty Fund.

Machiavelli, Niccolò. 1988. *Florentine Histories.* Trans. Laura F. Banfield and Harvey C. Mansfield. Princeton: Princeton University Press.

———. 1995. *The Prince.* Trans. David Wootton. Indianapolis: Hackett Pub. Co.

Machiavelli, Niccolò. 1996. *Discourses on Livy.* Trans. Harvey C. Mansfield and Nathan Tarcov. Chicago: University of Chicago Press.

Viroli, Maurizio. 2016. *How to Choose a Leader.* Princeton: Princeton University Press.

CHAPTER 6

Machiavelli and Inequality

Faisal Baluch

The standard diagnosis of our current age of populism is that it is symptomatic of increasing inequality. Deindustrialization and globalization have jeopardized the economic well-being of the working class in the West and they have reacted by endorsing populist leaders who promise a return to a golden age. But this diagnosis can be critiqued on the grounds that the impact of globalization has been felt for a long time. In other words, the timing cannot be explained on economic grounds. But the other problem with this explanation is that it fails to account for the nature of the populism that has arisen. For if one sees on the side of the electorate anger and a desire for change, populist leaders exhibit a disregard for precedent, especially in questions of family ties and business conflicts, and openly hold that their concern with personal interest is completely unproblematic. The leaders' populism is not limited to rhetoric that shows concern for the plight of common citizens, but is displayed more so as a disregard for the common and a concern with the personal. The leaders do not find it necessary to differentiate their stance toward the personal from that of private citizens, yet do not share the economic status of the people. Thus, economic inequality is combined with equality of a personalistic outlook. The age of populism thus puts on display both equality and

F. Baluch (✉)
College of the Holy Cross, Worcester, MA, USA

© The Author(s) 2018
M. B. Sable, A. J. Torres (eds.), *Trump and Political Philosophy*,
https://doi.org/10.1007/978-3-319-74427-8_6

inequality. In what follows, I show how Machiavelli's accounts of Rome and Florence reveal that it is precisely this type of equality and inequality that leads to the rise of populist leaders. Furthermore, the rise of such leaders is for Machiavelli a sign of corruption. Machiavelli's account of corruption, I argue, on the strength of the case of Florence, puts him at odds with those who defend commercial republics.

The chapter is organized as follows. I begin by distinguishing between three senses of the term equality that can be gathered from Machiavelli's texts. I then show how each sense manifested itself in Rome and Florence. I conclude by showing that Machiavelli's relevance when studying the rise of populist leaders is not limited to his analysis of Machiavellian leaders in the *Prince*.

Whether Machiavelli is viewed as an egalitarian depends to a consid erable extent on how he is read and which of his writings is emphasized. As the author of the *Prince*, calling for a singular savior for Italy, who he hopes is molded in the kiln that gave the world the great founders, the descriptor egalitarian does not seem to fit Machiavelli. But this impression is not limited to what might be called a vulgar reading of the *Prince*. The place of *un uomo solo* is prominent in the *Discourses*, and the focus of the third book of the *Discourses*. Yet we also have another Machiavelli. This Machiavelli warns against putting the guard of free- dom in the hands of the nobles, sees gentlemen as the source of trou- ble, and calls for poor citizens but a rich state. This Machiavelli is also best found in the *Discourses* celebrating Roman virtue. Therefore on first blush both the egalitarian Machiavelli and the inegalitarian Machiavelli seem true to the texts.[1] Thus, returning to the contempo- rary question at hand: what would Machiavelli make of the inequality and its relationship to recent political developments? The answer doesn't seem immediately evident.

This difficulty arises from the fact that Machiavelli does not use the term equality in only one sense. Equality appears in Machiavelli's writings in at least three senses. In the context of law and politics Machiavelli writes of civil equality [*civile equalità*]. Equality also appears as "equality of belongings" [*equalità di sustanze*], or what we would call economic equal- ity. Finally, equality also appears in Machiavelli's portrayal of individuals' attitudes and drives. The three senses relate broadly to the three dimen- sions of a polity: political, economic, and social.

POLITICAL EQUALITY

While in liberal democracies the main type of inequality under discussion is economic, Machiavelli conceives of another form of inequality which is even more pernicious. In a chapter in the *Discourses* dedicated to the question of inequality, Machiavelli writes the following: "To clarify this name of gentlemen such as it may be, I say that those are called gentlemen who live idly in abundance from the returns of their possessions without having any care either for cultivation or for other necessary trouble in living. Such as these are pernicious in every republic and every province, but more pernicious are those who, beyond the aforesaid fortunes, command from a castle and have subjects who obey them."[2] The first type of gentlemen are merely wealthy and thus are not driven by necessity to work and labor. But the "more pernicious type" are those who combine this wealth with what we would call militias. These latter are so problematic as to make a political way of life impossible. Understanding why such gentlemen make a political way of life impossible allows us to grasp the nature of political inequality.

These gentlemen with private militias are fundamentally a threat to a political way of life because they are not beholden to the law. A political way of life then is one governed by law. When, however, a portion of the population no longer feels the need to follow the laws then a political way of life is no longer possible. The first manifestation of political equality is that everyone is equal before the law. But while this principle of equality before the law now seems commonplace to us, Machiavelli's definition of the more pernicious type of gentleman suggests that respect for law depends on very particular conditions and cannot be taken for granted. Human beings do not of their own accord heed laws. The reason that gentlemen do not follow the laws is not because they are innately unconcerned with the law, rather their wealth makes it such that necessity does not bear on them and therefore they need not follow it.[3] Political equality requires that all citizens feel the necessity of following the law and this requires that private citizens not have forces that would allow them to stand up to the city.

Now faced with such gentlemen the prospect of setting up a republic is rather dim, unless a drastic step is taken. Here is Machiavelli's recommendation: "he who wishes to make a republic where there are many gentlemen cannot do it unless he first eliminates all of them."[4] For words and laws to have a hold, first steel must be used to create political equality.[5] Political equality does not only manifest itself through the hold of the law on all citizens. Respect for law offers all citizens a number of goods that make life in a republic worth living. In a proto-Lockean passage, Machiavelli writes of the life enjoyed by citizens of republics: "Riches are seen to multiply there in large numbers, both those that come from agriculture and those that come from the arts. For each willingly multiples that thing and seeks to acquire those goods he believes he can enjoy once acquired."[6] Citizens of republics enjoy material security, since all are subject to law no one can be arbitrarily denied the use of their property. Political equality, however, is also manifested in another important sense in republics. Citizens of republics, Machiavelli writes, in the same passage are more willing to procreate not only because material security means that their patrimony is secure but also because they know "not only that they are born free and not slaves, but that they can, through their virtue, become princes,"[7] Here we have the second manifestation of political equality defined. Political equality entails everyone being equally subject to law, on the one hand, and everyone having the opportunity to become a prince as long as they have the requisite virtue, on the other. The accident of birth neither determines whether one is subject to law, nor whether one can become a prince. In the eyes of the republic, all citizens are equal and all are eligible for the greatest honor should they prove themselves worthy of it.

Political equality in the second sense is also central to the health of republics. Machiavelli's discussion of *fortuna* in the *Prince* presents the problem of humans who aren't readily able to change, faced with fickle *fortuna*. *Fortuna* it turns out can be only partly conquered. The solution suggested by the *Prince* is that the way to battle with the unconquerable *fortuna* is to change the fighter. A republic that enjoys political equality will have the opportunity to pick a prince who fits the times regardless of the individual's station in society.

The importance of political equality for the health of republics is illustrated by the contrast between Rome and Florence. In Machiavelli's Rome there is most decidedly a class divide between patricians and plebs, yet the patricians cannot do without the plebs. The glory and wealth that the patricians seek is gained through conquest, which requires manpower provided by the plebs. Furthermore, respect for law is ensured since the plebs too have representation.[8] Finally, the plebs enjoy political equality in the second sense outlined above since they are not barred from the honor of being captains.

Contrast all this with Florence. In Machiavelli's telling the trouble for Florence begins with the conflict between families. When the

Amidei family felt slighted over a broken promise of marriage by a member of the Buondelmonte family, they, along with their relatives the Uberti, sought to have the Buondelmonte responsible for the broken promise of marriage killed. This murder led to reprisals until ultimately the entire city divided into two factions, with one led by the Buondelmonte and the other led by the Uberti, was at war. This would have remained a personal conflict, but "since these families were strong in houses, towers, and men, they fought for many years without dislodging the other."[9] Their use of private militias meant that matters were settled by force and disrupted the entire city. But what is critical for us here is to understand what led the head of the Buondelmonte family to break his promise. Machiavelli writes that he was inflamed with "such ardor" that he did not think of the "faith he had pledged or injury he did in breaking it [his promise]."[10] Such action undertaken under passion is characteristic of those who have been brought up to be gentlemen. While not a direct parallel, one is put in mind of the rape of Lucrece by a young patrician in Rome. Gentlemen with wealth and manpower see themselves as immune to the laws and customs of society.

The troubles that begin as a result of political inequality are also sustained by it, as becomes evident in *Florentine Histories* II.12. Here Machiavelli relates how Florence during a period of peace had the opportunity to put its own house in order. In pursuit of this aim, power and arms were given to the Gonfalonier of Justice who was tasked with upholding justice and using the arms he had under his control to ensure that the guilty did not get away with crimes. This well-intentioned effort, however, failed to keep the peace because the nobles continued to live outside the law. They could do so since they had their own wealth and arms, and could use this to silence and suppress witnesses against them. Laws and orders, Machiavelli shows us, are only effective to the extent that citizens comply with them. The hallmark of political inequality is that a certain class of citizens views itself as exempt from the laws and orders of the city.

Political equality then is a necessary precondition for a healthy republic. It first ensures that all citizens follow the laws and the laws makes exceptions for no one. A modified form of the Aristotelian adage applies: political equality ensures that everyone is able to be ruled, and secondly, that all those with the virtue to rule have an opportunity to do so.

Economic Inequality

Machiavelli lived at a time when the Medici were still ascendant in Florence. In the popular imagination, the Medici are viewed not just as political leaders but patrons of the arts, and bankers to the pope. Machiavelli thus lived at a time of artistic and economic ferment, but this did not inspire him to address these developments directly.[11] Despite his seeming lack of concern with the latter, we find that economic matters play an important role in his analysis of Rome and Florence.[12]

Early in the *Discourses*, Machiavelli defends his heterodox opinion that the greatness of Rome was the result of the tumults between the nobles and the people. He makes his case partly by showing that without such tumults one cannot get a state like Rome. Contrasting Rome with Sparta, Machiavelli argues that the latter avoided conflict both due to political and economic reasons. On a political level Sparta was able to create a balance between the nobles and the plebs through kings who protected the plebs. Furthermore, the Spartan political system, in Machiavelli's retelling, imposed strict ranks that quashed any hope of political power arising among the plebs. While this goes against Machiavelli's concern with political equality described above, he explains that the balance in Sparta was the result of a series of unique characteristics. Sparta, for example, in contrast to Rome, did not let in foreigners and thus did not grow much. There is, however, also one fundamental economic characteristic that allowed Sparta to avoid tumults. Lycurgus, Machiavelli writes, created an "equality of belongings [*equalita di sustanze*]" in Sparta. This equality of belonging "created an equality of poverty [*une equale poverta*]."[13] While this shows that economic inequality does figure in Machiavelli's analysis, given that he is arguing against Sparta as his preferred model, one cannot on the strength of this example establish whether he approves or disapproves of this equality of belonging and equal poverty.

One does not have to dig deep to find where Machiavelli's sympathies lie. Machiavelli unequivocally sides with poverty for citizens. In fact he makes the case that "keeping the public rich and private poor ... is the true way to make a republic great and to acquire empire."[14] Lest we be unsure of Machiavelli's conclusion on the matter, he recapitulates his position later in the *Discourses*: "we have reasoned elsewhere that the most useful thing that may be ordered in a free way of life is that the citizens be kept poor."[15] Despite these very clear articulations of his position, Machiavelli does offer republics one other option.

As mentioned above, book III of the *Discourses* deals with the actions of individuals. While Machiavelli deals with the actions of men who brought Rome back to its beginning, that is, men who were salutary to Rome's health, he also deals with those who endanger republics. Thus, in Chapter 16 Machiavelli writes about the danger posed by ambitious men who in times of peace find themselves unappreciated. Such men, Machiavelli argues, are further incensed by seeing others who are simply richer, made equal or promoted above them. Such a state of affairs is dangerous for a republic for these "great and rare men" are wont to create conflict in order to assert their superiority. Faced with this problem Machiavelli recommends two courses of action. First, he returns to his earlier recommendation "to maintain the citizens poor so that they cannot corrupt either themselves or others with riches and without virtue." But now he offers a second suggestion. Namely, that the republic be "ordered for war so that one can always make war and always has need of reputed citizens." After introducing these two means of dealing with the problem, Machiavelli quickly dismisses the first solution. Those republics, he argues, that do not follow Rome's way will "always run into them [inconveniences], and disorder will always arise when that neglected and virtuous citizen is vindictive and has some reputation."[16] This seems to suggest that keeping citizens poor is not a workable proposal on its own. Indeed, this is what we would expect from the author of the dictum that all humans "naturally wish to acquire." But it is Machiavelli himself who also told us that Rome was both expansionist and able to keep its citizens poor. This difficulty prompts him to wonder how, given the problem with the agrarian law, Rome succeeded in keeping its citizens poor.

The answer combines the two methods Machiavelli recommended in his treatment of ambitious men. By providing an outlet to ambition through its empire Rome was able to avoid the dangers posed by spirited men. This outlet also ensured that the way to gain prominence was not through wealth but one's actions. Rome remained poor, Machiavelli argues, because wealth was not a prerequisite for honors. Machiavelli thus does have very clear recommendations about how wealth is to be dealt with in a republic. Despite presenting two solutions to ambition, Machiavelli essentially concludes that the first solution—that of keeping citizens poor—is a by-product of the second solution—expansion—which disentangles honor and glory from wealth. Since, however, our concern here is with inequality we need to elicit from Machiavelli's texts his views on the distribution of wealth.

Machiavelli's position on the distribution of wealth can be adduced from the examples of the action of men who enjoyed levels of wealth exceeding those of their fellow citizens. Such examples can be found in both the *Discourses* and the *Florentine Histories*. In the *Discourses* Machiavelli relates the actions of Spurius Maelius during a famine in Rome.[17] Maelius, who was a wealthy plebian, used his wealth to buy grain and sell it at a lower price to the plebs. This gained him favor with the plebs but raised such concern about his intentions that he was called before the dictator. In Livy's account Maelius is then suspected of gathering arms in his home. Maelius attempts to escape when summoned before the dictator, and is killed by the Master of the Horse who had come to deliver the summons to Maelius.[18] In Machiavelli's telling, these details are not given. Most significantly, Machiavelli makes no mention of the accusation that Maelius was gathering arms. Yet Machiavelli presents Maelius's execution as a prudent step by the Senate. Why? In Machiavelli's view Maelius' actions, though generous, could have hidden under them a different intention. In particular, Maelius through his wealth might have sought to gain the favor of the plebs in order to gain political prominence. Thus, the Senate's concern was well-founded and the summons justified. This example makes evident the danger of inequality. Wealth can be used to manipulate those who have less. One need no longer have virtue and hard-won reputation, one need merely to have wealth to gain the latter and feign the former. When the distribution of wealth is grossly unequal those who are to be the guards of freedom can be corrupted. Harm thus comes not simply from the actions of the wealthy, but from the vulnerability of the poor. Machiavelli credits the Romans with having understood this and dealt with the danger early and in a decisive manner. Florence, however, did not act like Rome.

The fourth book of the *Florentine Histories* sees the rise of Cosimo de Medici. Florence is riven by divisions that are headed by prominent families, while also engaged in a military campaign in Lucca. In the midst of all this the "party of the nobles" attempts to "ruin" Cosimo either through exile or death. This proposal is brought by the party of the nobles before one of their compatriots, Niccolo da Uzzano. Machiavelli relates Uzzano's response in the form of a speech, which he introduces by announcing that Uzzano was opposed to "extraordinary ways." But the speech that Machiavelli puts in Uzzano's mouth suggests that the latter's opposition is not based simply on an aversion to "extraordinary ways." Uzanno's speech reads:

The deeds of Cosimo that make us suspect him are these: because he helps everyone with his money, and not only private individuals but the public ... because he favors this or that citizen who has need of magistrates; because by the good will that he has in the generality of people he pulls this or that friend to higher ranks of honor. Thus, one would have to allege as the causes for driving him out that he is merciful, helpful, liberal, and loved by everyone. So tell me: what law is it that forbids or that blames and condemns in men mercy, liberality, and love? And although these are all modes that send men flying to a princedom, nonetheless they are not believed to be so ...[19]

While in the *Prince* Machiavelli warns against liberality when the treasury of the republic is being used, Machiavelli here questions liberality even when using one's own treasury. Divergences in wealth allow individuals to use their liberality to gain favor with other citizens. This is problematic, for it is the route that can lead a republic to a principality. As Cosimo's case shows, what is even more pernicious about the deployment of these private modes of acquiring prominence is that those deploying them cannot be publicly blamed, for their actions are not bad in themselves. While private modes are pursued when public modes are not available, wealth inequality is an essential precondition for them to threaten republics.[20]

While the above may not have decisively established the importance of wealth and its distribution in Machiavelli's account, it does suggest that the theme is not absent. To establish its centrality, however, there is one more critical piece of evidence that we can bring to bear. Rome, or at least his imagining of it, is for Machiavelli the republic par excellence.[21] Yet this republic came to an end.[22] Part of the answer to the question of why Rome declines is to be found, according to Machiavelli, in the contention over the agrarian law.[23] This contention arose precisely because over time Rome strayed from the principle of keeping "the public rich and the people poor." Machiavelli's presentation of the agrarian reform is complicated since he seems to both bemoan the situation that created the necessity of reform, while also condemning the reform itself. The passage in question suggests that neither is Machiavelli's position simply to side with the people and emphasize the greed of the nobility, nor is he opposed to the principle behind the agrarian laws that limited land holdings. Machiavelli establishes early in the chapter that there was a "defect in the law." But he then goes on to specify what the defect was. He offers two possibilities: (i) the problem was the timing, the law was either not put in place early enough, or its implementation was delayed, and the second possibility,

(ii) the law put forth was well-ordered but became corrupt over time. Machiavelli's criticism of the law does not, however, explicitly question the principle behind the law. He is not, in other words, opposed to at least the principle of limiting property to ensure that the citizens remain poor.[24] While he does offer an assessment of the nobles asserting that they were more likely to share honors than property, the aim of the chapter is not simply to besmirch the reputation of the nobles. The chapter in fact begins with the statement that humans are made such that they wish to acquire endlessly, but only have a limited capacity to fulfill their desires. And his statement regarding wealth and property is offered not as applying to the nobles alone: "One also sees through this how much more men value property more than honors."[25]

Thus, despite his claim not to know about the silk and wool trade, Machiavelli's analysis in both the *Florentine Histories* and the *Discourses* highlights the importance of wealth distribution and in particular the dangers arising from an unequal distribution of wealth to the health of republics.[26] While the agrarian law is problematic since it creates tumults in the republic, the principle danger that arises from inequality is the rise of leaders who will use private modes to gain honors and ingratiate themselves with the people. The danger is not restricted to the leaders alone. Inequality also opens the people up to being corrupted. The use of private modes and the corruption of the people point to a deeper criticism of wealth in Machiavelli's account. This becomes evident when we consider the final form of inequality that features in Machiavelli's discussion of Rome and Florence.

Inequality of Spirit

In the account thus far provided Machiavelli has appeared as an egalitarian concerned with ensuring economic and political equality. Yet we have not dealt with the other Machiavelli, the one remembered primarily as the author of the *Prince*. This Machiavelli may be a defender of the people, but he most decidedly gives a prominent place in his accounts to extraordinary men. Indeed, that these extraordinary men stand apart from the people is evident not only in the *Prince* but also in the *Discourses*.

The figure of the founder held a unique fascination for Machiavelli.[27] To take a particular instance we can begin with Romulus. Romulus' action of killing his brother, Machiavelli argues, is justified because it led to the establishment of a long-lasting republic. The second justification Machiavelli offers is that founders cannot but be alone. While he later defends the judgment and desires of the people, he argues against deferring to the people at the founding moment. The founder must be alone since the people are unable to decide on the order to put in place.[28] The founder is both judged by a different standard and is endowed with superior judgment when it comes to the establishment of a polity. Despite Machiavelli's case for equality then, we find him setting the founder apart. If this example sets up the position of the founder as distinct from the people, Machiavelli's account in Book III of the *Discourses* makes the distinction even clearer.

Having dealt with the establishment and internal working of Rome in the first book of the *Discourses*, and the external affairs of Rome in the second, Machiavelli directs his attention to the renewal or refounding of republics in Book III. This refounding, Machiavelli tells us, requires that republics be taken back to their beginnings. And since the beginning is the work of an extraordinary individual, the refounding too must be the work of such an individual. These individuals are again set apart from the people, but this time in a clear way. These men, Machiavelli writes, must use extraordinary modes. Extraordinary modes are defined as actions undertaken outside of the law. So we come to the conclusion that these extraordinary men can act independent of the law. Acting outside the law, the examples in Book III suggest, involves the use of force. Indeed, one can recall here the great founders of the *Prince*, who Machiavelli reminds us, were all armed. Even the founder most associated with the law, Moses, Machiavelli reminds us was only able to succeed because he used force. While all the above has been well rehearsed and is not news to any reader of Machiavelli's texts, our aim here is to highlight what this means for Machiavelli's defense of political equality discussed above. Surely by putting these men in a separate category and indeed pointing out that they are above the law, the ideal of political equality seems to be put into question. While Machiavelli sets these individuals apart he does not defend a class hierarchy or hereditary succession. In fact, Machiavelli sets these individuals apart while arguing for leaving this position open to individuals of all social and economic stations. Despite this, however, his presentation of these individuals puts into question our use of the descriptor egalitarian when speaking of Machiavelli. Before conceding this, however, we need to consider how the type of differentiation that Machiavelli is suggesting interacts with economic inequality.

Honor and Wealth

Life in a republic Machiavelli tells us is attractive since security of life and property encourages citizens to work and accumulate. But as noted above, Machiavelli's case for republics extends beyond this. The other main attraction of a republic is that it gives hope to all that they or their progeny could become princes. In other words, not just the road to wealth but the road to honor also is open to all. Yet, when Machiavelli speaks of the founders he speaks often of glory and empire but seldom of wealth. This becomes salient when we consider the impact of wealth and its pursuit on those who seek honor.

We can begin by going back to Rome's agrarian reforms. Machiavelli's telling of Roman history reveals that it was not the type of polity that was founded with all the necessary orders in place. Rome was only perfected when the plebs got representation in the form of consuls. While this compromise took time to reach and was born of conflict between the two sides, the issue of land reform was not settled in a satisfactory manner. The latter ultimately contributed to the destruction of Rome. While earlier we considered Machiavelli's two hypotheses regarding the reasons for the failure of the law, here I want to focus on the divergent fates of the political and economic reforms.

Allowing the plebs to have their consuls gave the plebs a say in the political realm and thereby afforded them protection from the patricians. Consuls were granted because the patricians needed the plebs for war. The gains from war could not be made without the plebs playing their role. The plebs thus had leverage over the patricians. Yet this accommodation required willingness on both sides. When it came to land reform, however, matters turned out differently. Here the patricians were unwilling to agree. Machiavelli writes that this shows, "how much more willing men are to share honors than wealth." Now the question is whether this holds true in general about humans or applies only to the Romans. Machiavelli's phrasing suggests that he is talking about humans in general. By this account humans are more concerned with wealth than with honor. Indeed, this conclusion seems to be affirmed by Machiavelli's maxim that "men forget the death of a father more quickly than the loss of a patrimony."[29] If this is the case then how does Machiavelli explain the Roman example?

Machiavelli explicitly addresses this question when discussing the example of Cincinnatus. The reason that wealth was not valued in Rome is that all honors were open regardless of one's wealth. This suggests that ultimately men are not after wealth but honor, wealth is valued only to the extent that it offers one the ability to pursue honors. But this is in tension with the maxim about men being more concerned with their patrimony than with the death of their fathers, and it also does not jive with Machiavelli's diagnosis of the failure of the agrarian reforms. We can perhaps find our way if we look forward to Florence.

In Florence, the relationship between wealth and honor becomes more evident since we have one prominent family pursuing both. Cosimo's case is illustrative here. The move to private modes suggests not a move away from honor to wealth, but rather the introduction of the idea of honor through wealth. This of course is also evident in the Maelius example quoted earlier. While honor through wealth still suggests a concern with honor, ultimately the introduction of wealth seems to alter the ranking of the two goods. The best example of this is in military affairs. Those brought up on the idea of honor through wealth are more apt to pay for mercenaries as did Florence. Without repeating Machiavelli's case against mercenaries, in the context of our discussion it becomes evident that part of what is at stake is the fact that the honor through wealth equation breaks down. Victory through mercenaries does not bring honor. It is also in this context that we can read Machiavelli's statement that money is not the sinew of war. Thus, honor through wealth is the first step away from honor.

The move to honor through wealth has implications for the type of inequality we have been discussing in this section. What differentiates extraordinary men involved in founding and refounding is that they are not moved merely by security and wealth; they seek honor or glory. The move to honor through wealth fundamentally alters the nature of the polity. Opening the possibility of honor through wealth moves the polity away from the ideal embodied in Rome and celebrated by Machiavelli. Honor becomes increasingly open only to those with wealth. Thus, the identity of those seeking honors changes. Eventually men moved by honor alone become scarce in such a polity. Indeed, the second of the two benefits of political equality—that all those with the requisite virtue can become princes—is put into question. This change is best illustrated by Machiavelli's description of developments in Florence.

In the dedication to the *Florentine Histories*, Machiavelli writes that he has avoided flattery and will offer as proof the various speeches he puts into the mouths of protagonists in the story of Florence. Among the speeches that has elicited comment among Machiavelli's readers is the one found in Book III. The year is 1328 and internal divisions within Florence continue to cause unrest. Most of the plebs are divided into guilds based on their trade. The poorest of the plebs are part of the Wool Guild and have been involved in civil unrest, looting, and robbery. Unsatisfied and concerned with the punishment that may be meted out to them, one of their compatriots delivers a speech in which he encourages them to continue their violence. Since his compatriots see the wealthier citizens as their antagonists, to give his audience courage the speech maker assures them that there is no difference between them and their social superiors: "Do not let their antiquity of blood, with which they will reproach us, dismay you; for all men, having had the same beginning, are equally ancient and have been made by nature in one mode. Strip us all naked, you will see that we are alike, dress us in their clothes and them in ours, and without a doubt we shall appear noble and they ignoble, for only poverty and riches make us unequal."[30] As Florence becomes more commercial, society is divided based on occupation and wealth. People, the speech maker declares, are in fact fundamentally equal with only their wealth and what it can buy differentiating them. We have in other words an equality of spirit and an inequality of station. In as yet uncorrupt Rome the opposite holds true. The founders and refounders are not differentiated from others merely by their clothes and wealth but their actions that bring glory. Thus, as we move from Rome to commercial Florence one type of inequality is traded for another. Machiavelli's republic relies on inequality of spirit, for founding and refounding require exceptional men, but it also relies on equality which ensures that private modes are not adopted and the laws have a hold on all citizens. But Florence lacks both this type of inequality and equality. The speech at the Ciompi revolt thus offers an accurate assessment of Florence, for indeed there is little difference between the poor plebs and the rich except the latter's wealth. Thus, in a remarkably direct comment (given that the text is dedicated to a Medici) at the end of the first book of the *Florentine Histories*, Machiavelli bemoans the fact that Florence has fallen into the hands of men brought up in trade. Such men are either unconcerned with glory, or believe that they obtain it through wealth.[31]

We can then draw several conclusions form our discussion of inequality. First, in Machiavelli's analysis of republics, economic inequality is dangerous since it both opens the people to corruption and allows those not necessarily worthy of rule to gain power. Political equality too is necessary both to protect the people from power and to ensure that those most deserving rise to power. Second, increased concern with wealth has the detrimental effect of bringing to the political realm those concerned with personal accumulation. The corruption thus sets in as the channels available to vent ambition and the desire to acquire move from the public realm to the private realm, a change exemplified by the rise of men nurtured in trade rather than war. This development is problematic for such men are apt to pursue private modes to acquire honor and glory, and purchase it at the price of corrupting the people and neglecting the public. Furthermore, the emphasis on the role of wealth in this process of corruption pits Machiavelli against the later defenders of commercial republics. The easy peace promised through wealth creation and material security, in Machiavelli's eyes, leads to the public being sacrificed to the private. The change that takes place is not that humans are able to unleash their acquisitiveness, but rather in *how* this drive toward acquisitiveness is fulfilled. The very reasons that make gentlemen a danger –the fact that they are independent of the welfare and resources of the polity—also makes a move to a commercial republic dangerous. As wealth takes on a bigger role, the commercial republic gives rise to leaders and people who are more able to fulfill their ambitions and desires without concern for the public.

What does all this tell us about the rise of populism in the United States? A lot. And this should not come as a surprise. In the *Discourses,* Machiavelli bemoans the fact that his contemporaries look back to ancient art for inspiration but do not do so for politics. He argues that in doing so they act "as if heaven, sun, elements, men had varied in motion, order, and power from what they were in antiquity."[32] It is precisely to correct this error that Machiavelli offers his history of Rome. Thus, that we turn to his account of Rome and Florence to illuminate present day politics is very much in keeping with the spirit that animated Machiavelli's writings.

Increasing economic inequality combined with equality of spirit explains how an individual like Donald Trump can become the candidate of choice for the working class. Despite railing against the wealth that has become pervasive in the American political system, Americans elected the richest candidate in the field. And this candidate made no apologies for his wealth. Instead, he presented his wealth as a positive characteristic, for his success in acquiring private wealth was a proxy for his ability to bring wealth to the whole. That wealth accrues honor was not questioned. Indeed, wealth itself was viewed as qualifying the candidate for the honor. This changing equation between honor and wealth also explains Trump's questioning of the sacrifices of individuals who have served valiantly in the military. Finally, the all but complete vacation of honor from the public realm is exemplified by the use of the President's position to attack individuals in the media and entertainment industries.

Economic inequality thus opens the public to the rhetoric of those who promise easy solutions not on the backs of public success and sacrifice, but on private success in gaining wealth. In the current wave of populism, equality of spirit is manifested in the ever-shrinking divide between the personal and public. The employment of family members in the White House and their easy substitution for the President at international meetings is explained by the fact that such behavior aimed at promoting one's private interest is expected. Such behavior when dealing with a family business would not only be tolerated, but even expected. Now however the very same calculus is applied to the public realm.

Vox populi, vox dei. Restrictions apply.

NOTES

1. Pelczynski, Z. A., "Machiavelli: An Egalitarian?," in *Machiavelli, Hobbes, and Rousseau* (Oxford University Press, 2012).
2. D.I.55.4. I use the Mansfield translations of Machiavelli's texts. D = Niccolo Machiavelli, *Discourses on Livy*, trans. Harvey C. Mansfield and Tarcov Nathan (University Of Chicago Press, 1998); P = Niccolo Machiavelli, *The Prince*, trans. Harvey C. Mansfield, 2nd ed. (University Of Chicago Press, 1998); FH = Niccolo Machiavelli, *Florentine Histories*, trans. Laura F. Banfield and Harvey C. Mansfield (Princeton University Press, 1990). References are to book, chapter, and paragraph number.
3. "Men" Machiavelli reminds us "never work any good unless through necessity." D.I.3.2.
4. D. I.55.5.
5. Cf. Erica Benner, *Machiavelli's Ethics* (Princeton University Press, 2009), 273.
6. D.II.2.3.
7. Ibid.
8. D.I.3.
9. FH.II.3.
10. Ibid.
11. When he does bring up art he suggests that at least a similar amount—if not a greater amount—of attention ought to be given to politics. D.I.Preface.
12. I use the term economics to refer to matters concerning the generation and distribution of wealth.

13. D. I.6.2.
14. D. II.19.
15. D.III.25.
16. D.III.16.2.
17. D.III.28.
18. Livy, *The Early History of Rome: Books I-V of The History of Rome from Its Foundations*, trans. Aubrey De Sélincourt and S. P Oakley (London; New York: Penguin Books, 2002), bk. IV.13–14.
19. F.H. IV.27.
20. On the economic dimension of private modes see Eric Nelson, *The Greek Tradition in Republican Thought* (Cambridge, UK; New York: Cambridge University Press, 2004), chap. 2.
21. On Machiavelli's imagining of Rome, see Vickie B. Sullivan, *Machiavelli's Three Romes: Religion, Human Liberty, and Politics Reformed* (Northern Illinois University Press, 1996).
22. There is room for debate on whether Machiavelli envisions a perpetual republic. Even if we don't credit him with a cyclical view of history, his metaphysics seems to make such a republic an impossibility. "Human things" he reminds us, "are always in motion." D.I.6. See also FH.V.1.
23. D.I. 37.
24. John P. McCormick, "Machiavelli and the Gracchi: Prudence, Violence and Redistribution," *Global Crime* 10, no. 4 (October 22, 2009): 298–305. McCormick, however, goes too far when he insists that Machiavelli endorses redistribution.
25. D.I.37.3. Emphasis mine.
26. Machiavelli letter to Vettori, April, 9th 1513. James B. Atkinson and David Sices, eds., *Machiavelli and His Friends: Their Personal Correspondence* (Northern Illinois University Press, 2005), 225.
27. On the idea of Machiavelli himself being a founder see Leo Strauss, *Thoughts on Machiavelli* (University of Chicago Press, 1995), 83.
28. D.I.2.1.
29. P.XVII.
30. F.H. III.13.
31. F.H. I. 39.
32. D.I.Preface.

BIBLIOGRAPHY

Atkinson, James B., and David Sices, eds. 2005. *Machiavelli and His Friends: Their Personal Correspondence*. Northern Illinois: University Press.

Benner, Erica. 2009. *Machiavelli's Ethics*. Princeton: Princeton University Press.

Livy. 2002. *The Early History of Rome: Books I-V of The History of Rome from Its Foundations*. Trans. Aubrey De Sélincourt and S. P Oakley. London/New York: Penguin Books.

Machiavelli, Niccolo. 1990. *Florentine Histories*. Trans. Laura F. Banfield and Harvey C. Mansfield. Princeton: Princeton University Press.

———. 1998a. *Discourses on Livy*. Trans. Harvey C. Mansfield and Tarcov Nathan. Chicago: University of Chicago Press..

———. 1998b. *The Prince*. Trans. Harvey C. Mansfield. 2nd ed. Chicago: University of Chicago Press.

McCormick, John P. 2009. Machiavelli and the Gracchi: Prudence, Violence and Redistribution. *Global Crime* 10 (4): 298–305. https://doi.org/10.1080/17440570903248155.

Nelson, Eric. 2004 *The Greek Tradition in Republican Thought*. Cambridge/New York: Cambridge University Press.

Pelczynski, Z.A. 2012. Machiavelli: An Egalitarian? In *Machiavelli, Hobbes, and Rousseau*. Oxford: Oxford University Press.

Strauss, Leo. 1995. *Thoughts on Machiavelli*. Chicago: University of Chicago Press.

Sullivan, Vickie B. 1996. *Machiavelli's Three Romes: Religion, Human Liberty, and Politics Reformed*. DeKalb: Northern Illinois University Press.

CHAPTER 7

Thomas Hobbes' Defense of Liberalism, Populism and the Rise of Donald Trump

Kevin Slack

Part I: Hobbes and the Liberal State

Of Man Thomas Hobbes is often unfairly vilified as an opponent of free government. He was a classical liberal, and his project was to found a new political order, the commonwealth, as an alternative to those founded on priestly authority or feudalism, and the expansionist wars over resources that accompanied them. The instability of those orders was manifest in the religious wars in the 1500s, the Thirty Years War (1618–1648), the English Civil Wars, and Oliver Cromwell's ravaging of Ireland in the 1650s. Rootless mercenaries, fighting for the highest bidder, plundered cities. When unpaid, they sacked peasants' hovels, raping women and girls, and murdering men for sport. In the Thirty Years War, 20% of the total German population was wiped out by conflict, famine, and disease. This chaos was not unique—Hobbes called it the human condition. Replacing mercenaries with professional armies required popular support and undivided loyalty, but this was impossible with dueling claims to sovereignty. Using the analogy of a doctor, Hobbes diagnoses what is wrong with the political body of his time and gives counsel on the conditions for peace and civilization that will bring the organism back to health.

K. Slack (✉)
Hillsdale College, Hillsdale, MI, USA

© The Author(s) 2018
M. B. Sable, A. J. Torres (eds.), *Trump and Political Philosophy*,
https://doi.org/10.1007/978-3-319-74427-8_7

107

Hobbes begins his greatest political work, *Leviathan*, with a study of human psychology, regarding both the origins and limits of knowledge in the senses and the universal human passions. Beginning with human nature, he can create axioms for a political order that best provides for its flourishing. But the promise of a political science, which proceeds from clear definitions to right reasoning, confronts a fundamental problem: humans are only capable of reason because of speech, yet the abstractions of reason, mere words, are often modes of expression confused for mind-independent entities in reality. Unfounded and false assertions about God, nature, and man, unrelated to human felicity, become authoritative moral and political prescriptions. While reason should lead to "the benefit of mankind" (5 20), in morals (unlike math), perfect agreement is impossible, and "the parties must by their own accord set up for right reason the reason of some arbitrator or judge," or settle the controversy by violence (5.3). Mankind is trapped in this realm of opinion because reason tends to serve the passions instead of governing them. Men possess the same passions, but for different objects. Few are moved by curiosity, or a passion for science; most are guided by their imagination and often deceive themselves about what is good and their chances of attaining it. This uncertainty, discontentment with what one has, and hope for better, produces in all mankind a "restless desire of power after power, that ceaseth only in death" (11.2). Because man is a social animal, he measures himself by how others perceive his power. This is the origin of honor, which becomes a sort of currency in human relations.

Blinded by his passions, man's ignorance of "right, equity, law, and justice" (11.21) forces him to rely on tradition, which leads to endless disputes and violence. To understand why, Hobbes looks to the underlying religious character of claims to authority. Ignorance of nature makes man prone to posit causes, in spite of his uncertainty, because the claim to foresight can be a source of honor. Conversely, foresight is also the cause of anxiety, because humans, unlike animals, reflect upon their own death, and in their ignorance imagine and fear distant causes. Religion becomes a tool for control, to claim knowledge of future events as the basis of a present right to make laws. But religion "can never be ... abolished out of human nature" (12.23): new religions, founded on revelatory claims to authority, will always spring up and threaten political orders because they feed on man's proclivity to superstition.

But while religion is rooted in human nature, and is inevitably part of every political order, it alone is insufficient. Every religion is formed upon faith in some person who is believed to declare God's will supernaturally. The wisdom, sincerity, or love of every leader or his priests "necessarily" becomes "suspected" (12.24). "Natural reason" (12.25) challenges the contradictions in supernatural claims. The hypocrisy of religious leaders ("what they require other men to believe is not believed by themselves") and detection of their self-interest ("acquiring of dominion, riches, dignity, or ... pleasure") undermines faith in their sincerity and altruism (12.26-27). Finally, religious leaders must claim some practical effect—to perform miracles, predict the future, or make their followers extremely happy (12.28). But when problems arise that they cannot solve, they claim to be above mundane affairs, depend on cosmic justice, or promise it in the afterlife. "So that justice failing, faith also failed" (12.30). Priests desire the honor that comes from ruling without wanting to do the work of ruling; hence they do not understand, and are not good at, politics. Religion alone cannot sustain a political order: every successful religion must be upheld by "fear of the civil sword" (12.24).

Were there a vastly powerful and fearsome being on earth, there could be no division over opinion. But this is not so. Humans are naturally equal and free: they are equal because their inequalities of body and mind are inconsiderable, and free because all may do that which is necessary for preservation. As to physical strength, "the weakest has strength enough to kill the strongest, either by secret machination, or by confederacy with others" (13.1). There is even greater equality of mental faculties, leading to an equality of pride, and a sense of deserve, from which is born a war of "every man against every man" (13.8). The state of war is more than open battle; it exists whenever there is a known "will to contend by battle" (13.8). Its causes are: (1) competition over scarce resources, (2) diffidence (distrust of others that leads to securing those goods), and (3) glory— "pleasure in contemplating their own power in the acts of conquest" (13.4). There is little farming and no industry because one cannot be sure of receiving the fruits of his labor. There is no trade, arts, technology, or letters. Worst of all, there is "continual fear and danger of violent death" (13.9). In this state of war, "nothing can be unjust. The notions of right and wrong, justice and injustice, have there no place. Where there is no common power, there is no law; where no law, no injustice" (13.13). Nor is there property, for there is no "*mine* and *thine*" if all objects can be claimed by all. This state is not fictitious: Hobbes points to tribal societies that "have no government at all" (13.11). In foreign policy, all sovereigns remain in such a state with one another (13.12, 30.30). It exists whenever government breaks down and fails to achieve its proper ends. And it reemerges in civil society: who, Hobbes asks, does not lock his doors, or take precautions when traveling (13.10)? This is no reason to despise man; it is simply his nature, the study of which both alerts us to the disease and provides a remedy.

The remedy, according to Hobbes, "consist[s] partly in the passions, partly in [man's] reason" (13.13). The passions that incline men to peace are fear of death, desire for commodious living, and a hope by industry to attain it. Reason, by consideration of human felicity, suggests articles of peace for such agreement, the laws of nature. The laws of nature are "not properly laws," but useful maxims, or "qualities that dispose men to peace and to obedience" (26.8), and make possible civilization. The first law is "*seek peace, and follow it*" (14.4), which leads to a second: All should lay down most of their rights (except inalienable rights like self-preservation), and be contented with the same liberty as others. But there is no reason to trust that others will perform their oaths without a common power set up over them, to give this agreement the force of law. Hence they appoint a sovereign, who remains in the state of nature, and by enforcing these maxims, makes them proper laws. Fear of the sovereign makes possible the just relations between men that do not exist outside of political societies.

Competition remains, but the state of war disappears. First, scarcity is ameliorated by industry and technology, which frees all from starvation. Second, when men adopt the moral code of the law of nature they create an environment of trust. While Hobbes inverted the Golden Rule as the law of nature (14.5, 26.13, 42.11), not to do to others what you would not have done to yourself, he presents its fulfillment in the civil law as "*doing unto others as we would be done to*," and more, "*love thy neighbour as thyself*" (17.2, 30.13). The Golden Rule only works within a strong political order: Trust is secured in some by the desire to procure honor for being generous, and in others by fear of the sovereign. Finally, man's thirst for glory is satisfied as he is able to imagine his greatness in the commonwealth, which channels ambition into a hierarchy of honor awarded by the sovereign.

Of Commonwealth Hobbes describes a body politic as not unlike a human body: preservation, nutrition (economics), motion (morals and law), and reason (planning and judgment). The end of government, "preservation, and ... a more contented life thereby" (17.1), is achieved by defense "from the invasion of foreigners and the injuries of one another" (17.13), thereby securing life, liberty, and property. This is not just protection of "bare preservation, but also all other contentments of life" (30.1), which subjects lawfully acquire "by their own industry and by the fruits of the earth" (17.13). The commonwealth is more than an aggregation of individuals. It is a common mind: "This is more than consent, or concord; it is a real unity of them all, in one and the same person, made by covenant of every man with every man" (17.13). The nation-state is a mean between the city-state (17.3-4) and empire: it is neither a small republic, which encourages invasion, nor is it a chaotic multitude, whose diverse opinions rend it apart into factions (17.4, 18.16).

To achieve this end, the sovereign, whether an individual or an assembly, is conferred vast rights "by the consent of the people" (18.2). Neither the sovereign, nor the form of government, may be changed, nor may subjects become judges of breaches of the contract. The sovereign speaks for all, dictates what is just, establishes legal forms of property, and arbitrates disputes over right in courts of law. To defend property, it must have the right to make war, levy taxes, raise armies, and appoint officers, as well as the power to punish, by physical force, fines, or shame. While the sovereign remains in the state of nature, and is limited by no man, it is bound under God to observe the laws of nature (21.7, 24.7). If it gives away or fails to exercise these rights, to protect the subjects, it de facto is no longer sovereign, and all return to a state of nature: "The end of obedience is protection" (21.21).

Upon this foundation of a strong sovereign, Hobbes builds the modern commercial state, whose limited government encourages economic growth, or "the Nutrition and Procreation of a Commonwealth" (24). In bodies politic, "the power of the representative is always limited" (22.5). Where the sovereign has prescribed no rule, "there the subject hath the liberty to do or forbear, according to his own discretion" (21.18). These include "the liberty to buy, and sell, and otherwise contract with one another; to choose their own abode, their own diet, their own trade of life, and institute their children as they themselves think fit" (21.6). Procreation first means literal childbearing, encouraging and supporting families, who birth the next generation of taxpayers. Liberty includes the right to private associations, which include "markets, or shows, or any other harmless end" (22.4).

The sovereign must encourage "labour and industry" in the cultivation of animals, vegetables, and minerals, and "man's labour also is a commodity exchangeable" (24.3-4). This means, first, a self-sufficiency that prevents dependence on foreign powers: "laws as may encourage all manner of arts (as navigation, agriculture, fishing, and … manufacture)" (30.19). Monopolies are disadvantageous both to competitors at home, and foreigners abroad, hence corporations should be "bound up into one body in foreign markets," and "at liberty at home, every man to buy and sell at what price he could" (22.19). The presumption is for free trade, but where trade may hurt the public, the sovereign must regulate "what places, and for what commodities, the subject shall traffic abroad" (24.9). If left solely "to private persons," some "would be drawn for gain," both to abet an enemy and hurt the commonwealth "by importing such things as, pleasing men's appetites, be nevertheless noxious, or … unprofitable." To encourage growth, the sovereign must first legally clarify and secure property in land and labor (24.5 6). It must secondly facilitate trade, "exchange and mutual contract," by legally setting the parameters for their validity and enforcement: "buying, selling, exchanging, borrowing, lending, letting, and taking to hire" (24.10). Finally, it must provide a sound, and not fiat, medium of currency (24.11-12).

For the preservation and health of the political body, the sovereign must (1) make and execute good laws (30.2) and (2) enforce morality by "the power of rewarding with riches or honour" (18.14). *The sovereign must rule by civil law: "rules which the commonwealth hath commanded … for the distinction of right and wrong"* (26.3). Law is enforcement of equal and rational rules (26.15)—the laws of nature. The end of all law is "to limit the natural liberty of particular men" so "they might not hurt, but assist one another, and join together against a common enemy" (26.8). The civil law, by which the sovereign implements natural law, must be written, along with signs that it proceeds from the sovereign will (26.16). The sovereign cannot transfer or delegate its lawmaking power to another, else it renounces its sovereignty (30:3), and only it or an obedient interpreter can interpret the law, else by craft, "the interpreter becomes the legislator" (26.20).

The sovereign has a duty to make "good laws" (30.20), which are necessary, clear, and short. Laws must be for the public good: "the good of the sovereign and people cannot be separated" (30.21). A sovereign is only great by a strong, free people. Laws that encourage liberty are "hedges … not to stop travelers, but to keep them in the way." "Unnecessary laws are not good laws, but traps for money which … are superfluous" and "insufficient to defend the people." Subjects cannot obey the law if they do not know what it is (26.12). Where there is no clear, promulgated, civil law, there can be no crime (27.3). If laws are too short, they are "easily misinterpreted," but longer laws are worse: they are unnecessarily ambiguous, and encourage both the diligence to evade them, and "unnecessary processes," or bureaucracy (26.21, 30.22). Growth in the number of laws creates "a contention between the penners and pleaders of the law ... and ... the pleaders have got the victory."

All subjects must be treated equally under the law. This first means equal protection: "that justice be equally administered to all degrees of people" (30.15). The "poor and obscure," and not just the "rich and mighty," must be protected from injury. Similarly, there must be equal prosecution of offenders: "the great may have no greater hope of impunity" than the "meaner sort." Education, wealth, or birth must not provide exemption from the prosecution or punishments applied to "poor, obscure, and simple men" (27.13). Second, subjects possess equal duties to the commonwealth: equal taxes, labor to secure a livelihood, and defense of the country. In civil courts, subjects may equally sue one another, and even the sovereign (21.19). In criminal cases, equity demands due process: innocence until guilt is proven; confronting witnesses; trial by jury of both fact and right (26.27). Because all must be equally preserved, one may break the law in defense of his person or property, or when "destitute of food or other thing[s] necessary for his life" (27.26). Hence the sovereign must provide welfare, or a safety net for those who are unable to work, and force those with "strong bodies" to work (30.18-19).

The sovereign cannot rule by force alone, but uses "public instruction" to educate the people in the morals of natural law, and the first principles of government, lest they be seduced to rebel (30.2). Hobbes reduces this instruction to the Ten Commandments, which falls into love of country (approbation of its founding), and love of one's neighbors (30.7-13). Tradesmen and laborers will learn these commandments from "divines in the pulpit" and "such others as make show of learning," who "derive their knowledge from the universities and from the schools of law" (30.14).

Of the Kingdom of Darkness Hobbes warns of the diseases of the commonwealth and the causes of its death. Economic diseases include insufficient and disproportionate taxation, along with government monopolies or subsidies that cause inequality of wealth (29.19), which leads to demagoguery (29.20), or "the immoderate greatness of a town" or of corporations that may rival the sovereign (29.21). There are also the diseases of imperialism, "the insatiable appetite, or *Bulimia*, of enlarging dominion," and effete luxury, "the *lethargy* of ease, and *consumption* of riot and vain expense" (29.22).

But far worse are diseases in morals, law, and judgment, and they proceed from "learned men" who undermine the teaching of natural law (30.6). Hobbes calls this subversion of the political order "the kingdom of darkness ... *a confederacy of deceivers*" who seek "*to obtain dominion over men in this present world ... by dark and erroneous doctrines*" (44.1). The three sources of the kingdom of darkness are (1) theologians, (2) lawyers, and (3) philosophers. Each group keeps the people in awe of its power by its claims to authority—revelation, tradition, and claims to wisdom—to stoke the superstitions and fear of the people, and subvert "the peaceable societies of mankind" (47.1).

The first diseases come from "unlearned divines," Catholic, Anglican, or Presbyterian, who, claiming knowledge of Scripture, "do what they can to make men think that sanctity and natural reason cannot stand together" (29.8). If the sovereign defers to these, it becomes content with less power than is necessary for peace and security. The clergy teach the seditious doctrines that every man is his own judge of good and evil, and that he cannot disobey his conscience, which disposes him to debate whether or not he should obey the law. By teaching that the Kingdom of God is the Church on earth, the clergy claims power to govern the people, even in "civil war against the state" (47.6). It also claims exemption from civil and criminal laws, and authority over moral virtue in civil matters.

The next diseases are introduced by lawyers, who teach that (1) sovereign power is subject to the civil laws, (2) one has absolute right in his property against the sovereign, and (3) the sovereign power may be divided. Lawyers appeal either to the "false measure of justice barbarously call[ed] ... precedent" (11.21) or to private interpretations of natural law. Both challenge the authority of the sovereign, and seek to make the law depend on their own learning. The lawyers proclaim that law, and not men, should govern, but then confuse mere parchment barriers with law, which requires a unitary sovereign. They create a legal labyrinth that benefits their interests, flatters their pride, and brings lawlessness. Moreover, they "extend the power of the law, which is the rule of actions only, to the very thoughts and consciences of men" (46.37). Such policing of the mind, writes Hobbes, "is against the law of nature."

The deadliest diseases are introduced by the professors' teachings on metaphysics, ethics, and politics. Instead of cautiously furthering science, they lead students to a *"supernatural philosophy"* (46.14). They teach frivolous distinctions, in unclear terms and obscure language, which hide the truth and conceal contradictions and errors. They invent words for causes of things to make others think that they have knowledge of the incomprehensible, such as God or essences, and so arrogate to themselves the honor properly reserved to God, and the authority properly reserved to the sovereign. Hobbes challenges the very meaning of the word *essence*, which links consequential facts, but is confused for a fact itself: we conceive of essences where there are only descriptions. Its origin may be traced to the esotericism of Aristotle, who knew it "to be false philosophy," but, "fearing the fate of Socrates" (46.18), taught it to conceal his heretical views. But Christian scholars combined Jewish legal tradition with Greek metaphysics to create an unholy mess. In the universities, philosophy became "a handmaid to the Roman religion" (46.13). The clergy use the idea of essences to pit the *"ghostly authority"* against the *civil* (29.15), multiplying sovereigns and bringing civil war. They teach incorporeal souls (separated from bodies) that experience corporeal pleasures and pains in incorporeal places like heaven and hell. Subjects become too willing to give their bodies up, to sacrifice them for imaginary goods or virtues.

Ethically and politically, the professors praise the supposed virtues of the ancient Greeks and Romans, and "the virtue of their popular form of government" (29.14), in order to indirectly criticize the sovereign and honor themselves. But the ancients confused natural virtue, or dispositions developed by use and experience (4.24), with moral virtue, which is artificial, or practiced for the sake of honor that flatters pride. Honor, the opinion of the *"value* or WORTH of a man" (10.16) considering his power, consists in comparisons with others in a political hierarchy. Hence natural virtue is a false measure for a commonwealth, which measures by law. The trust between virtuous men, extolled by the ancients, is really based on one party being too weak to break his oaths, or a rare "glory or pride in appearing not to need to break it" (14.31). But the latter is too rare to be presumed on—most pursue wealth, power, or pleasure. Similarly, the focus on the virtue of the individual, and not the citizen, ignores the political conditions for the education of such qualities. The professors speculate on revolution, and praise neighboring or ancient forms of government, yet they ignore "the frequent seditions and civil wars produced by the imperfection of [ancient] policy" (29.14). Hobbes argues for a better political order, whose limited ends are rooted in more dependable human passions, and drawn to more certain effects.

Hobbes urges the sovereign to use both the civil law and honor to destroy the kingdom of darkness and to encourage citizens and officers "both to serve [the public] as faithfully as they can, and to study the arts" to do so (30.24). Subversive religious and legal authorities must be "silenced by the [civil] laws of those to whom the teachers of them are subject" (46.42). If professors teach "rebellion or sedition," they should "be silenced, and ... punished." Most importantly, "The instruction of the people dependeth wholly on the right teaching of youth in the universities" (30.14), which will remain ignorant of politics until they adopt the true doctrine of natural law. To make the laws of nature fashionable, the sovereign rewards with wealth and symbols of merit, which, if attached to privileges, become honorable (10.49-54). By this it appoints "what order of place and dignity each man shall hold," and public and private signs of respect (18.15). Wherever the "opinion of power" challenges justice (10.48), Leviathan, king of the proud, channels the thirst for glory into its hierarchy, outside of which is condemnation.

The cure to pernicious theology is religious toleration (47.20), and prohibition of religions that reject the laws of nature, along with the teaching of God as a rational being, unifying religion with moral duty under the natural law. The cure to the lawyers is the excise of convoluted precedent in the courts and pernicious opinions in eminent law books that violate natural law. Finally, a true philosophy must supplement leisure with method (46.6, 11), which creates systems that both approximate and help man to better understand nature, "*to the end to be able to produce, as far as matter and human force permit, such effects as human life requireth*" (46.1). There are political conditions of philosophy, which cannot be equated with mere curiosity (46.6). Without method, philosophers fail to understand nature, and become mired in debates over mere words. He challenges the universities to perfect his political science: to plan a commonwealth that "will never perish except by external force" (30.5, OL ed.).

PART II: THE STATE OF NATURE AND THE RISE
OF DONALD TRUMP

Of Man Describing Trump's victory, pollster Frank Luntz said, "Never
has the political class/industry/elite so misread the electorate and so mis-
understood American priorities."[1] It is precisely here that Hobbes' advocacy of a strong sovereign that would follow the natural law and create the
conditions for a peaceful, free, wealthy, and powerful people is explana-
tory. Using a Hobbesian lens to view our current situation, we must focus
not on the opinions of Trump himself, but on the three parallel crises that
are the origin of his appeal: (1) *Of Man*—the failure to secure the ends of
government, (2) *Of Commonwealth*—lack of a clear sovereign that rules
by law; (3) The return of the *Kingdom of Darkness*, and the discrediting of
an elite class that rules by its claim to expertise. Trump's success and the
failures of the ruling elite throw into sharp relief the profundity of the
general Hobbesian critique.

According to Hobbes, government exists to secure life, liberty and
property, but it has failed to do so. There are an estimated 400,000 unprocessed rape kits in the United States.[2] Violent crime in white working class
neighborhoods has quadrupled since 1960. Parts of New Orleans and
Detroit have returned to a literal state of nature; in 2012 the Detroit
Police Union warned that the department was understaffed, and the city
unsafe for visitors.[3] In African-American neighborhoods, where an increasingly militarized police has, in large measure, brought about a breakdown
of trust, homicides are on the rise and increasingly unsolved.[4] This has led
to greater acts of public lawlessness—the riots in Ferguson and Baltimore.[5]
Trump successfully ran as a law and order candidate; this position was
solidified in the minds of blue-collar voters when Trump's supporters were
violently beaten while the San Jose police looked on.[6] May Day rioters
recently destroyed $1.5 million in property in Portland. The Proud Boys
and Antifa have effectively become small private armies waging private
wars; Berkeley police were ordered to stand down at the April 15, 2017
demonstrations, which resulted in a supervised brawl.[7] Actors, musicians,
and even politicians joke about killing Trump as tyrannicide—it was acted
out in New York theater days before a Leftist gunman wounded Republican
Majority Whip Steve Scalise.

Of course, for Hobbes, the end of government is not mere preservation, but commodious living, and hope for the future. Journalist Chris Matthews gave the clearest analysis of Trump's support on election night. While Rachel Maddow attributed Trump's victory to racism, Matthews explained that many of Barack Obama's voters also voted for Trump because he ran "a legitimate campaign" on three issues: "Trade, immigration and wars." "I think the country hates all these wars, the establishment in both parties have been supporting these wars, including Hillary [Clinton]. The fact that we don't have an immigration system that we enforce. Business wants the cheap labor, Democrats want the votes.... In terms of trade ... just drive through Michigan, drive through Wisconsin, and you'll see places that are hollowed out." Middle-class Americans no longer believe that practicing the basic virtues will get them ahead. Trump's claim that the "system is rigged" was also made by Obama, Clinton, and Bernie Sanders.

The average American faces major difficulties. (1) *Increasing inequality of wealth.* Despite increased productivity, real wages have been flat or falling since 1973, manufacturing and IT jobs are increasingly being outsourced, and higher education is barred to the children of middle class Americans by high tuition costs. (2) *Increasing public and private debt.* To bail out increasingly centralized banks (including foreign banks),[8] Congress does not cut spending or increase taxes; rather it borrows vast amounts of money, amassing huge deficits. Interest on that debt, some $300 billion per year, will reach an unsustainable $800 billion by 2025.[9] State, municipal, credit card, and student debt have reached crisis levels. The Federal Reserve has exhausted its power to lower interest rates to stimulate the economy, and in the next crisis will resort to extreme measures. (3) *Hopelessness.* The basic things that secured commodious living and gave most Americans hope for the future have been destroyed. A decent income and the ability to raise a family were protected by a business-friendly economy, unions, and sensible divorce law. Today 17% of all able-bodied males and 50% of young black males are unemployed. There is a 41% overall illegitimacy rate; 53% for Hispanics; 72% for African Americans. The sexual revolution, which freed men and women to pursue lengthy educations, made marriage a luxury for the better off, but left the imitative working class vulnerable to the myriad ills of single parenthood.[10] Middle-aged whites manifest this hopelessness in rising opioid use and suicide rates.[11] For these ills, the working class blames the ruling class, which cannot rule well because it does not rule by law.

Of Commonwealth Hobbes warned of a lack of clarity in the sovereign. Against his maxim, Congress has long delegated its lawmaking authority to administrative agencies, which write, enforce, and adjudicate the law. But the older rules were constrained by congressional oversight, and log-rolling to distribute pork-barrel projects in omnibus bills in the 1970s kept representatives accountable to their constituents. Since the Republicans' 1994 Contract with America, Congress has been dominated by party leadership, and tends not to function as a deliberative body. It refuses to direct administrative agencies on basic public policies like carbon emissions and net neutrality. Not having passed a budget since 1997, it keeps the government open through "cromnibus" spending bills that contain continuing resolutions and raise the debt ceiling, which it did nine times between 2002–12. John Conyers and Max Baucus openly mocked the idea of even reading the Affordable Care Act; as Nancy Pelosi said, "We have to pass the bill so that you can find out what's in it." The ACA was 381,517 words long, and by 2013 agencies had published 11,588,500 words of final regulations.[12] Without clear congressional direction, bureaucracy determines its own needs, free from legislative control. These lengthy, unclear regulations, Hobbes warns, encourage arbitrage by the powerful, and are incomprehensible and threatening to ordinary citizens.

In the almost total absence of sovereign control as Hobbes would have understood it, the public rightly perceives that there is no effective institutional check operating on its behalf. Instead, bureaucracy secures the interests of a class of political and business insiders. After politicians and their staffers write bills and work with bureaucrats in the agencies to give special favors, regulatory exemptions, and contracts to industry, they leave politics for lucrative corporate jobs. In the immensely corrupt Medicare Part D, Billy Tauzin and a gaggle of staffers denied the government the power to negotiate drug prices; at the same time, they negotiated for new jobs as lobbyists for drug companies. Dick Cheney and Michael Chertoff both directed private companies that profited from defense contracts they had secured in public office.[13] The Department of Defense, despite spending almost $1 trillion a year, refuses to be audited, while appropriations are filled with questionable programs like the F-35 fighter, M1 Abrams tank, and Littoral Combat Ship.[14] Scholars have noted the rise of a "double government" of bureaucrats who make national security decisions, and even resisted Obama's attempts to scale back the military in Iraq and Afghanistan, America's longest and most expensive wars.[15] With little benefit to national security or an effective analytic to assess its data, new intelligence agencies, along with 500,000 well-paid contractors, record the internet searches and travel of citizens.[16]

This rule-by-exception, Hobbes would warn, violates the very definition of law: equity, reason, and enforcement. Trump was able to capitalize on the issue of immigration because the law is both ill-defined and unenforced.[17] Regulations passed by agencies are neither promulgated nor standing: by their sheer volume and ambiguity, only a few can know them. Arcane regulatory requirements increase startup costs for small businesses and prohibit market entry, creating monopolies that drive up prices, as with the recent EpiPen scandal.[18] The EPA, responding more to internal pressures than to the public need for clear laws, defines its powers as broadly as possible and then qualifies its obvious overreach by listing a multitude of narrowly defined exceptions.[19] Agencies frequently rewrite or arbitrarily interpret environmental, energy, and tax laws. For example, the IRS has repeatedly rewritten ACA tax credit provisions.[20] While large corporations both use campaign donations for influence and to hire lawyers to exploit regulatory loopholes, congresspersons both extort corporations by threatening regulation and use their insider information to profit by market speculation.[21] Rules, enforced case-by-case, are not applied equally, as when the Consumer Product Safety Commission bans a product because it is of "low utility to consumers."[22] Those with powerful connections are not prosecuted, are exempted from regulation, or are given special favors. After issuing new emissions rules in January 2011, the EPA immediately exempted a General Electric subsidiary. Wind energy companies are exempted from paying the stiff fines for the 600,000 birds, including endangered species, they kill each year. In 2013 the EPA exempted one anonymous oil company from the renewable fuels mandate. The 2005 Energy Bill exempted fracking oil and gas companies from seven major federal environmental laws. Before the 2010 Deepwater Horizon oil spill, the Interior Department gave BP's lease a "categorical exclusion" from the National Environmental Policy Act.[23] And Congress, despite the ACA, preserved its health care subsidies by having itself declared a "small business" with fewer than 50 employees.[24]

Congress hands sovereign and politically difficult decisions to administrative agencies and the Supreme Court, whose reputation is harmed as being partisan. To make these decisions, the courts forge precedent that inverts the application of constitutional provisions. "Equal protection" means special recognition or exemption, not the law applied equally to all.

"Due Process" means substantive rights, not procedural protections from arbitrary measures. Wealthy universities silence accusations of rape in hidden meetings, and either suspend the male without due process, or drag out the investigation until the female graduates and drops her claim.[25] In family courts, litigants may be deprived of their rights to free speech, religion, confronting their accusers, and due process,[26] and they are subject, via capricious tests like "best interest" and "imputed income," to arbitrary decrees and fines. In a return to debt servitude, 13.2% of South Carolina's county inmates, in one 2009 study, were poor black males incarcerated for not paying child support, amounts of which need not legally correlate to their earnings. A 2007 study of nine large states found that 70% of arrears were owed by those earning less than $10,000 a year, and expected to pay, on average, 83% of their paychecks.[27]

For Hobbes, the state of nature returns when there is no legal channel, with universal and equal application, for resolution of grievances. Law is an equal playing field that frees citizens from the rule of nepotism, passion, and the pride of others concealed as generosity. Today's rule by exception, and not law, is the preference of an elite class, with a competing claim to authority.

The Kingdom of Darkness Revisited The elites' claim to rule, aside from wealth and birth, is their expertise, following an education at the best universities. This self-proclaimed meritocracy feels entitled to the profits of a new global market of 7.5 billion people, and from sincere concerns for global problems it often rejects as archaic claims for the national good.[28] But this claim to rule is undermined by the return of what Hobbes called the Kingdom of Darkness, which opposes his teaching of natural law and peaceful liberalism. Beginning in the 1950–60s, political philosophers of various schools in universities and think tanks attacked not just liberalism, but all "modernity," which they claimed was, or culminated in, fascism. As an alternative, they called for either a return to the ancient *polis*, or progress to a new global order. In law, a class of lawyers, often hired by special interests, has replaced necessary, clear, and short laws with thousand-page bills written in jargon. In religion, Hobbes' project to make religious doctrines reasonable has been replaced by a dogmatic, inflammatory atheism, reciprocated by an unreasonable postmodernism and illiberal religion that preach the evils of the nation state.[29] College classes lead students to endless parsing of identity, not unlike the metaphysical disputes in Hobbes' time. Subjective revelatory insights are codified in a jargon that serves as an instrument of power, both creating a hierarchy of privilege that subverts the universal categories necessary for the rule of law, and making claims upon others that restrict speech and opinions.[30] The word *micro-aggression* equates words with, and justifies reciprocation by, physical injury. *Safe Space* has come to mean insulating students from opposing opinions. Student protestors shout down and beat up heretics.[31]

Aside from the injustices that arise with the rule by exception and not law, Hobbes would remind today's elites of the efficacy of the rule of law. When elite rule and consensus is blinded to reality, it results in a failure to solve elementary problems. The infrastructure of the country, its roads and bridges, is crumbling.[32] Federal obligations total more than $17 tril lion. American foreign policy, crafted by experts, has been a disaster: spending billions on corrupt dictators, useless and cronyistic infrastructure projects, and well intentioned but ineffective programs.[33] Optimistic State Department talking points, which tout successes, reflect at best fallacious assessments of bureaucrats removed from failures on the ground, and at worst intentional deception.[34]

The great inefficacy of this elite class eventually undermines its moral authority, which takes on a revelatory quality, and becomes susceptible to the flaws Hobbes describes. First are rational challenges to statistics, reported by the bureaucracy, on inflation, unemployment, GDP, and public debt, that conflict with empirical reality. But if inflation is closer to 5%, or even 10%, and unemployment closer to 20%, it becomes self-defeating to insist on 1.7% and 4.4%. So too has the sincerity of the elites been discredited by the inequities of the legal system and the hypocrisy of the wealthy. Clinton attacked Wall Street, but received up to $225,000 per speech at Goldman Sachs. Celebrities and professors demand Americans shrink their carbon footprint, yet fly on private jets, travel to international conferences, and live in palatial homes. Morally, the elite laid the legal path to today's vulgar culture, in which Jay-Z is invited to the White House, but they chide Americans for ignoring Trump's vulgarities. The politics of gender does not apply to developing countries or Muslims, the politics of race does not apply to Silicon Valley or Hollywood, and the politics of class does not apply to the Ivy League.[35] Career politicians who pronounce on the economy have never had a private sector job. For these reasons, critics denounce identity politics as a jargon that conceals and secures the interests of an elite class.

The failure to solve basic problems in government and the perception of hypocrisy among the elites has led to a breakdown of trust both in government and in the media, and this in turn becomes the source of what Hobbes sees as more dangerous ideological appeals and divisions in the body politic. As there is no longer a shared moral code, truth in reporting becomes impossible because voters judge truthfulness by informational cues to determine interest; facts are perceived as selected for political control. As the motivations of the media have become suspect, it has lost its credibility. Trump voters simply refused to answer exit polls because they viewed the media as part of a hostile establishment.[36]

Last Word to Hobbes Hobbes would remind both political parties that Trump was elected by the same voters who elected Obama,[37] not because they are racist or love vulgarity, but because he promised to fix real problems. Democrats misinterpreted Obama's victory as a referendum on identity politics. They mistakenly believed they had won the "culture war"—one Harvard professor proposed de-Nazification for conservatives[38]—when it was really an enthusiastic bid to unify the country and move beyond divisive categories. Conversely, Trump's stunning success in the Rust Belt, and Republican control of Congress and state governments, will mean nothing without results. Ultimately his legacy, and political realignment, rests on policy successes. This may be good news for Democrats, who might put together a "Better Deal" to run against Republicans on core economic issues in 2020.[39] Political success, Hobbes advises, awaits whichever party can restore national unity by returning to the basic ends of government.

This first will require candidness with the American public on immigration, trade, unemployment, entitlements, and the public debt. With genuine statesmanship, another attempt at a "grand bargain," where Democrats and Republicans compromise on cutting expenditures and raising necessary revenues, is possible.[40] It will also require moral consistency and advocacy: both restoring hope for the working class and affirming a moral code that accompanies elite status. This coming together, a unification of both classes in a hierarchy of honor and shame, begins with civility and mutual respect that panders neither to vulgarity nor to elitist contempt. But all of this would require, Hobbes would say, a return to the rule of law: universal, equal, and enforced. All large governments require extensive administration, but a lack of clarity in sovereignty results in inefficiency, irresponsibility, and ultimately injustice and class division. This would mean more than reducing the number of arcane regulations and the arbitrary enforcement that benefit special interests—it would mean reclaiming sovereignty, with its concomitant responsibility, from the bureaucracy and private corporations, and that requires real leadership, or *Leviathan*.

Curing the body politic, argues Hobbes, begins in the universities. As a classical liberal, he would warn conservatives that their imperialism drains the nation of blood and treasure, and their bid for either the rule of a managerial class or populist revolt will bring back the disorders of seventeenth century Europe. Hobbes would warn neo-progressives that their project of dual sovereignty in a world confederation is impossible because sovereigns always remain in a state of nature, and insofar as it promotes a global empire, it will destroy liberty. Hobbes would urge professors to use greater caution before using anti-liberal rhetoric, and to affirm liberal principles: to support freedom of conscience and speech, and withstand zealots' demands to curtail it. He would advocate not just legal protection, but honor, for public debate, requiring both toleration and the clarification of terms. Distinguishing those motivated by a love of truth from those who desire the honor of political power, Hobbes hoped to direct the latter's ideas into political channels, with accountability, instead of allowing them to hide and fester in universities. The freedom and felicity of the commonwealth, Hobbes warns, are not inevitable: they require the renewal of liberal principles, and codes of honor that direct the desires of vainglorious citizens.

Notes

1. Frank Luntz, "What the Polls Were Never Going to Reveal," *Time*, Nov 11, 2016, accessed Jul 22, 2017 [unless otherwise stated, all articles hereafter were accessed Jul 22, 2017], http://time.com/4565560/frank-luntz-polls-never-reveal/.
2. Nora Caplan-Bricker, "The Backlog of 400,000 Unprocessed Rape Kits is a Disgrace," *New Republic*, Mar 9, 2014, https://newrepublic.com/article/116945/rape-kits-backlog-joe-biden-announces-35-million-reopen-cases.
3. "Enter At Your Own Risk: Police Union Says 'War-Like' Detroit Is Unsafe For Visitors," *CBS Detroit*, Oct 6, 2012, http://detroit.cbslocal.com/2012/10/06/enter-at-your-own-risk-police-union-says-war-like-detroit-is-unsafe-for-visitors/.

4. Martin Kaste, "Open Cases: Why One-Third of Murders in America go Unresolved," *NPR*, Mar 30, 2015, http://www.npr.org/2015/03/30/395069137/open-cases-why-one-third-of-murders-in-america-go-unresolved.

5. Dexter Filkins, "'Do Not Resist' and the Crisis of Police Militarization," *The New Yorker*, May 13, 2016, http://www.newyorker.com/news/news-desk/do-not-resist-and-the-crisis-of-police-militarization.

6. Jacob Rascon and Ali Vitali, "Protesters Assault Trump Supporters With Eggs, Bottles, Punches After Rally," *NBCNews*, Jun 3, 2016, http://www.nbcnews.com/politics/2016-election/protesters-assault-trump-supporters-eggs-bottles-punches-after-rally-n585096.

7. Emilie Raguso, "Berkeley police chief: 'Our people did exactly what we asked' in April 15 demo," *Berkeleyside*, Apr 19, 2017, http://www.berkeleyside.com/2017/04/19/berkeley-police-chief-people-exactly-asked-april-15-demo/.

8. Roisin McCord, Edward Simpson Prescott, and Tim Sablik, "Explaining the Decline in the Number of Banks since the Great Recession," *Federal Reserve Bank of Richmond*, Mar 2015, https://www.richmondfed.org/~/media/richmondfedorg/publications/research/economic_brief/2015/pdf/eb_15-03.pdf; Rep. Alan Grayson, "The Fed Bailouts: Money for Nothing," *HuffingtonPost*, Feb 4, 2012, http://www.huffingtonpost.com/rep-alan-grayson/the-fed-bailouts-money-fo_b_1129988.html.

9. Bob Bixby and Maya MacGuineas, "Why the Federal Debt Must Be a Top Priority for the 2016 Presidential Candidates," *Brookings Institute*, November 18, 2015, https://www.brookings.edu/wp-content/uploads/2016/07/Bixby-MacGuineas_FINAL.pdf.

10. Cara Newlon, "Hooking Up And Marriage: Luxury Goods For Educated Millennials," *Forbes*, Jun 19, 2014, https://www.forbes.com/sites/caranewlon/2014/06/19/hooking-up-and-marriage-luxury-goods-for-educated-millennials/#66431ba93d11.

11. Jessica Boddy, "The Forces Driving Middle-Aged White People's 'Deaths Of Despair'," *NPR*, Mar 23, 2017, http://www.npr.org/sections/health-shots/2017/03/23/521083335/the-forces-driving-middle-aged-white-peoples-deaths-of-despair.

12. John Graham, *Obama on the Home Front* (Bloomington, IN: Indiana University Press, 2016), 171.

13. Rebecca Leung, "All in the Family," *CBS*, Apr 25, 2003, http://www.cbsnews.com/news/all-in-the-family-25-04-2003/; Kimberly Kindy, "Ex-Homeland Security chief head said to abuse public trust by touting body scanners," *Washington Post*, Jan 1, 2010, http://www.washingtonpost.com/wp-dyn/content/article/2009/12/31/AR2009123102821.html.

14. William D. Hartung, "How Not to Audit the Pentagon," *LATimes*, Apr 10, 2016, http://www.latimes.com/opinion/op-ed/la-oe-hartung-pentagon-waste-20160410-story.html.
15. Michael J. Glennon, "National Security and Double Government," *Harvard National Security Journal*, Vol. 5, Iss. 1 (2014), 1–113; see Bob Woodward, *Obama's Wars* (New York: Simon & Schuster, 2010), 301–17.
16. John Avlon, "The Military-Industrial Complex Is Real, and It's Bigger Than Ever" *The Daily Beast*, Jun 12, 2013, http://www.thedailybeast.com/the-military-industrial-complex-is-real-and-its-bigger-than-ever; John Napier Tye, "Meet Executive Order 12333," *Washington Post*, Jul 18, 2014, https://www.washingtonpost.com/opinions/meet-executive-order-12333-the-reagan-rule-that-lets-the-nsa-spy-on-americans/2014/07/18/93d2ac22-0h93-11e4-b8e5-d0de807676 ?_story.html.'utm_term=.5d8e/t09c9b1;   Devlin Barrett, "U.S. Spies on Millions of Drivers," *Wall Street Journal*, Jan 26, 2015, https://www.wsj.com/articles/u-s-spies-on-millions-of-cars-1422314779.
17. Kathleen Hennessey, "Immigration stands as Obama's most glaring failure," *PBS*, Jul 4, 2016, http://www.pbs.org/newshour/rundown/immigration-stands-as-obamas-most-glaring-failure/; Caitlin Dickerson, "Obama Administration Is Quietly Delaying Thousands of Deportation Cases," *New York Times*, Oct 6, 2016, https://www.nytimes.com/2016/10/07/us/delayed-deportations-illegal-immigrants.html.
18. "Sen. Rand Paul: EpiPen Scandal is a Perfect Example of Crony Capitalism," *Time*, Sep 7, 2016, http://time.com/4482179/sen-rand-paul-epipen-scandal/.
19. Michael Greve and Ashley C. Parrish, "Administrative Law without Congress," *George Mason Law Review* 22, No. 3 (2015), 501–47.
20. Jonathan Adler, "How the IRS repeatedly rewrites Obamacare tax credit provisions," *Washington Post*, Apr 14, 2015, https://www.washingtonpost.com/news/volokh-conspiracy/wp/2015/04/14/how-the-irs-repeatedly-rewrites-obamacare-tax-credit-provisions/?utm_term=.ca251ba569fd.
21. Peter Schweizer, *Throw Them All Out* (New York: Houghton Mifflin Harcourt, 2011); *Extortion* (New York: Houghton Mifflin Harcourt, 2013).
22. Sohrab Ahmari, "Craig Zucker: What Happens When a Man Takes on the Feds," *Wall Street Journal*, Aug 30, 2013, https://www.wsj.com/articles/craig-zucker-what-happens-when-a-man-takes-on-the-fed-1377903129.
23. Juliet Eilperin, "U.S. exempted BP's Gulf of Mexico drilling from environmental impact study," *Washington Post*, May 5, 2010, http://www.washingtonpost.com/wp-dyn/content/article/2010/05/04/AR2010050404118.html.

24. Timothy P. Carney, "Obama issues global warming rules in January, gives GE an exemption in February," *Washington Examiner*, Feb 2, 2011, accessed Feb 3, 2011, http://washingtonexaminer.com/blogs/beltway-confidential/2011/02/obama-issues-global-warming-rules-january-gives-ge-exemption-febr#ixzz1CugJME1a; Brian Seasholes, "Angry Birds? No, But Obama's Wind Energy Subsidies Have Them Very Frightened," *Forbes*, Jul 13, 2013, https://www.forbes.com/sites/realspin/2013/07/16/angry-birds-no-but-obamas-wind-energy-subsidies-have-them-very-frightened/#4fdb0af679f5; Kimberley A. Strassel, "Behind an Ethanol Special Favor," *Wall Street Journal*, Aug 13, 2013, https://www.wsj.com/articles/strassel-behind-an-ethanol-special-favor-1376437980; "Safety First, Fracking Second," *Scientific American*, Nov 1, 2011, https://www.scientificamerican.com/article/safety-first-fracking-second/; Kate Rogers, "Is Congress a small business? The stubborn Obamacare challenge," *CNBC*, Mar 6, 2015, https://www.cnbc.com/2015/03/05/is-congress-a-small-business-the-stubborn-obamacare-challenge.html.

25. Emily Yoffe, "The College Rape Overcorrection," *Slate*, Dec 7, 2014, http://www.slate.com/articles/double_x/doublex/2014/12/college_rape_campus_sexual_assault_is_a_serious_problem_but_the_efforts.html.

26. See Steven Baskerville, *Taken Into Custody* (Nashville, TN: Cumberland House, 2007), 75–109.

27. Frances Robles and Shaila Dewan, "Skip Child Support. Go to Jail. Lose Job. Repeat," *New York Times*, Apr 19, 2015, https://www.nytimes.com/2015/04/20/us/skip-child-support-go-to-jail-lose-job-repeat.html; Elaine Sorensen, Liliana Sousa, and Simone Schaner, "Assessing Child Support Arrears in Nine Large States and the Nation," *The Urban Institute*, Jan 14, 2009, http://www.urban.org/research/publication/assessing-child-support-arrears-nine-large-states-and-nation/view/full_report; Christopher Mathias, "One-Eighth of South Carolina Inmates were Jailed over Child Support Payments," *Huffington Post*, Apr 10, 2015, http://www.huffingtonpost.com/2015/04/10/walter-scott-child-support-_n_7036174.html.

28. Chrystia Freeland, "The Rise of the New Global Elite," *The Atlantic*, Jan/Feb 2011, https://www.theatlantic.com/magazine/archive/2011/01/the-rise-of-the-new-global-elite/308343/.

29. For one assessment, see Helen Pluckrose, "How French 'Intellectuals' Ruined the West," *Areo Magazine*, Mar 27, 2017, https://areomagazine.com/2017/03/27/how-french-intellectuals-ruined-the-west-postmodernism-and-its-impact-explained/; John Zmirak, "Illiberal Catholicism," *Aleteia*, Dec 31, 2013, https://aleteia.org/2013/12/31/illiberal-catholicism/.

30. "Noam Chomsky: Postmodernism is an Instrument of Power," *Youtube*, https://www.youtube.com/watch?v=WwTfHv5dpPw.
31. See Conor Friedersdorf, "UC Berkeley Declares Itself Unsafe for Ann Coulter," *The Atlantic*, Apr 20, 2017, https://www.theatlantic.com/politics/archive/2017/04/uc-berkeley-declares-itself-unsafe-for-ann-coulter/523668/; Allison Stanger, "Understanding the Angry Mob at Middlebury That Gave Me a Concussion," *New York Times*, Mar 13, 2017, https://www.nytimes.com/2017/03/13/opinion/understanding-the-angry-mob-that-gave-me-a-concussion.html.
32. American Society of Civil Engineers, "America's Infrastructure Scores a D+," http://www.infrastructurereportcard.org/.
33. Matthew Rosenbergapril, "With Bags of Cash, C.I.A. Seeks Influence in Afghanistan," *New York Times*, Apr 28, 2013, http://www.nytimes.com/2013/04/29/world/asia/cia-delivers-cash-to-afghan-leaders-office.html, Dion Nissenbaum, "Roads to Nowhere: Program to Win Over Afghans Fails," *Wall Street Journal*, February 10, 2012, https://www.wsj.com/articles/SB10001424052970203554104576655280219991322; Lucy Westcott, "U.S. Paid $335 Million for a Power Plant in Afghanistan No One Is Using," *Newsweek*, Aug 13, 2015, http://www.newsweek.com/us-paid-335-million-power-plant-afghanistan-no-one-using-362574; Josh Rogin, "After $200 Million, Afghan Soldiers Still Can't Read," *DailyBeast*, Jan 28, 2014, http://www.thedailybeast.com/after-dollar200-million-afghan-soldiers-still-cant-read.
34. Peter Van Buren, *We Meant Well* (New York: Metropolitan Books, 2011); "Is This What Winning Looks Like?" *Vice Media*, May 27, 2013, https://www.youtube.com/watch?v=Ja5Q75hf6QI; Sarah Chayes, *Thieves of State* (New York: W.W. Norton, 2015).
35. Robert Cherry, "Black and Muslim Women are Invisible to the Feminist Movement," *National Review*, May 16, 2017, http://www.nationalreview.com/article/447660/linda-sarsour-and-feminists-blindness-women-color; Allison Griswold, "When It Comes to Diversity in Tech, Companies Find Safety in Numbers," *Slate*, Jun 27, 2014, http://www.slate.com/blogs/moneybox/2014/06/27/tech_diversity_data_facebook_follows_google_yahoo_in_releasing_the_stats.html; "2014 Hollywood Diversity Report," *Ralph J. Bunche Center for African American Studies*, http://www.bunchecenter.ucla.edu/wp-content/uploads/2014/02/2014-Hollywood-Diversity-Report-2-12-14.pdf; Michele Hernandez, "Poor Students—Rich Ivies: Seeking Real Diversity at Ivy-Level Colleges," *Huffington Post*, Dec 15, 2016, http://www.huffingtonpost.com/dr-michele-hernandez/poor-students-rich-ivies-_b_13656152.html.
36. Luntz, "What the Polls Were Never Going to Reveal," *Time*, Nov 11, 2016.

37. Alex Roarty, "Democrats say they now know exactly why Clinton lost," *McClatchy*, May 1, 2017, http://www.mcclatchydc.com/news/politics-government/article147475484.html.
38. Mark Tushnet, "Abandoning Defensive Crouch Liberal Constitutionalism," *Balkinization*, May 6, 2016, https://balkin.blogspot.co.il/2016/05/abandoning-defensive-crouch-liberal.html.
39. Mike Allen, "Dems want to rebrand as the economic party," *Axios*, Jul 22, 2017, https://www.axios.com/better-deal-economic-agenda-house-democrats-plan-2463550316.html.
40. Sarah Ferris, "Showdown scars: How the $4 trillion 'grand bargain' collapsed," *The Hill*, Feb 10, 2016, http://thehill.com/policy/finance/268857-showdown-scars-how-the-4-trillion-grand-bargain-collapsed.

Bibliography

Ahmari, Sohrab. 2013. Craig Zucker: What Happens When a Man Takes on the Feds. *Wall Street Journal*, August 30. https://www.wsj.com/articles/craig-zucker-what-happens-when-a-man-takes-on-the-fed-1377903129.

American Society of Civil Engineers. *America's Infrastructure Scores a D+*. http://www.infrastructurereportcard.org/.

Baskerville, Steven. 2007. *Taken into Custody*. Nashville: Cumberland House.

Boddy, Jessica. 2017. The Forces Driving Middle-Aged White People's 'Deaths of Despair'. *NPR*, March 23. http://www.npr.org/sections/health-shots/2017/03/23/521083335/the-forces-driving-middle-aged-white-peoples-deaths-of-despair.

Caplan-Bricker, Nora. 2014. The Backlog of 400,000 Unprocessed Rape Kits Is a Disgrace. *New Republic*, March 9. https://newrepublic.com/article/116945/rape-kits-backlog-joe-biden-announces-35-million-reopen-cases.

Chayes, Sarah. 2015. *Thieves of State*. New York: W.W. Norton.

Filkins, Dexter. 2016. 'Do Not Resist' and the Crisis of Police Militarization. *The New Yorker*, May 13. http://www.newyorker.com/news/news-desk/do-not-resist-and-the-crisis-of-police-militarization.

Freeland, Chrystia. 2011. The Rise of the New Global Elite. *The Atlantic*, January/February. https://www.theatlantic.com/magazine/archive/2011/01/the-rise-of-the-new-global-elite/308343/.

Glennon, Michael J. 2014. National Security and Double Government. *Harvard National Security Journal* 1 (5): 1–113.

Graham, John. 2016. *Obama on the Home Front*. Bloomington: Indiana University Press.

Greve, Michael, and Ashley C. Parrish. 2015. Administrative Law Without Congress. *George Mason Law Review* 22 (3): 501–547.

Hobbes, Thomas. 1994. *Leviathan*, Ed. Edwin Curley. Indianapolis: Hackett Publishing Company, Inc.

Kaste, Martin. 2015. Open Cases: Why One-Third of Murders in America Go Unresolved. *NPR*, March 30. http://www.npr.org/2015/03/30/395069137/open-cases-why-one-third-of-murders-in-america-go-unresolved.

Luntz, Frank. 2016. What the Polls Were Never Going to Reveal. *Time*, November 11. http://time.com/4565560/frank-luntz-polls-never-reveal/

Newlon, Cara. 2014. Hooking Up and Marriage: Luxury Goods for Educated Millennials. *Forbes*, June 19. https://www.forbes.com/sites/caranewlon/2014/06/19/hooking-up-and-marriage-luxury-goods-for-educated-millennials/#66431ba93d11.

Paul, Rand. 2016. EpiPen Scandal Is a Perfect Example of Crony Capitalism. *Time*, September 7. http://time.com/4482179/sen-rand-paul-epipen-scandal/.

Ralph. J. *Bunche Center for African American Studies*, 2014 Hollywood Diversity Report. http://www.bunchecenter.ucla.edu/wp-content/uploads/2014/02/2014-Hollywood-Diversity-Report-2-12-14.pdf.

Roarty, Alex. 2017. Democrats Say They Now Know Exactly Why Clinton Lost. *McClatchy*, May 1. http://www.mcclatchydc.com/news/politics-government/article147475484.html.

Robles, Frances, and Shaila Dewan. 2015. Skip Child Support. Go to Jail. Lose Job. Repeat. *New York Times*, April 19. https://www.nytimes.com/2015/04/20/us/skip-child-support-go-to-jail-lose-job-repeat.html.

Schweizer, Peter. 2011. *Throw Them All Out*. New York: Houghton Mifflin Harcourt.

———. 2013. *Extortion*. New York: Houghton Mifflin Harcourt.

Scientific American. 2011. Safety First, Fracking Second. November 1. https://www.scientificamerican.com/article/safety-first-fracking-second/.

Seasholes, Brian. 2013. Angry Birds? No, But Obama's Wind Energy Subsidies Have Them Very Frightened. *Forbes*, July 13. https://www.forbes.com/sites/realspin/2013/07/16/angry-birds-no-but-obamas-wind-energy-subsidies-have-them-very-frightened/#4fdb0af679f5.

Sorensen, Elaine, Liliana Sousa, and Simone Schaner. 2009. Assessing Child Support Arrears in Nine Large States and the Nation. *The Urban Institute*, January 14. http://www.urban.org/research/publication/assessing-child-support-arrears-nine-large-states-and-nation/view/full_report.

Van Buren, Peter. 2011. *We Meant Well*. New York: Metropolitan Books.

Woodward, Bob. 2010. *Obama's Wars*. New York: Simon & Schuster.

Yoffe, Emily. 2014. The College Rape Overcorrection. *Slate*, December 7. http://www.slate.com/articles/double_x/doublex/2014/12/college_rape_campus_sexual_assault_is_a_serious_problem_but_the_efforts.html.

CHAPTER 8

Hope, Hate and Indignation: Spinoza and Political Emotion in the Trump Era

Ericka Tucker

INTRODUCTION

Americans are angry. After an economic collapse, slow recovery, and the resulting increase in inequality between economic classes, those in the dwindling middle classes are angry. The anger of many of these people has been channeled by sources like Fox News and right-wing radio, internet sites and social media into hatred of and resentment toward immigrants, refugees, Muslims, and African-Americans. Throughout the Obama presidency Donald Trump amplified some of the most fact-challenged of these propaganda organizations. As a "birther", Trump championed the idea that Barack Obama was a Muslim born in Kenya after all evidence pointed to the contrary. This theory, however, served as an organizing tool for those who believed their country had been "taken over" by those who did not look like them and who they believed threatened their way of life. The resentment and anger, for which it was a lightning rod, was a potent political force in the 2016 election. This resentment and anger brought Donald Trump into the White House.[1]

Although the circumstances of the U.S. Election in 2016 are far from the 17th Century world of philosopher Spinoza, his views on the role of

E. Tucker (✉)
Philosophy Department, Marquette University, Milwaukee, WI, USA

© The Author(s) 2018
M. B. Sable, A. J. Torres (eds.), *Trump and Political Philosophy*,
https://doi.org/10.1007/978-3-319-74427-8_8

emotions in human behavior and their results for political philosophy are, I propose, relevant insofar as hope, fear, and anger are still being employed as tactics to create political agreement, and insofar as there remain humans with the capacity to feel anger, fear, and even hope.

While less well known than Hobbes or Machiavelli, Spinoza offered a new set of arguments for why political leaders should take into consideration the emotions of the populace, and indeed, to build policy and institutions to shape these emotions for the good of the state. Spinoza's views are often at odds with these better-known theorists. A key difference is Spinoza's insistence that fear and hatred are emotions that diminish both the power of individual humans and the states of which they are part.[2] Following from this, Spinoza proposes that the state gains its power from that of its citizens, and thus, should try to organize it's policies and institutions to empower its citizens either through emotions like 'joy' or through more active participation in and knowledge of the activities of the state. Before we take Spinoza to be too naive a philosopher to take politics seriously, he also worried about the role of hope in individual lives and in politics. Hope, he argued, was a variety of fear, and as such made individuals in its grip less powerful than they might otherwise be.

In this chapter, I will set out the ideas of Spinoza on the political emotions while using the extended example of Donald Trump's campaign and early presidency. While all presidential elections arouse strong emotions, the Trump campaign and early presidency have seemed to arouse two kinds of emotions that Spinoza thought to be quite dangerous for the state, and enervating for both those who experienced them and the state of which they were a part: hatred and indignation. Before delving into these, I'll begin with an emotion that one might think would be good, namely, hope to see it as Spinoza might have: an emotion which, once disappointed, can turn into hate.

Trump's Emotional Politics

On the surface, one could hardly imagine two more different presidential campaigns than that of Barack Obama in 2008 and Donald Trump in 2016. Obama's campaign was built on the idea of grassroots community organizing, and explicitly campaigned on the idea of hope—that the future could be better than the past and the present.[3] Hope was a keyword in his 2004 keynote address to the Democratic National Convention.[4] Obama's book, *The Audacity of Hope*, set out a program of creating a better future and realizing the hope of inclusion through increasing public participation in democracy and in civic engagement.[5]

Barack Obama appealed to the hope for better times in 2008—a moment of widespread fear after a major international economic collapse. Obama offered the nation a hopeful vision of the future. He was also a candidate seemingly without a history. He had not been a politician for long before his inspiring speech at the 2004 Democratic National Convention. In 2016, after eight years of an obstructionist congress, a less progressive president than many were hoping for and the expansion of right-wing propaganda into mainstream media, Americans were angry.[6] Hope had turned to anger.

Trump's appeal to that anger was highly emotive, and ultimately successful. Trump's campaign was characterized by many as focused on fear-mongering and hate.[7] Trump insisted that the United States was under siege, and that threats to Americans were coming from both the outside and within from Muslim terrorists to Mexican immigrants.[8] His solutions were in the broadest sense 'protective' and 'exclusionary'.[9] To prevent these threats, Trump argued, we must ban Muslims from entering the country, restrict immigration in general, and build a border wall between the United States and Mexico.[10] Trump's campaign, while promising to "Make America Great Again" was more critical of the contemporary state of the United States, arguing that America needed to be "taken back".[11] In a campaign rally in Wisconsin, Trump argued, "This is your last chance ... to take back power from all the people who've taken it from you over so many years."[12] The rhetoric of taking back our country could be an innocuous campaign promise. The parties that the country has to be taken back from are not identified so that those who hear it can read into it whatever they like. However, some argue that the phrases "take America back" or referring to the country as "under siege" are so-called 'dog whistles'. Dog whistles are seemingly innocuous phrases that are associated with white nationalist organizations and support for racist policies that are socially unacceptable to back openly.[13] Hate groups have taken Trump's policies and statements as veiled endorsements of their activities.[14] Some argue that Trump's rhetoric has emboldened racists, and indeed hate crimes in the United States are rising.[15] At the same time, Trump has cut funding to the groups that monitor hate groups and attempt to ameliorate their influence.[16] After the events of August 12, 2017 in Charlottesville, Virginia, the connection between Trump and white-supremacist movement took a more direct turn, when he was slow in condemning hate groups initially, and then after a few days, appeared to offer support to the white nationalist cause.[17] As I write this in August 2017, these events are still developing. For the purposes of this study, I am interested in the fact that hate, fear and indignation played a role in making Mr. Trump's campaign for President of the United States in 2016 successful.

Political psychologist Drew Westen has argued that Democrats are less successful at gauging and responding to affective politics—issues that arouse strong emotional states in citizens. In Westen's view, Democrats are not as savvy as Republicans at understanding the emotions of the electorate. Democratic candidates often take rational and measured stances on issues that are emotionally charged. While this rational or unemotional approach is lauded by other Democrats, Westen argues that this approach is ineffective among many. Westen proposes that this approach makes Democratic candidates appear untrustworthy and as individuals who do not understand the importance of an issue.[18] When a candidate seems to have the wrong emotional response, or no emotional response to important issues, those who are not already supporters tend to find such a candidate unappealing.[19] Many scholars of politics have argued that a large swath of the American public feels resentment toward minorities, angry and disconnected from American public and political life,[20] and disempowered in a globalizing economy. Given this, Trump's appeal to and cultivation of the anger of the multitude who voted for him is not just unsurprising, but indeed, brilliant strategically.

Trump was able to recognize, and then to gain the trust of those who, like him, felt angry and resentful about perceived changes in the United States. While some of these are economic, many have to do with cultural phenomena that have seemingly little to do with general wellbeing. Many Trump voters, while genuinely afraid of Islam and immigration, noted their anger at "political correctness" as a reason for their vote.[21] Trump tapped into this anger. He acknowledged and amplified this anger. With every racial slur, with every rude comment toward women, Trump gained the trust of those who wanted someone to "tell it like it is". Despite his much-documented untruth, Trump was seen by his supporters as honest for this reason: he was willing to say out loud their own hatred in a way they no longer felt comfortable doing.[22] Recognition is an incredibly powerful force.[23] Trump's acknowledgement of this anger, resentment, and petty emotions of a large group of people won him the election in 2016. Winning elections, however, is different than governing, and this may be where the efficacy of appealing to and cultivating hate diminishes. In the next section, I will examine Spinoza's view of the relative efficacy of hope and hate as emotions to use for governing. This will take us first through Spinoza's theory of the emotions, and his view of how the emotions of individuals affect the political communities of which they are parts.

SPINOZA AND EMOTIONS

In Book Three of the *Ethics*, Spinoza begins setting out his theory of emotions. First, he proposes that there are three basic emotions: pain, pleasure and desire.[24] Now, desire turns out to be a bit more than an emotion, but for our purposes, the first two are the most important. Pain and pleasure are the basic emotions from which all other emotions derive. All of what we might call the 'positive' emotions are pleasure modified by the idea of an object, a temporal dimension, a modal dimension and a proximity dimension. This sounds complicated, but is as simple as the following: our joy for seeing our family (object) might be increased given its nearness to us in time, the degree of likeliness of this visit, and whether or not there are likely circumstances that could block this visit, etc. Love, for Spinoza, is the feeling of pleasure with the idea of an object, often a person, as the cause. This may sound bloodless to many, but it's really just an attempt to come up with a theory of how emotions can be based on relatively few basic emotions.[25] Spinoza defines hope as "inconstant pleasure arising from the idea of a thing future or past, of whose outcome we are in some doubt."[26] When we become more certain about the outcome of some event, our hope becomes joy should it go our way,[27] and disappointment should we have been wrong.[28] All of the positive emotions are based on pleasure relating to our idea of some object, be it an individual or event. Our ideas about that individual or event modify our degree of pleasure, and some of these modifications are significant enough to merit their own names as specific emotions. Among the positive emotions Spinoza identifies are honor, pride, esteem, joy, approbation, inclination and love.

What we might call negative emotions are all those emotions based on pain, but with the same sort of modifications as the positive emotions. Hate, for example, is defined as "pain accompanied by the idea of an external cause."[29] Fear is defined as "inconstant pain arising from the idea of a thing future or past of whose outcome we are in some doubt."[30] Careful readers will notice the parallel between hope and fear—each is an emotion involving inconstancy and uncertain outcomes. Hope, for Spinoza, is thus, is always intermixed with fear and thus, is a negative emotion.[31] Our ideas about the object that we believe cause us pain can increase that pain or diminish that pain. Should we consider something that we hate to be unfree, for example, Spinoza argues that our hatred will ebb.[32] Our emotions build on one another and our ideas about their objects. Should we fear something, we will hate it.[33] Should we hate something, we will try to destroy it.[34] Spinoza defines anger as the desire to destroy that which we hate.[35] The negative emotions that Spinoza defines include: fear, anger, hatred, aversion, disappointment and indignation.

Thus far, I have been using the terms 'positive" and "negative" emotion without explaining the significance of this distinction. For Spinoza, all emotions based on pleasure, insofar as they are not intermixed with emotions based on pain, express an increase in our power of acting and thinking.[36] They are, in a straightforward sense, good for us. All emotions based on pain, diminish our power acting and thinking, and are always bad for us.[37] It's possible, for Spinoza, for us to increase our power further, through understanding the causes of our pain and pleasure. This understanding is the best way to increase our power of acting and thinking; however, emotions based on joy help us to achieve this increased power as well.[38]

For Spinoza, the human individual seeks to free itself from pain,[39] This means that, for example, when we're confronted with something that diminishes our power, something that causes us pain, we try to imagine that thing destroyed or even act to destroy it in order to regain our sense of wellbeing or power.[40] In this sense, for Spinoza, pain and other emotions that are species of pain doubly enervate individual power—they diminish an individual's power in the first place, and then require that that individual focus on their negative emotions to destroy the object which they believe causes the pain. This is why, for Spinoza, an affect like hatred can never be good.[41] While pain may have its place in an affective economy, hatred can never be good. Further, Spinoza insists, the emotions of hope and fear in themselves can never be good.[42]

For Spinoza, emotions like hatred, anger, fear and even hope diminish humans' power of thinking and acting, leading us to make worse decisions, have less reasonable ideas than if we had emotions based on pleasure such as joy or love. Further, Spinoza insists, when our power is diminished, and when we experience the emotions of fear and anger, we tend to be at odds with one another.[43]

The objects of our love or hate, and our ideas about them can be incredibly complex. We can, Spinoza insists, hate love or fear just about anything,[44] depending on our ideas of that thing. Our ideas are often wrong, so we often hate things we should love, etc., and more to the point we often misidentify the causes of our emotions.[45] Our ideas about the world are shaped by those around us, and indeed, according to Spinoza we tend to emulate the emotions of those we identify with and whom we love.[46] Again, for Spinoza, just because we take something to be like us we may take on their emotions and ideas as our own, but whom we take to be like us and why is an incredibly complex process. Although, for Spinoza, all other humans are like us and are beneficial for us,[47] he recognizes that we rarely recognize this, and come to love and hate other human beings based on a variety of contingent features[48] about them which may not relate to us in the ways that we think and which inspire our love or hate. Throughout Book 3 of the Ethics, Spinoza sets out how it is that our affects and ideas shape one another, and are shaped by what we believe others to think and to feel.[49] Negotiating our own affects through this process of socialization is one that can lead to error, but which also creates social groups whose likes and dislikes, emotions and ideas are shared. Even if the ideas and emotions of others are confused, being in a group, for Spinoza, is always better than being alone.[50] Being in a group and sharing the emotions of a group does not always mean we agree on everything. Indeed, as Spinoza argues, we can be wrong about what others think and feel about anything, and we can be wrong about what they think of us. His example of this is somewhat appropriate: "It can easily happen that a vain man may be proud and imagine that he is popular with everybody, when in fact he is obnoxious."[51]

In the next section, I will set out how Spinoza's thought about the emotions—particularly of hope, fear and indignation—work when he considers humans living together in political communities.

It is not that important who sits in the White House if the structures of democracy are strong. If the structures of democracy are strong—you can have a madman or madwoman for four years or even eight, and then he or she is gone, and the nation's freedoms live.[52]

EMOTIONS AND INSTITUTIONS: SPINOZA'S POLITICAL THOUGHT

Spinoza based his political philosophy on his theory of emotions[53] developed in the *Ethics*. We have seen above that, for Spinoza, emotions like hate and fear diminish the power of individual humans, and in the political works, he argues that although fear may be useful at times, it should be avoided given that an individual or populace overcome by fear is weak. However, while Spinoza's sage-like figure in the *Ethics* sought individual perfection and reason, Spinoza did not seek perfection in the political realm. Spinoza is clear at the very beginning of his *Political Treatise*, that those who would seek to perfect human nature in either governance or citizenship were dreaming of a 'golden age' that never existed.[54] We cannot rely on a leader or citizen's virtue for the freedom or stability of a state, we need institutions that shape the emotions, ideas and actions of humans so that they can live together. In the political realm, hope and fear are the major engines of affective organization of the multitude. While both are dangerous for individuals, given that reason cannot be expected in large numbers, Spinoza agrees with Hobbes and Machiavelli that they have political utility. Spinoza insists that the best leader ought to govern with kindness, with limited appeals to hope and fear, and other passive affects like hatred. In the following section I will set out his views of how these emotions.

Hope, according to Spinoza, is a dangerous emotion for individuals. However, given the choice between hope and fear as tools of governance, Spinoza leaves open room for the use of hope. Hope, in political life, is a better tool for a government to use to coordinate its populace, because it is a species of pleasure. For individuals, it is contraindicated because of the measure of fear intermixed with this pleasure; however, pleasure beats pain in Spinoza's calculations of the power of human emotions. Pleasure increases human power, while pain or fear diminishes it.[55] Thus, even a pleasure intermixed with fear is better than fear alone. Like a fearful individual, a fearful population is dangerous and weak.[56] Their weakness, however, does not give the state more power, but rather, gives the state an inordinate number of potential individuals to worry about while diminishing its overall power.

The weakest form of state for Spinoza is one where there are very few who govern and a large population that is governed but has no say in either advising or in making decisions in the commonwealth. This is how Spinoza understands monarchy. Monarchy, traditionally, is the rule of the one, but Spinoza argues that each monarchy is really a hidden aristocracy, since the monarch is only a single human individual, and needs help to govern. Monarchies on Spinoza's view, have characteristic problems, namely, they exclude the multitude of citizen-subjects from rule, and thus must create ways in which to either include these individuals in government (which is what Spinoza suggests), but more often tend to try to find ways to diminish the power of this multitude, so that the monarch need worry less about the development of powerful individuals, factions, or even general revolt.[57] Diminishing the power of one's people, however, diminishes the power of the state. If the state weakens the multitude, this same multitude will be too weak to act collectively or to carry out state policies. Should the state need to, for example, counter foreign invasion, raise capital for infrastructure, or prepare for and recover from natural disasters, the multitude of individuals whose power has been diminished to make them innocuous, also makes them too weak and disorganized to act together as successfully as they might otherwise have done. Weakening one's own population may allow one (or a few) to rule without worry, but they cannot govern effectively or hope for any large-scale collective action or collaboration. This is one way in which to work out how fear weakens the state according to Spinoza's view. Fear diminishes the potential power of a state, which is held in the persons which make it up and their manner of organization. By making citizen subjects fearful and suspicious of one another—a natural outgrowth of fear—the collective power of the state is weakened.[58]

Disappointed hope leads to fear, hatred and indignation.[59] This indignation can lead to what we might call 'nihilism', but what Spinoza characterized as having "nothing to hope or fear from the state".[60] Those who believe that they have nothing to hope or fear from the state may not be correct—they may gain all sorts of advantages from the state or they may indeed have much to lose if the state were to act against them—however, our beliefs are not determined by what is the case. The feeling of indignation, for Spinoza, combined with the belief that one has nothing to hope or fear from the state, creates a citizenry that poses the most serious danger.[61] A ruler who evokes the indignation of the majority puts the very existence of the state in jeopardy. While fear and hate diminish the power of the individuals in a state and the state itself, indignation threatens the very status of a state.

While Spinoza is ambivalent about the usefulness of hope, he is unequivocal about the destructive power of hate and anger. Hate, for Spinoza, is always bad. Thus, if a political figure seeks to appeal to anger, this is always a bad or destructive action. That's not to say it wouldn't be successful—in the short term. Indeed, hatred of something can be shared. The object of shared hatred can briefly unify a group, and their shared power can be used to destroy the object of their hatred. However, hatred is not a force that unifies for long. Spinoza recognizes that anger against a common enemy can, briefly, be a source of political unity.[62] However, he argues it is not a good basis for collective association.[63] As hate is a species of pain, it weakens individuals, and thus, weakens the groups of which they are part.

According to Sharp, Spinoza insists that, "Peace, or political unity, depends upon organizing our social relations to counter one of the most prevalent emotions among human beings: *odium*"[64] Odium, or hatred, as an individual emotion enervates an individual's power to think and act, and as a collective emotion, or as a way of organizing a group, makes the group weaker than they would otherwise be. Recently, philosopher Myisha Cherry has argued that anger can be good. Cherry argues that a species of anger, which she calls "moral anger" is an important motivator to political action and as a proper response to, for example, injustice.[65] Another source of arguments in favor of anger as 'good' or at least 'proper' can be found or derived from the literature in ethics on the fittingness of emotions.[66] Feminist philosopher Marilyn Frye has argued that anger, particularly women's anger, has been repressed, and that to free repressed anger is genuinely liberatory.[67] For Spinoza, no passive emotion like hatred can ever be liberatory. However, understanding ones emotions and their causes can be. Indeed, for Spinoza, knowing ourselves as part of the natural world, with emotions that are caused often by external forces that are also natural, is the only real way in which people become free and how we overcome hatred—but that is another matter.[68] Reason, like perfection, is not a requirement of political participation for Spinoza.

If we cannot expect reason in either our leaders or our citizenry, how can we expect to have a stable state? Spinoza does not think that we can make people live wisely, but we can "guide" them to feelings that conduce to the greater good of the commonwealth by laying a good foundation for the state.[69] States derive their power from the individuals that make them up and the way they are coordinated or how they agree. Widespread indignation is a sign, for Spinoza, that governments have failed to do so. For some scholars, Spinoza's notion of indignation is akin to a concept of resistance. It is the point at which human power can take down the state. Indignation may be a cousin of Cherry's notion of moral anger. Filippo Del Lucchese proposes that the notion of indignation indicates that Spinoza believed that people sought an incorruptible state.[70] Thus, when something appears to shake the foundations of a state, the people become indignant. Indignation is the limit of the power of the state.[71] For Spinoza, human power always makes up the power of the state.[72] For Spinoza, the state has no juridical limit to its power. More extreme even than Hobbes' view: for Spinoza the state is in the state of nature. Nothing limits its right other than its power.[73] The only limit to the power of the state is the indignation of the people. The power of the state is limited by what the people will allow. Their indignation is resistance to the state. Spinoza derives from this a prescription to any state leader or functionary: if one wishes a state to persist, one must avoid creating the kinds of laws that will cause the people indignation, and avoid the kind of behavior that will rile up the multitude against the state.[74] These are two separate suggestions, based on the idea that the indignation of the people is a (and perhaps the only) limit on the state's use of power. When the hatred of the populace is focused on the state or the rulers of the government, this is certainly one way in which the state can topple, but this is hardly a good result for Spinoza. Spinoza sought ways to create strong political institutions;[75] he did not hope for their destruction. The essential insight of these thinkers, and the work of Alexandre Matheron on which they are based, is the idea that, for Spinoza, the limit of the power of the state is the power of the multitude.[76] The limit of this power is what the multitude of individuals will agree to, and their collective indignation marks the limit of that to which they will agree. Like the quotation above from Wolf et al, for Spinoza, strong democratic institutions can withstand a bad leader or vicious citizens. If a state cannot rein in a bad leader, then its institutions have failed.[77]

The state, and its leaders, can act only insofar as the people allow. That is, when the people become indignant—angry at the leaders of the state—the power of the state and its leaders are diminished. Spinoza sets out some prudential advice for leaders of a state, based on his undemanding of human emotions and how the most destructive of these emotions are aroused. For Spinoza, indignation is caused by the widespread perception that the leaders are acting in any one of the following ways:

- Acting viciously: that is, the leader is or has been found to indulge in vices, illegal acts, corruption, or other acts that are widely condemned.[78]
- Violating the norms of the state. Even when the leader is not engaging in illegal or vicious acts, they may violate the political, social or even basic comportment norms of the state. The most serious of these is when a leader violates the basic principles or fundamental laws of a state.[79]
- Removing basic freedoms. When a ruler attempts to rescind a freedom or a right that is basic to the citizens.[80]

Any leader who does the above, or who is thought to have done the above is in danger of arousing the indignation of the multitude of citizens, thereby losing power and undermining the power of the state.

TRUMP: FROM HATE TO INDIGNATION

Indignation, the anger of the multitude toward the rulers and institutions of government, is a perilous situation for any state.[81] As I write this, the approval ratings for Trump are 38 per cent.[82] The disapproval rate is 54.7 per cent.[83] Hate groups are emboldened, the leader of North Korea believes that the President of the United States has declared war,[84] and Trump has called for the firing of dozens of players in the National Football League.[85] Between the hatred and anger candidate Trump used and cultivated to get elected and the anger and indignation mounting against Trump as President, these are dangerous times for the United States. Do we have Spinozist reasons to worry about Trump? In a word: yes.

Trump's campaign and his early presidency have made extensive use of fear and hatred. For Spinoza, to the extent a leader uses fear and hatred, he weakens the civil state. This can be elaborated in a number of ways: with hate crimes on the rise, we have more violence and to an extent social peace and trust are eroded. Angrier citizens are weaker citizens. Weaker citizens lead to a weaker state, on Spinoza's view. Perhaps more worrying is that Trump's actions have fulfilled the criteria listed above for the kinds of things that tend to arouse the indignation of the people. Trump's flouting of norms of presidential comportment through texting national policy decisions, false assertions, calling for the firing of private citizens, name calling, nepotism, failing to release his taxes, and failing to strongly disconnect his personal financial dealings from policy have all put Trump in Spinoza's danger zone for arousing indignation.

Now, some may say, we certainly have had presidents who have done similarly outrageous things; however, the proposal here is just that these are norms that have been flouted. For Spinoza, social norms shape our attitudes.[86] To be part of a society is to, generally speaking, accept and expect that the norms of one's community are followed. Thus, when any norm is flouted any and all members of the community generally notice this, and excluding previous commitments, will generally condemn the flouting of a community norm. Some with the previous commitment to support the norm-flouter, might be happy about the flouting of a norm. We see this with Trump supporters who argue that his use of Twitter for calling out private citizens shows that he will not take an insult lying down, etc.

Another set of worries for Spinoza is the leader who tries to undermine or significantly change the political institutions of the civil state. In this, I think Trump may be in a worrying position with respect at least to the right to vote and the right to the privacy. This is a norm against which states have fought back, when the Trump administration requested sensitive voter information.[87] For others, the Trump administration's continuing attack on immigrants and attempts to exclude immigrants and visitors to the United States based on their religion has undermined crucial features of the U.S. Constitution—what Spinoza would understand as the fundamental laws of the state. Indeed, as of the writing of this, each version of the Trump administration's rules restricting immigration and entry into the U.S. based on religion have been rejected as unconstitutional.[88] This shows that there is widespread recognition that many of the policies and strategies of the Trump administration conflict with basic ideals, norms and values. These conflicts have led to people disregarding (or overturning) these policies. This, for Spinoza, is the foundation of indignation, and the signs that the power of the state and its rulers is diminishing.

From Indignation to Rational Hope

Where do we go from hate and indignation? Does Spinoza provide a solution to states that are mired in indignation, anger and hate? The short answer is yes. Indeed, Spinoza's turn to politics was inspired by the dark days leading up to the murder of the architects of the United Province's Golden Age.

In the mid-1660s, Spinoza set aside working on his book the *Ethics,* to try and write a book about politics. He wrote to his friends and colleagues that he felt he needed to intervene into the debates of his own time, which he felt were becoming dangerously violent.[89] What emerged from this was the *Theological-Political Treatise*. In this work, Spinoza seeks to argue that freedom to philosophize should be allowed both for the stability of the state and for the safety of religion. In this, he was arguing against the grain of his own time. The United Provinces was in the middle of a constitutional crisis, and many in the United Provinces worried that the unfettered investigation into the natural world might challenge religious, political and social norms.[90] Spinoza worried that Calvinist ministers were engaging in politics from the pulpit, fomenting anti-scientific and anti-Republican sentiments. His fears were warranted. In 1672 the Republican leaders of Amsterdam were killed and mutilated in the streets of The Hague, just blocks from Spinoza's home.[91] With this ultimate act of barbarism, as Spinoza saw it, he finished the Ethics and turned to write the *Political Treatise*, in which he offers a chastened view of politics, but one which the central aim of all political institutions is to understand and coordinate the emotions of the multitude of passionate individuals who could either form a destructive mob or a flourishing state.[92]

For Spinoza, the only solution to a state organized or disorganized through fear and indignation is a turn toward democracy. For Spinoza, this meant massive democratic councils, where individuals could build collective agreement without having to trust that anyone else was looking out for their interests. Fear undermines social trust.[93] For Spinoza, rebuilding social trust requires institutions that do not require much trust in the political system or in representatives of the whole. For Spinoza, even advisory councils—non-decision-making bodies—could be effective in creating the kind of political consensus that would be strong enough to build trust in the state.[94] Spinoza argued that these councils should be large—massive really—large enough that they could involve the participation of as many citizens as possible.[95] He believed that this active participation of regular, not necessarily virtuous citizens was the best way of recreating a stable political culture and a strong state.[96]

It's important here to note that while Spinoza argued in favor of large deliberative councils, he did not believe that those participating were necessarily rational or virtuous. He believed that any agreement made by such a large group of imperfect individuals would be better than anything any particular one of them could devise. Such an agreement would be better, Spinoza thought, both on its individual merits and because the deliberative process created stakeholders of those deliberating. Given the tendency for deliberation to be interpreted as rational communication, I prefer using the term "communication" to emphasize that Spinoza did not rely on the rationality of any particular member of the group to yield an agreement that could be considered rational.

For Spinoza, recovering from a state of fear required massive political participation. This participation was meant to create hope in each individual that his or her desires might be realized through participation. Hope, as we've seen, is an unstable emotion. However, in this circumstance, Spinoza proposed that hope merely brings participants to the democratic table. The process of democracy—communication, advising and creating new agreements for the future of the state—creates new affective alignments for those participating. This process rebuilds citizens as it rebuilds the state or political community—ideally on firmer ground than hope alone.

If one can see echoes of the Obama campaign's attempt to build community through community service and volunteering, that's no mistake. The idea of active democratic participation runs from Spinoza to Marx to the 2008 Obama campaign.[97] This is not to say that Obama is a Marxist, but rather that they share the idea that building community capacity inoculates populations against the corrosive effects of hate and fear. The failure of the Obama program of active democratic participation does not undermine the fact that such an approach is, according to Spinoza's theory, the only way to effectively rebuild social trust, and thereby the power of a state.

This passage from the *Political Treatise* is particularly apt:

And what we have written will, perhaps, be received with derision by those who limit to the populace only the vices which are inherent in all mortals ... as for the populace being devoid of truth and judgment, that is nothing wonderful, since the chief business of the dominion is transacted behind its back, and it can but make conjectures from the little, which cannot be hidden. For it is an uncommon virtue to suspend one's judgment. So it is supreme folly to wish to transact everything behind the backs of the citizens, and to expect that they will not judge ill of the same, and will not give everything an unfavorable interpretation. For if the populace could moderate itself, and suspend its judgment about things with which it is imperfectly acquainted, or judge rightly of things by the little it knows already, it would surely be more fit to govern, than to be governed. But, as we said, all have the same nature. All grow haughty with rule, and cause fear if they do not feel it, and everywhere truth is generally transgressed by enemies or guilty people; especially where one or a few have mastery, and have respect in trials not to justice or truth, but to amount of wealth.

The *Political Treatise*, as anyone who has read it will attest, is a fairly disappointing book. It was written after Spinoza had lost his youthful hope in the possibilities of his political present, and after he had witnessed turbulent political events that had been unthinkable. The writer of the *Political Treatise* is a chastened political philosopher, who can no longer write about people and about democracy as he once did in the *Theological-Political Treatise*—a book that looks positively upbeat in its hopefulness about the naturalness and inevitability of democracy. However chastened, the writer of the *Political Treatise* is still a democrat. He still thinks that the only way to seek peace is to include as many people as possible. He argues in the passage above that those who would deride the populace should not—since human nature is everywhere the same, echoing his dictum from the TTP that good citizens are not born, they are made.[98] Thus, the ignorance, foolishness, and violence of the multitude is to be expected. They are ignorant of the workings of the state, because these workings are hidden from them—they take no active part in it, so they have no knowledge of how things work. What little they do know may be false, inflammatory or both. So, it is no wonder that they act badly. Blaming people for acting badly, when their actions could have been avoided is not just bad form, it's shirking responsibility to engage and include the populace.

I take from this passage and Spinoza's writings in general two clear messages: (1) If we seek truth, enlightenment, freedom or salvation, we must not deride those elements of human nature that seem to bar us from attaining them— our emotions, our tendency to mistake consequence for cause or to believe other falsities, and our desires. Neither can we deride the emotions of others—the hate, anger and fear that motivate their political choices needs to be understood. Instead of judging and bemoaning our collective fate, we must try to understand our emotions, desires, and ways of thinking and knowing as if they were 'rocks and stones'—that is, fully intelligible and morally neutral objects of inquiry. This is true not just for our own emotions, desires and minds, but also for those of the 'multitude' or aggregation of other humans among whom we live. Rather than fearing or hating them, or deriding their judgment and passions, we must understand them. We must understand their emotions, their beliefs and their desires. These may be odious to us, they may seem ridiculous or just false, but if we do not understand them, we can never change their minds or improve their circumstances. (2) The second lesson I take from Spinoza is as follows: for our own sake, that is, for our own enlightenment, empowerment and freedom, we must do just that—improve the minds and circumstances of the multitude among which we live.[99] Most importantly, the lesson from Spinoza seems to be that to empower the multitude requires that we create institutions that include them, that allow them to communicate their beliefs, emotions, desires and interests to as many others as possible.

Following Spinoza, our aims must be to improve and not perfect—since this is impossible. Our aims must be to understand, and intervene carefully to build institutions that foster empowerment in regular, imperfect, passionate humans. These institutions will be communicative and participatory, and they must include as many as possible. The lesson of Spinoza's life and work, for us, in the time of Trump is to retain our belief in democracy by working to make it stronger, more inclusive, and more participatory. In order to avoid tyrants and fools for leaders, we need strong, educated, and healthy citizens. This, from a Spinozist point of view, is the work to be done in a time of anger, indignation and hate.

Notes

1. Nearly every U.S. citizen has a view on how Donald Trump won the election of 2016. I am not proposing here a complete forensic investigation of the circumstances of the election. My account is consistent with a host of other causes: foreign intervention into the election and the role of the GOP changes to its primary and caucus rules, gerrymandering, the usual party-change in the white house after 8 years of a Democrat in charge, etc. I seek only to address the role of emotion in the recent election, and to understand how it might be understood in terms of Spinoza's theory of the role of emotions in politics

2. E3P11S; I employ the standard abbreviated references to Spinoza's work: E3P11S is a reference to *Ethics*, Book 3, Proposition 11, Scholium. Abbreviations of Spinoza's writings: E (*Ethics*), TTP (*Theological-Political Treatise*), TP (*Political Treatise*); Ep (Letters). Other abbreviations: A (Axiom), P (Proposition), C (Corollary), Pref (Preface), App (Appendix), DefAff (Definition of the Affects), D (Definition), L (Lemma), S, (Scholium). Unless noted, all quotations are from: Spinoza, *Ethics* in Shirley (trans.), *Spinoza: Complete Works*. (Indianapolis: Hackett, 2002).

3. Mark S. Ferrara, *Barack Obama and the Rhetoric of Hope* (Jefferson, North Carolina: McFarland & Company, Inc., Publishers, 2013); Deborah F. Atwater, "Senator Barack Obama: The Rhetoric of Hope and the American Dream," *Journal of Black Studies* 38, no. 2 (November 2007): 121–29; Kevin Coe and Michael Reitzes, "Obama on the Stump: Features and Determinants of a Rhetorical Approach." *Presidential Studies Quarterly* 40, no. 3 (July 13, 2010): 391–413.

4. "Obama, B. (2004). Barack Obama: 2004 Democratic National Convention Keynote Address. Retrieved from http://www.americanrhetoric.com/speeches/convention2004/barackobama2004dnc

5. Barack Obama, *The Audacity of Hope: Thoughts on Reclaiming the American Dream* (Edinburgh: Canongate, 2008).

6. Lilliana Mason, "Why are Americans so angry this election season? Here's new research that helps explain it." *The Washington Post*, March 10, 2016, https://www.washingtonpost.com/news/monkey-cage/wp/2016/03/10/why-are-americans-so-angry-this-election-season-heres-new-research-that-helps-explain-it/?utm_term=.a8029f5bf144; Lilliana Mason, "A Cross-Cutting Calm: How social sorting drives

affective polarization," *Public Opinion Quarterly*, Volume 80, Issue S1, 1 January 2016, 351–377; "Journalists explore impact of anger, trust and faith in 2016 election." *Georgetown Initiative on Catholic Social Thought and Public Life*. September 14, 2016, https://www.georgetown.edu/faith-anger-trust-catholic-social-thought-gu-politics; Niraj Chokshi, "The year of 'enormous rage': Number of hate groups rose by 14 percent in 2015", *The Washington Post*, February 17, 2016, https://www.washingtonpost.com/news/acts-of-faith/wp/2016/02/17/hate-groups-rose-14-percent-last-year-the-first-increase-since-2010/?utm_term=.a15d62caed91; J.M. Bernstein, "The Very Angry Tea Party." The New York Times. 6/16/2010. https://opinionator.blogs.nytimes.com/2010/06/13/the-very-angry-tea-party/; Claudia Wallis and Katherine J. Cramer, "Trump's Victory and the Politics of Resentment." *Scientific American*, November 12, 2010. https://www.scientificamerican.com/article/trump-s-victory-and-the-politics-of-resentment/; Katherine J. Cramer, The Politics of Resentment: Rural Consciousness in Wisconsin and the Rise of Scott Walker (University of Chicago Press, 2016); Quin Hillyer, "No good reason for angry Americans," *The Washington Post*. March 9, 2017, http://www.washingtonexaminer.com/no-good-reason-for-angry-americans/article/2616914; Paul Starobin, "Social rage as a measure of the country's moral and political wellbeing." *The Atlantic Monthly*, January/February 2004,   https://www.theatlantic.com/magazine/archive/2004/01/the-angry-american/302885/; Susan J. Tolchin, The Angry American: How Voter Rage Is Changing the Nation. 2nd ed. *Dilemmas in American Politics*. Boulder, CO: Westview Press, 1999; Sharon R. Krause, *Civil Passions: Moral Sentiment and Democratic Deliberation*. (Princeton: Princeton University Press, 2008); Nussbaum, Martha Craven. Anger and Forgiveness: Resentment, Generosity, Justice. New York: Oxford University Press, 2016; Myisha Cherry, "Anger Is Not a Bad Word" TEDx. Chicago, 2015. https://www.youtube.com/watch?v=uysTk2EIotw.

7. Southern Poverty Law Center, "SPLC: 100 Days in Trump's America: Stoking Hatred." (Southern Poverty Law Center, April 27, 2017), https://edit.splcenter.org/20170427/100-days-trumps-america; Philip Bump, "How Donald Trump dominated Nevada, in one word: Anger," *The Washington Post*, February 24, 2016, https://www.washingtonpost.com/news/the-fix/wp/2016/02/23/early-data-suggest-an-angry-nevada-electorate-that-should-favor-donald-trump/?tid=a_inl&utm_term=.6d48af0b00db.

8. Jenna Johnson and Abigail Hauslohner, "'I Think Islam Hates Us': A Timeline of Trump's Comments about Islam and Muslims," *The*

Washington Post, May 20, 2017, https://www.washingtonpost.com/news/post-politics/wp/2017/05/20/i-think-islam-hates-us-a-timeline-of-trumps-comments-about-islam-and-muslims/?utm_term=.8721969004b4; Julie Hirschfield Davis, "Trump Orders Mexican Border Wall to Be Built and Plans to Block Syrian Refugees," *The New York Times*, January 25, 2017, https://www.nytimes.com/2017/01/25/us/politics/refugees-immigrants-wall-trump.html.

9. Bethany Albertson and Shana Kushner Gadarian, *Anxious Politics: Democratic Citizenship in a Threatening World* (New York: Cambridge University Press, 2015).

10. Eli Watkins and Joyce Tseng, "Trump's Policies and How They'll Change America—in Charts," *CNN Politics*, n.d., http://www.cnn.com/2017/03/14/politics/donald-trump-policy-numbers-impact/index.html.

11. Stephen Piggott, "Hate in the Race," *SPLC Intelligence Report*, July 6, 2016, https://www.splcenter.org/fighting-hate/intelligence-report/2016/hate-race.

12. Donald Trump, Campaign Speech in West Bend, Wisconsin, 8/16/2016. Video accessed: https://patch.com/wisconsin/shorewood/donald-trump-speak-milwaukee-tuesday; https://www.youtube.com/watch?v=B4aey0l6hrw.

13. Robin Eberhardt, "Ex-NAACP Leader: Trump 'Blowing a Racial Dog Whistle,'" *The Hill*, August 15, 2017, http://thehill.com/homenews/administration/346587-ex-naacp-leader-trump-blowing-a-racial-dog-whistle-by-retweeting-far.; Addy Baird, "The Subtle Dogwhistle in Trump's Belated Condemnation of White Supremacists," *Think Progress*, August 14, 2017, https://thinkprogress.org/the-hidden-dogwhistle-in-trumps-belated-condemnation-of-white-supremacists-d283d1f97914/; Frida Ghitis, "We All Heard Trump's Dog Whistle Giving White Supremacists His OK," *Miami Herald*, August 13, 2017, http://www.miamiherald.com/opinion/op-ed/article167019122.html#storylink=cpy.; Charlie Shelton and Frank Stasio, "How Dog Whistle Politics Is Changing Under Trump," *The State of Things* (WUNC 91.5 North Carolina Public Radio, March 2, 2017).

14. Judd Legum, "White Supremacists Cheer Trump's Response to Charlottesville Violence," *Think Progress*, August 12, 2017 https://thinkprogress.org/white-supremacists-cheer-trumps-response-to-charlottesville-violence-3d0d50196c52/; Stephen Piggott, "Hate in the Race," *SPLC Intelligence Report*, July 6, 2016, https://www.splcenter.org/fighting-hate/intelligence-report/2016/hate-race.; Sarah Posner and David Neiwert, "How Trump Took Hate Groups Mainstream The Full Story of His Connection with Far-Right Extremists," *Mother Jones*, October 14, 2016, http://www.motherjones.com/politics/2016/10/donald-trump-hate-groups-neo-nazi-white-supremacist-racism/.

15. A.C. Thopson and Ken Schwenke, "Hate Crimes Are Up — But the Government Isn't Keeping Good Track of Them," *ProPublica*, November 15, 2016, https://www.propublica.org/article/hate-crimes-are-up-but-the-government-isnt-keeping-good-track-of-them.

16. Melanie Zanona, "Trump Cuts Funds to Fight Anti-Right Wing Violence," *The Hill*, August 14, 2017, http://thehill.com/policy/national-security/346552-trump-cut-funds-to-fight-anti-right-wing-violence.

17. Glenn Thrush and Maggie Haberman, "Trump Gives White Supremacists an Unequivocal Boost," *The New York Times*, sec. Politics, 8/15/17, https://www.nytimes.com/2017/08/15/us/politics/trump-charlottesville-white-nationalists.html?emc=eta1; Julia R. Azari, "Presidential Responses To Racial Violence Have Often Been Weak, Trump's Is Weaker.," *FiveThirtyEight*, August 13, 2017, https://fivethirtyeight.com/features/trump-charlottesville-racial-violence/; Christine Wang and Kevin Breuninger, "Read the Transcript of Donald Trump's Jaw-Dropping Press Conference," *CNBC Politics*, n.d , https://www.cnbc.com/2017/08/15/read-the-transcript-of-donald-trumps-jaw-dropping-press-conference.html; "Sympathy for the Devils. Trump Defends 'Very Fine People' at Nazi Rally," *The New York Daily News*, August 16, 2017; Robin Eberhardt, "Fox & Friends' Guest: Anyone Who Defends Trump Is 'morally Bankrupt,'" *The Hill*, August 16, 2017; Michael D. Shear and Maggie Haberman, "Trump Defends Initial Remarks on Charlottesville; Again Blames 'Both Sides,'" *The New York Times*, August 15, 2017, https://www.nytimes.com/2017/08/15/us/politics/trump-press-conference-charlottesville.html?hp&action=click&pgtype=Homepage&clickSource=story-heading&module=b-lede-package-region&region=top-news&WT.nav=top-news; Jacob Pramuk, "Trump Again Blames All Sides for Virginia Violence in Bizarre, Chaotic News Conference," *CNBC Politics*, August 15, 2017.

18. Drew Westen, *The Political Brain: The Role of Emotion in Deciding the Fate of the Nation* (New York, NY: Public Affairs, 2008), 87–88.

19. Drew Westen, *The Political Brain: The Role of Emotion in Deciding the Fate of the Nation* (New York, NY: Public Affairs, 2008), 69–70.

20. Naomi Wolf, Alicia Garza, Linda Tirado and May Boeve, "Trump: 100 days that shook the world – and the activists fighting back." *The Guardian*, April 23, 2017, https://www.theguardian.com/us-news/2017/apr/23/trump-100-days-shook-the-world-and-the-activists-fighting-back.

21. For a small sample of such pieces: Gordon Marino, "Telling It Like It Is," *Commonweal*, November 10, 2016, https://www.commonwealmagazine.org/telling-it-it; "Why Trump's war on 'political correctness' is good news for hate speech." *Vanity Fair*, August 9, 2016, https://www.vanityfair.com/news/2016/08/donald-trump-political-incorrectness; James Taranto, "Trump vs. Political Correctness," *Wall Street Journal*, Nov. 15, 2016,

https://www.wsj.com/articles/trump-vs-political-correctness-1479233123;
Leonardo Bursztyn, Georgy Egorov, and Stefano Fiorin. "From Extreme to
Mainstream: How Social Norms Unravel." Cambridge, MA: National Bureau
of Economic Research, May 2017; Jason Willick, "How Trump Affected
Political Correctness," *The American Interest.* May 26, 2017, https://www.
the-american-interest.com/2017/05/26/how-trump-affected-political-cor-
rectness/; Anthony Brooks, "Trump's War On 'Political Correctness' Is At
The Center Of His Appeal." *Here and Now,* WBUR. Airdate: July 22, 2016.
http://www.wbur.org/politicker/2016/07/21/trump-political-correct-
ness; Conor Friedersdorf, "A Dialogue With a 22-Year-Old Donald Trump
Supporter: He lives near San Francisco, makes more than $50,000 per year,
and is voting for the billionaire to fight against political correctness." *The
Atlantic,* May 27, 2016, https://www.theatlantic.com/politics/
archive/2016/05/a-dialogue-with-a-22-year-old-donald-trump-sup-
porter/484232/.

22. Bursztyn, Leonardo, Georgy Egorov, and Stefano Fiorin. "From Extreme
to Mainstream: How Social Norms Unravel." Cambridge, MA. National
Bureau of Economic Research, May 2017.

23. Nancy Fraser and Axel Honneth. *Redistribution or Recognition?: A
Political-Philosophical Exchange.* London ; New York: Verso, 2003;
Godman, M., M. Nagatsu, and M. Salmela. "The Social Motivation
Hypothesis for Prosocial Behavior." *Philosophy of the Social Sciences* 44, no.
5 (September 1, 2014): 563–87; Macherey, Pierre, and Stephanie Bundy.
"Judith Butler and the Althusserian Theory of Subjection." *Décalages,* Vol.
1, Iss. 2, Art. 13, 2014; Honneth, Axel. "Recognition or Redistribution?
Changing Perspectives on the Moral Order of Society." *Theory, Culture
and Society* 18 (2–3) (n.d.): 43–55; E. Tucker, "Recognition and Religion
in Spinoza's Social Thought," M. Kahlos, H. Koskinen, and R. Palmen
(Eds.) *Reflections on Recognition: Contemporary and Historical Studies.*
(Oxford University Press, forthcoming: 2018).

24. E3P11S.

25. Antonio Damasio, *Looking for Spinoza: Joy, sorrow, and the feeling brain.*
Houghton Mifflin Harcourt, 2003; Jesse Prinz, "Which Emotions Are
Basic?" In in D. Evans and P. Cruse (Eds.), Emotion, Evolution, and
Rationality, Oxford University Press (2004); Jaak Panksepp and Douglas
Watt. "What is basic about basic emotions? Lasting lessons from affective
neuroscience." *Emotion Review* 3, no. 4 (2011): 387–396; Paul Ekman,
"An argument for basic emotions." *Cognition & emotion* 6, no. 3–4
(1992): 169–200.

Ekman, Paul. "Are there basic emotions?." Psychological Review, vol.
99, no. 3 (1992): 550–553; Carroll E. Izard, "Basic emotions, natural
kinds, emotion schemas, and a new paradigm." *Perspectives on psychological*

science 2, no. 3 (2007): 260–280; Jaak Panksepp, *Affective neuroscience: The foundations of human and animal emotions.* Oxford University Press, 2004.

26. E3DefAff12.
27. E3DefAff16.
28. E3DefAff17.
29. E3DefAff7.
30. E3DefAff 13.
31. E3P18, E3DefAff13.
32. E2P49.
33. E3P13.
34. E3P28.
35. E3P39S, E3P40S, E3DefAff 36.
36. E3P11S.
37. E3P11S, E3P59S; Emotions based on pain are always bad, except in the few situations where our pleasure has gotten out of control, E4P47.
38. Ursula Goldenbaum, "The Affects as a Condition of Human Freedom in Spinoza's Ethics." *Spinoza on Reason and the Free Man.* Ed. Yirmiyahu Yovel and Gideon Segal. (New York: Little Room Press, 2004). 149–166.
39. E3P12, E3P13, E3P13S.
40. E3P40S, E3P20.
41. E4P45.
42. E4P47.
43. E3P11S, E3P13, E4P37S.
44. E3P15, E3P15S.
45. E3P15, E3P16.
46. Def Aff 33.
47. E4P18.
48. E3P15, E3P16.
49. E3P19-E3P3.
50. E4P18S.
51. E3P30.
52. Naomi Wolf, Alicia Garza, Linda Tirado and May Boeve, "Trump: 100 days that shook the world – and the activists fighting back." *The Guardian,* April 23, 2017. https://www.theguardian.com/us-news/2017/apr/23/trump-100-days-shook-the-world-and-the-activists-fighting-back.
53. TP1. 1.3, TP 7.2.
54. TP1.5.
55. E3P11S.
56. E3P11S, E4P37S, TP3.9.
57. TP, Chapter 6.
58. E3P11S, E4P37S.

59. E3P19, DefAff12, DefAff13 Explication.
60. TP 2.14, 686; TP 3.8, 692–693.
61. TP 3.9.
62. E4P32S, TP6.1.
63. E4P32S, TP3.9.
64. Hasana Sharp, *Spinoza and the Politics of Renaturalization.* (Chicago: The University of Chicago Press, 2011), 171.
65. Myisha Cherry, "Anger is not a bad word" April 14, 2015 [Video File]. Retrieved from: https://www.youtube.com/watch?v=uysTk2EIotw.
66. Allan Gibbard *Wise Choices, Apt Feelings: A Theory of Normative Judgment.* (Cambridge, Mass. Harvard University Press, 1990); Krister Bykvist, "No Good Fit: Why the Fitting Attitude Analysis of Value Fails." (*Mind* 118(469): 1–30).
67. Marilyn Frye, *Politics of Reality: Essays in Feminist Theory.* (Freedom, California: The Crossing Press, 1983).
68. E5P10.
69. TP 10.6.
70. Filippo Del Lucchese, *Conflict, Power, and Multitude in Machiavelli and Spinoza: Tumult and Indignation.* (New York; Gordonsville: Bloomsbury Academic Macmillan, 2011), 60–62.
71. TP 3.9, Alexandre Matheron, "L'indignation et le conatus de l'Etat spinoziste," in M. Revault D'Allones, H. Rizk (eds.), Spinoza: Puissance et ontologie (Paris: Kimé, 1994) pp. 153–165.
72. TP 3.9.
73. TTP Chapter 16, TP 2.15.
74. TP 4.4.
75. TP 7.2.
76. Alexandre Matheron, "'L'indignation et Le Conatus de L'état Spinoziste'." In *Spinoza : Puissance et Ontologie*, edited by M. D'Allones and H. Rizk. Paris: Éditions Kimé, 1994.
77. TP 4.2.
78. TP 4.4.
79. TP 4.1, TP 4.4.
80. TP 3.9, TP 4.1-4.4, TTP, Chapter 20.
81. E. Tucker "Affective Disorders of the State," Journal of East-West Thought, Vol. 3, No. 3 (Summer 2013): 97–120.
82. https://projects.fivethirtyeight.com/trump-approval-ratings/.
83. https://projects.fivethirtyeight.com/trump-approval-ratings/.
84. https://www.cnbc.com/2017/09/25/we-have-right-to-shoot-down-strategic-us-bombers-even-if-they-are-not-in-north-korean-airspace-nk-foreign-minister-says.html.

85. https://www.washingtonpost.com/news/early-lead/wp/2017/09/22/
donald-trump-profanely-implores-nfl-owners-to-fire-players-protesting-
national-anthem/?utm_term=.b04199bc2279. Some have argued that
this decision is illegal; however, this is only if the President is effective in
influencing the decisions made by NFL owners. 18 U.S. Code § 227.

86. E. Tucker, "Spinoza's Social Sage: Emotion and the Power of Reason in
Spinoza's Social Theory" *Revista Conatus*, Volume 9, July, 2015.

87. Liz Stark and Grace Hauck, "Forty-Four States and DC Have Refused to
Give Certain Voter Information to Trump Commission." *CNN*, July 5,
2017.   http://www.cnn.com/2017/07/03/politics/kris-kobach-letter-
voter-fraud-commission-information/index.html.

88. Matt Zapotosky, "Federal judge blocks Trump's third travel ban " *The
Washington Post*, October 17, 2017 https://www.washingtonpost.com/
world/national-security/federal-judge-blocks-trumps-third-travel-
ban/2017/10/17/e73293fc-ae90-11e7-9e58-e6288544af98_story.
html?tid=a_inl&utm_term=.454bd284a6e8, Matt Zapotosky, "Second
judge rules against latest entry ban, saying Trump's own words show it was
aimed at Muslims." *The Washington Post*, October 18, 2017. https://
www.washingtonpost.com/world/national-security/second-judge-rules-
against-latest-travel-ban-saying-trumps-own-words-show-it-was-aimed-at-
muslims/2017/10/18/5ecdaa44-b3ed-11e7-9e58-e6288544af98_
story.html?utm_term=.ae186dbb39f4.

89. Letter 29 from Oldenburg Letter 30 to Oldenburg, 1665 in Spinoza,
Complete Works. Ed. Samuel Shirley, (Indianapolis, IN: Hackett Pub,
2002), 842.

90. Jonathan Israel, *The Dutch Republic: Its Rise, Greatness and Fall, 1477–
1806.* (New York: Oxford University Press, 1998); J.L. Price, *The Dutch
Republic in the 17th Century.* (New York: St. Martin's Press, 1998); Samuel
Shirley, editor's note 100, Spinoza, *Complete Works*. Ed. Samuel Shirley,
(Indianapolis, IN: Hackett Pub, 2002); Letter 30 to Oldenburg, 1665,
Complete Works (2002), 844

91. Jonathan Irvine Israel, *The Dutch Republic: Its Rise, Greatness, and Fall,
1477–1806*, Paperback with corrections, Oxford History of Early Modern
Europe (Oxford: Clarendon Press, 1998); Steven M Nadler, *Spinoza: A
Life* (Cambridge, U.K.; New York: Cambridge University Press, 2001);
Antonio Negri, *L'anomalie sauvage: puissance et pouvoir chez Spinoza*
(Paris: Editions Amsterdam, 2007).

92. E. Tucker, "Spinoza's Multitude" in Santos-Campos (Ed.) *Spinoza: Key
Concepts.* (Academic Imprint, 2015).

93. Kenneth Newton, "Social and Political Trust in Established Democracies," in
Pippa Norris (Ed.), *Critical Citizens*. (Oxford University Press, 1999); Paul
Stoneman, *This Thing Called Trust: Civic Society in Britain.* (Basingstoke:

Palgrave Macmillan, 2008); Robert J. Blendon, '*Changing Attitudes in America*', *Why people don't trust government* (Harvard University Press, 1997); Linda Trinkaus Zagzebski, *Epistemic Authority: A Theory of Trust, Authority, and Autonomy in Belief.* (Oxford: 2012); Mark Warren, *Democracy and Trust* (Cambridge University Press 1999); Joseph Cooper (ed.) *Congress and the Decline of Public Trust.* (Boulder, Colo: Westview Press, 1999); Chris Bodenner, "The U.S. Has Fallen Into a State of Political Nihilism," *The Atlantic,* December 12, 2016, https://www.theatlantic.com/notes/2016/12/state-of-utter-political-nihilism/510314/.
94. TP 6.15, TP 6.17, TP 8.13.
95. TP 6.15, TP 6.17, TP 7.18, TP 7.27, TP 8.13.
96. TP 1.5.
97. Pew Research Center Journalism and Media Staff, "Engagement and Participation," September 15, 2008.
    http://assets.pewresearch.org/wp-content/uploads/sites/13/legacy/CAMPAIGN_WEB_08_DRAFT_1V_copyedited.pdf
98. TTP Chapter 3, 418; TTP, Chapter 17, 548–9.
99. TIE, Sections 14–15; ST, Chapter 6, p.71; E4P37S.

Bibliography

Albertson, Bethany, and Shana Kushner Gadarian. 2015. *Anxious Politics: Democratic Citizenship in a Threatening World*. New York: Cambridge University Press.

Atwater, Deborah F. 2007. Senator Barack Obama: The Rhetoric of Hope and the American Dream. *Journal of Black Studies* 38 (2): 121–129.

Blendon, Robert J. 1997. *'Changing Attitudes in America', Why People Don't Trust Government.* Cambridge: Harvard University Press.

Bursztyn, Leonardo, Georgy Egorov, and Stefano Fiorin. 2017. *From Extreme to Mainstream: How Social Norms Unravel.* Cambridge, MA: National Bureau of Economic Research.

Bykvist, Krister. 2009. No Good Fit: Why the Fitting Attitude Analysis of Value Fails. *Mind* 118 (469): 1–30.

Cherry, Myisha. 2015. Anger Is Not a Bad Word. *TEDx.* Chicago. https://www.youtube.com/watch?v=uysTk2EIotw.

Coe, Kevin, and Michael Reitzes. 2010. Obama on the Stump: Features and Determinants of a Rhetorical Approach. *Presidential Studies Quarterly* 40 (3): 391–413.

Cooper, Joseph, ed. 1999. *Congress and the Decline of Public Trust.* Boulder: Westview Press.

Cramer, Katherine J. 2016. *The Politics of Resentment: Rural Consciousness in Wisconsin and the Rise of Scott Walker.* Chicago: University of Chicago Press.

Damasio, Antonio. 2003. *Looking for Spinoza: Joy, Sorrow, and the Feeling Brain.* Boston: Houghton Mifflin Harcourt.

Del Lucchese, Filippo. 2011. *Conflict, Power, and Multitude in Machiavelli and Spinoza: Tumult and Indignation*, 60–62. New York: Bloomsbury Academic Macmillan.

Ekman, Paul. 1992a. An Argument for Basic Emotions. *Cognition & Emotion* 6 (3–4): 169–200.

———. 1992b. Are There Basic Emotions? *Psychological Review* 99 (3): 550–553.

Ferrara, Mark S. 2013. *Barack Obama and the Rhetoric of Hope.* Jefferson: McFarland & Company, Inc.

Fraser, Nancy, and Axel Honneth. 2003. *Redistribution or Recognition?: A Political-Philosophical Exchange.* London/New York: Verso

Frye, Marilyn 1983. *Politics of Reality: Essays in Feminist Theory* Freedom: The Crossing Press

Gibbard, Allan. 1990. *Wise Choices, Apt Feelings: A Theory of Normative Judgment.* Cambridge, MA: Harvard University Press.

Godman, M., M. Nagatsu, and M. Salmela. 2014. The Social Motivation Hypothesis for Prosocial Behavior. *Philosophy of the Social Sciences* 44 (5): 563–587.

Goldenbaum, Ursula. 2004. The Affects as a Condition of Human Freedom in Spinoza's Ethics. In *Spinoza on Reason and the Free Man*, ed. Yirmiyahu Yovel and Gideon Segal, 149–166. New York: Little Room Press.

Honneth, Axel. n.d. Recognition or Redistribution? Changing Perspectives on the Moral Order of Society. *Theory, Culture and Society* 18 (2–3): 43–55.

Israel, Jonathan. 1998. *The Dutch Republic: Its Rise, Greatness and Fall, 1477–1806.* New York: Oxford University Press.

Izard, Carroll E. 2007. Basic Emotions, Natural Kinds, Emotion Schemas, and a New Paradigm. *Perspectives on Psychological Science* 2 (3): 260–280.

Krause, Sharon R. 2008. *Civil Passions: Moral Sentiment and Democratic Deliberation.* Princeton: Princeton University Press.

Macherey, Pierre, and Stephanie Bundy. 2014. Judith Butler and the Althusserian Theory of Subjection. *Décalages* 1 (2): 13.

Mason, Lilliana. 2016. A Cross-Cutting Calm: How Social Sorting Drives Affective Polarization. *Public Opinion Quarterly* 80 (S1): 351–377.

Matheron, Alexandre. 1994. L'indignation et le conatus de l'Etat spinoziste. In *Spinoza: Puissance et ontologie*, ed. M. Revault D'Allones and H. Rizk, 153–165. Paris: Kimé.

Newton, Kenneth. 1999. Social and Political Trust in Established Democracies. In *Critical Citizens*, ed. Pippa Norris. Oxford: Oxford University Press.

Nussbaum, Martha Craven. 2016. *Anger and Forgiveness: Resentment, Generosity, Justice.* New York: Oxford University Press.

Obama, Barack. 2008. *The Audacity of Hope: Thoughts on Reclaiming the American Dream*. Edinburgh: Canongate.

Panksepp, Jaak. 2004. *Affective Neuroscience: The Foundations of Human and Animal Emotions*. New York: Oxford University Press.

Panksepp, Jaak, and Douglas Watt. 2011. What Is Basic About Basic Emotions? Lasting Lessons from Affective Neuroscience. *Emotion Review* 3 (4): 387–396.

Price, J.L. 1998. *The Dutch Republic in the 17th Century*. New York: St. Martin's Press.

Prinz, Jesse. 2004. Which Emotions Are Basic? In *Emotion, Evolution, and Rationality*, ed. D. Evans and P. Cruse. Oxford: Oxford University Press.

Sharp, Hasana. 2011. *Spinoza and the Politics of Renaturalization*, 171. Chicago: The University of Chicago Press.

Spinoza. 2002. Ethics. In *Spinoza. Complete Works*, trans. Shirley. Indianapolis: Hackett

Stoneman, Paul. 2008. *This Thing Called Trust: Civic Society in Britain*. Basingstoke: Palgrave Macmillan.

Tolchin, Susan J. 1999. *The Angry American: How Voter Rage Is Changing the Nation*, Dilemmas in American Politics. 2nd ed. Boulder: Westview Press.

Tucker, E. 2013. Affective Disorders of the State. *Journal of East-West Thought* 3 (3 Summer): 97–120.

———. 2015a. Spinoza's Social Sage: Emotion and the Power of Reason in Spinoza's Social Theory. *Revista Conatus* 9 (17): 23–41.

———. 2015b. Spinoza's Multitude. In *Spinoza: Key Concepts*, ed. Santos-Campos. Exeter: Academic Imprint.

———. 2018. Recognition and Religion in Spinoza's Social Thought. *Reflections on Recognition: Contemporary and Historical Studies*, ed. M. Kahlos, H. Koskinen, and R. Palmen. Oxford: Oxford University Press, forthcoming.

Warren, Mark. 1999. *Democracy and Trust*. Cambridge: Cambridge University Press.

Westen, Drew. 2008. *The Political Brain: The Role of Emotion in Deciding the Fate of the Nation*, 87–88. New York: Public Affairs.

Zagzebski, Linda Trinkaus. 2012. *Epistemic Authority: A Theory of Trust, Authority, and Autonomy in Belief*. New York: Oxford University Press.

CHAPTER 9

Preserving Liberty in Mass Society: Locke and the 2016 Presidential Election

Cole Simmons

I would like to begin with a word about my procedure. I understand that it is possible to view Trump as a base opportunist, whose vulgarities should have "disqualified" him from ever being a president of the United States. If indeed Trump wants to be a tyrant, or is a tool of foreign influences, or anything else equally terrible, then of course any of the eminent thinkers discussed in this book would strongly disapprove and have many creative ways of voicing their disapproval. Therefore, my focus is on the planks of Trump's platform that are defensible and appealed to his electorate, in order to discuss Locke's political science and the right-wing that developed in American politics during Trump's campaign. I will begin by explaining Trump's rise by describing what made him appealing and why that appeal was sufficient to produce his electoral victory. Then I will give a brief overview of Locke's political science, or at least the side of it that is pertinent to the 2016 election. The final third of the chapter will be an examination of Trump's rise according to Lockean political science.

C. Simmons (✉)
University of Dallas, Irving, TX, USA

© The Author(s) 2018
M. B. Sable, A. J. Torres (eds.), *Trump and Political Philosophy*,
https://doi.org/10.1007/978-3-319-74427-8_9

TRUMP'S ELECTORAL VICTORY

Trump does not owe his victory to a brilliant set of transparent and easily understandable policy proposals. (I do not even know if those exist any longer.) There was nothing "wonkish" about his victory. His electorate consisted of traditional Republicans, excepting a number of well-known conservative intellectuals who thought his rhetoric and populism represented a dangerous departure from a salutary public decorum. Instead he won blue-collar workers in Pennsylvania, Ohio, and across the country by stealing the working-class appeal from the Democratic Party and adding to it the "America first" flavor.

Trump's populism would not have won over blue collar workers if it lacked this "America first" flavor. His argument was that the political establishment had found a way to profit at the expense of the American people. That is, he argued that the establishment did not derive its power from the people but through corruption, mainly in the form of receiving large donations to campaigns and political organizations operated as charities. The problem with this argument is that candidates still need votes to win. If the people still have the power of electing their representatives, how can these representatives derive their power from anywhere other than the people? That is, how can the people feel powerless or overpowered if they elect those in power? The liberals diagnosed the problem in the following way. The white middle class is used to holding power, but their demographic is shrinking and they are fearful of losing their ruling prerogatives to other races and foreigners. This diagnosis is too cynical and will likely produce racists, which I imagine is not the objective.[1] A better diagnosis would be, middle class citizens are used to living in a world where their influence matters. The less state and local governments matter, the bigger their world becomes and the smaller they become. Tellingly, Trump won 2,626 counties to Clinton's 487.[2] When we consider that Clinton won the majority of votes, it is easy to see whose electorate is accustomed to having more influence over politics. Trump's voters are much more capable of influencing their representatives than Clinton's voters, the majority of whom reside in large metropolitan areas. These disparities equalize the higher up the chain one goes; the Electoral College is one of the last impediments to national dominance by large metropolitan areas and a corresponding diminution of everyone else. The people in the large metropolitan areas are inured to having little influence. The middle class and rural populations are very upset by having little influence. This difference translates into views of freedom. Those inured to having little influence interpret freedom as being allowed to do many things. Those who are accustomed to wielding influence believe freedom is never having to be "allowed" to do anything, and therefore never wanting to do anything that might diminish their influence. They *should* say with Locke, a "state of liberty ... is not a state of license."[3]

Trump did not need to tell his electorate that their influence was shrinking. He told them why it was shrinking: they were being squeezed from the top and the bottom. The people at the top were enriching themselves and making use of the people at the bottom to do it. International trade deals were allowing people at the top to profit by taking manufacturing jobs overseas, and the remaining low-income jobs were being filled with immigrant labor, which not only was cheaper, but would provide votes for Democrats.[4] Hitherto, the Republican party had let this stranglehold develop, being wed to "free trade" and hoping that they could co-opt the newly arrived immigrants.[5] Trump promised to put an end to this. He promised to bring manufacturing jobs home, renegotiate trade deals, and prevent large numbers of unskilled immigrants from coming into the country. He suggested that the current views of immigration were a result of politically correct views and disconnected from any rational consideration of the nation's interests.

The immigration issue had become a moral issue, rather than a simple question of whether or not American citizens would benefit. People who opposed immigration were called bigots, racists, and "deplorables." Trump told middle class and blue-collar Americans that they were not immoral, and that it was good that they were not sensitive like "the elites." He told them that the government exists to serve the citizens and no one else. These arguments appealed to the moral sentiments of blue-collar workers, while also telling them that the Republicans under Trump's guidance would change their tune and do more to fight for manufacturing jobs. This combination delivered electoral victories in Pennsylvania and Ohio.[6] Furthermore, after years of eroding support among the middle class for Democratic politicians, Trump's message led to staggering victories throughout many middle class communities that Obama had won in 2008.[7]

The question of this chapter is what Locke would think of Trump's rise to the presidency. If American politics is a mere back and forth, then in this election Locke would have approved of the direction, but worried about the degree of oscillation.

LOCKE AND LIBERTY

I will discuss the two ways Locke sought to secure liberty in the modern world. The first way involved protecting natural right while promoting the conditions for trade and manufacture in a *large* commonwealth. The second way involved protecting natural right by teaching the prudential and principled reasons for political and religious toleration. Locke thought the size of the commonwealth would produce many material and spiritual goods, but that these goods would prove to be mixed blessings.

Trade and Manufacture in a Large Commonwealth

The foundation of Lockean political science is natural right. In a time when the "race of men have now spread themselves to all the corners of the world, and do infinitely exceed the small number [that] was at the beginning," Locke gives a political teaching that seeks to harness the latent powers of these relatively new multitudes, while staking out boundaries that promote the natural right of individuals in the midst of these increasingly large nations.[8]

Locke's promotion of large populations committed to manufacture and trade is evident in the *Second Treatise*, where he promotes the industrious and rational man while denigrating aristocrats whose substance was drawn from vast landholdings rather than manufacture and trade. Two places in Chap. **5** of the *Second Treatise* illustrate this choice. In section 34, Locke prophesies that "God gave the world to men in common; but since he gave it to them for their benefit, and the greatest conveniences of life they were capable to draw from it, it cannot be supposed he meant it should always remain common and uncultivated. He gave it to the use of the industrious and rational, (and labor was to be his title to it;) not to the fancy or covetousness of the quarrelsome and contentious." That is, although a man or group of men may possess a large landholding, and thereby draw their substance from it without any waste and at great leisure, that land can be put to much better use. That land could support many more men, if they devoted themselves to cultivation (farming, not gardens) and manufacture. Later in the chapter, in section 42, Locke again invokes a divine sanction favoring large societies. He says that "numbers of men are to be preferred to largeness of dominions; … and that prince, who shall be so wise and godlike, as by established laws of liberty to secure protection and encouragement to the honest industry of mankind … will quickly be too hard for his neighbors."[9] He sums this position up well in a minor essay titled "Trade." He writes, "Power consists in numbers of men, and ability to maintain them. Trade conduces to both these, by increasing your stock and your people, and they each other."[10] Locke believes this combination of numerous citizens, manufacture, and trade, is the way forward for peoples. There is, however, a downside to this combination for power. It may well make the prince unbearable to his subjects.

An unjust government is always more onerous in proportion to the power it has, which means, in proportion to the number of people who have consented to lend their power to it. When Locke argues against absolute kingship, he makes this case: "I desire to know what kind of government that is, and how much better it is than the state of nature, where one man, *commanding a multitude*, has the liberty to be judge in his own case, ... much better it is in the state of nature."[11] Near the end of the work, Locke is trying to assuage the concerns of readers who fear his teachings will lead to lawlessness. He replies that their worries are misplaced, for "it being as impossible for one, or a few oppressed men to disturb the government, *where the body of the people do not think themselves concerned in it*, as for a raving mad-man, or heady malcontent to overturn the well-settled state."[12] That is, honest and just men can be run over, so long as the power base of the government remains undisturbed. In this situation, just men are treated the same as lunatics. Locke compares these powerful governments, when they have become unjust, to the giant cyclops, whose size allows him absolute and unjust rule in his own domain.[13] So while Locke sets out to encourage men to draw power from large societies, he nevertheless is a very sober and responsible man and tries to simultaneously encourage tendencies which would ameliorate the excesses of these potential cyclopes.

Locke teaches that all men are by nature "equal and independent," and that "no one ought to harm another in his life, health, liberty, or possessions."[14] By making the ownership of property a right, because it is necessary to life, health, and liberty, Locke also secures the right to *acquire* property.[15] This right to acquire produces a negative view of whatever influences impede acquisition: taxes for the poor, prodigal vices, arbitrary (lawless) government, lots of lawyers, large standing armies, and needless waste of all kinds.[16] This right and its corollaries provide men who wish to acquire, that is, to grow larger in some sense, the moral grounding upon which they can assert themselves. Self-assertion on behalf of the right to acquire and preserve property is the heart of political liberty for Locke. Men who cannot acquire are burdens, either justly or unjustly. That is, some are pitiable and some are blameworthy. In his "An Essay on the Poor Law," Locke proposes forced labor for those who are unjust burdens on the property of others, and a tax for the relief of those who are truly incapable of acquiring any property and so are burdens, but cannot be blamed for their incapacity. In that essay, he is very severe toward "vagabonds" (beggars who have no right to beg) and proposes methods of capturing them, holding onto them (he complains of their often slipping away), and putting them to work.[17] This bit about vagabonds demonstrates that Locke is clearly willing to restrict the movement of those who are not industrious. The large commonwealth is healthy when its citizens are growing self-sufficient and wealthy. If the large commonwealth ceases to be stocked by industrious citizens, the liberty of the "industrious and rational" man is endangered by the increasing needs of the idle and contentious. This group includes vagabonds and idle aristocrats, men who are idle and contentious, though for different reasons. In Locke's commonwealth, the goal is for as much acquisition as possible, which redounds to the individual and to the commonwealth; it is when the commonwealth begins to ask productive citizens to become smaller, to stop growing, *to give way*, that the large commonwealth becomes inimical to liberty.[18] In his minor essay promoting the naturalization of immigrants, Locke holds up neighboring Holland as an example of a country that is "crammed with people [and] abounding in riches," whereas he finds "very inconvenient laws for maintaining the poor" if the citizens are numerous and the commonwealth is not prosperous.[19]

Toleration in a Large Commonwealth

The promotion of property rights serves to protect industrious and rational men from the pressing multitudes, by producing as much independence and material wealth as possible, and by justifying growth, or acquisition. However, there are other threats to these men that worried Locke, namely, threats to their intellectual and moral liberty.

The source of these threats is not merely cynical rulers oppressing dissidents as they try to hold onto power. Nor are these threats merely the result of economic poverty which is usually connected with parochial ignorance. These are dangers, to be sure. Locke spent no small amount of time haranguing hypocritical princes for their cynical use of religion.[20] He also understood the effects of economic poverty on the intellectual and moral development of people.[21] However, he thought the sincere errors of men were the greatest threat to intellectual and moral liberty.

Locke was concerned primarily with the dangerous opinions that religious belief produced. So I will start by explaining how sincerely held religious opinions threaten the liberty of others, though it should be kept in mind that *religious* fanaticism is merely one manifestation of fanaticism. Let us say that finding the right path to Heaven is very difficult, intellectually and morally. Let us also say that not getting into Heaven is terrible: eternal fire and damnation. These extremities produce corresponding powers in the government and clergy, the means always being equal to the ends. Such dangerous situations require heightened sensitivity. Locke describes such a situation in his work *A Letter Concerning Toleration*. He first describes a situation secured by a large degree of economic independence. "In private domestic affairs, in the management of estates, in the conservation of bodily health, every man may consider what suits his own convenience, and follow what course he likes best. ... no body murmurs, no body controls his him; he has his liberty." He then goes on to discuss the pressing lack of moral liberty: "But if a man do not frequent the Church, if he do not conform his behavior exactly to the accustomed ceremonies ... this immediately causes an uproar. The neighborhood is filled with noise and clamor. Everyone is ready to be an avenger of so great a crime."[22] The public reacted this way because they keenly felt the danger of deviation, that is, of a man exercising his liberty contrary to the common usages of the day. This anger was felt because Hell is no small terror, and if it is very easy to end up in Hell, men must be very sensitive to those around them lest they, even accidentally, do something to cause other people to lose their way and end up in Hell. The grave danger to which all are exposed imposes a corresponding burden on all the citizens of the commonwealth. In such a situation, "He that considers [thinks or questions] is a foe to orthodoxy, because possibly he may deviate from some of the received doctrines there." So, just as indigent men who faced dangers related to penury endangered the liberty of others to grow and acquire property, so too do men "without any industry or acquisition of their own, inherit local truths" and thereby, out of a desire to protect themselves and their loved ones, endanger the liberty of other men to grow intellectually.[23] In sum: exaggerated dangers are not only pretexts for the cynical increase of power, they can be sincere attempts to end human suffering that become oppressive.

In *A Letter Concerning Toleration* Locke addresses the problem of exaggerated fears, but only incidentally. That is, he does not elaborate a theological position wherein things are not so dire or terrifying. Such a teaching would include a wide path to Heaven, which was relatively easy to find and follow and a corresponding diminution of the terrors of Hell. Instead, he takes pains to "grant unto these zealots" that Hell is terrible and the way to Heaven narrow, believing he can show that these fears, even if real, should not impinge upon the intellectual and moral liberties of others.[24] Locke argues that the narrow way can only be profitably walked if sincerely walked. If a man were to be forced onto the narrow way, his unbelief would tell against him on judgment day, no matter how many church services he was forced to attend. Locke says that this sincerity cannot be produced by force.[25] When this argument met with stiff opposition from an Anglican clergyman, who argued that force could produce the conditions for sincere belief, Locke ceased granting points to zealots and argued that belief could never amount to knowledge and that honest men should never force upon others what they themselves could not possibly know.[26]

Furthermore, Locke promotes intellectual and moral growth by praising the usefulness and dignity of inquiring into questions, rather than accepting the views of others. He teaches that "no one sees all, and we generally have different prospects of the same thing, according to our different, as I may say, positions on it." Men would do well to speak freely with others of different views, which, of course, requires the freedom to air different views.[27] Forcing men to forego the conclusions of their own reasoning runs counter to their growth and self-respect, because "men would be intolerable to themselves, and contemptible to others, if they should embrace opinions without any ground, and hold what they could give no manner of reason for."[28]

Locke's promotion of a populous society combined with his concern for liberty within that society, make him a voice we would do well to hear. Our society may have reached a size that goes well beyond Locke's idea of a "large society," and we may face problems that date Locke's political science. Nevertheless, the 2016 election was fought over questions that Locke addressed.

LOCKE'S VIEW OF TRUMP'S VICTORY

Economics

Trump's populist message appealed to Americans in two important ways, as I pointed out earlier. He told the nation's labor force that he would seek to preserve and increase the number of jobs available to them and told average Americans that they were not guilty of insensitivity or moral obtuseness.

Locke would approve of Trump's focus on manufacturing, but he would be dismayed at the reasons American companies take jobs overseas. The corresponding methods of bringing those jobs back would also dismay him. Fundamentally, Locke's view of national wealth amounted to the very straightforward view outlined above. Namely, numbers of people and wealth go hand in hand and the dangers associated with this position should be mitigated by good laws. Several American founders expressed grave doubts about Locke's straightforward view. Franklin, Madison, and Jefferson all held similar views of large manufacturing populations. Franklin explained, "Great establishments of manufacture require great numbers of poor to do the work for small wages; these poor are to be found in Europe, but will not be found in America, till the lands are all taken up and cultivated, and the excess of people, who cannot get land, want employment." These considerations led Franklin to oppose government subsidies for manufactures. A related concern was Madison's, who worried that these centers of manufacturing would corrupt the laws. When men have no property and "no means or hope of acquiring it, what is to secure the rights of property?" Likewise, Jefferson voiced concerns about the negative effects of "great cities," where "the want of food and clothing necessary to sustain life has begotten a depravity of morals."[29] Locke thought this evil could be mitigated, but I cannot believe he thought it could be indefinitely avoided.

Locke defended a general naturalization movement in England, knowing that the added immigrant labor could very well lower the wages of workers. The immigrants would make English laborers "work cheaper and better ... and can that be counted an inconvenience which will bring down the unreasonable rates of your own people or force them to work better?"[30] Unlike Franklin, Madison, and Jefferson, he did not believe this to be a danger, so long as the commonwealth's laws and morals promoted work, for "if there be any such poor amongst us already who are able to work and do not, 'tis a shame to the government and a fault in our constitution and ought to be remedied ... but if people have here no permission nor encouragement to be idle amongst us the more we have the better."[31] The loss of manufactures to foreign labor markets deprives citizens of work, and suggests that our nation ought to reform its laws and morals along Lockean lines. Without such reforms, increasing the pool of potential laborers would not be suitable for our nation. Locke would agree with Trump, that bringing manufacturing jobs back to America is important. He would agree, that immigration is only justifiable if it is useful. But unless he could be convinced that our labor situation was too crowded, he would promote immigration. We face a few problems Locke did not face that, if put to him today, may have altered his opinion, not about immigration as such, but about what we ought to be doing with our immigration policy. For example, a Trumpian might ask Locke if there is any chance that our politicians could successfully shrink our entitlements and reduce the incentive to idleness. Locke urges the poor to be kept, by legal means, away from alcohol and gambling as much as possible.[32] Does any successful politician contemplate such reforms? A Trumpian could also point out the decreasing demand for human hands in manufacturing and retail, a fact that threatens to antiquate Locke's view that more is always better. These appeals to the practical situation we face today would be taken seriously by Locke.

Political Correctness

The polls before the election were all wrong. The majority of political commentators were also wrong. Trump's most eloquent defenders wrote under pseudonyms. There was something louche about supporting Donald Trump. When Trump attacked political correctness, he did it by flouting the conventions politically correct speech enforces. He did not marshal complex arguments against politically correct speech. Indeed, how would one go about arguing in our nationally televised "debates" that measures taken against racism or sexism can be bad? Instead of this approach, which would have surely ended in failure, Trump implied in his bombastic way that political correctness was for wusses and hypocritical politicians. He implied that the left's care and concern was contemptible and getting in the way of important things. "Make America Great Again" was an effective slogan, not because of the words themselves, but because Trump used them to suggest what many Americans felt. The slogan suggested that America is greater when America is more bombastic than nice, which is why his supporters called themselves "Deplorables" with impish pride.

Locke would have had the normal reservations any reasonable conservative has about Trump's fight against political correctness. Conservatives cannot afford to lose that fight, and Trump may not be the most trustworthy figurehead for the conflict. Locke would approve of the fight, not only as a proponent of free speech, but as a philosopher who sought to protect the middle class type of man in the midst of increasingly large societies. The litany of politically correct objectives all tend toward forcing independent men to become smaller in order to become less dangerous, which was the tendency Locke's promotion of property and free speech was meant to counteract. That is, Locke opposed an alliance between the "imperiled" and "vulnerable" people, the nation's clergy, and their political allies. This alliance sought to impress uniformity for the sake of protection against a danger Locke thought was exaggerated. I think we a see a similar alliance today, which is why today, as in Locke's time, the proponents of free speech are often seen as defenders of violence toward the helpless.

Locke's approval of Trump and his supporters would be qualified. The opposition to political correctness is important, and Trump's electorate is right to think people should toughen up. When they label outrageously insolent college kids as "snowflakes" and the like, they are expressing a desire to stop the downward trend. They are saying that the claims of these students are irrational because the people making the claims are not truly suffering, and if they are suffering it is suffering that should be counteracted by "toughening up" rather than compelling other people to change the way they live and think. However, the opposers of political correctness too often voice their opposition with such vulgarity that they end up affirming the view of their opponents rather than drawing it into question. Trump is guilty of this as are many of his supporters. No philosopher discussed in this book would approve of this "approach," or lack thereof. A good point of comparison between Locke's reasonable approach and our own dangerously extreme approach is the Muslim ban Trump proposed during his campaign.

The Muslim Ban

As one part of his general anti-immigration and anti-political correctness positions, Trump spoke more forcefully and constantly about Muslim refugees and "Islamic terrorism" than any of the other candidates. Can Trump's campaign promise to put an end to Muslim immigration for a number of years, or his "travel ban," be justifiable on Lockean grounds?

At first glance, Trump's campaign promise appears perfectly justifiable on Lockean grounds, for no church can claim any "right to be tolerated by the magistrate, which is constituted upon such a bottom, that all those who enter into it, do thereby, *ipso facto*, deliver themselves up to the protection and service of another prince." Locke's example of such men in the *Letter* are Muslims. He writes, "It is ridiculous for any one to profess himself to be a Mahumetan only in his religion ... whilst at the same time he acknowledges himself bound to the Mufti of Constantinople."[33] Locke elaborates elsewhere, that "No peace and security, no not so much as common friendship, can ever be established or preserved amongst men, so long as this opinion prevails, that dominion is founded in grace, and that religion is to be propagated by force of arms."[34] The grounding of civil law in religious law is antithetical to the commonwealth and an unnatural subordination of the civil to the religious. Now, whether or not Islam requires this subordination is not a question I can answer in this chapter. However, is it not the case that many people believe this? Sincere Muslims often believe this. This does not preclude them being good people, but it is a belief that must be seen as inimical to liberal institutions. The supporters of Trump are right to view this as a danger that should be faced. Furthermore, it is wrong to refuse to face the danger out of a fear that speaking openly and intelligently about it could produce feelings of alienation. Locke would support those who wish to address the danger publicly, so long as they were reasonable and measured in their speech. Locke knew that in the large commonwealth, speaking about dangers could inflame public passions and produce injustice. That is, reasonable men could incidentally produce injustice because their concerns were taken up by zealots who always mishandle even the best of causes.[35] Knowing this about men, Locke opposes those religious opinions that are incommensurable with the foundations of the commonwealth, but tempers this opposition so as to avoid giving comfort and aid to zealotry.

To this end, Locke teaches that what was intolerable can become tolerable. Near the end of the *Letter*, Locke says, "Nay, if we may openly speak the truth, and as becomes one man to another, neither Pagan, nor Mahumetan, nor Jew, ought to be excluded from the civil rights of the commonwealth, because of his religion. ... It is not the diversity of opinions, (which cannot be avoided) but the refusal of toleration to those that are of different opinions, (which might have been granted) that has produced all the bustles and wars."[36] By his inclusion of "Mahumetans," Locke suggests that the situation he addressed before could, and perhaps should, be viewed differently. Whereas earlier he said it was impossible to be both a sincere Muslim and a good citizen of a commonwealth, it now becomes possible, with the help of toleration. It sounds impious, but Locke is suggesting that regardless of the "genius" or "nature" of any given religion, the religion itself is never the "cause of those evils charged upon religion;" rather, "the principle of persecution" is the cause of the evils.[37] The implication is that "the principle of persecution" is either never inherent in any of the religions Locke mentions, or that, if inherent to a religion, can be excised in one way or another. Tolerating Pagans, Muslims, Jews, and Christians can purify the religions of the principle of persecution; the religions can be changed so that the principle of toleration replaces the principle of persecution. Recognize the danger, but if you can, smother the danger before it grows into an existential threat. Again, Locke would never say, "smother that religion." He would say exactly what he did say: zealots are dangerous, and if you can, you should tolerate them out of existence.

During his campaign, Trump insisted on using the phrase "radical Islamic terrorism" and issued a press release (December 7, 2015) which stated, "Donald J. Trump is calling for a total and complete shutdown of Muslims entering the United States until our country's representatives can figure out what is going on." Trump defended this ban on numerous occasions afterward, as a necessary step to securing America's civil interests. At no point that I am aware of did Trump justify the proposed Muslim ban by saying that the Muslim religion is false or evil. Locke would be pleased that a religious community is not being (and most likely cannot be) barred from entering the United States for religious reasons. Nevertheless, Locke's teaching, that oppression produces dangerous dissidents, suggests Trump's travel ban could be counterproductive.

The ban could be counterproductive because men become dangerous to the civil order if they are stigmatized and excluded, especially if the speech used to stigmatize them is overly passionate. Even if a religion taught one of the doctrines abhorrent to Locke, that political dominion is founded on grace and religion should be propagated by force of arms, Locke suggests you might be able to improve or overcome this religion by loving it. Show its zealous followers again and again that they sacrifice peace, friendship, and the comforts of civil society. If not all men, at least enough men will end up preferring these goods to the promises of their religious leaders. Common sense may suggest to the citizens of a country to resist a foe with all their might, but Locke suggests that some foes should be assimilated. This suggestion avoids giving any aid or comfort to zealots on either side. If "Lockeans" constituted a numerous and powerful political party, and went around rooting out any and all of the religious opinions that are contrary to the commonwealth, injustices perpetrated by these "Lockeans" would multiply and doom to failure the very people who were putatively fighting for a just and tolerant social order.

I end by restating my central contention concerning Locke's political science and its application to the 2016 election. In the midst of increasingly large societies, Locke promoted the interests of the middle class and spiritual dissidents by ennobling acquisition and freedom of religion. His program does not map perfectly onto Trump's, which should be no surprise. Locke would approve of Trump's economic platform aimed at supporting middle class and blue-collar citizens, as well as Trump's denunciations of increasingly odious restrictions on speech. This agreement would be qualified, because Locke refused to give aid and comfort to zealots of any variety. Perhaps this is merely the luxury of theory, but it is a luxury our politicians should at least strive to enjoy.

Notes

1. How could this diagnosis produce racists? It frames the electoral struggle as the struggle of overt and microaggressive white supremacists, and not everyone has the mental wherewithal to break out of their enemy's frame of reference. I like the example of the Salem Witch Trials. Massachusetts, always a hotbed of moral fervor, was filled with anxiety over, and hatred of, witches. One of the terrible things witches did was dance in the woods. So what did rebellious teenagers do? They danced in the woods. One self-proclaimed practitioner of witchcraft hated the family she worked for. Who did the family she work for hate? They hated witches. What did she become? A witch.
2. Associated Press. "Trending story that Clinton won just 57 counties is untrue." https://apnews.com/fb5a5f7da21d460bbffb6985cb01cb2c/trending-story-clinton-won-just-57-counties-untrue (accessed August 2, 2017).
3. Locke, John. 1980. *Second Treatise of Government*. Indianapolis, IN: Hackett Publishing: 9. I emphasize "should" because the middle class is largely to blame for its shrinking size and influence.
4. Politico. "Donald Trump's jobs plan speech." http://www.politico.com/story/2016/06/full-transcript-trump-job-plan-speech-224891 (accessed September 4, 2017).
5. TIME staff. "Here's Donald Trump's Presidential Announcement Speech." http://time.com/3923128/donald-trump-announcement-speech/ (accessed September 4, 2017). Speaking of Republicans, Trump said, "And they don't talk jobs and they don't talk China. ... You don't hear it from anybody else. And I watch the speeches." See also, LA Times Staff. http://latimes.com/politics/la-na-pol-donald-trump-immigration-speech-transcript-20160831-snap-htmlstory.html (accessed September 4, 2017). "The fundamental problem with the immigration in our country is that it serves the needs of the wealthy donors, political activists and powerful, powerful politicians."

6. Maria Panaritas, Dylan Purcell, Chris Brennan, and Angela Couloumbis. "How Trump took Pennsylvania: Wins everywhere (almost) but the southeast." http://www.philly.com/philly/news/politics/presidential/201661110_How_Trump_took_Pennsylvania_wins_almost_everwhere_but_the_southeast.html (accessed July 9, 2017).

   Dan Horn, and Jeremy Fugleberg. "How Donald Trump won Ohio." http://www.cincinnati.com/story/news/politics/2016/11/09/how-trump-won-ohio/93560164 (accessed July 9, 2017).

7. Ruth Igielnik. "GOP gained ground in middle-class communities in 2016." http://www.pewresearch.org/fact-tank/2016/12/08/gop-gained-ground-in-middle-class-communities-in-2016/ (accessed July 25, 2017). "Of the 221 areas examined, there are 57 such solidly middle-class areas, and they were almost equally split in 2008, with 30 areas voting for Democrats and 27 for Republicans. In 2016, Trump successfully defended all 27 middle-class areas won by Republicans in 2008. In a dramatic shift, however, Hillary Clinton lost in 18 of the 30 middle-class areas won by Democrats in 2008."

8. Locke (1980, 23).

9. Locke (1980, 21 & 26).

10. Locke, John. 2006. *Locke: Political Essays*. Ed. Mark Goldie. Cambridge: Cambridge University Press: 222.

11. Locke (1980, 13 emphasis added).

12. Locke (1980, 106 emphasis added).

13. Locke (1980, 115).

14. Locke (1980, 9).

15. Locke (1980, 19).

16. Locke (2006, 222).

17. Locke (2006, 186).

18. These metaphorical statements on size pertain almost exclusively to acquisition, property, and speech. Locke suggests many ways that men ought to become smaller and give way, but these suggestions have a limit and have as their aim the promotion of the industrious and rational man. For example, Locke teaches that it is rational to tolerate other religions, which of course may make things feel a bit cramped at times, to a certain kind of person.

19. Locke (2006, 322 & 324).

20. Locke, John. 1983. *A Letter Concerning Toleration*. Indianapolis, IN: Hackett Publishing: 24–25.

21. Locke (2006, 191–192). Here Locke focuses on ameliorating the effects of poverty on children ages 3–14. He notes that without some care given by the parish, their bodies would fail to grow healthy. He also laments the poor parents' "loose way of breeding up" their children. That is, he fears that without some additional attention from the community, the children

will turn out unhealthy and morally coarse. These unhealthy characters make them dangerous to the laboring classes. As adults with unhealthy bodies and narrowed minds, these poorly reared men will not only need more sustenance, they can procreate and may participate in the political life of the commonwealth.

22. Locke (1983, 34).
23. Locke, John. 1996. Eds. Ruth W. Grant and Nathan Tarcov. *Some Thoughts Concerning Education and Of the Conduct of the Understanding*. Indianapolis, IN: Hackett Publishing: 212. It should be noted, "inheriting local truths" is simply what normally happens. The local truths Locke addresses tended to produce "zealous bigots," which was the nub of the problem. That is, the problem is not belief itself, but belief in exaggerated threats.
24. Locke (1983, 36).
25. Locke (1983, 27 & 38).
26. Adam Wolfson ably presents and explains this argument of Locke's. Adam Wolfson. 2010. *Persecution or Toleration. An explication of the Locke – Proast Quarrel, 1689–1704*. Lanham, MD: Lexington Books: 59–78.
27. Locke, John. 1996. Eds. Ruth W. Grant and Nathan Tarcov. *Some Thoughts Concerning Education and Of the Conduct of the Understanding*. Indianapolis, IN: Hackett Publishing: 169.
28. Locke (1996, 176).
29. All quoted in: West, Tom. 2017. *The Political Theory of The American Founding: Natural Rights, Public Policy, and The Moral Conditions of Freedom*. Cambridge: Cambridge University Press: 386–388.
30. Locke (2006, 325).
31. Locke (2006, 326).
32. Locke (2006, 184).
33. Locke (1983, 50).
34. Locke (1983, 33).
35. Locke himself taught that men should "enter into some religious society … to own to the world that they worship God" (1983, 38–39). But was disgusted by the irrational thirst for vengeance that erupted when some decent men did not bring their children to church or attended the "wrong" church (1983, 34).
36. Locke (1983, 55).
37. Locke (1983, 54–55).

Bibliography

Locke, John. 1980. In *Second Treatise of Government*, ed. C.B. Macpherson. Indianapolis: Hackett Publishing.

———. 1983. In *A Letter Concerning Toleration*, ed. James H. Tully. Indianapolis: Hackett Publishing.

———. 1996. In *Some Thoughts Concerning Education and of the Conduct of the Understanding*, ed. Ruth W. Grant and Nathan Tarcov. Indianapolis: Hackett Publishing.

———. 2006. In *Locke: Political Essays*, ed. Mark Goldie. Cambridge: Cambridge University Press.

West, Tom. 2017. *The Political Theory of The American Founding: Natural Rights, Public Policy, and The Moral Conditions of Freedom*. Cambridge: Cambridge University Press.

Wolfson, Adam. 2010. *Persecution or Toleration. An Explication of the Locke – Proast Quarrel, 1689–1704*. Lanham: Lexington Books.

CHAPTER 10

Civic Dignity in the Age of Donald Trump: A Kantian Perspective

Susan Meld Shell

In addressing the subject of citizenship in the wake of the election of Donald Trump I am inspired by my mother, who recently passed away at 100, in full command of both her wits and a memory stretching back to the election of 1924 (four years after the passing of the 19th amendment), in which she accompanied her own immigrant mother to the polls to help her with reading English.

This was not primarily an election directed against women or driven by misogyny as some immediately rushed to conclude. Many voters who derided Clinton would no doubt have happily voted for Sarah Palin, or some other woman differently encumbered politically and biographically. Nor, I suspect, was it mainly an expression of "white backlash"—at least not in the sense in which the left generally understands the term.

The stark facts: the loss of jobs among the formerly industrial white working class, the hollowing out of small-town and rural America, amply documented both by the numbers and by the eloquent testimony of authors like J.D. Vance in *Hillbilly Elegy* and Arlie Hochschild in *Strangers in Their Own Land*, the declining wages across the board for the less

S. M. Shell (✉)
Boston College, Chestnut Hill, MA, USA

© The Author(s) 2018
M. B. Sable, A. J. Torres (eds.), *Trump and Political Philosophy*,
https://doi.org/10.1007/978-3-319-74427-8_10

educated—in short, a falling tide and shrinking pie for vast sectors of the country, stretching from the Maine border all across America, both north and south, almost all the way to the Pacific coast—speak a hard and harsh truth. The question is how to interpret that truth.

Here's a try.

POLITICAL FAILURES LEADING TO TRUMP'S ELECTION

People want respect more than they want hand-outs. Hand-outs can be a symbol of <u>respect</u>—a share in spoils, as it were, that one deserves—or they can be the opposite, a sign that one is pitiable. I think that Democrats across the board have tended to ignore this fact. As Thomas Hobbes once suggested [see *Leviathan*: chapter 15], most men would rather hazard their lives than not be revenged (i.e., get their respect back). What drove the Sanders folks was arguably less a desire for "more free stuff" than an eagerness to punish free-loading bankers and others who had robbed the young of their deserved right to rise (to coin a phrase). And Hilary's dismissal of a quarter of the population as a "basket of deplorables" whom she called "unredeemable" evoked a moral narrative that was particularly likely to repel a demographic group already freighted by many on the left with the burden of a "white privilege" as innate (for no one chooses one's white skin or one's ancestors) as the "original sin" on which it is seemingly modeled, and from which they could never hope to fully extricate themselves, given the increasingly shrill demands of this or that self-perceived victim. According to this moral narrative, white men (and women) of the small towns and rural south were in a state of permanent moral disgrace, as Shelby Steele has noted. Trump's uncivil (and frequently outrageous) assaults against "political correctness" were wildly effective in their implicit promise of honorable redemption. One suspects that what Trump immediately delivered to his most fervent audiences was not the promise of more jobs (about whose details he was evasive) or a halt on immigration (again, few campaign details) but a first installment on restored respect. For me the most telling fact about the Clinton campaign was its failure to include in what was otherwise a spectacularly competent and well-run Democratic National Convention a single visible representative of the male white working class—as if to signal that their sort—union men and other traditional stalwarts of the Democratic Party—were not wanted.

At the same time, free-enterprise purists have in my view been equally if not more remiss, not only for habitually discounting the condition of the economic losers in a global free-market place, but also for a moral narrative too eager to equate financial success with civic virtue, or to see every problem as a nail for which "free markets" are the only hammer. It was also a grave mistake, in my opinion, to dismiss growing concern with inequality as nothing more than an expression of class envy. The more recent response to inequality by some on the libertarian right—namely, data purporting to show that the wealthy are less happy (and, presumably, that the poor, like the happy peasants of yore, should therefore be content with their lot)—was no more persuasive. I was therefore both heartened and dismayed to read a recent column by Arthur Brooks, in which he speaks, empathetically, of a "hunger for dignity" on the part of many of the poor or underemployed who voted for Trump "Dignity," yes; but "hunger," in my view, puts things exactly the wrong way. One does not "hunger" for respect, one demands—one even fights for it. To hunger for respect is already in a sense to merit just the opposite.

A similar condescension prevailed at a Harvard post-election panel that I attended. The moderator did not fail to reassure the audience that it was in a "safe space." A renowned economist rolled out the woeful statistics documenting the falling incomes of those in the bottom educational tercile, especially white men, along with the rising income of those (like himself) who taught and studied at places such as Harvard. He then guiltily confessed: "they trusted us and we failed them." But his answer: fuller use of various routine tools from the progressive economist's tool-kit, from earned income-credits to job retraining (to charter schools), did not inspire great confidence. There was also a whiff, however unintended, of "I, the great white hope, must do a better job, next time I descend among the natives."

And the Democrat's studied indifference to their traditional union base, along with crucial states of the Midwest surely didn't help.

Every political order, Aristotle tells us, is guided by a ruling conception of justice. Such conceptions are always fractious at best, and at worst prone to civil war and dissolution. If Lincoln remains the best weaver of our fundamental national narrative, it is one that has in recent days increasingly threatened to come undone. Lincoln once spoke of a new nation brought forth upon this continent, "conceived in liberty and dedicated to the proposition that all men are created equal." That image was arguably high-jacked following the failure of Reconstruction, a time in which "birth of a nation" came literally to refer (as in the highly popular if controversial 1915 film that bore the title *Birth of a Nation* and was itself based on an equally popular novel by Thomas Dixon Jr. called *The Clansman*) to the emerging "Aryan" union of the North and South out of the cinders of civil war under the shared banner of white supremacy. It took the civil rights movements of the 1960s to return us to Lincoln's original vision, from which we once again have strayed, both on a left driven by identity politics, and more recently, a newly emboldened so-called alt-right.

For Lincoln, the phrase "free labor" was not an end in itself but a means to a life of broadly shared dignity and achievement. But Lincoln also knew better than anyone the limits of "spontaneous order" and the crucial importance of governmental power, shrewdly and imaginatively deployed, for securing the nation whose image he so powerfully evoked at Gettysburg. Tocqueville, in other words, may be less helpful at this point than Lincoln, and with him, thinkers like Kant (and Hegel,) whose remedies for the excesses of the "administrative" state and "free markets" alike may better suit the conditions of the contemporary world.

If there is one generally acknowledged "take away" from the election of Donald Trump, it may be that the old ideological divisions between right and left no longer hold. Trump base supporters were aroused less by the appeals to "small government" and free enterprise that moved earlier Tea Partiers, than by anger against a liberal elite whose perceived condescension and indifference to their own deeply held moral beliefs and sense of personal dignity could not outweigh that elite's self-proclaimed intention to promote the interests of the economically less well-off. Trump, by way of contrast, combined the promise of individual prosperity with that of a renewed common share in national "greatness." And he reminded all of us that the primary responsibility of a president is to the well-being of his own country—to *our* greatness, so to speak—not to the directives of some unelected global official or to the endless demands of an abstract and shapeless "other."

At the same time, and more disturbingly, Trump's hyperbolic rhetoric and gleeful channeling of popular vitriol—be it against illegal immigrants, the mainstream press (or—with ever shrinking credibility—Wall Street), bears an eerie resemblance to the opening moves of Erdogen and Putin, leaders whom Trump professes to admire and about whose subsequent manner of governing he has expressed few if any reservations. Indeed, Trump's perceived contempt for established constitutional limits, including "checks and balances" as conceived by the Framers, seems bound to weaken, if not altogether undermine, the civic rituals and habits necessary to free government. Finally, and not least, Trump's ongoing flirtation with White Nationalism and seeming ignorance of if not outright hostility to core principles of the Declaration of

Independence now borders on the shocking. As Trump swings between occasional bows to moderation and blatant and increasing excess—this or that reasonable statement or appointment, on the one hand, and wild swings at his enemies, real or imagined, on the other—one is left wondering where we are heading. The "managerial state" surely has its defects; but it is also, as Hobbes well knew, the ultimate check, when all else fails (or divided government has broken down) against the ravages of a wayward absolutism. It is also difficult to see how the shared prosperity that Trump has promised can be accomplished without *some* managed restrictions on the market beyond tariffs and presidential jaw-boning (not to speak of greater taxes on the wealthiest), or how national security can be adequately assured if *some* line is not drawn between professional intelligence gathering and immediate political expediency.

Finally and not least, Trump's ongoing encouragement to the worst elements of the far right betrays a dangerous obliviousness, at best, to the inherent fragility of every constitutional order. The terrible and tragic civil war that once proved necessary to sustain our "nation" left us with the task, as Lincoln saw it, of "binding up the nations wounds," not of fighting it anew. Trump, along with some around him, can sometimes seem to wish, with an unnerving casualness, such a war upon us once again.

We *are* an exceptional nation, in Lincoln's terms: not born, primarily, from a peculiar ethnic or racial soil but *in liberty* and through an explicit act of dedication to the principle that all men are created equal. That principle flies in the face of some cruder, if all too familiar, understandings of national greatness. We must be for ourselves, yes, but what we are—what primarily distinguishes us as a nation—is, at least on Lincoln's account, our shared commitment to the claim that *all* men are created equal. One can only hope that the ensuing complications, and accompanying passions, do not overstrain the bonds of civic friendship, or darken our vision of the world beyond the truth, but instead continue to call forth what Lincoln called, in even bleaker times, the better angels of our nature.

KANT AND CIVIC DIGNITY

The affinities between Kant's and Lincoln's understanding of a liberal civic order deserve special emphasis in the age of Trump, in which the civic bond is under challenge arguably not seen since Lincoln's time.[1] Kant's potential untapped contribution to contemporary political discourse can here be discussed only briefly; but it can hopefully suffice to indicate and more fruitful approach to the claims of liberal citizenship, in keeping with the spirit of Lincoln, than any currently on offer by the conventional left and right, while also addressing some of the problems that contribute to Trump's appeal.

To be sure, much about Kant's approach to citizenship, elaborated under an absolutist Prussian monarchy in which serfdom had not yet been fully abolished and praise of republican principles could land one in prison can easily seem outdated at best. One of Kant's most disturbing civic claims, for modern readers, lies in his distinction between active and passive citizens, only the former of whom may vote or otherwise actively participate in the management of state affairs.[2]

That puzzlement is partly allayed by taking into account the political/ historical context, and in particular—the fact that Kant's categories of "active" and "passive" citizen are lifted almost verbatim from the French Constitution of 1791, following the recommendations of Abbe Siéyès. In adopting these categories—as Kant's contemporary audience would surely have recognized—Kant was also laying down a political marker, in favor of the French constitutional moderates and against radicals like Robespierre who was closely identified with the cause of universal suffrage.[3] To call for universal suffrage, in such a context, would be close to endorsement of the Terror that had quickly followed Robespierre's rise.

At the same time Kant's own treatment of active and passive citizenship diverges from contemporary French practice in a number of important ways. First: Whereas the National Assembly, following Siéyès, had made the right to vote conditional upon possession of a degree of taxable (productively derived) wealth, Kant rests that right, more formally and abstractly, on what he calls "self-subsistence" [Selbstständigkeit].[4] Second: whereas Siéyès had defined the "nation" as a "society" or "body of associates living under common laws and represented by the same legislative assembly," Kant specifically distinguishes the people qua "society" from the commonwealth [gemeine Wesen], or state, by which that society is, as Kant puts it, "made." [6: 306–7] Finally: whereas Siéyès includes within the "nation" only members of the productive class, or "third estate" (as distinguished from the non-productive first and second estates—i.e., the clergy and nobility—or anyone laying claim to exceptional political privilege), Kant includes all willing to join in constituting a people.

The essential attributes of a citizen, according to Kant, are (1) "freedom" in the sense of obeying no law other than one to which one has consented; (2) "equality" in the sense of regarding no one among the people as superior to oneself in moral capacity to bind others, and

(3) "self-reliance" or "self-subsistence" in the sense of owing one's preservation to one's own "rights" and "forces" as member of the commonwealth. Kant's verbal linkage between the "essence" [Wesen] of the citizen and the commonwealth as, literally, the "common essence" [gemeine Wesen] drives home the integrative character of civic *Selbständigkeit*. The citizen is self-subsistent not in an autarkical sense but only in relation to and as integral member of the whole.[5]

That all members of the people are not "self-subsistent" in this sense "makes necessary" a distinction, however, between active and passive citizens, only the former of whom may vote or otherwise actively participate in managing affairs of state.

> The qualification to be a citizen is constituted only by the capacity [Fähigkeit] for voting [Stimmgebung]; this, however, presupposes the self-sufficiency of one among the people who would be not only a part [Theil] of the commonwealth but also a member [Glied] of it, that is to say, an acting [handelnder] part in community with others from his own Willkür. The latter quality, however, makes necessary the distinction of *active* [activen] from *passive* citizens, even though the concept of the latter seems to stand in contradiction with that of a citizen in general. [6: 314]

Kant is sensitive to the difficulty, bordering on contradiction, that this "necessity" poses, given his essential definition of a citizen as a "law-giving" member of the "state" understood as a *societas civilis*. [6: 313–14] Kant responds with a series of clarifying examples of those who are only fit to be passive citizens—e.g., the journeyman or apprentice in comparison with the master craftsman, the servant or day-laborer in comparison with the carpenter or blacksmith (who can place the products of their labor up for sale), and the house tutor in comparison with the schoolteacher, as well as, in general, "all women":

> The woodcutter whom I employ in my yard, the blacksmith in India who goes house to house with iron with his hammer, anvil and bellows to work with iron, in comparison with the European carpenter or blacksmith who can place the products of his labor publicly up for sale as wares; the house tutor in comparison with the schoolteacher; the tenant farmer in comparison with the lease-hold farmer, and so forth, are mere handy-men [Handlanger] of the commonwealth, because they must be under the direction or protection of other individuals and thus possess no civil self-subsistence. [6: 314]

What each of these figures has in common is a shared need to be "under the direction or protection" of another. Whereas Siéyès had considered such a condition akin to slavery,[6] Kant himself *distinguishes* slavery, which is a fundamental violation of the innate right of each to be his own master (*sui iuris*) [6: 237–38], from dependence in the sense here intended, a dependence entirely consistent with that innate right, according to Kant, so long as it is based either on one's natural status as a minor (as with children), or arrangements arising from one's own choice, and limited by the rights of humanity in one's own person. [6: 276–284; 285]. (An additional, final proviso, namely that nothing stand in the way of passive citizens "working their way up" to active status. [6; 315]) Indeed, it is only through due recognition of this innate right to freedom and equality—a right that those who enter into such relations of dependence are incapable of forfeiting—that the state is possible at all.

Kant's own distinction between active and passive citizenship might thus be put as follows: On the one hand, the passive citizen, like all citizens, participates in that general will by which all are united to give a law in which "each wills for all and all for each," a law that is necessarily just in accordance with the principle that "no one can do himself an injustice." On the other hand, the "organized" power [Gewalt] thereby authorized, through which subsequent positive laws are to be introduced, is to be conceived, on Kant's view, as a separate community in its own right. The members of community, unlike the general members of society at large, have what he here calls "civil personality" [bürgerliche Personalität] [6: 314], as distinguished from the "moral personality," both internal and external, that no human being is capable of giving up. [6: 223].[7]

In sum: qua *citizen*, the passive citizen is a full-fledged member of the people and with it the general will by which the people both constitute the state and subject themselves to the latter's three-fold authority [Gewalt]: legislative, executive, and judicial. [6: 315–16] Qua *passive* citizen, however, he is subject to the legislative authority to which he has ideally given his consent as member of the general will, without, unlike the active citizen, playing an ongoing role in organizing or otherwise "cooperating" in "the introduction of specific laws." [6: 314–15]

If this is indeed the right way to understand Kant's distinction between active and passive citizenship, how might it bear on issues of redistributive justice, and, in particular, the duty/authorization to compel those with means to provide for those in need? And in what way, if at all, might the requirement that that passive citizens "be able to work their way up" to active citizenship (if the category of passive citizenship is to remain consistent with citizen's innate right to freedom and equality) translate into the duty or authorization of the state to actively enable those in a position of dependence to thus work their way up?

I would suggest the following two-tiered answer. The **first** stems from what Kant calls the "duty of the people" to provide for the most basic natural needs of those who, through no fault of their own,[8] cannot provide for themselves, either "self-sufficiently" (in the manner of active citizens) or through other voluntary arrangements (e.g., by temporarily "hiring out" to another the "use of [their own] forces" [6: 285; 330]). Such provision might be likened to other policies with redistributive implications, policies that Kant might endorse on similar grounds. Given flexible and rising standards of what it means to have one's basic natural needs unmet (e.g. lack of access to inoculation against common infectious diseases), such provision might, indeed, prove quite expansive, including access to adequate health care services, decent housing, nutritional support, and so on, so long as care were taken that such provision not become a "means of acquisition" for the lazy and thereby unjustly burden the people as a whole.

The **second** basis for redistributive policies stems from the requirement that nothing prevent passive citizens from "working their way up" to active status. On a "minimalist" reading, to be sure, this would demand no more than that there be no legal bars to such advancement (of a sort that still existed in contemporary Prussia, where serfdom had not yet been completely abolished, and noble status remained necessary for placement in the upper military ranks, as would remain the case until the end of World War One.) But that Kant himself had more in mind is suggested by his frequent flirtations with the idea of universal state supported education—a policy that had, in principle if not in practice, been in place in Prussia since the early 18th century. His objection to state, as opposed to privately supported education, was based not on the worry that it might unjustly burden taxpayers, but on the likelihood of it resulting, under current political conditions, in popular moral and religious indoctrination inimical to the cause of freedom. That children had a *right* to education— a right directed, in the first instance, against their parents—Kant had no doubt; and it seems reasonable to assume that he would have urged, in cases in which parents could not fulfill this obligation, that the state make it available, either indirectly or directly.

At the same time, the *content* of the education that Kant favored (as described in his Lectures on Pedagogy) suggests the limits he would probably have placed on positive state efforts to help citizens advance from passive to active status: namely, that such policies not unwittingly subvert a citizen's *own* efforts to become able to maintain himself through his own forces. It here becomes especially important to distinguish *Selbständigkeit* in the sense of being self-supporting from "independence" as understood by contemporary scholars (following the work of Phillip Pettit, Quentin Skinner, and others).[9] Whereas "independence" (the term commonly used to translate "Selbständigkeit") places the emphasis, especially if understood in Pettit's sense, on freedom *from* domination by another's will, Kant himself places the emphasis on the positive ability to be "self-supporting" [9: 486; 491 92], i.e., to rationally manage one's own affairs on the basis of one's own resources [Vermögen], whether material or mental, as member of the commonwealth

But "to be one's own master" in a juridical sense is *not* the same, on Kant's understanding, as self subsistence. Savages, for example, may enjoy independence in the sense of freedom from domination by another will (and are properly sui iuris) and yet manifestly lack the qualities necessary for *Selbständigkeit* as Kant himself defines it. To be self-subsistent in this sense is, in Kant's own words, to be "an acting [*handelnder*] part in community with others from [one's] own choice." One who is thus qualified "can thank for his existence and maintenance" his "own rights and forces as member of the commonwealth," rather than depending another's choice, in the acquisition and deployment of the means needed for his own support. [6: 314; cf. 213]

Such qualities include not only skills and discipline for which culture and civilization are necessary, but also a certain strength of character that can only be acquired through personal effort, be it (to cite the ideal case) during a properly guided childhood and youth, in the manner sketched in Kant's own Lectures on Pedagogy, or otherwise.

Kant may well have conceived of passive citizenship as a useful form of civil and moral education, at least potentially, particularly for those without access to the sort of ideal youthful education that he favored. Indeed, if, as Kant elsewhere insists, true maturity, both civil and moral, rarely occurs before the age forty, then a prolonged state of civil "journeyman-ship"[10] may be unavoidable, whatever one's actual material means. If this suggestion has merit, passive citizenship (in an extended sense) might have its own necessary uses, especially given the imperfect state of education.[11] Abraham Lincoln may have had something similar in mind when he hoped that employees who made up the ranks of what was then called "free labor" might at some point in their lives have the opportunity to work for themselves—at some point, but not immediately.[12] And that aspiration lives on in the dream, not only American, of "being one's own boss," a status not generally thought inconsistent with starting out as an employee under the direction and management of others.

I am far from urging that we revert to the sort of limited suffrage embraced by Kant, French moderates like Siéyès, and the Framers of the US Constitution. Still, the appeal of Trump to what has been called the "low-information" voter might give pause to those who have perhaps too readily assumed that higher voting rates are always politically beneficial. And it might reframe the "welfare" vs. "dependency" debate in ways that make (temporary) dependency a condition to be welcomed rather than regretted, at least when linked with opportunities for civic and moral maturation, opportunities increasingly limited, in today's US, to the economically privileged. We tend to applaud, rather than deplore, those who spend years attending college and in unpaid internships in preparation for careers and later marriage and childrearing; similar opportunities that foster civic self-sufficiency in a roughly Kantian sense might be offered to others currently less fortunate. This might include not only the "free college" often promised but also extended vocational apprenticeships, along with moving and housing help. And it might assuage the civic resentment and anxiety currently felt by a significant portion of the electorate who have come to believe, not altogether without reason, that the current "system" is stacked against them.

Understood in this light, Kant's distinction between active and passive citizenship not only suggests certain necessary limits on any positive policies in support of citizens' ascent from passive to active status; it also sheds light on Kant's argument for the duty of the people, and related authorization of the state, to compel the wealthy to provide for those who are truly needy (i.e., who, through no fault of their own, cannot meet their most basic natural needs). What is juridically pertinent about such a condition is not "neediness" as such, but lies, rather, in its relation to the end and act of the juridically constitutive general will, which unanimously intended the ongoing existence of the "people." It is not his own individual existence that each member of the general will must be presumed to have had in view, but his own existence only insofar as it counted neither more nor less than that of others. The duty of the wealthy to those in need is thus one of reciprocity: the wealthy have already enjoyed no less benefit from the protection of the commonwealth than they are now obliged to give. This reciprocal dependence is precisely in keeping with the equality of rich and poor as subject members of "society" in general, as distinguished from the juridical "civil society" or "commonwealth," in whose necessitating authority only those capable of rationally managing their own affairs are fit to actively participate.[13]

In short: the civic duty of those "with means" both to provide for the poor, and to make sure that opportunities for advancement toward civic self-sufficiency are and remain widely available, is rooted in their common citizenship: i.e., on the united will of all to sustain the "nation" as the state's necessary (naturally rooted) correlate and matrix.

"Birth of a Nation" Reconsidered

A "nation [Nation]" in a juridically relevant sense is, as Kant understands it, a specifically *political* union, arising through an act of mutual submission to a common legal framework through which an aggregate of individuals (previously united, in the ordinary course of things, by language or culture) become fellow citizens:

> The human beings who constitute a people [*Volk*] can be represented as born from the soil [*Landeseingeborne*] according to an analogy of reproduction from a common ancestral stem [*Elterstamm*] (congeniti), even though this isn't so: yet in an intellectual and juridical sense, they can be represented as born from a common mother (the republic), so as to make up, as it were, a family (gens, natio), whose members (state citizens) are of equal birth, and who avoid, as ignoble, any commingling with those (savages [Wilden]) who may live around them in a state of nature. [6: 343]

States are the vehicle through which a people in a merely cultural or ethnic sense becomes a civic "nation." All states are in this sense "nation states." The double analogy of a 'common derivation' (both from the soil, 'as it were,' and from the commonwealth (or gemeines Wesen)) helps explain the transformation of human beings into citizens, with distinct and potentially overriding rights and duties from which other human beings might be properly excluded. (The process also works the other way: when Kant wants to explain natural organic form, he compares it to the organization of a state.)[14] Citizenship implies a reciprocal, coercively enforced obligation to uphold the rights of other citizens—an obligation that does not apply with the same force and in the same way to others.

Citizens, according to Kant's adaptation of an ancient and a more recent political conceit, are familially related in a double sense: first, as still-savage children, as it were, of a common soil, second, as jointly ennobled sons of the republic. Without this shared double 'natality,' for which being human is not enough, men, in their capacity as purely moral beings, would hover over the world like angels (to borrow a conceit from Pierre Manent). Juridical man is embodied man (a 'child of the earth') who takes up space and thus comes into potential conflict with other human beings. Everyone excludes others from some portion of the globe, beginning with the place where he or she is placed by birth without their willing it. Peoples arise, in both fact and right, from the debt of support that parents owe their children for bringing them into the world "without their consent." Kant's account of citizenship acknowledges this debt, while subordinating it to an ideal of civic re-creation (and the principles of freedom and equality therein embodied), an ideal brought to life in the peculiar 'spirit' of a nation, and accessible, in principle, to peoples everywhere. At the same time, Kant regards the state so conceived (along with the "patriotism" that properly accompanies it) as the best possible school for inculcating respect for humanity at large.

How does such a conception of citizenship articulate with the primary, territorially rooted ethnic affinity that Kant associates with [naturally emerging] peoples? If civil ordering converts culturally united peoples into "nations," can states include a plurality of peoples, or is national unity necessarily linked to that of a single populus? What defines a populus as a 'whole'? And what happens when two or more peoples claim a common territory?

Kant indirectly addresses such questions by conceding that each of the 'nations' of Europe is composed of many peoples. Over time, at least, separate peoples can come to form a single nation, whose members regard themselves as 'co-descended,' in as much as the 'union of the members is (presumed) to be inherited.' Juridical "peoplehood," in other words, overrides peoplehood in its pre-political form.

To what extent, then, can our civic 'rebirth' as citizens override linguistic and ethnic differences? Republican self-government, according to Kant, cannot flourish without what Lincoln later called a "political religion." Toleration is not enough[15]; and it is, in any case, not possible without damaging the essence of republican citizenship. Citizens need not constitute a single ethnically rooted people; but they must be able to accept sub-populations as co-contributors to a common civic purpose and as co-subscribers to a related national creed—not merely as irritations to put up with.

Unlike contemporary formulas of 'union in diversity' Kant does not emphasize respect for 'otherness' as such, but instead stresses the differing positive contributions of each people (according to its own individual gifts) to a common national project. Kant's conception of the nation-state (unlike that of, say, Herder or Fichte) is supple enough to support the existence of multiple peoples within a common constitutional framework (for example, ethnic Lithuanians and Poles within a territorially expanded Prussia).[16] But it also requires, if that framework is not to be a hollow one, a common national creed—a shared, historically adapted vehicle of the "republican spirit."

The United States is, arguably, the country that has carried furthest the promise of nationhood in accordance with the Kantian model: one that is rooted not in common historical habits or ethnic bonds but in a shared allegiance to core constitutional principles of liberty, equality, and self-reliance. It is this sort of American "exceptionalism" that Trump's election and subsequent performance increasingly places in question. Trump's apparent contempt for the basic principles of a decent constitutional order may be more threatening to the American nation as championed by Lincoln than Trump's covert appeals, however odious, to racism and "white identity."

At the same time, those who are unwilling to accept the common principles that have heretofore unite us both constitutionally and politically, lack what Kant calls "the quality of a citizen" and hence are not true members of the "nation," whatever their own ethnic background:

> [A people], or the part of it that recognizes itself as united into a civil whole by common derivation, is called a nation [Nation; gens]. That part which excepts itself from these laws (the savage [wilde] group in this people) is called rabble [Pöbel; vulgus], which, uniting against the law, becomes a mob [Rottiren; agere per turbas]—behavior that excludes them from the quality of a citizen. [7: 311]

As the debate unleashed by Trump's election and subsequent performance as president continues, we could do worse than keep in mind not only the promise of national citizenship as both Kant and Lincoln understood it, but also, on the same understanding, its inherent fragility.

Notes

1. For a discussion of some of these links, see also the chapter in this volume by John Burt; see also his *Lincoln's Tragic Pragmatism* (2013).
2. See, for example, Beiner (2011).
3. On Kant's relation to Siéyès and the constitutional moderates, see also Maliks (2014).

4. When Kant's speaks of the innate right to "independence" from the elective wills of others, he uses "Unabhängigkeit," rather than "Selbständigkeit," a term he here exclusively reserves for citizenship in the "active" sense. (Cf., however, *Vorarbeiten* [19: 351]; and *Theory and Practice* [8: 295], where Kant equates Selbstandigkeit with being sui iuris.).

5. Kant's understanding of self-sufficiency thus not only falls outside Isaiah Berlin's famous distinction between positive and negative freedom, but also is not to be identified with the "third concept of freedom" more recently championed by Quentin Skinner. On Berlin's two concepts of freedom in relation to Kant see also Williams (2013).

6. Siéyès, *Arch Parl.*, 27 August 1789, tome VIII, p. 503.

7. A "person" is a subject "whose actions may be imputed to him." "Moral personality" is the freedom of a rational being under moral laws," from which it follows, Kant says, that "a person is subject to no laws other than those he gives himself (either alone or at least along with others) " [6: 223]

8. I.e., who have not willfully made poverty a "means of acquisition." Kant's own striking example of such no-fault neediness is that of abandoned children, whom the state is to charge the people "with not allowing to perish knowingly." [6: 326–27]

9. See, for example, Pettit (2001), Skinner (1998).

10. See note 10 above.

11. In the *Anthropology* and *Lectures on Pedagogy*, Kant suggests that the "idea of education" has not yet been fully worked out and, indeed, may never be.

12. See Abraham Lincoln, "Address to the Wisconsin State Agricultural Society: September 30, 1859.

13. That wealth and active citizenship are not identical categories can be illustrated by the example of wealthy minors, whose funds are administered by others.

14. See *Critique of Judgment* [5: 375n.].

15. See Kant, 'What is Enlightenment?': an 'enlightened' prince, who considers it his duty, in religious matters, not to prescribe anything to his people, 'will reject the arrogant name of *tolerance*.' [8: 40] From a Kantian point of view, mere toleration (implying as it does an evil one chooses to put up with) would not be enough, while 'celebration' of difference for its own sake (as some contemporary ethicists urge) would be equally misguided.

16. "Nachschrift eines Freundes," [8: 445].

BIBLIOGRAPHY

Beiner, Ronald. 2011. Paradoxes in Kant's Account of Citizenship. In *Kant and the Concept of Community*, ed. Chalton Payne and Lucas Thorp. Rochester: University of Rochester Press.

Kant, Immanuel. All references are to volume and page number in the Academy Edition of Kant's Work [*Kant's Gesammelte Schriften*] (Berlin: De Gruyter, 1968–). (These references also appear in the standard Cambridge University Press edition of Kant's work in translation).

Maliks, Reidar. 2014. *Kant's Politics in Context*. Oxford: Oxford University Press.

Pettit, Philip. 2001. *A Theory of Freedom*. Oxford: Oxford University Press.

Skinner, Quentin. 1998. *Liberty Before Liberalism*. Cambridge: Cambridge University Press.

Williams, Howard. 2013. Kant and Libertarianism. In *Kant on Practical Justification*, ed. Mark Timmons and Sorin Baiasu. Oxford: Oxford Unviersity Press.

CHAPTER 11

The Ideological Rhetoric of the Trump Platform and Edmund Burke's Theory of a Generational Compact

Douglas Jarvis

The baby boomer generation, and the various movements of the 1960s and 1970s, has been viewed as the central driving force behind contemporary political tensions and fragmented forms of social identity. Since the late 1960s, we have found ourselves increasingly defined according to an identity politics culture based on our perceived sense of self. Moreover, the amplified social atomism of modern mass society, within a neo-liberal capitalist framework of temporary work and disposable consumerism ("the gig economy"), has fueled this sense of a divided political community. The political rise of Trump arguably reflects the overall effects of both of these historical trends. Trump's election, as probably the last member of the sixties generation to hold power, can probably be seen as the endpoint of the post-war era. In the United States, as in the rest of the Western world, we are no longer a "people" sharing a sense of solidarity. It is the growing lack of political connectedness among individuals, in the midst of both greater social pluralism and economic class retrenchment, which has driven greater ideological tension between Americans. The resentment of the Tea Party

D. Jarvis (✉)
Lakehead University, Orillia, ON, Canada

© The Author(s) 2018
M. B. Sable, A. J. Torres (eds.), *Trump and Political Philosophy*,
https://doi.org/10.1007/978-3-319-74427-8_11

Movement and the utopian aspirations of the Occupy Movement over the past decade have now morphed into dangerous movements that feed off of the mob-like dimensions of us-versus-them demagoguery.

These movements are spearheaded by a variety of activist organizations and internet sources representing a multitude of identities and interests (BLM, Antifa, Daily Stormer, RedIce, Infowars, etc.). It is the lack of social cohesion between Americans, not just absurdly intense market competition, which has allowed for the growing problem of potential political violence. This new form of political violence, as exemplified in the Berkeley Campus riots of 2017, the "silencing" efforts against controversial speakers at university campuses such as Charles Murray at Middlebury College, and the racial hatred seen in the violent 2017 Unite the Right Rally in Charlottesville, is fueled by mob anger and exclusionary identity politics. The attempt to constructively address and remedy this problem is one of the greatest cultural challenges faced by moderate conservatives and liberals alike. At the same time, by addressing this issue, some headway can be made toward a reconfigured consensus of values among liberals and conservatives (and even social-democrats): the kind of consensus which America has not seen since the early-post war era.

It is my intention in this chapter to analyze this problem according to the foundational values of classical conservatism articulated by Edmund Burke, and its concern with generational solidarity, on both a political and spiritual level. In essence, the rhetoric of Trump's campaign claimed to reverse the assumed nihilistic effects of American generational solidarity breaking down due to new left social progressivism, as best reflected in the "Make America Great Again" motto. However, the ideological zealotry and populist demagoguery of the Trump platform places it far outside the norms of classical conservatism. For Burke, a political community is cemented by an inter-generational contract of societal care for the purpose of order. He points to a religiously transcendental connection existing among the living, dead and unborn. Burke's generational compact centers itself on cherishing proven civil practices and institutions that maintain both political stability and moral gravity. It is this aspect of Burkean political thought that directly challenges the normative value of the Trump platform, both in its rhetorical promise of revolutionary leadership and the reactionary ideological perspective on historical development.

This chapter will initially explore how Trump's populist rhetoric promotes an idea of politics that exists far outside the classical conservative norms of Burke. Next, the chapter assesses how the alt-right historicist dimension of Trump's electoral platform undermines the Burkean understanding of history's importance to political rule. This will be accomplished through a critique of Steve Bannon's cinematic works on American politics, which both preceded and shaped the Trump election message.[1] Finally, Burke's historically grounded concept of a generational compact will be critically applied to the ideological divide between the new left and alt-right. Throughout this chapter, Burke's thought will be presented as a key prescriptive tool for addressing the divisive ideological forces currently at play in American politics.

THE RHETORIC OF 'SWAMP TALK' IN THE TRUMP PLATFORM AS AN ANTI-BURKEAN APPROACH TO LEADERSHIP

By its very nature, the Trump campaign slogan "Make America Great Again" (MAGA) is centered on historical consciousness. The phrase presents a clear message as to how one should view American history. The slogan praises a past era, rejects the present state of affairs, and promises a better future. The phrase also bemoans a decaying American generational compact through its suggestions surrounding the current day direction of American life. Most importantly, the phrase articulates a populist agenda in explicitly "popularist" terms.[2] The populist dimension of MAGA attempts to address the average American's frustration with the current political climate. The phrase is "popularist" due to its rhetorical simplicity being accessible to any citizen, regardless of their level of civic education. According to Steve Bannon in his 2017 interview with CBS' 60 Minutes, this symbiotic connection between his own populist worldview and Trump's popularist outlook on politics is central to understanding Trump's Presidential campaign.

Bannon stated that he views himself as "populist" because his understanding of phrases like MAGA and "drain the swamp" are centered on a concern for the material needs and conventional mores of America's 'ordinary citizens.' Trump, who, according to Bannon, is an avid reader of Carl Jung, views his approach to political leadership primarily through the need to discuss ideas in a popularist manner[3]: The most important thing is that his message, especially in comparison to other public figures, is always understandable and accessible to all 'ordinary citizens.' Jung saw the human psyche structured by core archetypal ideas and values. Trump is focused on projecting messages that tap into archetypal values and mental images existing throughout the electorate. This stands especially true if these messages include the large voter pool of what Richard Hofstadter once described in *Anti-Intellectualism in American Life* as America's anti-intellectual, but essentially democratic circles. Hence Trump's famous statement during the campaign, "I love the uneducated voter."

It is this mixture of populism and popularism—Bannon's ideological fervor and Trump's demagogic sophistry—that placed the Trump election platform outside the norms of Burkean classical conservatism. Most importantly, the radical populist outlook of Bannon and the Jungian sophistry of Trump's communication methods have created a "revolutionary" approach to American conservatism. On one level, the populism of the Trump platform, in its wish to "drain the swamp" as its main electoral promise, is a direct challenge to Burke's reliance on the continued suste nance of institutional governance through mediated politics On the other level, Trump's popularist rhetoric is focused on breaking down popular political opinion to its lowest common denominator for the egoistic interest of power acquisition. This section will explore the anti-Burkian dimension of both the populist rhetoric behind the phrase "drain the swamp" and the despotic implications of Trump's rhetoric.

The populist phrase "drain the swamp" was eventually translated publicly by Bannon into policy terms as "the deconstruction of the administrative state." This agenda is driven by an ongoing neo-conservative/libertarian struggle against the American welfare-state, e.g. the liberal heritage of the New Deal era. The extent to which Trump may or may not fulfill this agenda is beyond the scope of this chapter. However, there is still a radical dynamic to this rhetorical phrase that places it outside the tenets of classical conservatism, because Bannon sees the Trump Presidency as the first movement toward a new "carte blanche" America. This new America will not only reject social-progressivism as a governing philosophy, but will also void the reforms of the New Deal liberal project.

For Burke, pragmatic reform, rather than radical change, is central to the continued sustenance of any political order. Regardless of the grave problems a society may face because of past policy decisions or entrenched institutional settings, possible solutions are only valid if they balance the value of the existing order with assumed opportunities. As Burke states in the *Reflections on the Revolution in France*:

> I cannot conceive how any man can have brought himself…to consider his country as nothing but *carte blanche*…A disposition to preserve, and ability to improve, taken together would be my standard of a statesman. Everything else is vulgar in the conception, perilous in the execution.[4]

This statement by Burke was directed against the civic republican aspirations of the French Jacobins and English Reformers. However, it is also equally applicable to the populist project of "draining the swamp." As Burke further elaborates in the *Reflections*, radical deconstruction of any institutional setting, despite its failings, puts the overall good of society at risk due to the "long habit" that social actors have developed in their vital relations to these institutions.[5]

With many Trump supporters, classical conservatives would share an equal disdain for the problems of welfare dependency, identity politics centered norms of the new left, and Washington cronyism. Despite that fact, the populist agenda of "draining the swamp" indicates that American right-wing politics under Trump has radically divorced itself from classical conservative values. Welfare-reform is a central point of concern for conservatives, but a radicalized movement to rapidly dismantle the historical legacy of the New Deal for the sake of a rhetorical mission of "draining the swamp" shows itself as highly dangerous. As former CIA official and Treasury Dept. advisor Brian O'Toole has noted, the Trump administration's populist "drain the swamp" approach to the public sector has established a rapid exodus of civil service professionals, and a dearth of aspiring public sector applicants, in needed government work in fields ranging from administrative law and civil engineering to parks/forestry care and intelligence gathering.[6] In the hopes of creating what Burke dismissed as a future "carte blanche" situation for America through the "deconstruction of the administrative state," the populist rhetoric of the Trump platform neglects what Burke described as the "long habits" a citizenry forms with its government for the continued care of the nation.

Even more troubling is the "popularist" nature of Trump's personal approach to political rhetoric. As the *Dilbert* cartoonist Scott Adams noted well before Trump's victory in late 2016, Trump, from the very start of the primaries, was using a very psychologically advanced approach to mass communication centered on simple messaging. These messages appealed to archetypal mental imagery among the citizenry. Most importantly, no matter what Trump said, his phrases and policy proposals were designed to be always memorable and understandable according to the electorate's "universal vocabulary," as something opposed to the "confirmation bias" displayed by Trump's detractors.[7] This idea of a "universal vocabulary" among the American masses is where Bannon's claim that Jung is a huge influence on Trump rings true.

The most Jungian aspect of Trump's rhetoric is in his us-versus-them definition of the Washington establishment as a globalist "swamp." Trump's opponents increasingly tried to demonize his personal character during the election. On the other hand, Trump successfully countered their character attacks with the idea that there were a mass of innocent American citizens under threat from a globalist elite agenda, directed by Washington insiders. Trump's campaign strategy was effective because it directly appealed, in its lowest common denominator form, to the universal value system of what Jung described as the defining characteristic of the "mass man." As Jung states:

> The "average man," who is preponderantly a mass man, acts on the principle of realizing nothing, nor does he need to, because for him the only thing that commits mistakes is that mass anonymity conventionally known as "State"....The mass man...has the privilege of being at all times "not guilty" of the social and political catastrophes in which the whole world is engulfed.[8]

Trump's Jungian understanding of the American electorate is revealed by his effective application of the principle described above to mass communication through carefully chosen but easy-to-understand phrases. It is on this point that one can confirm Trump as a true political genius. The rhetorical notion of a "swamp," or what Jung refers to as the "State," gave moral legitimacy to many Americans to decide to make a reactionary vote for Trump. On the Jungian level, "draining the swamp" is the archetypal wish of all "mass men," especially when it comes to how they feel they could best be relieved from their varied personal problems.

It is also this Jungian approach to political communication that identifies Trump as a possible demagogue opposed to Burkean principles of statesmanship. One of the central concerns that Burke had about revolutionary approaches to politics is that revolutionary leaders desire to shape public opinion through mass social engineering efforts. For Burke, political society was meant to be established through mediated representation, which maintained both the customs of order and the richness of social diversity. As Russell Kirk stated, this core value of Burke is what places him as the modern forefather of classical conservatism, despite himself being an 18th century Whig in an era of "Enlightened" reform.[9] Most importantly, the attempt to break down the electorate into a massive cohesive whole, which can be molded through enforced policy or despotic rhetoric, is anathema to Burke's principle of conservatism. As Burke states about the Jacobin project:

They reduce men to loose counters merely for the sake of simple telling, and not to figures whose power is to arise from their place in the table...they have levelled and crushed together all the orders which they found...all securities to a moderated freedom fall behind it...This is to play a most desperate game.[10]

These phrases from Burke were directed against the revolutionary destruction of the estate system in the French ancien regime. However, the moral quandaries involved in Trump's powerful grasp of modern political communication are equally reflected in Burke's fear of despotically leveling a social order to its lowest common denominator through communication methods centered on the principle of "simple telling." There is no more "simple telling" phrase than MAGA, just as there is no more "leveling together" solution than "drain the swamp." It is exactly this approach to rhetoric that placed the Trump platform radically outside the conventions of classical conservatism. How the rhetoric of the Trump platform found its historical context now needs to be explored.

UNDERSTANDING STEVE BANNON'S APPROACH TO AMERICAN POLITICS: THE COUNTER-CULTURE AND REAGAN REVOLUTION AS THE FOUNDATION OF ALT-RIGHT HISTORICISM

Trump, through his MAGA rhetoric, tapped into the long-standing assumption in contemporary American conservatism that something went horribly wrong for American civilization with the advent of baby-boomer generation values. A good example is Irving Kristol, who influenced American conservative leaders ranging from Ronald Reagan and Newt Gingrich to George W. Bush and Rick Santorum. As Kristol admitted in the early 1980s, if it were not for the tumultuous generational cleavages borne out of the 1960s era counter-culture, and his own revulsion toward their leftist implications, he would have probably remained a liberal Democrat.[11]

The counter-culture represented the beginning of a generational crisis in the American political fabric. Over much more than just simply control of resources or positions of power, the counter-culture represented a major shift in values as to what it means to be an American. By coming of age within an era of unseen material abundance and technological advancement, the American baby boomer generation found itself able to retranslate culture at its core. In essence, civic and religious tradition could be replaced by a new society centered on self-expression and pluralistic progressive-secular change. A fundamental generational continuity links the liberal identity politics of McGovern's 1972 "American Promise" platform and Obama's "Change" slogan of the 2008 Presidential campaign. One should remember that although Obama appealed to younger voters, by being born in the early 1960s, he still stands as a bona fide member of baby boomer leadership. However, as sociologist Michael Brake explains, the counter-culture, which was supposed to replace the early post-war era civic culture, found itself completely dependent on both the consumerism and technocratic comforts of modern industrial life provided by past generations. The plastic artificiality of 1960s era consumerism was replaced with chemically manufactured drugs, holistic medical approaches were promoted in the midst of birth control pill dependency for a freer lifestyle, money was not important because there was an abundance of monetary wealth, etc.[12] The contradictions of the counter-culture, and its dependence on technocratic consumerism, would morph America toward the self-expressive consumerist values of the neo-liberal era.[13] Perhaps the greatest icon of this shift in values during the 1980s was none other than Donald Trump himself.

The Trump Presidency, as reflected in the worldview of Steve Bannon, has tapped directly into the generational tensions born from the counter-culture. Bannon's documentary, *Generation Zero*, centers itself explicitly on the historical transition from the counter-culture to neo-liberalism. Bannon has stated quite forcefully, merely through the film's title, what the letter "Z" really represents for today's emerging youth in their assigned generational category. The whole point behind *Generation Zero* is that the baby boomer generation has, in its hyper-hedonistic live for today values, completely unglued the pre-existing Burkean generational compact for American civilization.

Generation Zero declares that America is moving toward an apocalyptic age during the 21st century. For Bannon, today's youth face an either-or choice, a revolutionary paradigm of life and death survival. This crisis for today's youth has been brought on by the assumed moral degeneracy of a past baby boomer generation (ironically, the generation of Bannon and Trump). In essence, Bannon has transformed the "Act Now" 1960s era slogan of the new left into the "Fight Now" creed of the alt-right. It is this aspect of Bannon's approach to conservatism that places him, and possibly the Trump Presidency, outside the pragmatic and stable tenets of classical Burkean conservatism. Most importantly, when *Generation Zero* is watched in conjunction with Bannon's 2004 film *In the Face of Evil: Reagan's War in Word and Deed ("Face of Evil")*, this apocalyptic scenario in American history is connected to humanity's eternal conflict against the "The Beast." For Bannon, "The Beast" is an entity consistently morphing itself into new political ideologies that threaten American freedom. According to *Face of Evil*, this metaphysical entity ontologically defines the symbolic contours of a now eternal political force determined to destroy American liberty. Indeed, *Face of Evil* argues that "The Beast" disguised itself as communism in the 20th century and has now re-emerged as radical Islamism during the 21st century. Most importantly, Ronald Reagan is presented as a central world-historical figure—as America's premier 20th century 'warrior saint' in the divine struggle against "The Beast" in its Soviet-communist form.

The worldview expressed in Bannon's films is very similar to the World War II era writings of the Italian fascist and occultist Julius Evola. In fact, Bannon personally cited Evola during conferences with the Vatican City.[11] Evola, in his defense of the Axis cause during World War II, argued that Indo-Aryan tradition was centered on two guiding principles. First, all political conflicts and social relations in the material world are mystically symbolic of a very real supernatural struggle between the cosmic forces of light and darkness.[15] Evola's influence within Bannon's cinematic worldview is revealed in the *Face of Evil*. The film presents the 1980s as a time when the 'light side' of history's supernatural forces stand behind Ronald Reagan's spiritual struggle against the politically metamorphic 'dark side' force of "The Beast." Secondly, Evola claims that human excellence is only attained by concretely engaging, through ascetic dedication, in a permanent life and death struggle for spiritual meaning within the material world. Perpetual conflict is undertaken for what the Norse myth of Valhalla deemed the Viking warriors' glory of being subsumed in "celestial fire."

According to Evola, this holy baptism of exclusive immortality for warriors is attained through an ancient Indo-Aryan honor code, which is dedicated to subduing the cosmic "black wolf" that stalks humanity's material world. This spiritualist rite of passage, attained through the celestial fire of honor and ascetic driven armed combat, is the passport to the metaphysical realm of Valhalla (or Brahma, Nirvana, Jannah, etc.). In this ecumenical Valhalla, one has the godlike honor of eternally guarding against the "black wolf" in its pure metaphysical and supernatural form, and one is equally celebrated as a Herculean hero of humanity.[16] Evola presented the Valhalla myth in ecumenical terms that were compatible with the extremist variations of military honor culture found among any specific heritage. Bannon's films present the esoteric outlook developed by Evola according to the neo-conservative narrative of American exceptionalism.

It is the assumed inescapable need to confront the spiritually intangible and mystically vague "black wolf" of the human condition (or "Beast" in Bannon's terms), for the purpose of existential meaning, that places the alt-right dangerously in line with previous far-right authoritarian traditions. Moreover, by assuming to have a complete understanding of the laws of history, Bannon's films also falls into the potential totalitarian pitfalls of historicism and its wizard-like certainty surrounding "right" political action. If there is an invisible force behind history that must always be confronted in a war-like manner by the youth of today, then it is impossible to revere the transcendental connection existing between the generations of a civilization. Customary maintenance of the political order must inevitably take a back seat to perpetual struggle. In the absence of customary stability as an anchor against perpetual strife, the alt-right, like the Jacobins of the 1790s, becomes a nihilistic and potentially destructive force for humanity.

To fully showcase the inherent dangers in this revolutionary approach to conservatism, some historical comparison is necessary. As Jeffrey Tucker states in his description of the alt-right approach to history:

> Whereas libertarianism speaks of individual choice, alt-right theory draws attention to collectives on the move...Each of us only matters when our uniqueness is submerged to a group. This group in turn calls forth a leader. It takes something mighty and ominous like a great leader, an embodiment of one of these great forces, to make a dent in history's narrative.[17]

Bannon's *Generation Zero* presents to the viewer this exact same notion of history. An ominous force in history has ripped apart the Burkean generational compact of America. *Generation Zero* promotes a reactionary perspective on history that subtly calls for a great leader, while never explicitly stating the need for one. It puts the weight on the shoulders of the youth to fully survive the forthcoming "Armageddon" on their own. It attempts to leave the viewer, especially if they are young, wishing that there was a Zarathustra-like leader that can tap into their anxieties under the weight of history and help them regain their lost sense of greatness as Americans.

Now compare Tucker's description of the alt-right approach to history with the following quote about the Nazi approach to history from Utz Ulrich, a curator of the Nuremberg Museum:

> You had to believe you were coming from a very important past and going into a very important future. The whole [regime] was a theatre of memories picked together from whatever was good and interesting for them, forgetting the rest; and they mixed them together in a way never seen before. There was a fascinating cocktail of never-happened history.[18]

I do not quote Ulrich to promote some extremist viewpoint that America is following a path toward of Nazi Germany, nor to make a vulgar comparison between the personal character of President Trump or Mr. Bannon with senior Nazi leaders. However, both Tucker and Ulrich delineate the fundamentally collectivist form of authoritarianism, which subordinates individuality to the conflict-centered dynamics of assumed historical forces. If the patterns of history are known without doubt, dissent against "right action" is both unnecessary and undesirable. Indeed, quashing dissent can appear more as a necessary moral act, rather than as just a desired convenience. By attempting to create a radical prescription against political correctness, the alt-right has, in its historicist trappings, fallen into a shared position of authoritarianism with the far left. Unlike classical conservatism, there is no place for dissenting opinion when one perceives oneself playing an all-stakes game for total control of the political arena.

Bannon, by his own admission, is heavily influenced by the generational cycle interpretation of American history put forth by Neil Howe and Richard Strauss in their book *The Fourth Turning*. This is clearly shown by the extensive interviews of Neil Howe in *Generation Zero*. The questionable accuracy of the Strauss-Howe theory of generational cycles in history is beyond the scope of this chapter. Nor is a debate over whether historicist perspectives are inherently authoritarian within the focus of this chapter.[19] What is important though is that any historicist perspective articulated within the academic fields of history and sociology does have ramifications for how authority is perceived. If one is absolutely certain about how history unfolds, one is certain as to what is the "right action" for authority regardless of pre-existing arrangements within a political community. In many ways, ideological adherence to a historicist world-view implies an inevitable lack of respect for the moral gravity of history itself.

Bannon's film *Generation Zero* does regrettably fall into that trap. Burke's theory of a generational compact recognizes the moral gravity of history, but analyzes that weight as the anchor necessary for stability and civil decency. For the Burkean generational compact, history is a rich resource of wisdom for a people in their political inquiries, not a social-climatological pattern that demands radical or reactionary political leadership. As Mark Lilla states, Burke's idea of history is not one where we are being carried by impersonal forces toward fixed points. Such a mindset can easily be used to justify grave crimes.[20] In Bannon's zeal to "de-construct the administrative state" for the purpose of adapting America to a specific narrative of history, he has fallen into a reaction against 20th century American history similar to what Burke bemoaned regarding the Jacobins and the French ancien regime. One should never forget that despite genuine and well-deserved frustrations with the Washington establishment among working Americans, the Trump promise to "drain the swamp" reflects as much a reaction against historical tradition as what Burke feared about the late 18th century Jacobin left. Liberating society from a particular political setting in the name of a proper and absolutely accurate interpretation of history has been a basis for a multitude of destructive political movements. Like Trump, Jacobins, Soviets, Fascists and Maoists have all promised to "drain the swamp" in their respective polities. At no point in the Burkean generational compact is a "swamp" to be drained. Under the Burkean generational compact, past experiences, whether they stand as successes or failures, are to be the means of cultivating the 'living garden' of a stable constitutional order.

While *Generation Zero* does acknowledge the Burkean generational compact, the film declares this principle as now determinately lost in contemporary America. Furthermore, the historicist perspective of the movie presents a view of American politics in which classical conservative values must inevitably become extinct in the current state of affairs. During his life, Burke confronted the French Jacobins and English Reformers in their zeal to liberate European society from the shackles of history in the name of a better present. For these austere founders of the modern left, this project was pursued in the republican name of attaining a new form of civic virtue, which was centered on the absolute "natural rights" of man. In the early 21st century, we need the Burkean principle of customary adherence to political stability—through an inter-generational reverence of the past—in order to escape the political determinism of a far-right movement directed by a historicist political ideology. Most disturbingly, this ideological outlook may be potentially leading us toward perpetual conflict and chaotic theatrics.

Burke's Generational Compact and the Ideological Divides of the Trump Era

The above section should make it clear that Burke is essential to maintaining the moral vigor of American conservatism. Through Burke's influence, classical conservatism views itself as self-consciously attempting to create working political orders for future generations through a pragmatic retention of proven traditional ways. On the one hand, Burkean political thought exposes prospective weaknesses of the alt-right in failing to properly address the post counter-culture breakdown of the American generational compact. On the other, the general civic inclusivity of Burke's generational compact checks the identity politics obsessed weaknesses of the contemporary Obama era left. Generational tensions over social and political values during the 1960s were the embryonic source of both the alt-right and contemporary radical social-progressivist movements. The demagoguery throughout the contemporary ideological spectrum is predicated on the tensions existing between the so-called alt-right and "social justice warriors." The alt-right recognizes the unraveling of the generational compact but rejects any classical conservative prescription. The social progressivist camp simply dismisses the generational compact as unimportant, or at worse, oppressive. A substantive classical conservative ethos in contemporary America is needed in order to help quell this problem. To make the first steps toward this direction, one needs to more fully examine Burke's theory of a generational compact and how it differs in its virtues from the trappings of both social progressive and alt-right thought.

Any attempt to engage with Burke on a scholarly level is difficult. First, he, like Cicero and Goethe, are enmeshed in their historical context. Their greatness on a philosophical level was matched by extensive practical political experience in matters of historical importance. Burke is not only a central character in the canon of modern conservative thought, but also played a major role in the issues of his time, such as the 'Irish Question,' the American Revolution, the French Revolution and the moral direction of the British Empire in regard to its Asian holdings. He was also a central figure in romanticism through his assessment of the esthetic relationship between beauty and the sublime. As someone who had to politically navigate the major historical events and issues of the late 18th century, a singular coherent doctrine of theoretical thought is difficult to find in the vast archive of his writings and speeches.

Nonetheless, three central characteristics held strong throughout Burke's life and career. First, he showed a keen faith in a certain relationship existing between philosophy and politics. For Burke, argument directs human judgment in matters of philosophy, but judgment in political matters must ultimately refer to the rhetorical strength of moral claims.[21] Unlike the Jacobins, who concerned themselves with transforming the private virtues into a new model of enlightened citizenship, Burke kept focus on the moral questions relating to public policy and political affairs. It is for this reason that the study of history was for Burke integrally entwined with all matters of political inquiry and action. As Burke stated in 1770, "History is a preceptor of prudence."[22] Secondly, if history is the source of prudence, moral principles cannot be discovered exclusively through ahistorical theories of political organization, whether they are legitimized by liberal-utilitarian arguments or appeals to abstracted notions of natural right. Despite Burke's reverence toward the wisdom of history, historiasm has no real place in the Burkean approach to politics. History teaches only inductively. To Burke, history's value—especially in questions of political action—is based on a pragmatic and open-ended discussion of how our understanding of the follies of the past is connected to the potential prosperity of the future. As Stephen Browne has argued, the great error of the academic community in its reading of Burke lies in its wish to simply assess the content of Burke's criticisms of both utility and natural right according to their theoretical implications. For Burke, as modernity's Cicero, political ideas must be assessed and discussed in a manner that avoids the ethical pitfalls of either idealistic principle or amoral expedience.[23] Thirdly, as Leo Strauss has persuasively argued, what distinguishes Burke most fully from the social contract theorists of his Enlightenment era contemporaries was his differing view on the relationship between nature and right. For Burke, history validates the moral stability of civil society, through customary relations, over the anarchic and nihilistic implications of what "rights to survival" actually mean in a 'State of Nature' devoid of civilization. Therefore, the "great primeval contract" maintains civilization and sustains human morality across generations, through the principle of conventional duties, rather than institutional adherence to "natural rights."[24]

Burke's notion of a generational compact through civic duty cements a living "holy covenant" within a political community, because proper morals within a civil society depend on a fundamental religious foundation directed toward stable civic goals. Like the great father of historicism Hegel, Burke asserts the organic totality of society. For Burke, this is based on the fact that every society represents a "partnership in all science; a partnership in all art; a partnership in every virtue, and in all perfection."[25] Unlike Hegel, Burke does not describe this pursuit of perfection in explicitly historicist terms, whereby the ends of politics, art and religion become providentially realized in the rationally determined completion of history. Instead, Burke maintains that there is a permanent sacred oath passing through historical time between all members of a civil society, whether they are dead, alive or unborn. This "contract" is based on a now "eternal society" that connects the "lower and higher natures" of the social order. This principle underlines classical conservatism, in its concern for both stability and preservation, and differentiates it from current day libertarianism, neo-conservatism and alt right reaction.

Unlike the social-progressive call for "CHANGE", or the alt-right/libertarian demand for deconstruction of the administrative state, Burke's generational compact demands that stability and pragmatism, through civil political discussion, be placed above zealous demands for a new order. This stands true whether these demands for extreme political action are expressed in revolutionary or reactionary terms. For example, regarding society's institutions,

> The municipal corporations of that universal kingdom are not morally at liberty at their pleasure...to separate and tear asunder the bands of their subordinate community, and to dissolve it into an unsocial, uncivil, unconnected chaos of elementary principles. It is the first and supreme necessity only, a necessity that is not chosen but chooses, a necessity paramount to deliberation, that admits no discussion, and demands no evidence, which alone can justify a resort to anarchy.[26]

This passage from Burke's *Reflections on the Revolution in France* is central to understanding the driving force behind his moral approach to politics in both practice and theory. It also directly touches upon the major fault-line of the alt-right versus "social justice warrior" dichotomy of Trump era culture wars.

Moreover, Burkean conservatism recognizes that anarchy and despotism inevitably follow from adopting "CHANGE" as the primary moral directive for political leadership. This stands especially true when the abstracted ideal of post-modern era 'social justice' supplants the more classical modern idea of natural right or utility in legitimizing social engineering reforms. There can be little doubt that in the past twenty-five years, the new left has taken on policy ventures that could be seen by many to potentially destabilize markets, governments and especially family units. This has been driven by either non-historical reflection on the abstracted ideal of social justice or unidimensional revisionist narratives about historically produced forms of victimhood. As Mark Lilla has noted in his liberal critique of identity politics and victim narratives, charitable faiths can only be inculcated by notions of duty that integrally connect the "privileged with the disadvantaged."[27] Burke's theory of a generational compact addresses this need for civic unity decried as deficient by Lilla when it comes to the approach of contemporary liberalism. As the 2016 U.S. Presidential Election showed, Burke's prophecy of inevitable anarchic demagoguery in the midst of engineered "CHANGE" has been largely vindicated. The radical social progressivism borne out of the Obama era was by its very nature a direct challenge to the foundational belief system of classical conservatism. The politically righteous fervor for "CHANGE"—or as Canada's current Prime Minister Justin Trudeau so famously said, "Because it's 2015!"—attempted to overturn traditions shared over many generations, thus quickly realizing the anarchy described by Burke.

The trajectory of the French Revolution, from the Tennis Court Oath to the perpetual warfare of the despotic Napoleon Bonaparte, shows how the choice not to honor the generational compact of keeping civil society together quickly reveals its poisonous flower. It was this very loss of America's generational compact in the baby boomer era that enabled the populist forcefulness of the Trump Presidency. It was the self-conscious recognition among many Americans that the generational compact was being permanently lost during the early 21st century which so dramatically raised the ante of the American culture wars during the 2016 U.S. Presidential Election. One of the fundamental reasons that Trump is the current President and not Hillary Clinton is an irony: Despite his non-classical conservative alt-right leanings, Steve Bannon, more than anyone else in the American elite, and especially the Democratic Party establishment, understood that problem for the American people in its concrete Burkean form.

CONCLUSION

Given the rich depth of Burke's political life and thought, this chapter has had to overlook much of Burke's relevance to the current Trump era of American politics. As someone who grappled with both the moral issues of the British Empire and the political turmoil of 18th century Europe, Burke could easily be applied to evaluate Trump's "America First" foreign policy. Burke's discussion of property and luxury are equally essential to thoughtful discussions about the future of specific economic and social policies alongside Bannon's self-acclaimed mission to "deconstruct the administrative state". This chapter focused on the still important issue of how Burke's theory of a generational compact is connected to the dema goguery witnessed in the America's culture wars emerging between the alt-right and "social justice warriors". It has also focused on how this paradigm is central to the ideological forces at play in the electoral campaign of the Trump Presidency. Most importantly, by examining Burke's theory of a generational compact in light of the Trump Presidency, one can fully gauge how far outside the boundaries of classical conservatism is the political scenery of the Trump era. Classical conservatism is fundamental for understanding Trump era politics precisely because its primary tenets are missing from the emerging spectrum of contemporary American conservatism, i.e., between alt-right and libertarian tendencies.

In essence, the alt-right movement is borne out of the neo-conservative recognition that the American generational compact has been dismantled by the counter-culture and its varying effects since the late 1960s. However, the classical conservative tenets of Burkean political thought reject the nihilistic reactions of the alt-right approach to this problem through its historicist approach to political action. Tradition is not a matter of mystical and esoteric identity as the fascists believed. Instead, it is a theologically-grounded "holy" venture centered on pragmatic civic custom and principled political discussion. By the same token, the socially progressive mantra of "CHANGE" borne out of the Obama era is equally susceptible to Burke's historically grounded criticism that there are moral consequences of not honoring a generational compact that has developed over time within a polity. Perhaps the traditions of a society and its cross-generational institutions cannot be validated in mystical terms, but their value to a political order is holy in the sense that they connect the national identity existing between those who live today and those who have or will exist in the passage of history. "CHANGE" is not a directive for institutional and social reform, but rather a cosmic force that must be adapted to pragmatically through custom and compromise. Moreover, Burke's classical conservatism is founded on the principle that neither a revolutionary nor a reactionary approach to history and politics can tolerate dissent. A nation must fall into either anarchy or despotism, as proven by the violent demagoguery currently seen across the ideological spectrum in America's current culture wars.

One of the central problems for American conservatism is that America's republican roots as a revolutionary nation are predicated on natural right. Classical liberalism, rather than the Tory traditionalism found in Britain, Europe and Canada, has been the primary soil for future notions of what it means to be an American conservative.[28] As this chapter has highlighted, Americans, right up to the rise of the counter-culture of the 1960s, did not really have to concern themselves with a generational compact.[29] The civic virtues of American republicanism were simply seen as aligned with a providence that ensured the relative liberty and prosperity found in the 'American Dream.' It is the counter-culture, along with the subsequent rise of neo-conservatism and the new left during the baby boomer era, which has made the question of a generational compact central for American civilization. Trump attained the presidency largely by recognizing this problem and making an alt-right reactionary promise to "Make America Great Again." It is the dwindling presence of classical conservative ideas in the American right, as brought on by the growing prevalence of libertarianism, neo-liberalism and neo-conservatism, which has helped fuel this phenomenon. Classical conservative Americans now have the rare historical opportunity to go back to the drawing board in re-imagining the American generational compact, even if the current political environment appears most dreadful due to the rise of hateful demagogy. Burke's theory of the generational compact, and its essential desire to balance custom with reform, property with social care, and authority with dissent, is a central tool in this monumental task of retrieving conservatism from the pitfalls of alt-right nihilism.

NOTES

1. Mr. Bannon was President Trump's Chief Election Executive and Senior White House Advisor until he resigned from his government post on August 18, 2017.
2. I differentiate between "populism" and "popularism" because Bannon himself says this is the key difference in understanding him from Trump. I will make this distinction clearer in what follows.

3. CBS *60 Minutes,* Sept. 10, 2017.
4. Edmund Burke, *Reflections on the Revolution in France,* Stanford University Press, 2001, p. 328.
5. Ibid., p. 328.
6. Brian O'Toole, "The Danger of Forsaking America's Civil Service", *The Hill,* Sept. 18, 2017.
7. *The Rubin Report,* Interview with Scott Adams, Sept. 1, 2016.
8. Carl Jung, "On the Nature of the Psyche," *The Basic Writings of C.G. Jung,* Modern Library Edition, 1993, p. 100.
9. Russell Kirk, *The Conservative Mind: From Burke to Eliot,* Regnery Publishing Inc., 2001, p. 19.
10. Edmund Burke, pp. 358–9.
11. Walter Goodman, "Irving Kristol: Patron Saint of the New Right", *New York Times,* Dec. 6, 1981.
12. Michael Brake, *Comparative Youth Culture: The Sociology of Youth Cultures and Youth Sub-Cultures in America, Britain and Canada,* Routledge, 1985, p. 94.
13. Thomas Frank, *The Conquest of Cool,* University of Chicago Press, 1998, p. 232.
14. Jason Horowitz, "Steve Bannon Cited Italian Thinker Who Inspired Fascists", *New York Times,* Feb. 10, 2017.
15. Julius Evola, "The Aryan Doctrine of Combat and Victory", *The Metaphysics of War: Battle, Victory and Death in the World of Tradition,* Arktos Media Ltd., 2011, p. 97.
16. Ibid., p. 98.
17. Jeffrey Tucker, "Five Differences Between the Alt-Right and Libertarianism", Foundation of Economic Education, Aug. 26, 2016, https://fee.org/articles/five-differences-between-the-alt-right-and-libertarians/
18. *The Living Dead: On the Desperate Edge of Now* (BBC), 1995.
19. Since Hegel, many historicist works in both philosophy and social research have richly defined the intellectual outlook of the modern era. I am not as keen as someone like Karl Popper, in his two volume work *The Open Society and Its Enemies,* to dismiss all historicist work of political thought as authoritarian at its core.
20. M. Lilla, *The Shipwrecked Mind: On Political Reaction,* New York Review Books, 2016, p. xi.
21. Richard Bourke, *Empire and Revolution: The Political Life of Edmund Burke,* Princeton University Press, 2015, p. 3.
22. Edmund Burke, *Thoughts on the Cause of the Present Discontents,* Project Gutenberg, 1770, http://www.gutenberg.org/files/15043/15043-h/15043-h.htm#Page_433

23. Stephen Browne, *Edmund Burke and the Discourse of Virtue*, University of Alabama Press, 1993, p. 102.
24. Leo Strauss, *Natural Right and History*, University of Chicago Press, 1965, p. 296.
25. Edmund Burke, *Reflections on the Revolution in France*, p. 261.
26. Ibid.
27. Mark Lilla, *The Once and Future Liberal: After Identity Politics*, Harper Press, 2017, p. 126.
28. Patrick Deneen, "Conservatism in America? A Response to Sidorsky," *American Conservatism*, New York University Press, 2016, p. 155.
29. Early post-war conservatives such as Russell Kirk and Richard Weaver did see the 'writing on the wall' when it came to America's generational relations.

BIBLIOGRAPHY

60 Minutes, CBS, September 10, 2017.

Bourke, Richard. 2015. *Empire and Revolution: The Political Life of Edmund Burke*. Princeton: Princeton University Press.

Brake, Michael. 1985. *Comparative Youth Culture: The Sociology of Youth Cultures and Youth Sub-Cultures in America*. Britain and Canada: Routledge.

Browne, Stephen. 1993. *Edmund Burke and the Discourse of Virtue*. Tuscaloosa: University of Alabama Press.

Burke, Edmund. 1770. *Thoughts on the Cause of the Present Discontents*, Project Gutenberg. http://www.gutenberg.org/files/15043/15043-h/15043-h.htm#Page_433.

———. 2001. *Reflections on the Revolution in France*. Stanford: Stanford University Press.

Deneen, Patrick. 2016. Conservatism in America? A Response to Sidorsky. In *American Conservatism*, ed. Sanford Levinson, Joel Parker and Melissa Williams. New York: New York University Press.

Evola, Julius. 2011. The Aryan Doctrine of Combat and Victory. In *The Metaphysics of War: Battle, Victory and Death in the World of Tradition*. Budapest: Arktos Media Ltd.

Frank, Thomas. 1998. *The Conquest of Cool*. Chicago: University of Chicago Press.

Goodman, Walter. 1981. Irving Kristol: Patron Saint of the New Right. *New York Times*, December 6.

Horowitz, Jason. 2017. Steve Bannon Cited Italian Thinker Who Inspired Fascists. *New York Times*, February 10.

Jung, Carl. 1993. On the Nature of the Psyche. In *The Basic Writings of C.G. Jung*, Modern Library Edition.

Kirk, Russell. 2001. *The Conservative Mind: From Burke to Eliot*. Washington, DC: Regnery Publishing Inc.

Lilla, Mark. 2016. *The Shipwrecked Mind: On Political Reaction.* New York: New York Review Books.

———. 2017. *The Once and Future Liberal: After Identity Politics.* New York: Harper Press.

O'Toole, Brian. 2017. The Danger of Forsaking America's Civil Service. *The Hill,* September 18.

Strauss, Leo. 1965. *Natural Right and History.* Chicago: University of Chicago Press.

The Living Dead: On the Desperate Edge of Now (BBC), 1995.

The Rubin Report, Interview with Scott Adams, September 1, 2016.

Tucker, Jeffrey. 2016. *Five Differences Between the Alt-Right and Libertarianism.* Foundation of Economic Education, August 26, 2016, https://fee.org/articles/five-differences-between-the-alt-right-and-libertarians/.

CHAPTER 12

The Aim of Every Political Constitution: The American Founders and the Election of Trump

Zachary K. German, Robert J. Burton,
and Michael P. Zuckert

The election of Donald Trump was an exceptional political event; few observers anticipated he could be successful in the Republican primaries, and even fewer expected him to triumph in the general election. As a result, his unforeseen electoral success generated a widespread examination of how his election came about and, for many, how it might have been otherwise. In the process, the Electoral College (EC) has once again been subject to increased scrutiny.[1]

In *Federalist* 57, James Madison wrote, "The aim of every political constitution is, or ought to be, first, to obtain for rulers men who possess most wisdom to discern, and most virtue to pursue, the common good of the society."[2] Alexander Hamilton was particularly confident that the delegates at the Constitutional Convention had achieved that aim with respect to the election of the president. The EC, he argued, "affords a moral certainty,

Z. K. German (✉)
Arizona State University, Tempe, AZ, USA

R. J. Burton • M. P. Zuckert
University of Notre Dame, South Bend, IN, USA

© The Author(s) 2018
M. B. Sable, A. J. Torres (eds.), *Trump and Political Philosophy*,
https://doi.org/10.1007/978-3-319-74427-8_12

215

that the office of president will seldom fall to the lot of any man who is not in an eminent degree endowed with the requisite qualifications"—indeed, "that there will be a constant probability of seeing the station filled by characters preeminent for ability and virtue."[3] As he wrote these words, Hamilton no doubt had statesmen like George Washington on his mind.

In the wake of the 2016 election cycle and the ultimate election of Donald Trump, many observers have failed to share Hamilton's "moral certainty" with respect to the EC. In fact, the EC's critics allege that it is undemocratic, that it is obsolete and/or pernicious, that it never had a good justification and never was more than an unprincipled concession.[4] The *New York Times'* editorial board captures much of this discontent by highlighting the fact that "a Wyoming resident's vote counts 3.6 times as much as a Californian's."[5] John Koza, the chair of NationalPopularVote.com, contends that there are other undemocratic effects of the EC in our contemporary politics—that the EC has led to the existence of a select few "battleground states," which receive outsized attention during presidential campaigns and disproportionate government perks between elections.[6] In short, the EC appears to represent a compromise with "our most fundamental political beliefs."[7]

The EC's contemporary advocates, for their part, worry about the drawbacks of a national popular vote. They frequently make the case, for instance, that the EC's formula for disproportionate representation ensures that rural, less populated areas maintain a meaningful voice in the federal government, circumventing the tyranny of the coasts and cities.[8] Allen Guelzo and James Hulme situate this defense of the EC in the context of federalism, writing that the EC "made a place for the states as well as the people in electing the president by giving them a say at different points in a federal process and preventing big-city populations from dominating the election of a president."[9] In other words, the EC promotes the election of truly *national* rather than strictly *majoritarian* chief executives; as Jeffrey Anderson explains, a successful presidential candidate "must appeal to the nation as a whole."[10]

Both sides of the debate tend to bypass how the EC was originally designed to function. The framers intended the EC to serve primarily as an intermediary body that channeled the sentiments of the people into the selection of a qualified candidate for president. As such, it was just one concrete manifestation of their broader theory of republicanism, one which sought republican remedies to counter dangers inherent in republican liberty. Notwithstanding the framers' original vision, the EC was soon supplanted by the arrival of the party system, but that development did not leave the selection of the president in an institutional vacuum. Rather, to varying degrees, American political parties themselves played (at least partially) the role initially assigned to the EC, functioning as mediating forces between rank-and-file party members and presidential nominees for nearly two centuries.

In 2016, however, both major parties displayed an incapacity to fulfill this mediating role effectually. Though the Democrats were finally able to nominate Hillary Clinton, party leaders struggled to combat the unendorsed and underfunded campaign of Bernie Sanders. On the other side, Republican leaders, almost without exception, opposed Trump and rallied around the sentiment, "Anybody but Trump." Yet Trump capitalized on a divided field, a disgruntled electorate, and an endless supply of free media. By the time of the Republican National Convention, party leaders lacked the ability to oppose Trump's nomination in any way that voters would have accepted as legitimate. Though convention delegates still technically controlled the nominating process, in practice the party was left with little recourse to avoid a candidate they perceived as toxic to the party's short- and long-term success. Whatever one's assessment of the merits of Sanders and Trump as presidential candidates, the unfolding of the 2016 election evinces the failure of the major parties to continue their function as truly mediating bodies in the choice of their presidential nominees. We argue that this failure is largely due to the changes in the nominating process that began in the Progressive Era and were brought to fruition in the Reform Era of the 1970s.[11] We discuss the unfolding of those changes below, but we also seek to revive an understanding of the original design and purpose of the EC and, more generally, the role of mediating bodies in facilitating a thriving and sustainable republic. In so doing, we hope to provide a reminder of the enduring thesis that the dangers inherent in republicanism require creative republican remedies.

THE ORIGINAL DESIGN AND EVOLUTION OF THE ELECTORAL COLLEGE

In order to assess the EC in its different historical forms, it is important to disaggregate its various features so that we can determine which characteristics are responsible for the blame (and praise) that it garners. Adopted as part of the original Constitution, the EC allowed each state to appoint a certain number of "electors" equal to the total number of its representatives (members of the House and Senate) in Congress. These electors could not be federal officeholders, guarding the separation of powers by ensuring that those who chose the president were not already members of the federal government. Electors would cast their votes for president in their respective states as a means of fostering deliberation and preventing collusion.

The constitutional method of casting and counting electoral votes was somewhat mind-boggling, but deliberately designed. Each elector cast two votes, one of which could not be for a candidate from their own state, to encourage the rise of more nationally representative candidates. The candidate with the most votes above a certain threshold (the threshold being a majority of the number of electors, not a majority of the electoral votes) became president. However, because each elector had two votes, it was possible that more than one candidate could pass the threshold and reach a tie. In such a scenario, the House of Representatives, voting as state delegations (with one vote per state), would decide between tied candidates.[12] If no candidate managed to pass the threshold, the House would vote in the same manner, choosing from among the five candidates with the most votes. The candidate with the second most electoral votes became vice president.

However, after the turbulent election of 1800, the Founding generation amended this process through the Twelfth Amendment. This amendment created separate elections for president and vice president, with one of each elector's two votes being cast for each office. By cutting the total number of votes for president in half, the amendment eliminated the possibility that more than one candidate could pass the threshold of a majority of electors and thus decreased the likelihood that an election would be thrown to the House. Since ratification of the Twelfth Amendment, only the election of 1824 has been decided by the House.

The foregoing explanation constitutes the entirety of the *constitutionally* instituted system for presidential selection.[13] However, an extra-constitutional element of the EC dubbed the "unit rule" has become one of the EC's defining elements, in great measure because of the criticism it has garnered. Between the Constitution's ratification and the election of 1824, states experimented with their constitutional prerogative of selecting electors, some opting for selection by state legislatures, while others put electors to the ballot, either in winner-take-all statewide elections or in proportional electoral districts. However, as the Federalist and Democratic-Republican parties emerged, majorities in state legislatures sought to solidify their party's strength in the EC by requiring that *all* of a state's electoral votes go to the candidate with the largest plurality (a "winner-take-all" system), a policy now known as the "unit rule."[14] By the election of 1820, an equal number of states chose electors through statewide elections as through state legislatures.[15]

Noting this trend, Madison expressed his disapproval of the unit rule and considered it to be contrary to the intent of the delegates at the Constitutional Convention of 1787, contending that "the district mode [as opposed to statewide "unit rule" elections] was mostly, if not exclusively in view when the Constitution was framed and adopted."[16] The unit rule had gained prominence only because, once adopted by some states, no state wished to be left behind, making its adoption "the only expedient for baffling the policy of the particular States which had set the example." Madison even proposed a constitutional amendment to remedy the problem, yet by 1838, all states except South Carolina implemented the unit rule. As of 2017, only two states—Nebraska and Maine—depart from the unit rule, employing a form of electoral districts instead.

The widespread implementation of the unit rule is largely responsible for criticism of the EC, due to its facilitation of counter-majoritarian outcomes. Because there is no meaningful difference between winning a state by a single vote and winning by a large margin, the unit rule rewards campaign strategies (or luck) that capture some states by close margins and lose others in landslides. Thus, we just witnessed Donald Trump triumph nationally in a context in which he won a crucial state like Michigan by less than 11,000 votes (for a plurality of 47.25%), while losing California by more than 4,200,000 votes (with only 31.49%).[17]

One implication of this counter-majoritarian dynamic is that votes in safe states are "worth less" or "count less" than those in swing states, in the sense that superfluous votes seem not to have any meaningful impact on the electoral outcome. But if the superfluity of these votes is foreseeable prior to Election Day, we might expect voter turnout to be depressed in non-competitive elections, affecting down-ballot races and popular vote tallies in the process. Moreover, if voters lack the motivation to participate in their own states' non-competitive elections, presidential candidates lack incentive to pay them any attention. The unit rule is thus responsible for the phenomenon of "battleground states." To make this point clear, imagine, for a moment, that states allotted electoral votes according to the proportion of the popular vote, rather than according to the unit rule. In that case, winning a close contest in a battleground state would be mostly symbolic: a bare plurality or majority of votes would only yield a bare plurality or majority of electoral votes. Consequently, the minimal benefit of nail-biting victories would entail that battleground states, as a meaningful category for campaign strategy, would cease to exist. With the unit rule firmly in place, however, battleground states receive intensive campaign and media attention, and some argue that they continue to receive disproportionate consideration throughout the ordinary operations of the government.[18]

In short, however compelling one finds the blame laid at the EC's feet, the EC, as originally designed, is not culpable for much of the blame that has been attributed to it, which would be more accurately leveled against the unit rule introduced later. The misattribution of that blame has regrettably led to the neglect, among both its defenders and detractors, of the main purpose of the EC -that electors, using their individual judgment, would function as a filtration device for the will of the people. While Trump's election has drawn attention to the unit rule's operation, it also highlights the present day EC's departure from its original purpose.[19]

THE ELECTORAL COLLEGE AND THE FEDERALIST THEORY OF REPUBLICANISM

To fully understand the EC and the filtering effect the Founders created it to perform, one must first come to terms with their theory of representation and republicanism more generally. While they considered a republican government founded on the people's consent to be the only legitimate form of government, their historical analysis convinced them that republics had a terrible track record with regard to both political stability and the protection of liberty. Since they valued not only republican legitimacy but also other governmental qualities, as Herbert Storing explains, "the great architectural principle of the American government ... is precisely that responsiveness to public opinion is a necessary but *not* a sufficient condition of good government."[20] Thus, the framers' constitutional challenge amounted to the quest for republican cures to republican diseases. If they failed in that quest, Hamilton concludes that "the enlightened friends of liberty" would have to abandon all hope for republicanism. Fortunately, "[t]he science of politics ... has received great improvement," enabling the American people to apply those scientific advances to the challenges inherent in republicanism.[21]

One of those challenges, as Madison explains in *Federalist* 37, is that the various qualities of good governance are sometimes in tension with one another. While one institutional mechanism may be productive of one quality, it may be counterproductive of another. In that vein, while provisions characteristic of direct democracy may be conducive to republican liberty or "safety," they tend not to cultivate other essential governmental qualities, such as energy, stability, and wisdom. Put differently, the people, when directly and frequently involved in making political decisions, including the selection of their leaders, do not always make the right decisions or choose the right people for the right jobs.

Questioning the people's competency for direct, active participation first requires one to acknowledge, as the Founders did, an essential difference between political legitimacy and political right: a legitimate government requires the consent of the people, yet those same people may, at times, desire that which is imprudent or unjust. If political legitimacy and political right are not always the same, then we may anticipate occasions when what is right must prevail over the people's immediate desires and when statesmanship calls for more than simply conveying or enforcing those desires. The uneasy relationship between legitimacy and right is central to Madison's discussion of faction in *Federalist* 10, where the liberty of the people, though the only legitimate foundation for a government, is "to faction, what air is to fire" and, if not refined by an extended, *representative* republic, will fail to protect "the public good and the rights of other citizens."[22] The Founders' theory of republicanism thus acknowledged the sovereignty of the people, while seeking to *filter* or *channel* that sovereignty through representatives who could respect and ultimately answer to the people, but also exercise independent judgment in pursuit of right and prudent policies. In other words, the Founders wished to incorporate the "input" of popular consent and participation while at the same time generating the "output" of good government.[23]

The Founders were able to create a system that reconciled legitimacy and right, in part, because of their precise conception of republican legitimacy. Direct participation by the people and the straightforward reflection of their immediate will were not mandated by the principle of republicanism to which the Founders were both practically and normatively bound. As Madison defined a republic, "It is essential to such a government, that it be derived from the great body of the society, not from an inconsiderable proportion, or a favoured class of it ... It is sufficient for such a government, that persons administering it be appointed, either directly or indirectly, by the people," with either limited or indefinite tenures of good behavior.[24] The sufficient condition left the framers ample space to devise creative remedies for the ills of republican government. Thus, they staggered terms of office ranging from two years for members of the House to tenures of good behavior for the Supreme Court. State legislatures selected U.S. senators prior to the ratification of the Seventeenth Amendment, and presidents still appoint Supreme Court justices, with the advice and consent of the Senate. In the case of the presidency, the Founders sought to create an intermediary body that could overcome the people's shortcomings in presidential selection, while remaining grounded upon their consent.

The task was to design an arrangement which would ensure that the chief executive would possess the requisite qualities for good executive governance. They considered a national popular vote for the presidency, but, in addition to practical concerns revolving around the suffrage of slave and non-slave states, they doubted the people's capacity to choose the type of person who could be a genuinely national leader. They worried that the people would be attracted to local and regional favorites, rather than national statesmen, and they suspected that the people would lack the knowledge and discernment to determine who those statesmen were. Thus, though they expected that the extended republic would exert its salutary influence on a national popular vote, they were not persuaded to leave presidential elections directly in the hands of the people.

The institutional answer upon which they settled did not exclude the people from the electoral process altogether, but added an additional step to the process, instituting a temporary, intermediary body that would filter or channel the people's wishes toward a qualified candidate for president. Although the Founders doubted the people's capacity to choose a chief executive well, they believed that they could select individuals who, themselves, would have the knowledge and character to choose good national leaders. In other words, the Founders believed that the involvement of a uniquely situated, uniquely informed political class was both conducive to and necessary for the selection of a chief executive.

The EC was intended to be the institutional mechanism by which to guarantee the vital participation of that political class. In contrast to many of the Constitution's other institutional innovations, Hamilton begins *Federalist 68* by observing that it "is almost the only part of the system, of any consequence, which has escaped without severe censure, or which has received the slightest mark of approbation from its opponents."[25] The EC warrants this gentle treatment from the Constitution's virulent opponents, in Hamilton's estimation, for "it unites in an eminent degree all the advantages, the union of which was to be wished for."[26]

Those advantages are, according to Hamilton, five in number: first, the EC gauges "the sense of the people"—that is, it meets the baseline criteria of republicanism. Second, it leaves the ultimate decision to "wise electors," those "most likely to possess the information and discernment" to select a qualified president. Third, it promotes the tranquility and stability of society by avoiding the upheaval of a popular election. Fourth, it avoids the corruption, including that of foreign influence, that might infect a preexisting body charged with electing the chief executive. Finally, it secures presidential independence by eschewing reliance upon a permanent body like Congress; a president "might otherwise be tempted to sacrifice his duty to his complaisance for those whose favour was necessary to the duration of his official consequence."[27]

Each advantage and its absence in our contemporary electoral system relate in some way to concerns about the 2016 election. Hamilton places the last two in contrast to some of the proposals prominent during the Convention that would have allowed Congress to elect the president and vice president in ordinary, rather than exceptional, circumstances. Since these alternatives are beyond the realm of our contemporary discourse, we might pass over this point without further comment. However, given our current political context, we would be remiss not to note how Hamilton's analysis is applicable to the role of political parties in presidential elections. Jeopardizing the salutary independence that Hamilton praises, presidents may feel just as beholden to political parties as they would be to Congress, for they owe much to those parties for their election (and aspirations for reelection).

The first advantage of the EC that Hamilton mentions is that "the sense of the people [would] operate in the choice of the person to whom so important a trust was to be confided."[28] The American people would not suffer a hereditary monarch, and other modes of election would run the risk of allowing a political establishment to choose someone contrary to or with little regard to the sense of the people. The EC was not intended to defy the people's will; instead, the electors would serve to filter or channel popular sentiments—they would, like the extended republic generally, "refine and enlarge the public views," not ignore or repudiate them.[29] The people would choose their electors, with the understanding that those electors would deliberate and exhibit independent judgment in their choice, while nevertheless taking account of the "sense of the people." Their judgment would not thwart the public will, but embody it, as a constitutional manifestation of filtration. In other words, the point is not to reject the people's choice but to regulate their role in the process of selection, thereby allowing for the refinement of their views. As a result, what Madison argues in *Federalist* 10 is applicable to the EC: "it may well happen that the public voice, pronounced by the representatives of the people, will be more consonant to the public good, than if pronounced by the people themselves."[30]

Madison's statement captures the second advantage of the EC, that the selection of a president will be better when made "by men most capable of analyzing the qualities adapted to the station, and acting under circumstances favourable to deliberation, and to a judicious combination of all the reasons and inducements that were proper to govern their choice."[31] It is often noted (though not always followed) that judges ought to be indirectly appointed, because their offices require a special set of skills, knowledge, and character; but it is less often recognized that Hamilton advances an analogous argument for the presidency. The extensive electoral district, coupled with the mediation of electors, would constitute a double-layered filtration device that would foster sound political judgment in the selection of presidents.

Some scholars argue that more pressing concerns than the desire for such filtration drove the framers' adoption of the Electoral College as their ultimate method of presidential selection.[32] They were much more preoccupied, so the argument goes, with the potential re-eligibility of the executive and his independence from Congress, the distribution of electoral influence between states of different sizes and regions, and the improbability that the people would coalesce around national figures. Of course, these considerations are not incompatible with a concern for mediation. Indeed, they underline to some extent the filtration function of the EC. For instance, while the delegates ultimately concluded that the need for presidential independence rendered election by Congress inadvisable, Jack Rakove explains that election by Congress "had the advantage of placing the decision in the nation's most knowledgeable leaders."[33] The EC presented an alternative that jeopardized neither the executive's qualifications nor his independence. Likewise, whereas the delegates anticipated that, due to citizens' partial knowledge and the states' partial interests, direct election by the people would lead to a competition among local favorites, the EC increased the likelihood that more "continental" figures might be selected.

Finally, Hamilton refers to one more advantage that is particularly salient in the wake of the divisive 2016 presidential campaign and its restless aftermath. "It was also peculiarly desirable," he observes, "to afford as little opportunity as possible to tumult and disorder." Long prior to the gradual expansion of executive power, Hamilton foresaw that civil unrest "was not least to be dreaded in the election of a magistrate, who was to have so important an agency in the administration of the government." He detected a distinctly democratic phenomenon that Alexis de Tocqueville observed firsthand in America forty years later, whereby society is convulsed by the momentous event of a presidential election. Tocqueville describes the scene as follows:

> As the election approaches, intrigues become more active, agitation more lively and more widespread. Citizens divide into several camps, each of which takes the name of its candidate. The entire nation falls into a feverish state; the election is then the daily text of public papers, the subject of particular conversations, the goal of all reasoning, the object of all thoughts, the sole interest of the present.[34]

Tocqueville considered this spectacle to be "a cause of agitation, not of ruin."[35] Hamilton, on the other hand, worried about the consistent historical example of tumultuous democracies, was understandably predisposed to circumvent any social upheavals that he could. Thus, he praised the cooling effect of the EC: "The choice of *several*, to form an intermediate body of electors, will be much less apt to convulse the community, with any extraordinary or violent movements, than the choice of *one*, who was himself to be the final object of the public wishes."[36] By placing an extra link in the chain of decision-making, Hamilton anticipated that the people would be less incited throughout the process and less incensed by its conclusion. In the heat of our present political climate, such a cooling effect would be deeply desirable, but the EC, as should now be clear, no longer plays the role that was initially envisioned for it.

THE RISE AND DECLINE OF PARTIES AS FILTERING MECHANISMS IN PRESIDENTIAL SELECTION[37]

Despite the Founders' efforts at "reflection and choice" in constitutional design, it appears that, at least in terms of presidential selection, "accident and force" quickly got the better of them. Some of the filtering role the

Founders originally assigned to the EC quickly shifted from the EC to the major political parties in the decades following the Constitution's ratification. However, due to electoral reforms undertaken in the Progressive Era and again in the 1960s and 70s, what filtering power parties possessed has continued to weaken, resulting, by the 2016 election, in both Democratic and Republican parties that struggled to control their nominating processes. In defining "party," we, like V.O. Key, Jr., differentiate between (a) the party in government, (b) the party organization, and (c) the party in the electorate.[38] When we say that a "party" acts as a filtering mechanism, we must distinguish between the elected officials of a particular party, the state or national party organization, and citizens who identify themselves as party members.

The Founders, including those who created the first political parties in America, were averse to the notion of political parties. This was, in part, because they associated contesting parties not only with different policy views, but with alternative visions of "the way in which society and government should be ordered."[39] Ceaser rightly notes that, having just decided on a form of government, the Founders were right to be cautious about divisive political parties associated with regime change: allowing permanent party competition "would mean legitimizing a continual struggle between different views about the very foundation of the political order."[40] However, by 1796, Jefferson, Madison, and others who supported a smaller national government were convinced that dangers posed by Hamilton's nationalist and commercialist policies were tantamount to a constitutional crisis. In what they believed was a necessary and temporary expedient, the Founders began dividing themselves into political parties.

The new parties' primary goal was to elect likeminded candidates to Congress and the presidency, and they did so by working at both the state and national levels. In the states, the parties exercised influence over who would be selected as electors. As more states instituted statewide elections and enforced the unit rule, delegates became bound to particular candidates and the electoral votes of whole states were allocated to the party's nominee. At the national level, the party in government—those affiliated with the party in Congress or the executive branch—gathered in what became known as "caucuses" to settle on a particular presidential nominee and throw their collective support behind him. The dominance of the caucus in presidential selection from about 1800–1828 has been termed the "Congressional Caucus System."[41] By controlling who could be nominated through the caucus and by exercising influence on the selection of electors at the state level, the parties essentially wrested the filtering role in presidential selection from the EC. Party caucuses, not electors, began filtering candidates based on their electability, appeal, and abilities.

However, the Congressional Caucus System was only able to perform certain parts of the five advantages Hamilton had ascribed to the EC. First, while parties may approximate the "sense of the people" through information shared by congressional representatives and through the "party in the electorate" as manifest in the local and state party organizations, because of parties' partisan nature, they are only interested in the "sense" of a particular group of people: their supporters and those they think will realistically become supporters. They have no incentive to gauge the "sense" of the other party's loyal patrons and, in some instances, may simply focus on "energizing" their supportive base and ignore swing voters altogether. Thus, parties can only partially claim to understand and represent the "sense of the people." More importantly however, the parties' domination of the EC institutionalized partisanship as part of the presidential selection process, something the Founders sought to institutionally discourage by making the EC a temporary political body whose "transient existence" and "detached situation" made political allegiances and corruption more difficult and less likely.[42]

Next, while those in congressional caucuses may have possessed the wisdom, information, and discernment originally expected from electors, the Congressional Caucus System undermined Hamilton's fifth advantage: preserving presidential independence. If Congress chooses the presidential candidates, the separation of powers Madison and others had so assiduously crafted at the Convention would be compromised. Thus, while the party system and congressional caucuses began performing, if imperfectly, at least part of the filtering functions the Founders originally assigned to the EC, many Founders and other political leaders thought it an unwanted development. Madison even proposed a constitutional amendment that would have eliminated the unit rule and pulled power in presidential selection away from Congress.[43] However, the amendment process proved unsuccessful, and with the creation of the Democratic Party under Andrew Jackson in 1832 and the Whig Party in 1834, the two-party system we know today was firmly established.[44]

1832 also witnessed an early manifestation of what would become a steady march toward greater openness and democratization in the American electoral system: as part of their anti-corruption and anti-establishment campaign, Jacksonian Democrats replaced the "corrupt" Caucus System of the previous decades with what has been termed the "Pure Convention System."[45] This new system, with presidential nominees chosen by delegates at party conventions, arguably did a better (although still partisan) job of "gauging the sense of the people," due to the mix of delegate and elite influence in the selection process. In addition, because power was diffused among the relatively larger group of convention delegates in contrast to the congressional caucus, conventions made parties less susceptible to corruption and foreign influence. At the very least, the convention system went a long way toward ensuring the independence of the presidency from another permanent political body, such as Congress. Finally, because the convention system largely mirrored the structure of the EC (delegates were sent to a convention for the purpose of candidate selection), it would seem plausible that convention delegates would likewise have the information, discernment, and wisdom the Founders ascribed to electors. The main difference between the original concept of the EC and the Convention System was, once again, the latter's partisan nature. However, once political parties became firmly entrenched in the American political system, the Convention System may have been the most workable alternative to the EC.

Notwithstanding their partisanship, party leaders shared a number of incentives which, though not synonymous with the Founders' purposes for the EC, were at least related to them. While leaders sought to elect a president partial to their views, they needed a candidate with sufficiently broad appeal to win a general election. They also faced, as institutions with a long-term political vision, the necessity of maintaining a successful party "brand" across time. These political realities, frequently combined with genuine concern for the country's welfare, incentivized party leaders to "filter" in favor of more qualified candidates.

Party leaders were able to filter candidates in a variety of ways. They could provide their preferred candidate with organizational support, coordinated endorsements, and information distribution. By organizing at the state level, parties could push for electors who favored the candidate of their choice. Once at the convention, multiple rounds of voting permitted party leaders to negotiate among the various factions. Throughout the 1800s and early 1900s, parties employed their control of vast numbers of patronage jobs to develop support for particular candidates.

By means of conventions, party leaders continued to act as filters in presidential selection until the rise of the Progressives in the early decades of the 20th century. The Progressives sought to purify politics of "corrupting" influences, including the inside negotiations that often occurred among party leaders at conventions.[46] In particular, Progressives campaigned to replace conventions with a more open and democratic "primary" system which, by having all party members cast ballots to elect their party's nominee, pulled the power of presidential selection away from party leaders (both in government and in the party organization) and toward the party in the electorate. At least in theory, the primary system would thus eliminate the party leadership's filtering role altogether. Primaries would also incentivize presidential aspirants to appeal directly to the people for support through personal electoral mandates, furthering the Progressives' goal of a "powerful president" who could "command public opinion and galvanize it to make the government act with greater energy."[47]

However, the Progressives were only partially successful in their attempt to reform the electoral system in an open and democratic direction. Party organizations still wielded significant influence at conventions, though it was more "checked" and "constrained."[48] Primaries provided some elected delegates who were bound to support a particular nominee and, at a minimum, provided evidence of a candidate's electoral appeal.[49] This "Mixed System" constituted an uneasy but effective balance between the leadership-driven Convention System and pure primary system advocated by Progressives. It was arguably less subject to corruption and influence than the Pure Convention System and certainly less so than the Congressional Caucus System. Yet it still left much decision-making to party leadership and, inasmuch as some delegates were not bound to a particular candidate, it provided space for the filtration function the Founders originally assigned to the EC.

Yet as the 20th century progressed, parties felt more pressure to "democratize." By the 1968 Democratic Convention, demonstrators protested against the lack of democratic openness and some delegates called for "complete direct democracy and for a national primary."[50] To examine these grievances, the party created the influential "McGovern-Fraser Commission," which eventually recommended a series of rules regarding the process of selecting delegates and essentially institutionalized a direct, democratic nomination vote.[51] The number of primaries increased significantly and delegate selection procedures were regularized and nationalized. Republicans soon followed in adopting many of the same reforms. Although both parties continued to tinker with their nominating systems and even adopted some less democratic elements a decade later (such as the Democrats' adoption of "superdelegates" in the 1980s), the democratization effect of the 1960s and 70s Party Reform Era has continued to the present day.

CONCLUSION

The innovations of the Progressive and Party Reform Eras certainly intended to increase the electoral system's ability to "gauge the sense of the people": the more a selection process approaches direct democracy, the more synonymous it will be with the people's "sense."[52] Yet whatever its merits in gauging the people's sense, the reforms obviated the parties' institutional ability to filter potential nominees, as both the Democratic and Republican 2016 primaries demonstrated. One could argue that although the Reform Era policies hollowed out the parties' *institutional* ability to filter candidates, both parties in the 1980s reacted to the hollowing of the progressive trade by centralizing their fundraising and organizational capacities, giving themselves *de facto* leverage in candidate selection. However, although there is evidence that the "money primary" (a candidate's fundraising ability) and "endorsement primary" (endorsements by prominent party leaders) have been good indicators of success in past presidential primaries, the 2016 election strongly suggests the limited capacity and effectiveness of these "soft" filtering abilities.

Examples of weakened filtering power appeared in both parties. Though Bernie Sanders was eventually able to raise comparable amounts of money as Clinton in the Democratic primary, he did so while receiving endorsements from only a handful of representatives and one senator, while Clinton's endorsements numbered over 100.[53] In the Republican primary, Trump spent less than forty-five percent of what was spent by rivals Ted Cruz and Jeb Bush.[54] Instead, he made the most of various forms of "free" media, such as social networking sites and cable news.[55] Neither was Trump's success contingent upon his performance in the "endorsement primary." While many Republican leaders failed to utilize the influence of their formal support, Trump nevertheless overcame the disadvantage that he faced from the few endorsements that he received.[56] During the primary season, he obtained the endorsement of only a single U.S. senator, Jeff Sessions of Alabama, and that endorsement was not announced until February 27, 2016.[57] When he had essentially wrapped up the nomination, Trump had garnered the endorsements of a mere handful of U.S. representatives and governors, all of which came either just days before or sometime after Sessions' endorsement. Trump's lack of support from party leaders stood in striking contrast to his primary opponents and, even more so, the precedents of past party nominees. Indeed, this was just one more manifestation of his anti-establishment brand. Trump's example indicates that the parties' already "soft" power may be softening further.

Though the party reforms never *guaranteed* the election of a Trump-like candidate, a lack of institutional checks on the people's passions left the republic much more susceptible to someone largely immune to parties' tempering power. While parties tried to compensate for their weakened influence through enhanced fundraising and influence coordination, the 2016 primaries in both parties manifest these efforts' impotence when confronting a frustrated and impassioned electorate. Yet weakened filtering institutions will cause no concern unless one accepts the Founders' fundamental principle that, although they are intimately connected, political legitimacy and political right are not synonymous. On the other hand, if one is open to the idea that democratic might does not necessarily make political right, then one may also wish to consider the role of institutional arrangements, including in the presidential selection process, that incentivize wise and judicious people to seek political leadership, provide a space for political leaders to exercise independent moral and political judgment and, as a result, provide some filtering or refining of the public views. Doing so does not deny the legitimacy of republicanism, what we today call democracy. Rather, if the Founders were correct in assessing the dangers republican liberty can present both to republicanism and to liberty, then the friends of liberty and republicanism ought to take the role of mediating institutions very seriously indeed.

NOTES

1. This is by no means the first time the EC has come under assault. Shlomo Slonim observes that "[c]lose to seven hundred proposals to amend the Electoral College scheme have been introduced into Congress since the Constitution was inaugurated in 1789." Shlomo Slonim, "Designing the Electoral College," in *Inventing the American Presidency*, ed. Thomas E. Cronin (Lawrence: University Press of Kansas, 1989), 33.
2. James Madison, "*Federalist* No. 57," in *The Federalist*, ed. George W. Carey and James McClellan, The Gideon Edition (Indianapolis: Liberty Fund, 2001), 295. All subsequent references to *The Federalist* are to this edition.

3. Alexander Hamilton, "*Federalist* No. 68," 354.

4. These general themes of critique are not new, as the debates in the 1970s, which spurred Martin Diamond's response, demonstrate, yet they arose with acute intensity in 2016–17. See Martin Diamond, *The Electoral College and the American Idea of Democracy* (Washington, DC: American Enterprise Institute for Public Policy Research, 1977).

5. The Editorial Board, "Time to End the Electoral College," *New York Times*. 19 December 2016. NYTimes.com. Web. Accessed 22 Sept. 2017.

6. John Koza, "Adopt Our Plan for a Popular Vote," *USA Today*. 10 November 2016. USAToday.com. Web. Accessed 22 Sept. 2017; and John Koza, "At the Next Presidential Election, the Popular Vote Must Win Out," *The Guardian*. 10 November 2016. TheGuardian.com. Web. Accessed 22 Sept. 2017.

7. Andrew Treen "The Electoral College Is No Way to Show Off Democracy," *USA Today*. 14 November 2016. USAToday.com. Web. Accessed 22 Sept. 2017.

8. See, for example, Larry P Arnn, "The Electoral College Is Anything But Outdated," *Wall Street Journal*. 14 November 2016. WSJ.com. Web. Accessed 22 Sept. 2017. See also Editorial Board, "The 'Excellent' Electoral College," *Wall Street Journal*. 14 November 2016. WSJ.com. Web. Accessed 22 Sept. 2017.

9. Allen Guelzo and James Hulme, "In Defense of the Electoral College," *The Washington Post*. 15 November 2016. WashingtonPost.com. Web. Accessed 22 Sept. 2017.

10. Jeffrey Anderson, "The Founders Knew What They Were Doing with the Electoral College," *The Weekly Standard*. 27 December 2016. WeeklyStandard.com. Web. Accessed 22 Sept. 2017.

11. Of course, one could also point to cultural and technological changes, the distinctive 2016 political climate, or even, more fundamentally, the pervasive egalitarian ethos in America that Alexis de Tocqueville described so well. In the 1970s, James Ceaser was already discussing the way that changes in communication technology altered the character of presidential elections in a way that the Founders did not anticipate. See James Ceaser, *Presidential Selection* (Princeton: Princeton University Press, 1979), 68.

12. James Madison admitted that the outsized role of states in breaking a tie and in selecting the president when no candidate received a majority was "an accomodation [sic] to the anxiety of the smaller States for their sovereign equality." See James Madison to George Hay, August 23, 1823, in *The Papers of James Madison*, Retirement Series, vol. 3 (1 March 1823–24 February 1826), ed. David B. Mattern et al. (Charlottesville: University of Virginia Press, 2016), 108.

13. The Twentieth Amendment superseded part of the Twelfth Amendment dealing with presidential succession, including the possibility that Congress fails to elect a candidate when the vote has been thrown to them, but it does not alter the nature of the EC.
14. Thomas E. Cronin, "Forward," in Judith Best, *The Choice of the People?: Debating the Electoral College.* (Lanham, MD: Rowman & Littlefield, 1996), xii.
15. John L. Moore, ed., Congressional Quarterly's Guide to U.S. Elections, 2nd ed. (Washington, DC: Congressional Quarterly, Inc., 1985), 254–56.
16. Madison to Hay, August 23, 1823, 109.
17. David Leip, "2016 Presidential General Election Data," *US Election Atlas.* uselectionatlas.org. Web. Accessed 25 July 2017.
18. To be clear, the unit rule does not have uniformly negative consequences: It seems to reinforce the federal nature of the system as a whole, and it tempers the influence of particularly partisan or ideological states. It is also worth noting that the unit rule is not the only potentially counter-majoritarian feature of the EC. The original formula for representation was disproportionate by design. However, this original disproportionality was rather modest, while the unit rule exacerbates its counter-majoritarian potential.
19. The original EC still faces another common charge—that it derived from a desire to protect the institution of slavery and is morally contemptible for that reason. By indirectly incorporating the Three-Fifths Clause into the formula for apportioning electors, the EC provided slave states with a disproportionate role in the selection of the president. This arrangement no doubt pleased some citizens of slaveholding states; however, this effect was not the main intent of the EC. To suggest otherwise requires one to dismiss the set of reasons they offered for rejecting alternative proposals, the reasons why they found the Electoral College favorable, and the compatibility between those reasons and their broader understanding of republican government and representation. A fuller response to this charge, unfortunately, is not possible within the constraints of this essay.
20. Herbert J. Storing, "In Defense of the Electoral College," in *Toward a More Perfect Union: Writings of Herbert J. Storing*, ed. Joseph M. Bessette (Washington, DC: AEI Press, 1995), 396.
21. Alexander Hamilton, "*Federalist* No. 9," 38.
22. James Madison, "*Federalist* No. 10," 43.
23. Storing, "In Defense of the Electoral College," 397–98.
24. James Madison, "*Federalist* No. 39," 194.
25. Hamilton, "*Federalist* No. 68," 351. Hamilton is not dissembling here. For how little the EC was an item of debate during the ratification strug-

gle, see, for instance, Forrest McDonald, *The American Presidency: An Intellectual History* (Lawrence: University Press of Kansas, 1994), 182–208; and Jack N. Rakove, *Original Meanings: Politics and Ideas in the Making of the Constitution* (New York: A.A. Knopf, 1996), 244–87.

26. Hamilton, "*Federalist* No. 68," 352.
27. Ibid., 352–53.
28. Ibid., 352.
29. Madison, "*Federalist* No. 10," 46.
30. Ibid.
31. Hamilton, "*Federalist* No. 68," 352.
32. See, for instance, Diamond, *The Electoral College and the American Idea of Democracy*; Slonim, "Designing the Electoral College"; and James P. Pfiffner and Jason Hartke, "The Electoral College and the Framers' Distrust of Democracy," *White House Studies* 3, no. 3 (2003): 261–71.
33. Rakove, *Original Meanings*, 259.
34. Alexis de Tocqueville, *Democracy in America*, trans. and ed. Harvey C. Mansfield and Delba Winthrop (Chicago: University of Chicago Press, 2000), I.1.8, 127.
35. Ibid., 124.
36. Hamilton, "*Federalist* No. 68," 352.
37. Particularly in this section, we wish to acknowledge our debt to the work of James W. Ceaser. One of the purposes of this essay is to bring Ceaser's work in *Presidential Selection* (1979) and *Reforming the Reforms* (1982) up to the 2016 election.
38. Marjorie Randon Hershey, *Party Politics in America*, 16th ed. (Pearson: Boston, 2015), 6.
39. Ceaser, *Presidential Selection*, 91.
40. Ibid.
41. See Hershey, *Party Politics in America*, 132; and James W. Ceaser, *Reforming the Reforms: A Critical Analysis of the Presidential Selection Process* (Cambridge, MA: Ballinger, 1982), 14.
42. Hamilton, "*Federalist* No. 68," 353.
43. Madison to Hay, August 23, 1823, 110. Madison's proposed amendment was as follows: "The Electors to be chosen by districts, not more than two by any one district; and the arrangement of the districts not to be alterable within the period of——previous to the election of President. Each Elector to give two votes: one naming his first choice, the other his next choice. If there be a majority of all the votes on the first list for the same person, he, of course to be President: if not, and there be a majority (which may well happen) on the other list for the same person, he then to be the final choice: if there be no such majority on either list, then a choice to be

made by joint ballot of the two Houses of Congress, from the two names
having the greatest number of votes on the two lists taken together."
44. Hershey, *Party Politics in America*, 18.
45. Ceaser, *Reforming the Reforms*, 11.
46. Hershey, *Party Politics in America*, 19–20; and Ceaser, *Reforming the Reforms*, 22–23.
47. Ceaser, *Reforming the Reforms*, 23.
48. Ibid., 27.
49. Ibid.
50. Ibid., 6, 31.
51. Hershey, *Party Politics in America*, 78; and Ceaser, *Reforming the Reforms*, 7.
52. Whether it, in fact, gauges the people's sense more rigorously is debatable. A sort of perverse filtering still characterizes primary elections. Primaries attract a disproportionate number of activists from the parties' ideological extremes. Extremely low voter turnout in primaries means that, in a two-party system, a fraction of largely activist citizens choose the final two candidates. In 2016, for example, just nine percent of Americans and fourteen percent of eligible voters voted for either Hillary Clinton or Donald Trump as nominees. See Alicia Parlapiano and Adam Pearce, "Only 9% of America Chose Trump and Clinton as the Nominees." *New York Times*, 1 Aug. 2016. NYTimes.com. Accessed 27 July 2017.
53. Aaron Bycoffe, "The Endorsement Primary." FiveThirtyEight.com. Updated 7 June 2016. Web. Accessed 22 Sept. 2017.
54. "Which Presidential Candidates are Winning the Money Race?" *New York Times*. 22 June 2016. NYTimes.com. Web. Accessed 19 Sept. 2017.
55. Nicholas Confessore and Karen Yourish, "$2 Billion Worth of Free Media for Donald Trump," *New York Times*. 15 March 2016. NYTimes.com. Web. Accessed 21 Sept. 2017.
56. Bycoffe, "The Endorsement Primary"; Aaron Bycoffe, "A Huge Number of GOP Leaders Aren't Endorsing This Year," FiveThirtyEight.com. 15 April 2016. Web. Accessed 21 Sept. 2017.
57. Eli Stokols, "Sen. Jeff Sessions endorses Trump," Politico.com. 28 February 2016. Web. Accessed 21 Sept. 2017.

Bibliography

Ceaser, James W. 1979. *Presidential Selection*. Princeton: Princeton University Press.
———. 1982. *Reforming the Reforms: A Critical Analysis of the Presidential Selection Process*. Cambridge, MA: Ballinger.

Cronin, Thomas E. 1996. Forward. In *The Choice of the People?: Debating the Electoral College*, ed. Judith Best. Lanham: Rowman & Littlefield.

Diamond, Martin. 1977. *The Electoral College and the American Idea of Democracy.* Washington, DC: American Enterprise Institute for Public Policy Research.

Hamilton, Alexander, James Madison, and John Jay. 2001. *The Federalist*, ed. George W. Carey and James McClellan. The Gideon Edition. Indianapolis: Liberty Fund.

Hershey, Marjorie Randon. 2015. *Party Politics in America.* 16th ed. Boston: Pearson.

Madison, James. 2016. Letter to George Hay, August 23, 1823. In *The Papers of James Madison*, Retirement Series, Vol. 3 (1 March 1823–24 February 1826), ed. David B. Mattern et al. Charlottesville: University of Virginia Press.

McDonald, Forrest. 1994. *The American Presidency: An Intellectual History.* Lawrence: University Press of Kansas.

Moore, John L., ed. 1985. *Congressional Quarterly's Guide to U.S. Elections.* 2nd ed. Washington, DC: Congressional Quarterly, Inc..

Pfiffner, James P., and Jason Hartke. 2003. The Electoral College and the Framers' Distrust of Democracy. *White House Studies* 3 (3): 261–271.

Rakove, Jack N. 1996. *Original Meanings: Politics and Ideas in the Making of the Constitution.* New York: A.A. Knopf.

Slonim, Shlomo. 1989. Designing the Electoral College. In *Inventing the American Presidency*, ed. Thomas E. Cronin, 33–60. Lawrence: University Press of Kansas.

Storing, Herbert J. 1995. In Defense of the Electoral College. In *Toward a More Perfect Union: Writings of Herbert J. Storing*, ed. Joseph M. Bessette, 395–402. Washington, DC: AEI Press.

Tocqueville, Alexis de. 2000. *Democracy in America.* Trans. and Ed. Harvey C. Mansfield and Delba Winthrop. Chicago: University of Chicago Press.

CHAPTER 13

Tocqueville's Great Party Politics and the Election of Donald Trump

Jean M. Yarbrough

The mere thought of this elegant French aristocrat reflecting on the election of Donald J. Trump is enough to make the head spin. Alexis de Tocqueville, who visited the United States in 1831 when Andrew Jackson was president, was appalled by the "vulgarity and mediocrity" of American politics even then. After meeting Jackson, Tocqueville concluded that the low tone of American society started at the top.[1] As a general matter, Tocqueville wondered why the best men did not go into politics in democracies, and why a democratic people might not chose them if they did (DA, 188–190).[2] But the elevation of this uncouth Indian fighter to the highest office in the land raised these questions to a whole new level.

Trying to account for Jackson's rise, Tocqueville attributed it to his victory in the Battle of New Orleans, which he thought demonstrated the powerful influence that military glory exerted on the spirit of a people. Even a nation as commercial and unwarlike, indeed "prosaic," as the United States could be dazzled by the general's triumph in battle, and a minor battle at that. In Tocqueville's estimation, Jackson was "a man of violent character and middling capacity…"(DA, 265). Worse, he seemed to have no talent for politics: he rode "roughshod over his personal

J. M. Yarbrough (✉)
Bowdoin College, Brunswick, ME, USA

© The Author(s) 2018
M. B. Sable, A. J. Torres (eds.), *Trump and Political Philosophy*,
https://doi.org/10.1007/978-3-319-74427-8_13

237

enemies" in a way no president had hitherto done and treated members of Congress with "almost insulting disdain." (DA, 378). "[N]othing in all the course of his career had ever proved that he had the requisite qualities to govern a free people: so the majority of the enlightened classes of the Union had always been opposed to him."(DA, 265).

If this is what Tocqueville was willing to say publicly about Andrew Jackson, imagine what his first impressions of President Trump might be. Donald Trump, real estate mogul, host of "The Apprentice," owner of beauty pageants and backer of "WrestleMania," among other louche enterprises, would seem to confirm how even more debased the standards of the American people had become. And indeed, this is exactly what most members of today's enlightened class, even on the Republican side, seemed to think when, against all odds, he cinched the nomination for President. Donald Trump made history of a certain kind as the first man ever to run for President of the United States who had never before held any elective office, had not served in the military, and had thrice married beauty queens. His detractors were unanimous: Donald Trump was not a serious man, perhaps not even a decent man and, at least as important, he threatened to take the Republican held Senate and possibly even the House down with him. "Never Trump" became a badge of honor for the wise men and women of the Republican establishment, which some stalwarts refused to give up even after his surprise victory. Democrats saw the Republican response and raised it, vowing to "resist" the new president, as if their actions were comparable to the Resistance in Nazi occupied France.[3]

Yet putting aside for the moment Trump's demagoguery, his questionable character (he was hardly alone in these qualities), and his scant, or at least highly unusual, qualifications for office, Trump campaigned on issues that had a Tocquevillean resonance. To put it another way, Tocqueville highlighted certain dangers to democratic liberty and greatness that Donald Trump, it is safe to say, never having read a word of *Democracy in America,* instinctively seized on to battle his way to victory. Let me suggest four.

NATIONAL IDENTITY

Start with the most obvious—and contentious: Trump's campaign cry to build a wall to stop the flow of illegal immigration from Mexico into the United States. His proposal was met with criticism from within his own party, many of whose business interests favored cheap labor, and from Democrats, who looked to an influx of poor immigrants to boost their electoral prospects. Although there was undeniably something demagogic in Trump's rhetoric, the ideas behind it were eminently sensible: nations need secure borders and a strong sense of national identity. Citizenship, especially in a democratic republic, is too important to be held hostage to narrow commercial interests or crude electoral calculations. In so doing, Trump spoke to the long-range interest of American citizens in remaining free or what Tocqueville called their "self-interest well understood" (DA, 515).

To be sure, America had since its beginnings been a nation of immigrants, but most of these settlers had come from Great Britain. Tocqueville acknowledged this fact when he referred to the inhabitants of the United States as "Anglo-Americans," distinguishing them from both the French and the Spanish in the New World. The Anglo-Americans were largely Protestant, highly individualistic, acquisitive, and self-governing. Whatever their regional differences, they brought with them a heritage of political rights and entrepreneurial energy that set them apart from the European settlers to their north and south, giving them a distinct national identity (DA, 358).

Traversing the arc of French settlements from Quebec to New Orleans, Tocqueville was struck by the persistent differences in its people. The French in the New World continued to prize strong family connections and "love of one's birthplace," while the Anglo-Americans were far more enterprising, willing to pull up stakes in pursuit of their own fortunes (DA, 268, 272). In contrast to both, the Spanish were moved by ambition to maintain their armies and to fight among each other (DA, 293). For them, pride mattered more than the love of wealth and self-government or the quiet charms of domestic life. These differences in mores (*mœurs*) produced very different political communities. Looking ahead, Tocqueville predicted that French culture in America would gradually decline, and the New World would be left with only two rival civilizations: "the Spanish and the English" (DA, 392). In the great match up between culture and creed, Tocqueville put more weight on the side of culture or "homogeneity in the civilization" (DA, 158), paying scant attention to the universal principles announced in the Declaration.[4] It was not mankind as such who risked their lives, their fortunes, and their sacred honor, but a particular band of Anglo-Americans long schooled in the arts of self-government. Americans can be forgiven for wanting to hold on to their distinctive language and political culture; in short, for celebrating the Fourth of July and not El Cinco de Mayo.

Nevertheless, Americans also believed that the rights they proclaimed in the Declaration were the Creator's gift to all men. Accordingly, as the

United States expanded in size, America embarked on a great experiment, opening its doors to many different races and ethnic groups, at first from Europe, but eventually from Asia, Africa, and the Middle East as well, with the express goal of assimilating them to the American way of life. In this sense, all immigrants would become "Anglo-Americans" by adopting their political principles. In Abraham Lincoln's words, the principles of the Declaration were the "electric cord" that bound all patriotic and liberty-loving Americans together.[5]

Today, the whole project of assimilation, which once seemed so generous and welcoming (despite periodic opposition), has come under sustained attack. Multiculturalists reject the idea that immigrants should give up their native cultures, which they regard as authentic and perhaps even superior to the American way of life (even if they have to dial back their rhetoric on this last)[6]; globalists reject the idea of the nation-state and argue that peoples have an unlimited right to emigrate wherever they choose. Activists protest against the use of the term "illegal" immigrant, insisting on the more benign "undocumented" or "unauthorized."[7] Opposition is met with cries of "racism" and "xenophobia," even as many Americans worry that their distinctive way of life is slipping away, at least in the sense that unlimited and illegal immigration endangers property rights in the Southwest and threatens job opportunities elsewhere, to name but two of the prominent objections. During his campaign, Trump seized on these anxieties to reaffirm his commitment to secure borders and to preserving America's national identity. At the same time, he remained open in principle to immigrants from all nations. His foremost criterion was that the people who came here had to love America and not wish to do it harm. "Bad hombres," whether from south of the border or elsewhere, were not welcome. A sovereign country not only had the right to control its borders, but also to deport those who were living here illegally. Beyond that, he seemed to imply that loving America meant adapting to its ways. Tocqueville, who was struck by the distinctive American love of country, would not have been surprised by Trump's full-throated patriotism and its appeal to his enthusiastic supporters (DA, 226–227). Conversely, he would surely have been dismayed by the tendency of Trump's critics to champion such abstract ideas as multiculturalism and globalization, so deadly to the concrete love of liberty he most prized (DA, 415–416). This has certainly been the rallying cry of the modern day Tocquevillean, Pierre Manent, whose writings warn against the erosion of the European nation-state and with it the decay of political life.[8]

It is also worth recalling that for Tocqueville, national identity was very much bound up with religion, which in the United States (as in Europe) meant Christianity. *Democracy in America* addressed itself to the democratic revolution that was spreading across "the Christian universe," and considered what this would mean for "Christians in our day" (DA, 6). In contrast to Europe, especially France, where lovers of freedom regarded religion as their enemy, Americans had so conflated "the spirit of religion" and "the spirit of freedom" that it was impossible for them to conceive of one without the other (DA, 43). Tocqueville believed the Americans were right: "Despotism can do without faith, but freedom cannot." Religion is much more necessary in republics, "and in democratic republics more than all others" (DA, 282). Although the religions Americans embrace today are more diverse than the Christian sects Tocqueville discussed, the dividing line between people who view religion as a benign influence and those who do not has become more pronounced than ever.

As in much else, Democrats in the election of 2016 had moved much closer to the European understanding of the relation between freedom and religion, regarding Christianity in particular as an adversary, if not an outright enemy of freedom (DA, 287). At the Democratic Convention, party leaders removed all mention of God from the party platform, and a voice vote on the floor of the convention over whether to restore the reference to God erupted in boos. It was also the Democrats who subordinated the religious beliefs of the Little Sisters of the Poor to feminists' concerns about the availability of contraceptives in government run health insurance plans and compelled conservative Christian businesses to provide their services for gay weddings.

Ironically, it was Donald Trump, the twice divorced, lapsed Presbyterian, who took up the cause of beleaguered Christians, reaching out to Evangelical and Catholic leaders alike. (His daughter Ivanka had converted to Orthodox Judaism when she married, so that base was also covered.) Astonished Democrats could not believe that these devout Christians could be so easily taken in by a politician who did not even know how to cite Scripture properly and who seemed far more at home on the golf course than in church on Sunday mornings.[9] But these priests and pastors were less concerned with Trump's religious convictions than they were with his promise to stand up for them in their battles against the forces of secularism. He embraced their causes and promised to appoint conservatives to the Supreme Court who would protect their religious liberty. That was good enough for them. Here again, it is hard to see how Tocqueville could fault him, except for not setting a better example (DA, 282, 521).

Given that Tocqueville's audience was Christian Europe, it is difficult to know what he would have made of the current influx of immigrants into Europe and the United States from the non-Christian world. Tocqueville took the great religions of the world seriously, paying special attention to the ways in which they influenced politics and national identity. In preparation for his first trip to Algeria in 1840, he noted two salient facts about Islam: first, it "had war as its purpose," and second, it failed to separate mosque and state, making the Koran the "common source for religious and civil law, and even lay science...,"[10] It goes without saying that when "radical Islamic terrorism" is added to this mix, a phrase candidate Trump insisted upon using, it made sense to scrutinize individuals from countries that posed the greatest risks. Apart from the bumbling way in which the Trump administration first implemented its "extreme vetting" measures, it is difficult to see what fault Tocqueville, who served briefly as Foreign Minister in the short lived Second French Republic, would find in taking prudent precautions to ensure the safety and liberties of American citizens. The role of the lower federal courts and activist lawyers in thwarting these legitimate executive actions would surely have dismayed him (DA, 93–98, 142, 254–258).

GREAT PARTIES I: TAKING ON THE ADMINISTRATIVE STATE

In *Democracy in America* Tocqueville famously distinguished between "great parties," and "small parties." Great parties are "more attached to principles than to their consequences; to generalities, and not to particular cases; to ideas, not to men." As such, they generally have "nobler features, more general passions, more real convictions, and a franker and bolder aspect than others." Although selfish considerations are never completely absent in great parties, they generally hide themselves "under the veil of the public interest." By contrast, "small parties" are less elevated or concerned with noble objects; they are more selfish and coarse in their aims, debasing society by the search for profits, but never actually overthrowing it (DA, 167). In short, they seek to advance their economic interests without regard to larger, more disinterested objects of national concern.

According to Tocqueville, America once had great parties at the time of the founding. These were not as violent as those that shook France during its Revolution, but they "touched on immaterial interests of the first order": how far to extend popular power in the name of equality and independence. Although Tocqueville regarded the appearance of the Federalist Party as "one of the most fortunate events that accompanied the birth of the great American Union," (DA, 168) that party had, by the time of the Frenchman's visit, fallen victim to the inevitable triumph of democracy. With the tariff of 1828 and the nullification struggle as a backdrop, Tocqueville claimed that the parties that threaten the Union "rest not on principles, but on material interests." Great parties did, of course, reappear during the Civil War, during the heyday of the New Deal, and for a time with the Reagan Revolution. It is worth considering whether the campaign of Donald Trump has summoned them, however chaotically, once more into being.

Another of Trump's campaign promises was that he would "drain the swamp," by which he meant seriously scale back the administrative state that had risen up alongside America's three constitutional branches of government. The Framers of the United States Constitution had envisioned an administrative apparatus that would function as an arm of a politically accountable and limited federal government. But in an effort to extend the democratic principle, Andrew Jackson instituted the "spoils system," which rewarded his democratic supporters with government jobs. Jackson's move, in turn, led to charges of political corruption and incompetence, accompanied by calls for civil service reform. Backers of reform argued such measures accorded with the Framers' intentions, which made merit rather than political patronage the criterion for government positions.

In the post-Civil War era, however, civil service reform became entangled with a related, but very different, idea of administration that had far-reaching consequences. Americans who undertook post-graduate studies abroad (mostly) in German universities became enthralled with the German state theory. Reading Hegel, they became convinced that impartial civil servants would be *better able* to make and execute public policies than elected lawmakers. American legislators were simply too in thrall to local interests and too stymied by the Constitution's checks and balances to pursue the public good. Administrative rule promised to overcome both of these defects by relying on neutral experts, whose agencies would operate free of the separation of powers and federalism.[11]

Over the last century, the administrative state has continued to expand its reach, so that most of American public policy today is formulated by unelected and unaccountable bureaucrats promulgating administrative rules and regulations that have the force of law. What makes these edicts particularly dangerous is that the same agencies that make these rules also execute and judge them. This concentration of legislative, executive, and judicial power is, as Jefferson warned and James Madison agreed, "precisely the very definition of despotic government."[12] It is incompatible with America's constitutional design.

The rise of the administrative state thus undermines the power of the people to govern themselves and accustoms them to being ruled by faceless and unaccountable bureaucrats. In his chapter, "What Kind of Despotism Democratic Nations Have to Fear," Tocqueville famously predicted that democratic governments would centralize administrative power and use it to exercise greater control over their citizens, presumably for their own good. He imagined an "immense tutelary power," looming over a "crowd of like and equal men," each pursuing his own "small and vulgar pleasures." This power would be "absolute, detailed, regular, far-seeing, and mild. It would resemble paternal power if, like that, it had for its object to prepare men for manhood," but instead it aims "to keep them fixed irrevocably in childhood," enjoying their innocent pleasures. To keep them safe and secure, it smothers them in "a network of small, complicated painstaking, uniform rules," which in time reduces them to "a herd of timid and industrious animals of which the government is the shepherd" (DA, 663). Nothing could be more fatal to liberty and to republican self-government than this benevolent despotism, which removes the need to think, and becomes "absolute master" of each man's freedom and life (DA, 88).

As is clear from his discussion in *The Old Regime and the Revolution in France*, the country Tocqueville had in mind when he penned these warnings was France, where the Revolution did nothing to reverse the centuries old drive for centralization begun under the Old Regime. Indeed, as Phillip Hamburger has recently argued, the administrative state so beloved by Progressives, far from being a modern development, is really a throwback to the extralegal prerogative powers enjoyed by English monarchs and their continental counterparts in the Age of Absolutism.[13]

The Declaration of Independence threw off the yoke of despotic rule,[14] while the Constitution dispersed political power and subjected the executive to the rule of law. Tocqueville took special pains to explain this complex federal system to his countrymen and to distinguish between a desirable centralization of governmental powers and an equally beneficial decentralization of administrative powers, especially in the New England townships. These townships, unknown in modern France, testified to the Americans' "mature and reflective taste for freedom" (DA, 67). The federal pyramid, grounded on direct democracy, reached upward through the states to the national government. Thus, Tocqueville could write of the federal arrangement that it combined the advantages of the small republic with those of the large, distributing to each powers appropriate to their competency (DA, 150–154). However admirable, this diffusion of power did not last, undone by new economic conditions, but more importantly, by a new theory of administrative rule.

Starting with the Progressives, then moving on to the New Deal, and finally accelerating with the super-regulatory agencies in the 1970s, the United States has built up a powerful administrative state that has drawn to itself powers historically exercised by the people and their elected officials.[15] In so doing, it has undermined its own traditions of republican self-government, while installing a ruling elite that is unelected and unaccountable to ordinary citizens. Donald Trump understood these frustrations and gave voice to them. He promised to roll back intrusive regulations by executive order. To that end, he took on the powerful educational bureaucracy and called for more parental choice in the education of their children, especially in America's inner cities. He offered hope that the Obama era expansion of Title IX regulations affecting educational institutions receiving federal funds would be scaled back. He pledged to rein in the Environmental Protection Agency's ever-expanding regulatory powers. He vowed to reverse environmental regulations that were hampering energy independence and economic growth. In the international arena, he promised to take a hard look at the Paris Climate Accords, which imposed onerous new obligations on the United States, entered into by the executive branch alone, without the advice and consent of the Senate. He also promised to roll back financial regulations that were impeding the economic recovery, and to appoint conservative judges to the federal courts, especially to the Supreme Court. In pledging to nominate a worthy successor to Justice Scalia, President Trump made good on this important promise. He appointed and got confirmed a justice who appears even more willing than Justice Scalia to reconsider the proper role of the administrative state in the constitutional order. Once in office, he took on the intelligence agencies, firing the head of the F.B.I., and attacking former national security officials for their partisan manipulation of intelligence. By his outspoken, sometimes outrageous tweeting, he called out the "fake news" fed by entrenched partisan bureaucrats and former officials to an oppositional mainstream media.[16] In addition to rolling back the Obama regulatory regime, Trump also promised to work with Congress to enact legislation that would expand individual freedom. Chief among these was his promise to repeal and replace the Affordable Care Act, which with its spiraling costs and failing markets, was driving health insurance inexorably toward the single payer system favored by the left. In short, Donald Trump reignited a great party debate over the proper role of the administrative state in the American constitutional order. At stake was something more fundamental than material interests; it was the capacity of the people to govern themselves both directly and through their elected and accountable representatives.

GREAT PARTIES II: LIBERAL DEMOCRACY VERSUS EUROPEAN-STYLE SOCIAL DEMOCRACY

Not only did Donald Trump promise, in the words of his advisor Steve Bannon, to "deconstruct the administrative state" (sometimes ominously referred to as "the deep state" for its ability to obstruct and impede challenges to its power), but he also took on the activist left-wing of the Democratic Party that was pushing the country toward a European-style social democracy. The signs were troubling. Among the young, support for the one-time Socialist, Bernie Sanders, exceeded that of Hillary Clinton; for the first time, a majority of Americans under the age of thirty expressed a more favorable view of socialism than of capitalism.[17]

In *Democracy in America*, Tocqueville observed that although democratic peoples professed a sincere love for liberty, he worried that they would come to love equality even more (DA, 479). The "sublime pleasures" of freedom can only be understood in the long term and only by those disposed to enjoy them, whereas the "charms of equality" are immediately evident and "within reach of all" (DA, 481). What's more, given the choice between a "manly and legitimate equality" that inspires citizens to try to raise themselves up and a "depraved equality" that attempts to pull the strong down to the level of the weak, he feared that democrats (especially in continental Europe) would be sorely tempted by "equality in servitude" (DA, 52). But how far would this go? In *Democracy in America*, Tocqueville seemed uncertain. On the one hand, he speculated that "great revolutions," meaning revolutions rooted in great principles, would become more rare. In democratic ages, he thought, most inhabitants had become property holders, which made them unlikely to risk losing what they had. Attachment to their property would thus discourage them from entertaining new intellectual and political ideas, whatever these might be. Ambition would rarely reach great heights. Individuals might nibble at change around the edges, but society itself would become fixed and immobile, "so that the human race will stop and limit itself; that the mind will fold and refold itself around itself eternally without producing new ideas..." (DA, 617). In such passages, Tocqueville seemed to be flirting with his own version of the end of history.

Yet Tocqueville also saw that equality is not a static notion; it has a dynamic of its own. Whereas most men will be satisfied with a certain level of freedom, they will never be satisfied with their present degree of equality. In fact the more equal conditions become, the more the remaining inequalities will offend them, and the more "insatiable" their desire for an even greater equality will become (DA, 513). By the end of 1847, with revolution in the air, Tocqueville returned to this thought: was there another act still to be played out in the great democratic drama? Although the first stage of the French Revolution had abolished aristocratic social privileges, it left the right to property intact. Property owners should not, however, labor under any illusions about their situation: "they should not imagine that property rights are an unconquerable fortress because it has not yet been breached." These rights were the last surviving remnant of an aristocratic order; as such, they were, and remain, vulnerable to destructive democratic passions, especially envy. The looming political struggle, he predicted, will now be "between the haves and the have nots. Property will be the great battlefield, and the great political questions will be about how to change property rights and to what extent," to which he added in the *Recollections,* "Then we shall again see great public agitations and great political parties."[18]

It is true that by socialism Tocqueville had in mind something akin to the violent class struggle Karl Marx called for in his *Communist Manifesto,* published just in time for the revolutions of 1848. The challenge America now faces is more subtle. Democratic socialism does not advocate the violent overthrow of liberal democracy or the abolition private property rights. Rather, it envisions a gradual and peaceful transformation to a more egalitarian society with generous economic entitlements, brought about by high levels of taxation and the redistribution of wealth.

This idea is not exactly new in the United States; it can be traced back to the Progressive Era and later to the New Deal, both of which called for a new social contract between the people and government that would put in place policies akin to those in the European welfare states. Unlike in Europe, however, American mores have historically militated against democratic socialism. The Declaration of Independence proclaims that the purpose of government is "to secure these rights," not to promote greater economic equality. As Tocqueville noted, Americans have always been energetic and liberty-loving. As a people, they are less willing to surrender their individual rights to a distant centralized government (and this applies especially to Trump's supporters, who worry about what their children are taught in school, as well as environmental regulations that threaten their livelihood, to mention but two examples). They take property rights seriously, and are less concerned with income inequality at the top than with holding onto what they have and doing with it what they want. They are animated less by envy than by anger that they are losing control over their lives (DA, 298).

But all this may be changing—because the culture is changing, has in fact already changed, and politics is "downstream" from culture (DA, 295).[19] As the recent polling mentioned above suggests, an entire generation of young Americans has been poorly educated in the political principles that have made America both free and great. Starting in elementary school, they have been fed a steady diet of left-wing propaganda that focuses solely or disproportionately on the country's failings, especially its economic and racial inequalities, while painting in glowing colors the achievements of democratic socialism.[20] This view is then reinforced by the cultural elites in the news media, the academy, the law schools, and the entertainment industry, all of which lean strongly left.

What's more, the culture has changed in other important ways as well, reinforcing the millennials' slide toward socialism. Our immigration policies favor family reunification over job skills, requiring more economic assistance for an increasing number of immigrants. Add to that the growing number of children born in recent decades to unmarried mothers who depend on government programs to stand in for absent fathers. Finally, the increase in able-bodied adults who have dropped out of the workforce since the Great Recession and are collecting some form of public assistance increases the pressure to keep benefits flowing. In some sense, these are all economic issues, but Donald Trump sought to elevate them to "great party" cultural issues by empowering individuals and emphasizing hope over despair.

MAKE AMERICA GREAT AGAIN

The red "Make America Great Again" cap Trump sported throughout his campaign touches on the final Tocquevillean theme, which is really a question: can democracies achieve greatness or must they rest with content with a comfortable mediocrity that improves the day to day life of their people, but aims at nothing higher? (DA, 234–235) Tocqueville had worried about whether democracies were capable of pursuing great foreign policy goals, warning that democratic peoples lacked the patience and determination to see long-range policies through to the end (DA, 220). Ignoring Tocqueville's doubts, Trump promised to restore America's standing in the world. He vowed not to commit American blood and treasure to ill-defined objectives, or to fritter away hard won gains. His charge that Americans don't win wars anymore struck a raw nerve. He pledged to build up the United States' military, which had been allowed to decline to dangerously low levels of preparedness, so that if the country had to fight a war it would win. But he also vowed to make our allies assume more of the burden for their defense. The author of *The Art of the Deal* promised he would make new deals, or renegotiate old deals, that put "America First." He did not mean a policy of isolation or withdrawal from the world stage, though some of his more incendiary comments played into his opponents' hands.

So, too, did his strange affinity for Russian president, Vladimir Putin. Ironically, at the end of the first volume of *Democracy in America,* Tocqueville had written that there were "two great peoples on the earth today," the Russians and the "Anglo-Americans," with the United States standing for the principle of freedom and Russia that of servitude (DA, 395–396). This divide alone, confirmed by the history of the twentieth century, should have been enough to induce a certain wariness of Russian intentions in the Trump campaign. But like both the Bush and Obama administrations before him, he failed to take the true measure of his opponent.

Tocqueville had also marveled at Americans' unique commercial talents, finding in their efforts to sell tea for a penny less than the English merchants a kind of "heroism" (DA, 387). Trump promised to revive this spirit by making sure that the economic agreements into which the country entered did not disadvantage its entrepreneurs or workers. He pledged to reform the tax code to lure companies and jobs back to the United States, and jawboned American businesses to keep their factories and plants here at home. He promised to remove regulatory obstacles that impeded economic growth and to put Americans back to work.

Lastly, Tocqueville perceived a uniquely democratic greatness in the capacity of a free people to govern themselves (DA, 64–67, 293–294). In lashing out against "political correctness," Trump gave hope to the white working class men and women who had been sidelined, their economic prospects diminished, their way of life mocked. He stood up for law and order, principally the police and the military, and for small businesses. He visited factories and military installations, promising to renew American greatness. He spoke at churches and town halls in "fly-over" middle America. Largely unnoticed, his message also quietly resonated with more of the white educated classes than let on. Much to the surprise of everyone, including the world's most sophisticated pollsters, Donald Trump eked out an Electoral College victory over Hillary Clinton.

Whether President Trump can deliver on these Tocquevillean themes remains to be seen, however. Here again, it is best to let Tocqueville have the last word. Reflecting on the causes that preserve a democratic republic in the United States, Tocqueville considered first such accidental or providential causes as its fortuitous location and continental expanse. He noted also that the United States as yet had no great cities, though like Jefferson, he predicted that both the growth of these cities and "the nature of their inhabitants" would pose a "genuine danger" to the future of democratic republics in the New World (DA, 265–267). He next considered its laws, singling out for praise America's federal form, its institutions of local self-government that "give the people the taste for freedom and the art of being free," and the moderating influence of its courts (DA, 274). In attacking the excesses and pretensions of the administrative state and promising to appoint justices who interpret rather than make the law, Trump sought to reaffirm the country's proud commitment to republican self-government. It is, however, too early to know if he will succeed. The bureaucrats who run the administrative state have no intention of ceding their dominance over public policy without a serious fight, and there are plenty of Americans who, having benefitted from these policies, side with them despite the distortions to the Framers' constitutional design.

Finally, Tocqueville considered its mores, by which he meant not only those "habits of the heart," but also "the sum of ideas of which the habits of the mind are formed" (DA, 275). Here, Tocqueville considered religion as well as the character of the democratic family, including the distinctive way in which Americans understood the equality of men and women. He applauded the religious character of Americans and found "greatness" in the freely chosen virtue of their women (DA, 574–576). But since the cultural revolution of the 1960s, "the whole moral and intellectual state of a people" (DA, 275) has been radically transformed, throwing into question whether American mores are still favorable to republican self-government. The problem is that when mores have shifted, it is difficult to restore them. Laws alone will not bring them back (DA, 295). Thus, we are left depending upon accident or Providence to reform laws and mores in tandem. This will take time. The long march through the institutions carried out by the left was not accomplished overnight, and a counter-reformation will not be either. It will take patience and skill in the great art of leading a free people, an art Tocqueville believed Andrew Jackson did not possess. Whether Donald Trump has the steadiness of character and the political skills to carry out this supremely ambitious project also remains unclear. In the end, restoring American greatness and liberty may depend more on accidents or Providence, especially the latter.

NOTES

1. George Wilson Pierson. 1938. *Tocqueville in America*. Baltimore, MD: John Hopkins Paperback edition, 1966.
2. All citations to *Democracy in America* are from the translation by Harvey C. Mansfield and Delba Winthrop. 2000. Chicago, IL: University of Chicago Press.
3. For an opposing view, see David Gelernter, "The Conservative 'Resistance' Is Futile," *The Wall Street Journal*, July 6, 2017, A15.
4. Samuel P. Huntington. 2005. *Who Are We? The Challenges to America's National Identity*. London: Simon & Schuster.
5. Abraham Lincoln. 2012. "Speech at Chicago," July 10, 1858, in *The Writings of Abraham Lincoln*. Ed., Steven B. Smith. New Haven: Yale University Press, p. 148.
6. Two examples might be statements by Linda Sarsour, former executive director of the Arab American Association of New York, and LosUnidos, formerly the National Council of La Raza.
7. "Illegal, Undocumented, Unauthorized: The Terms of Immigration Reporting," Stephen Hiltner, *The New York Times*, March 10, 2017.
8. Pierre Manent. 2013. *A World Beyond Politics? A Defense of the Nation-State*. Trans. Marc A. LePain. Princeton, NJ: Princeton University Press, reprint edition.

9. See, for example, NPR's report on Trump's speech at Liberty University in January 2016, where he mistakenly referred to "Two Corinthians," instead of "Second Corinthians." "Citing 'Two Corinthians,' Trump Struggles To Make The Sale To Evangelicals," January 18, 2016. http://www.npr.org/people/404496424/jessica-taylor.

10. Cited in *The Tocqueville Reader*, Eds. Olivier Zunz and Alan Kahan. 2002. Malden, MA: Blackwell Publishers, Ltd., pp. 227–229.

11. See esp. *The Progressive Revolution in Politics and Political Science: Transforming the American Regime*. 2005. John Marini and Ken Masugi, eds. Lanham, MD: Rowman & Littlefield.

12. Thomas Jefferson, *Notes on the State of Virginia*, cited in *Federalist* # 48, p. 307. See also *Federalist* # 47, where Madison observes that "the accumulation of all powers, legislative, executive, and judiciary, in the same hands, ... may justly be pronounced the very definition of tyranny," p. 298. *The Federalist Papers*. 2003. Ed. Clinton Rossiter, with Introduction and Notes by Charles R. Kesler. New York: Signet Classics.

13. Phillip Hamburger, 2014 *Is Administrative Law Unlawful?* Chicago. University of Chicago Press.

14. Among the Declaration's indictments against King George III is this: "He has erected a Multitude of new Offices, and sent hither Swarms of Officers to harass our People, and eat out their Substance."

15. Jean M. Yarbrough, *Theodore Roosevelt and the American Political Tradition*. 2012. Lawrence, KS: University Press of Kansas, pp. 163–169.

16. For Tocqueville's analysis of the "coarse" spirit and "sketchy" education of American journalists, DA 177. For the journalistic call to arms against Trump as candidate, see Jim Rutenberg, *New York Times*, August 7, 2016.

17. Catherine Rampell, "Millennials have a higher opinion of socialism that of capitalism," *Washington Post*, February 5, 2016.

18. Zunz and Kahan, pp. 223, 236.

19. The phrase, which dates back to 2000, is variously attributed to Don Eberly and Bruce Chapman.

20. "The Port Huron Statement," issued by Students for a Democratic Society in 1962 advised young radicals not to bother trying to win control of the Democratic Party, but to take over the universities. On the success of this project, see Roger Kimball. 1990. *Tenured Radicals: How Politics Has Corrupted Higher Education*. New York: HarperCollins and *The Long March: How the Cultural Revolution of the 1960s Changed America*. 2000. San Francisco: Encounter Books.

BIBLIOGRAPHY

Hamburger, Phillip. 2014. *Is Administrative Law Unlawful?* Chicago: University of Chicago Press.

Hamilton, Alexander, and et al. 2003. *The Federalist Papers.* Edited by Clinton Rossiter, with an Introduction and Notes by Charles R. Kesler. New York: Signet Classics.

Huntington, Samuel P. 2005. *Who Are We? The Challenges to America's National Identity.* London: Simon and Schuster.

Kimball, Roger. 1990. *Tenured Radicals: How Politics Has Corrupted Higher Education.* New York: Harper Collins.

———. 2000. *The Long March. How the Cultural Revolution of the 1960s Changed America.* San Francisco: Encounter Books.

Lincoln, Abraham. 2012. *The Writings of Abraham Lincoln*, ed. Steven B. Smith. New Haven: Yale University Press.

Manent, Pierre. 2013. *A World Beyond Politics? A Defense of the Nation-State*, Trans. Marc LePain. Princeton: Princeton University Press.

Marini, John, and Ken Masugi, eds. 2005. *The Progressive Revolution in Politics and Political Science: Transforming the American Regime.* Lanham: Rowman & Littelfield.

Pierson, George Wilson. 1968. *Tocqueville in America.* Baltimore: Johns Hopkins Paperback. [orig. pub. 1938].

Tocqueville, Alexis de. 2000. *Democracy in America*, Trans. Harvey C. Mansfield and Delba Winthrop. Chicago: University of Chicago Press.

———. 2002. *The Tocqueville Reader: A Life in Letters and Politics*, ed. Olivier Zunz and Alan S. Kahan. Oxford: Blackwell Publishers.

Yarbrough, Jean M. 2012. *Theodore Roosevelt and the American Political Tradition.* Lawrence: University Press of Kansas.

PART III

Continental Perspectives

CHAPTER 14

Power, Resentment, and Self-Preservation: Nietzsche's Moral Psychology as a Critique of Trump

Aaron Harper and Eric Schaaf

Introduction

Donald Trump refused to campaign like any presidential candidate before him. His off-the-cuff statements were a hallmark of his rallies, and he communicated through Twitter at all hours of the day. His surprising statements and strategies were often ridiculed, and his campaign was declared "dead" on multiple occasions. Yet on Election Day Trump won key states, despite losing the popular vote by nearly three million votes, to claim the presidency. His successful primary and presidential campaigns seem inexplicable for much of modern political theory. Trump's ideas did not emerge victorious in a marketplace of ideas; he did not win debates or convert the voting public with prepared campaign speeches. Most economic and historical metrics predicted a close race regardless of the candidates, but none predicted a convincing electoral victory by the most

A. Harper (✉)
West Liberty University, West Liberty, WV, USA

E. Schaaf
Lincoln College, Lincoln, IL, USA

© The Author(s) 2018
M. B. Sable, A. J. Torres (eds.), *Trump and Political Philosophy*,
https://doi.org/10.1007/978-3-319-74427-8_14

257

unpopular candidate in modern American political history. Although the unexpected nature of Trump's victory may challenge political theory in numerous ways, we believe that Friedrich Nietzsche's analysis of modernity provides useful tools to understand and assess Trump and his associated movement in the 2016 election.

Our focus here is not directly on political theory or what is purportedly Nietzsche's explicit "political" work. Rather, the most perplexing questions regarding Trump pertain to his popularity.[1] Trump's electoral success, despite his unique and often puzzling candidacy, combined with extreme devotion among a segment of the population, should be the central issue for scholars to examine. How did he maintain appeal despite the many actions that were expected to derail his campaign? And why did he receive such strong support from communities that have the most to lose given his policy proposals on issues like health care and trade? In modern parlance these have been labeled political questions, but for Nietzsche they are fundamentally issues of (moral) psychology, which his work is particularly well-suited to answer. Nietzsche offers his most thorough discussion of the political implications of his moral psychology in *On the Genealogy of Morality*. Thus, our analysis of Trump primarily draws from the arguments and themes presented in Nietzsche's mature philosophy of the 1880s.

Our argument proceeds as follows: We begin with a discussion of our methodological approach to Nietzsche's politics. We then analyze two purported Nietzschean explanations of Trump—power and resentment—that have been put forth in popular and scholarly works. While these have some merit, we contend that they are largely superficial or, at best, incomplete. Nietzsche's *Genealogy* instead leads us to consider Trump's strategy in the context of the instinctual need for self-preservation. His amplification of this need through his rhetoric and associated negative emotions, including resentment, has led to a revaluation that diminishes humanity. We conclude by drawing out the implications of Nietzsche's view, revealing a forceful Nietzschean critique of Trump's methods and values.

Nietzsche's Politics

Most political philosophers have an identifiable approach to politics, even though we may debate their respective methods and insights. A political philosophy offers theories and facilitates analysis of political phenomena, like the emergence of Trump. However, it is not obvious to us that Nietzsche offers a political philosophy. More precisely, we do not believe the many political comments that Nietzsche makes can be organized into a coherent political theory which could address our current political situation. To this end, Andrew Huddleston distinguishes a political philosophy from what he calls a political agenda, which is comprised of ideas for transforming institutions or culture through political mechanisms.[3]

Huddleston's distinction illuminates our approach in this essay. While Nietzsche may not have a political philosophy, he clearly has a political agenda, and we should understand his politics accordingly. In addition, our contention is that we are better served by inquiring into the political *implications* of Nietzsche's broader philosophical work. Nevertheless, this strategy has not proven to be as fruitful as scholars have hoped.[4] We believe so many fundamental disagreements surround Nietzsche's work largely due to the ambiguity of the subject matter. At a more fundamental level, some would resist even the modest proposal that Nietzsche has a political agenda. After all, he disavows any interest in the subject, famously describing himself as the "last *anti-political* German" (EH "Wise" 3).[5]

At the same time, it is not surprising that Nietzsche has been treated as a political philosopher. Nietzsche routinely makes political claims or advocates political action, and he raises the possibility of a "great politics" for the future of Europe to which his work may contribute (BGE 208). Accordingly, some defend an aristocratic Nietzsche who envisions a political system designed to cultivate great individuals.[6] Yet the fundamental question remains whether Nietzsche's comments on politics are substantive enough to comprise an identifiable theory that undergirds and motivates his work. Defenses of an underlying political theory must rely on scattered comments found in different contexts, with significant use of unpublished writings or essays written early in Nietzsche's philosophical career. The considerable difficulty of reconstructing a political theory from these sources, when combined with Nietzsche's anti-political comments, leads many scholars to share a view captured by Brian Leiter: Nietzsche "occasionally expresses views about political matters, but, read in context, they do not add up to a theoretical account of any of the questions of political philosophy."[7]

Nietzsche's remarks on democracy illustrate the peril of attempting to extrapolate a political theory from his work. Specifically, Nietzsche criticizes democracy, at one point describing "the democratic movement to be not merely an abased form of political organization, but rather an abased (more specifically a diminished) form of humanity, a mediocritization and depreciation of humanity in value" (BGE 203). However, Nietzsche also proposes a reinterpretation of equality into a form that is uplifting, not leveling.[8] His critique of European democracy appears

directed at the uses it is put to, i.e., as a mechanism driving the diminution of humanity, not as an inherent failure of democracy. Such an interpretation would seem to unite Nietzsche with 19th Century advocates
of democracy like Tocqueville, Emerson, and Mill, who all expressed
similar concerns that democracy could level human beings and stifle the
development of human excellence.[9]

Any scholar can see that Nietzsche offers political insights, such as his
suggestive, yet underdeveloped, reinterpretation of democracy, but these
seem insufficient to call him a true political theorist. Other scholars worry
we may miss his political views because his work has been sanitized to be
more palatable to the post-war reader. In the 1950s and 1960s Walter
Kaufmann rehabilitated Nietzsche for mainstream philosophy, presenting
him as an existentialist-humanist. Anti-political individualism was, arguably, the price paid to reclaim Nietzsche.[10] Hugo Drochon claims that we
are now free to once again embrace Nietzsche's great politics. While
Drochon's interpretation of Nietzsche's political program—with its
emphasis on remaking culture and fostering the creation of genuine
philosophers—is intriguing, his work as a whole makes less progress
toward a theory than we might hope. Again we find that Nietzsche's
work is political in addressing modern society and the exercise of power
therein, but these are incomplete grounds for attributing to him an over-
arching political theory.

When we consider Nietzsche's political agenda instead of looking for
an underlying political theory, we find that other important features of his
work contribute to and inform this agenda. We claim that moral psychology is an essential contributor to Nietzsche's political agenda, and by the
time of his later works, one could argue that for Nietzsche politics *is* moral
psychology. We believe this convergence provides a window into Trump's
success in American politics. Nietzsche's interest is not in electoral victory
but in the transformation of culture and the implementation of new
values. We will now turn to an examination of key elements in Nietzsche's
moral psychology, looking at his treatment of power, resentment, and
self-preservation.

POWER

To gain a better understanding of Trump, and the peculiar appeal he holds
with his supporters, one might initially look to the fact that, by many measures, he is a powerful man in a country that esteems power. With this idea

in mind we turn our attention to a brief exchange in *The New York Times* in July 2016. Peter Wehner, critiquing Christians' embrace of Trump, claims that we can better understand him through the lens of Nietzsche.[11] In emphasizing the primacy of power in Nietzsche's work, Wehner identifies a shared value between them.[12] A week later, no less an authority on Nietzsche than Richard Schacht weighed in.[13] Schacht points out the folly of such an association between Trump and Nietzsche, noting that Wehner's "summary … is a simplistic caricature," going on to suggest that, while "power for Nietzsche is the name of the game," it is by no means a "blanket endorsement of all expressions of the basic disposition he calls 'will to power.'"

Unfortunately, associations like the one Wehner makes are nothing new. We agree with Schacht, and would add that the attempt to link Trump with Nietzsche's notion of power is predicated on a superficial and mistaken reading of power. There is no doubt that power is a central element of Nietzsche's mature philosophy, but the nature of power, how we should understand it, and just what role it plays in Nietzsche's thought, continue to be points of debate among scholars. To this end, in the last thirty years several sophisticated and philosophically rich treatments of the will to power have been written, most notably in the work of Schacht, Maudemarie Clark, and John Richardson.[14]

In the last decade, Bernard Reginster entered the debate by offering an interpretation that has opened new ways of understanding power in Nietzsche's writings. Playing a central role in the basic project he attributes to Nietzsche—responding to the problem of nihilism—Reginster understands the will to power as "the will to overcoming resistance."[15] Reginster thinks other, mistaken interpretations focus on the consequences of the pursuit of power, like appropriation and domination. Instead, he turns to what the pursuit of power consists in. Will to power should be understood as a kind of insatiable striving, i.e., continuous striving that seeks challenges and resistance.[16] We find this reading to correctly describe power as an activity, specifically "the activity of confronting and overcoming resistance."[17]

Importantly, this is not to say that the will to power is a will to there being resistances that perpetually frustrate a person. Rather, we should recognize resistances and challenges as being essential to the project of self-overcoming. We can see this if we understand that the will to power "is a kind of desire that does not allow for permanent (once-and-for-all) satisfaction."[18] Consider the example of someone learning a musical instrument. She desires to learn music that is neither too easy, such that it presents no challenge, nor pieces that are too difficult, such that she simply gives up, unable to take the challenge on. Rather, the will to power requires a particular dissatisfaction to motivate the pursuit. Thus, what she is learning must include frustration in the pursuit of obstacles, which is necessary to spur her self-overcoming as a musician.

While Nietzsche's rhetoric can be used to support a reading that extols the value of power as aiming at domination and control over others, to do so is to accede to a superficial interpretation that fails to look at the philosophical meaning behind Nietzsche's rhetorical choices. One virtue of Reginster's interpretation is that it explains how some of the more questionable elements of Nietzsche's account of power, e.g., identifying it with "appropriation" and "exploitation," are mistaken [19] Reginster helpfully points out that for Nietzsche appropriation and exploitation are *consequences* of pursuing power, not an explanation of power in itself.

Those who make up Trump's base interpret all of his actions as clear evidence that he is a powerful figure, using his will to upend the status quo in Washington and "drain the swamp." Every decision Trump enacts reinforces the belief that he is a man who gets things done, i.e., a powerful man in the mold of other powerful figures. And his successes in business and real estate reveal the ability to overcome obstacles in these pursuits. Yet on Reginster's interpretation of the will to power, it becomes very difficult to find evidence of power, that Trump has sought out resistance or worked to overcome it. This is a man who angrily denounces any and all criticism, has prevented certain news organizations from attending press conferences (for fear of critical questions), and has gone so far as to paint journalists as the enemy (even advocating jailing or suing some of them). He is prone to wanton outbursts of anger at the most trivial of issues, as well as any perceived challenges to his authority. And his most common tactic of avoiding conflict is to simply dismiss what is critical as "fake news." Overall, Trump's actions reveal, among other things, a strong disdain for any genuine confrontation with challenges and resistance.

Our argument can be supplemented by Nietzsche's distinction of the master and slave types from the first essay of the *Genealogy*. Appealing to Nietzsche's treatment of the master and slave types helps to illuminate the moral psychology underpinning the politics of power. In almost every way, Trump seems to evince not the traits of the master type, but rather the slave type. To see this, let us quickly summarize how Nietzsche characterizes the master type and then the slave. As Nietzsche characterizes the master type, he says 'yes' to himself; he is strong and active; he feels himself to be happy; he is confident and honest with himself; he does not take enemies or misfortunes seriously for long, and when he feels resentment, it is quickly discharged before it has time to poison him; the master type is healthy and life-affirming. In contrast, the slave is tame and mediocre, weak and life-denying; he says 'no' to all that is 'other'; he is not honest with himself; he is poisoned by resentment, cannot forget his enemies, and constructs an imaginary revenge on these enemies.

Given this typology, an assessment of Trump reveals a characteristically weak type.[20] In the end, Nietzsche's notion of power is such that we can understand Trump as a small man who mistakenly equates power with being able to dominate others. To claim that Nietzsche would identify Trump as representative of the ideal he envisioned is absurd. After all, Nietzsche remarks that the "highest feelings of power and self-assurance" evince a "power that does not need to prove itself" (TI "Skirmishes" 11). Yet Trump seems obsessed with continually proving himself and defending his past triumphs. Against this, Nietzsche maintains that once an obstacle has been overcome and an accomplishment has been achieved, one must move on to the next challenge.

Robert Pippin offers a penetrating remark about the kind of power Nietzsche valorizes in contrast with the kind of power people have traditionally esteemed: "The ability to bully and tyrannize someone into cooperation is one thing; the ability to inspire true service is another."[21] Trump's *modus operandi* seems built around bullying and tyrannizing others to get his way, a strategy that has suited him well in his business life, which he has continued into the beginning of his presidency. Setting the matter of bullying aside, the second half of Pippin's remark should catch our attention, as it does seem to be the case that Trump has been very successful in inspiring his base. However, he has not achieved this solely through positive inspiration but rather manipulation. Among his voters Trump provoked strong visceral attachments primarily rooted in negative emotions. Thus, fear or resentment might provide more adequate explanations for why voters are drawn to Trump.

Resentment

Numerous 2016 post-election autopsies held resentment as the key element of Trump's victory. Jill Filipovic described the election as "the revenge of the white man," with voters feeling "anger and resentment" at the progress and inclusiveness perceived as unfair to those who used to hold advantageous positions in society.[22] Helena Bottemiller Evich attributed Trump's victory largely to rural voters galvanized by "years of declining electoral power, driven by hollowed-out towns, economic hardship and a sustained exodus."[23] And Matt Vespa described the election as fundamentally "the revenge of the white working class."[24] Nietzsche recognizes the significance of anger and resentment, which he connects to "the deepest and most sublime hate," an "ideal-creating, value-reshaping hate whose like has never before existed on earth" (GM I: 8). In the first essay of the *Genealogy*, he makes resentment of elites a central psychological phenomenon in culture.[25]

Manfred Frings captures our ordinary understanding of ressentiment; it is a persistent, possibly incurable, feeling of hating or despising rooted in persistent impotences and weaknesses.[26] These impotences generate negative emotions that can produce false beliefs and promote a claim or moral system. Nietzsche's notion is more precise, and Reginster defines it as a "repressed vengefulness" that arises when a person is inhibited (by "weakness") from leading a type of life she deems valuable, yet she retains the original pretensions and refuses to accept the inability to realize these values.[27] *Ressentiment* motivated the revaluation of values, where the initial 'master' morality was reversed in favor of 'slave' morality, thereby elevating weakness into an accomplishment. The slave revolt was spurred by the self-interest of those oppressed by the nobles. *Ressentiment* became "creative," effectively precipitating a new human ideal and altering the political and social power structure.

The aforementioned post-election analysis used resentment to connote sour grapes of disaffected groups (e.g. white or rural voters), but attempts to explain Trump by appealing to sour grapes have no relationship to Nietzsche's work. Some interpreters have presented Nietzsche's *ressentiment* in similar terms.[28] However, in sour grapes an individual convinces herself that the object she desires is not actually the thing she wanted. This serves to revalue only the means by which values are attained, i.e. the grapes are sour and will not bring about an experience of sweetness. In contrast, *ressentiment* alters the values themselves, devaluing the highest values and offering new values in their stead.[29]

Other recent studies of resentment uncover a deeper phenomenon than sour grapes. Katherine Cramer's research into the role of resentment in Wisconsin politics provides a representative example.[30] She identifies resentment as a phenomenon of social identity and insecurity, reinforcing political differences and adding a personal component to what she calls 'rural consciousness.' Resentment appears to be an effective strategy for addressing the loss of political power or social status.[31] Nevertheless, the efficacy of such work must explain why resentment arises rather than some other response or reactive attitude, like envy or spite. Envy typically has a more specific object than resentment, which is marked more by frustration at some general inability or weakness. Spite tends toward the self-destructive. Reginster offers two additional possibilities in lieu of resentment. When frustrated by weakness, an individual could resign herself to the condition, or she could simply abandon the higher values. Unlike these two strategies, resentment fails to resolve the basic tension, and the resentful person remains unsatisfied, with no path forward to achieve that which she values most.

Cramer provides a persuasive account of rural consciousness; rural voters have a distinct view of political power and resources. Voters sometimes vote against their apparent self-interest due to their identity rooted in place.[32] Politicians like Donald Trump and Scott Walker have embraced the politics of resentment, exploiting these deep divides. Yet Cramer does not show why resentment of Nietzsche's sort was the response to the condition rather than some other emotion.[33] For instance, Arlie Russell Hochschild performed similar research in Louisiana. She also found her subjects felt marginalized in society, as if others were being allowed to cut in front of them as they pursue the American Dream.[34] Hochschild describes them as feeling betrayed, anxious, and fearful. She includes resentment as well, yet she presents it as derivative of these other feelings and not a unique political force. Based on such research, we can feel confident that emotional responses toward candidates are playing outsized roles in determining who wins elections.[35] However, these do not seem to implicate resentment in Nietzsche's sense.

Ressentiment emerges in the conditions of a particular kind of deprivation that is systematic in nature. R. Jay Wallace characterizes the specific systematic deprivation as one occasioned by invidious comparisons to others who are able to enjoy an abundance of enjoyable things to which the resentful person is systematically excluded.[36] The intense desire and systematic exclusion make *ressentiment* personal and hostile, distinguishing it again from envy. Eventually, it is transformed into a vengeful hatred, but it retains a distinct personal animus.[37] Common to the various political analyses discussed above, personal animus is motivated more by fear than resentment, with individuals worrying that others will take away what is rightly theirs. Contemporary resentment may be motivated by structural inequalities, but the deprivation is not seen as systematic. Rather, individuals are responding to what is perceived as preferential and unequal treatment benefitting others. Even if there are, as some have suggested, implicit racial or nationalistic biases underlying their conception of fairness, it is clearly distinct from the *ressentiment* characteristic of Nietzsche's slaves.

The structure of *ressentiment* reveals another dissimilarity with contemporary resentment. Much of the recent work makes *ressentiment* "strategic," meaning that actions motivated by *ressentiment* intend to harm or punish. Three primary arguments have emerged from recent scholarship against this strategic reading of Nietzsche's slave revolt. First, revaluation is an impractical means of pursuing revenge, since the creation of a new value schematic is convoluted and indirect. The process transpires over generations, rendering it an ineffective response for individuals at the beginning of the process. It also misunderstands the nature of valuing, since values, desires, and beliefs cannot be changed through a simple act of conscious willing. Second, Wallace argues that a strategic revaluation of values is self-undermining because it succeeds only when valuations are internalized. Revaluation is undertaken as a means of revenge, so it cannot also function as a fundamental framework for evaluation, deliberation, and criticism.[38] Third, the slaves, as Nietzsche depicts them, lack the cunning and understanding to develop such a nuanced form of revenge.

We contend that Wallace's expressivist account provides the most successful interpretation of Nietzsche's *ressentiment*, whereby it became creative when the tensions among the powerless slaves led them to internalize a new set of values. The systematic deprivation of that which they value most led to a negative orientation, characterized by hostility toward those things that have been recognized as good and desirable, eventually manifesting itself in hatred of those who possess what they lack. The frustration of desire was unsustainable, and such psychic tension only finds satisfaction in a new table of values. Resentful people develop or adopt new values that make sense of their condition, coming to value that which they can actually acquire. Accordingly, the slaves adopted a new evaluative framework or emotional orientation that reconceptualized how things matter to them.

Understood this way, Nietzsche's conception of *ressentiment* contributes little to explaining Trump and Trumpism. Certainly there are structural and systemic inequalities that deprive many people of their basic goods and highest values. However, these have not resulted in the widespread deprivation that creates Nietzsche's distinct kind of psychic tension. The vote for Trump did not reflect a complete shift in values. If we accept the evidence provided in the works discussed above, today's resentment results from a feared loss of identity and social position rather than a frustration of desire. Negative emotions do seem to correlate with Trump's success, but the proposed explanations for how these orientations arose do not mirror the processes of Nietzsche's slave revolt.

To understand Trump, we need not identify any sort of slave revolt in the population. Nietzsche's insights lead us to consider not the location of resentment but how it is put to use. The slave revolt interests Nietzsche not because of the presence of resentment but due to its power to induce moral and political changes. The 2016 election cycle seems to be another instance where resentment became manifest in an uncommon manner, leading to a surprising political outcome. Jeremy Engels identifies such situations as amplifications of resentment, which he finds intertwined with victimization and violent rhetoric. Engels understands resentment as a hostile reaction to injustice or injury, but in its current amplified form it becomes a new way of being in the world. He finds our present condition reminiscent of Nietzsche's *ressentiment*.[39] Given our interpretation of Nietzsche's expressivist *ressentiment*, we disagree with Engels's precise characterization of the concept, but we accept his broader point. The management and manipulation of resentment is more politically noteworthy than its mere presence.

In Nietzsche's account, the priests would benefit most from overturning the status quo. They recognize that a political revolt occurs when the internalization of values implicitly challenges the traditional authorities. Therefore, the priests direct *ressentiment* as a means to increase their own power. The priests cultivate the expressivist *ressentiment*, but their revenge is a secondary phenomenon in Nietzsche's story of revaluation. He directs us to the political implication of elites exploiting negative emotions for their own purposes, which we explore with respect to Trump in the next section.

The Politics of Self-Preservation

The central issue goes beyond the question of electoral success. Akin to the slave revolt in the *Genealogy*, what warrants an explanation is how Trump's movement seemingly changed (or revalued) the policy and moral preferences of so many people in such a quick manner. For instance, unlike traditional Republican and conservative politicians, Trump supported Medicaid, pledged to protect LGBTQ rights, and advocated friendly terms with Russia. Additionally, the fact that many of these changes appear to harm the same supporters makes the success of his movement that much more unexpected. This abrupt transformation seems to be an example of corruption, which Nietzsche defines as when a species or individual prefers that which will harm it (A 6). Throughout all of this, we are inundated with charges of "fake news," undermining the political realm itself. As Nietzsche writes, "…[T]o deny one's own 'reality'—what a triumph!" (GM III: 12). Nietzsche's moral psychology provides the resources to address these phenomena.

Nietzsche's investigations in the *Genealogy* locate a "Trump-like" figure in the ascetic priest, a type Nietzsche abhors yet simultaneously admires for its power. The priests bear a complex relation to both the masters and slaves in Nietzsche's account. The priests are of noble birth, but they have more in common with the slaves than the masters. Nietzsche remarks that the priest must be "sick himself" before immediately clarifying that to understand the sick he must only be "related to the sick and short-changed from the ground up" (GM III: 15). The priests retain their will to power, which puts them in a position of power and influence.

Trump's origin story shares many priestly characteristics. Trump is, obviously, of a different upbringing and class from many of his most ardent supporters. Trump grew up in New York City and inherited wealth from his father. Revealingly, while Trump is thoroughly urban, he found his electoral success in rural America. Like these voters, Trump shares a distrust of many New York elites. Yet it is clear that Trump's beef with them is rooted in his desire for recognition and legitimacy, evident in his repeated claims that he only lost the popular vote due to massive, unsubstantiated voter fraud. He wants to be seen as a success by those he recognizes as his peers, and he feels short-changed when he finds his economic accomplishments diminished, which we have seen in public feuds with figures like Mike Bloomberg.

Trump's peculiar standing vis-a-vis his voters only deepens the puzzle of how a revaluation could so quickly transpire. We claim that Nietzsche's notion of the ascetic ideal can help to explain this puzzle. We are not arguing here that Trump represents the ascetic ideal, but Nietzsche's account is instructive. The ascetic ideal emerges from the *"protective and healing instincts of a degenerating life* that seeks with every means to hold its ground and is fighting for its existence" (GM III: 13). The need for self-preservation is a basic instinct of self-defense (EH "Clever" 8). People will pursue nearly any means in order to protect their lives, even if the preconditions and values of life must be altered or replaced.[40] Thus, Nietzsche's work reveals that self-preservation can motivate shifts in value and politics of the sort we find with Trump and Trumpism, with the ascetic ideal explaining an analogous historical shift. From the outside these alterations appear paradoxical or self-undermining, but in the context of preservation we can understand them in the service of life.

That many Trump voters feel the need for self-preservation is evident in the anger and resentment discussed in the previous section, albeit at a more conscious level than with Nietzsche's ascetic ideal. In particular, the research performed by Cramer and Hochschild shows that the anxieties felt by this voting bloc pertain more to a sense of identity and are not primarily economic in nature. Large segments of the American population see their livelihood at risk as the country, in their view, changes to accommodate other groups of people who gain unfair advantages. Believing these other groups now receive opportunities no longer afforded to them, many people feel marginalized and hopeless.

The priests have an interest in keeping their dominion over others. Likewise, Trump has little incentive to upend current forms of valuation, since he trades in a profession that is highly valued in the status quo and, by traditional metrics, has been quite successful. The priests use the need for self-preservation as a means to power. Nietzsche contends that they exacerbate the condition, or "poison the wound," in order to make themselves essential to the masses as the only means to survive their dire situation (GM III: 15). The priests worsen the condition by turning *ressentiment* inward and fostering self-hatred. Then they address the increased suffering by offering strategies to anesthetize the pain, which they insist only priests can administer.

Trump's campaign seems to have reached the same conclusion.[41] Of course, all politicians claim to offer cures for what ails society, but Trump's strategy is priest-like in at least two ways. First, he makes a personal case that only he can provide salvation, as in his Republican convention speech where he insisted, "I alone can fix it!" Second, as we will show below, he intensifies the problem, creating a worse situation that requires a more dramatic solution. If traditional political means no longer appear successful, then "Trumpian salvation" becomes a more palatable, if not necessary, response. Nietzsche is surprisingly vague when it comes to the specific priestly techniques, yet we should note an important difference in Trump's strategy. While the priests used internalization and provoked self-hatred, Trump cultivates the need for self-preservation through identification of external threats. His rhetoric contains what Nietzsche calls "explosive material" (GM III: 15). He brings people to the very edge, stopping just short of chaos that undermines his very attempt to organize a campaign.

Trump's nationalist rhetoric has provided his most reliable explosive material. Encapsulated in his maxim to "build the wall," Trump has identified myriad threats to the people of United States, including those of terrorism, crime, and drug cartels. These threats, often attributed to foreign sources, are directly connected to the well-being and identities of his voters. Also, he highlights trade and immigration as threats to American jobs and entitlements. Nietzsche argues that this sort of nationalist rhetoric alienates people from each other (BGE 256). He connects this strategy with short-sighted politicians enamored with old, and weak, forms of nationalism. Nietzsche identifies other failures of the nationalist statesman who incites passions that lead to anger, competing "truths," and what he terms "spiritual leveling" (BGE 241). We find this most clearly in Trump turning media outlets themselves into the enemy. It presents a world filled with danger and doom, where "the American Dream is dead." Not only is he the only one who can fix the situation, but he is the only one who can differentiate real threats from fake ones.

Trump also uses revaluation as a tactic to aggravate the need for self-preservation. Nietzsche recognizes that those under siege seek new pride in their identity. They claim for themselves the mantle of virtue, while others are labeled unjust (GM III: 14). The parallels to Hochschild's analysis of Louisiana voters are clear, since outsiders are seen to be given unequal and unfair treatment. Trump's call to "Make America Great Again" allows his supporters to claim a heritage of traditional virtue for themselves. At the same time, the failures identified in the status quo justify moving in some new directions. Already we have seen that Trump revalued elements of the Republican platform. Of particular note is his radical approach to international relations, dismissing European allies while embracing authoritarian leaders of Russia, Turkey, and the Philippines, effectively creating a new world of imaginary or exaggerated threats hitherto unrecognized by Americans. By changing the usual notions of what is safe and unsafe, Trump disrupts the traditional responses to these threats. Moreover, by highlighting failures of U.S. intelligence—again, traditionally supported by Republican candidates—Trump undermined traditional political solutions. The threat to the livelihood of voters makes Trumpism a preferred solution for many.

The revaluation of moral norms has been even more striking. The Republican Party has long adopted the moral platform of the Christian right. Trump embraced evangelical voters, yet he made numerous comments, including many of a sexual nature, that would seem antithetical to Christian virtues. By the same token, many Trump voters engaged in a similar revaluation, accepting behaviors they previously considered immoral. Parts of this revaluation seem purposeful, although much is unintentional in nature. The need for self-preservation overrides other considerations; individuals adapt to survive when their very identity is at stake. Thus, like the priests, Trump's campaign was able to "discharge this explosive in such a way that it does not blow up either the herd or the shepherd" (GM III· 15). The result has been a form of faith that Nietzsche associates with fanaticism, which is "always most desired and most urgently needed where will is lacking; for will, as the affect of command, is the decisive mark of sovereignty and strength. That is, the less someone knows how to command, the more urgently does he desire someone who commands" (GS 347). In studying Trump through the optic of Nietzsche, we understand more precisely how the need for self-preservation, enflamed by rhetoric and other strategies, reveals Trump as the "cure" society seeks.

NIETZSCHE'S CRITIQUE OF TRUMP

We have argued that attempts to offer a Nietzschean explanation of Trump by appealing to power and resentment are inadequate, as they rely on conceptions of these ideas that are either superficial or do not reflect Nietzsche's actual work. Using Nietzsche's insights, we maintain that Trump has cleverly manipulated voters for his own ends. For example, he uses both rhetoric and revaluation that plays to and amplifies the need for self-preservation by magnifying and exaggerating the threats to traditional notions of social identity, status, and livelihood. Drochon makes a more dramatic charge against Trump, suggesting that he is a kind of Last Human Being, a "demagogue, telling the people that he's going to make things great again, which is to say simple and how they once were – and they love him for it."[42] We disagree that Trump himself is like the Last Human Beings, who are incapable of finding meaning and genuine happiness but exist in a condition marked by small goals and "wretched contentment." Yet our argument identifies similar political concerns, with Trump serving to diminish humanity rather than building humanity up. His movement, which embraces petty politics, has also used the emotional responses of the community for self-serving aims, amassing power and wealth through lip service to populism, with little evidence of support for populist policies.

Building on these concerns, in section II we highlighted Nietzsche's claim that democracy could foster uplifting values and genuine political engagement, but often serves instead to weaken humanity. Our subsequent analysis reveals that Trump reflects a distinct and troubling challenge. Political polarization has been identified as a similar challenge to democracy, but Trump's politics of self-preservation both exacerbates the problem and makes it different in kind. As we have described, Trump's strategies exploit democracy, but they are particularly insidious by instilling further change in politics itself. Most notably, issue and value-based arguments become even less effective. Voters will support a candidate who they believe best protects their life and basic interests, even when doing so contradicts prior values and commitments.[43] Politicians seem to recognize that people sacrifice themselves and their long-held commitments if convinced they will otherwise lose themselves. And it is Trump's politics which steers people toward self-preservation.

Additionally, Nietzsche's treatment of power and resentment provides grounds for a forceful critique of Trump, even apart from his damaging effects to politics. Trump has achieved great power by traditional metrics, though we agree with Jacob Golomb's analysis that the power expressed by Trump is closer to a caricature of Nietzsche's *Übermensch*, the 'Superman' who is measured by traditional, material successes.[44] Trump better resembles what Nietzsche calls "the great man of the masses" (HH 460). We could imagine Nietzsche's assessment of Trump paralleling the way he spoke of Thomas Carlyle. Speaking of "that fatuous dolt, Carlyle," Nietzsche describes him as, "that half actor and rhetorician who tried to conceal under impassioned grimaces what he knew about himself: namely, what he *lacked*— real *power* of intellect, real *profundity* of spiritual vision . . ." (BGE 252).[45]

We have argued that Trump evinces only a simulacrum of power which masks weakness; genuine expressions of power evince a striving to overcome resistance and challenges. The process of doing so is continuous. It requires a person to persistently work to achieve goals while desiring and pursuing further challenges, committing to a task while being willing to abandon it based on new developments. Based on the evidence of passages like *Zarathustra's* "On Self-Overcoming," GM II: 12, and GS 347, Pippin argues that this self-overcoming process entails "the ability to foster in oneself constant dissatisfaction with one's own achievements."[46] Accordingly, we find compelling arguments that the will to overcoming resistances is intimately connected to self-overcoming, where power is specifically power over oneself.

Connecting the will to power with power over oneself brings to mind Kaufmann's claim that "the highest degree of power consists in self-mastery."[47] The self-mastery required to pursue and overcome resistances involves commanding oneself and one's desires.[48] By this standard, Trump routinely appears on the precipice of losing control of himself—if he hasn't yet lost control—most evident in is frequent Twitter outbursts. Additionally, we find little evidence of Trump fostering "dissatisfaction with one's own achievements." Instead, we have Trump's continued interest in his winning electoral map, which he is said to bring up unsolicited and to hand out at interviews. By all effective measures, Nietzsche's notion of power is such that we can understand Trump as a small man who erroneously equates power with being able to dominate others, while possessing minimal self control. Trump lacks self-mastery, but, more importantly, such power is not even valued in Trumpism.

We can better capture a Nietzschean critique of Trump by looking to Nietzsche's remarks on health and sickness. Nietzsche's understanding of health is admittedly elusive, but we can highlight several intriguing features. For Nietzsche, becoming healthy is primarily a task of overcoming negative elements of human life, yet he also posits a higher health predicated on developing positive elements beyond the level of mere health.[49] Nietzsche characterizes this higher health as an "ideal of a human, super-human well-being," which involves, among other things, becoming "stronger, craftier, tougher, bolder, and more cheerful" (GS 382).

Where resentment is grounded in a persistent, and possibly incurable, hatred, we can locate a standpoint of health in Nietzsche's notions of laughter and cheerfulness. This laughter is grounded in love, and it is found in those who exude joy and seek out challenges. Additionally, it captures a kind of assuredness, a confident ability to take on all things that life throws at her in stride.[50] Nietzsche's Zarathustra admonishes the higher men, emphasizing the need to "learn to laugh at yourselves as one must laugh!" (Z IV: "On the Higher Men" 15). In contrast, Trump and many of his supporters mock others, through means like Trump's derisive tweets and name-calling. These aim to diminish others and to provoke negative emotions, serving to maintain differences between people by delegitimizing others. Such laughter is rooted in resentment and fear, shifting attention to others, yet finding nothing of value in oneself.

Learning to laugh in the way Nietzsche desires is something one develops through experience. It necessitates being able to distance oneself from these experiences, seeing them in new ways, seeing the limits, and seeing beyond those limits. Such distancing is a component of what Nietzsche calls the ability to forget, which he claims is "an upholder of psychic order" (GM II: 1). This ability is vital insofar as it's a kind of letting go of the past—including both what is bad and good—even as the past is incorporated into one's life. Forgetting can be understood as a continuous process of psychic archiving. Nietzsche applauds being "able to shake off with a single shrug a collection of worms that in others would dig itself in" (GM I.10). Otherwise one is liable to be poisoned by resentment. We have offered many examples that show Trump is unable to forget; he continually returns to past battles and holds on to grudges.

Trump has succeeded through his manipulation of the political system, primarily by amplifying and exploiting the need for self-preservation, not due to his purported power or the resentment felt by his voting base. Trump's appeal is understandable from a Nietzschean perspective once we recognize the political import of his moral psychology. Yet through this same perspective and corresponding political agenda, we have argued that Trump's methods and values are condemnable.

NOTES

1. Popularity here, of course, is relative. Trump was elected with higher unfavorable and lower favorable ratings than even his unpopular opponent Hillary Clinton. Nevertheless, he remained popular enough to win the Electoral College, which in American presidential politics is the name of the game.
2. Trump himself, in a moment of surprising self-awareness, boasted at a rally in Iowa that "I could stand in the middle of 5th Avenue and shoot somebody and I wouldn't lose voters."
3. Andrew Huddleston, review of *Nietzsche's Great Politics*, by Hugo Drochon, *Notre Dame Philosophical Reviews*, December 18, 2016 http://ndpr.nd.edu/news/nietzsches-great-politics/.
4. Shaw aptly writes that the results have been so diverse one might conclude that Nietzsche's "ethical and epistemological views do not themselves have any very determinate political consequences." Tamsin Shaw, *Nietzsche's Political Skepticism* (Princeton: Princeton University Press, 2007), 2.
5. We have employed parenthetical citations of Nietzsche's works using the following abbreviations:

   A = *The Antichrist*, in *The Antichrist, Ecce Homo, Twilight of the Idols, and Other Writings*, ed. Aaron Ridley and Judith Norman, trans. Judith Norman (Cambridge: Cambridge University Press, 2005).

BGE = *Beyond Good and Evil*, ed. Rolf-Peter Horstmann and Judith Norman, trans. Judith Norman (Cambridge: Cambridge University Press, 2002).

EH = *Ecce Homo*, in *Basic Writings of Nietzsche*, ed. and trans. Walter Kaufmann (New York: The Modern Library, 1967).

HH = *Human, All Too Human*, trans. R. J. Hollingdale (Cambridge: Cambridge University Press, 1996).

GM = *On the Genealogy of Morality*, trans. Maudemarie Clark and Alan J. Swensen (Indianapolis: Hackett Publishing, 1998).

GS = *The Gay Science*, ed. Bernard Williams, trans. Josefine Nauckhoff and Adrian Del Caro (Cambridge: Cambridge University Press, 2001).

TI = *Twilight of the Idols*, in *The Antichrist, Ecce Homo, Twilight of the Idols, and Other Writings*, ed. Aaron Ridley and Judith Norman, trans. Judith Norman (Cambridge: Cambridge University Press, 2005).

Z = *Thus Spoke Zarathustra*, ed. Adrian Del Caro and Robert Pippin, trans. Adrian Del Caro (Cambridge: Cambridge University Press, 2006).

6. Detwiler offers what might be the most common version of a Nietzschean political theory, which he calls "the politics of aristocratic radicalism." See Bruce Detwiler, *Nietzsche and the Politics of Aristocratic Radicalism* (Chicago: University of Chicago Press, 1990).

7. Brian Leiter, *Nietzsche and Morality* (London: Routledge, 2002), 296.

8. "The thirst for equality can express itself either as a desire to draw everyone down to oneself…or to raise oneself and everyone else up" (HH 300). In this vein, Maudemarie Clark argues that democratic institutions are not necessarily bound to values like egalitarianism. "Nietzsche's Antidemocratic Rhetoric," *Southern Journal of Philosophy* 37, no. S1 (1999): 133.

9. See James Conant, "Nietzsche's Perfectionism: A Reading of *Schopenhauer as Educator*," in *Nietzsche's Postmoralism*, ed. Richard Schacht (Cambridge: Cambridge University Press, 2001), 226–228.

10. See Hugo Drochon, *Nietzsche's Great Politics* (Princeton: Princeton University Press, 2016), 1. See also pp. 1–3, 49–51.

11. Peter Wehner, "The Theology of Donald Trump," *New York Times*, July 5, 2016, accessed July 28, 2017, https://www.nytimes.com/2016/07/05/opinion/campaign-stops/the-theology-of-donald-trump.html.

12. This seems to be representative of a common view of Nietzsche on Trump vis-a-vis power. Among many other examples, see Damon Linker, "How Nietzsche Explains the Rise of Trump," *The Week*, August 11, 2015, accessed July 30, 2017, http://theweek.com/articles/570977/how-nietzsche-explains-rise-donald-trump.

13. Richard Schacht, "Donald Trump and Nietzsche," *New York Times*, July 12, 2016, accessed July 28, 2017, https://www.nytimes.com/2016/07/13/opinion/donald-trump-and-nietzsche.html.

14. See Richard Schacht, *Nietzsche* (New York: Routledge, 1983), esp. Chapter 4; Maudemarie Clark, *Nietzsche on Truth and Philosophy* (Cambridge: Cambridge University Press, 1990), esp. Chapter 7; John Richardson, *Nietzsche's System* (Oxford: Oxford University Press, 1996). See also the discussion on the will to power between Clark, Schacht, Richardson, and David Owen in *International Studies in Philosophy* 32, no. 3 (2000).

15. Bernard Reginster, *The Affirmation of Life* (Cambridge, MA: Harvard University Press, 2006), 126.

16. "What is happiness?" Nietzsche asks. It is "the feeling that power is *growing*, that some resistance has been overcome" (A 2). See also, BGE 19 and TI "Skirmishes" 38.

17. Reginster, *The Affirmation of Life*, 136

18. Reginster, *The Affirmation of Life*, 138.

19. As a representative example, consider the following: "'Exploitation' does not belong to a corrupted or imperfect, primitive society; it belongs to the *essence* of being alive as a fundamental organic function; it is a result of genuine will to power, which is just the will of life" (BGE 259). Cf., GM II: 12.

20. Admittedly, if we were to be faithful to Nietzsche's text, the fact of the matter is that Trump is probably, like most people, a mix of the master and the slave type. See BGE 260, where Nietzsche writes, "In fact, you sometimes find [these moralities] sharply juxtaposed – inside the same person even, within a single soul."

21. Robert Pippin, *Nietzsche, Psychology, & First Philosophy* (Chicago: University of Chicago Press, 2010), 118.

22. Jill Filipovic, "The Revenge of the White Man," *Time*, November 10, 2016, accessed February 20, 2017, http://time.com/4566304/donald-trump-revenge-of-the-white-man/.

23. Helena Bottemiller Evich, "Revenge of the Rural Voter," *Politico*, November 13, 2016, accessed February 20, 2017, http://www.politico.com/story/2016/11/hillary-clinton-rural-voters-trump-231266.

24. Matt Vespa, "Losers: Clinton Campaign Ignored Bill's Advice and Felt White Working Class Voters Weren't Worth the Time," *Townhall*, November 13, 2016, accessed February 20, 2017, https://townhall.com/tipsheet/mattvespa/2016/11/13/losers-clinton-campaign-ignored-bills-advice-and-felt-white-working-class-voters-werent-worth-the-time-n2245095.

25. Nietzsche uses the French *ressentiment* in his work. When possible, we use '*ressentiment*' to denote Nietzsche's specific conception of the more general phenomenon for which we use 'resentment'.

26. Manfred Frings, introduction to *Ressentiment*, by Max Scheler (Milwaukee: Marquette University Press, 1994), 5.

27. Bernard Reginster, "Nietzsche on *Ressentiment* and Valuation," *Philosophy and Phenomenological Research* 57, no. 2 (1997): 286–287.

28. For example, Bittner offers the fable of the fox and sour grapes to illuminate what he takes to be the important aspects of Nietzsche's view. See Rüdiger Bittner, "*Ressentiment*," in *Nietzsche, Genealogy, Morality*, ed. Richard Schacht (Berkeley, CA: University of California Press, 1994), 130–131.

29. See Reginster, "Nietzsche on *Ressentiment* and Valuation," 290–291. Furthermore, Sinhababu contends that treating ressentiment as a form of sour grapes wrongly minimizes the vengefulness of the slaves, See Neil Sinhababu, "Vengeful Thinking and Moral Epistemology," in *Nietzsche and Morality*, ed. Brian Leiter and Neil Sinhababu (Oxford: Oxford University Press, 2007), 268.

30. Katherine J. Cramer, *The Politics of Resentment* (Chicago: University of Chicago Press, 2016).

31. Green argues that resentment is necessarily unsuccessful because frustration cannot transform the unsatisfied desire, Michael S. Green, "Nietzsche on Pity and *Ressentiment*," *International Studies in Philosophy* 24, no. 2 (1992): 66. We agree with Babich's response that Nietzsche's problem with resentment must be precisely that it is successful. See Babette E. Babich, "Commentary: Michael Green, 'Nietzsche on Pity and *Ressentiment*'," *International Studies in Philosophy* 24, no. 2 (1992): 74.

32. Cramer, *The Politics of Resentment*, 15, 145, 192.

33. We want to emphasize that our primary question here pertains to whether these scholars are tapping into Nietzsche's sense of resentment, and not whether they are well-researched and compelling feats of scholarship, which they certainly are.

34. Arlie Russell Hochschild, *Strangers in Their Own Land* (New York: The New Press, 2016), 135–139.

35. And as Hochschild puts it, Trump "is an 'emotions candidate.' More than any other presidential candidate in decades, Trump focuses on eliciting and praising emotional responses from his fans rather than on detailed policy prescriptions." Hochschild, *Strangers in Their Own Land*, 225.

36. R. Jay Wallace, "*Ressentiment*, Value, and Self-Vindication: Making Sense of Nietzsche's Slave Revolt," in *Nietzsche and Morality*, ed. Brian Leiter and Neil Sinhababu (Oxford: Oxford University Press, 2007), 116.

37. Wallace, "*Ressentiment*, Value, and Self-Vindication," 117.

38. See Wallace, "*Ressentiment*, Value, and Self-Vindication," 114.

39. Jeremy Engels, *The Politics of Resentment* (University Park, PA: Pennsylvania State University Press, 2015), 127.

40. Individuals will go to the extreme for self-preservation, and this extends to the need for a goal. Humanity would rather "will *nothingness* than *not* will" (GM III: 1).

41. The priests are not the only ones to take advantage of the instinct for self-preservation; according to Nietzsche Socrates used a similar strategy. He "understood that the world *needed* him" for self-preservation, so he offered his own method and cure in order to gain influence (TI "Socrates" 9).
42. Sean Illing, "What Nietzsche's Philosophy Can Tell Us about Why Brexit and Trump Won," *Vox.com*, June 11, 2017, accessed July 10, 2017, https://www.vox.com/conversations/2016/12/20/13927678/donald-trump-brexit-nietzsche-democracy-europe-populism-hugo-drochon.
43. "An article of faith could be refuted to [man] a thousand times; as long as he needed it, he would consider it 'true' again and again" (GS 347).
44. Jacob Golomb, "The Case of Nietzsche Against Trump," *The Critique*, January 15, 2017 http://www.thecritique.com/articles/nietzsche-against-trump/.
45. "Carlyle ... *needs* noise. A constant, ardent *dishonesty* towards himself—that is his *proprium*, that is what makes and keeps him interesting" (TI "Skirmishes" 12).
46. Robert Pippin, review of *The Affirmation of Life*, by Bernard Reginster, *Philosophy and Phenomenological Research* 77, no. 1 (2008): 289, note 15.
47. Walter Kaufmann, *Nietzsche: Philosopher, Psychologist, Antichrist.* 4th ed. (Princeton: Princeton University Press, 1974), 252.
48. Pippin, *Nietzsche*, 118.
49. We owe this basic idea on the relationship between the nature of health and higher health to William Schroeder.
50. Lippitt writes, "Zarathustra is showing the required flexibility and openness to experience, in accepting his need to continually integrate his traits, habits and patterns of action; always remaining open to what his future might bring, and surely, to be able to view this prospect with amusement, he must have attained the practical distance from his own current self necessary to this humorous attitude towards life." John Lippitt, "Nietzsche, Zarathustra and the Status of Laughter," *British Journal of Aesthetics* 32, no. 1 (1992): 45.

BIBLIOGRAPHY

Babich, Babette E. 1992. Commentary: Michael Green, 'Nietzsche on Pity and Ressentiment'. *International Studies in Philosophy* 24 (2): 71–76.

Bittner, Rüdiger. 1994. *Ressentiment*. In *Nietzsche, Genealogy, Morality*, ed. Richard Schacht, 127–138. Berkeley: University of California Press.

Clark, Maudemarie. 1990. *Nietzsche on Truth and Philosophy*. Cambridge: Cambridge University Press.

———. 1999. Nietzsche's Antidemocratic Rhetoric. *Southern Journal of Philosophy* 37 (S1): 119–141.

Conant, James. 2001. Nietzsche's Perfectionism: A Reading of *Schopenhauer as Educator*. In *Nietzsche's Postmoralism*, ed. Richard Schacht, 181–257. Cambridge: Cambridge University Press.

Cramer, Katherine J. 2016. *The Politics of Resentment*. Chicago: University of Chicago Press.

Detwiler, Bruce. 1990. *Nietzsche and the Politics of Aristocratic Radicalism*. Chicago: University of Chicago Press.

Drochon, Hugo. 2016. *Nietzsche's Great Politics*. Princeton: Princeton University Press.

Engels, Jeremy. 2015. *The Politics of Resentment*. University Park: Pennsylvania State University Press.

Frings, Manfred. 1994. Introduction to *Ressentiment*, by Max Scheler, 1–18. Milwaukee: Marquette University Press.

Golomb, Jacob. 2017. The Case of Nietzsche Against Trump. *The Critique*, January 15. http://www.thecritique.com/articles/nietzsche-against-trump/.

Green, Michael S. 1992. Nietzsche on Pity and Ressentiment. *International Studies in Philosophy* 24 (2): 63–70.

Hochschild, Arlie Russell. 2016. *Strangers in Their Own Land*. New York: The New Press.

Huddleston, Andrew. 2016. Review of *Nietzsche's Great Politics*, by Hugo Drochon. *Notre Dame Philosophical Reviews*, December 18. http://ndpr.nd. edu/news/nietzsches-great-politics/.

Illing, Sean. 2017. What Nietzsche's Philosophy Can Tell Us About Why Brexit and Trump Won. *Vox.com*, June 11. https://www.vox.com/conversations/2016/12/20/13927678/donald-trump-brexit-nietzsche-democracy-europe-populism-hugo-drochon.

Kaufmann, Walter. 1974. *Nietzsche: Philosopher, Psychologist, Antichrist*. 4th ed. Princeton: Princeton University Press.

Leiter, Brian. 2002. *Nietzsche and Morality*. London: Routledge.

Lippitt, John. 1992. Nietzsche, Zarathustra and the Status of Laughter. *British Journal of Aesthetics* 32 (1): 39–49.

Nietzsche, Friedrich. 1967. *Ecce Homo*. In *Basic Writings of Nietzsche*, ed. and Trans. Walter Kaufmann. New York: The Modern Library.

———. 1996. *Human, All Too Human*. Trans. R. J. Hollingdale. Cambridge: Cambridge University Press.

———. 1998. *On the Genealogy of Morality*. Trans. Maudemarie Clark and Alan J. Swensen. Indianapolis: Hackett Publishing.

———. 2001. *The Gay Science*, ed. Bernard Williams, Trans. Josefine Nauckhoff and Adrian Del Caro. Cambridge: Cambridge University Press.

———. 2002. *Beyond Good and Evil*, ed. Rolf-Peter Horstmann and Judith Norman, Trans. Judith Norman. Cambridge: Cambridge University Press.

———. 2005a. *The Antichrist*. In *The Antichrist, Ecce Homo, Twilight of the Idols, and Other Writings*, ed. Aaron Ridley and Judith Norman, Trans. Judith Norman. Cambridge: Cambridge University Press.

———. 2005b. *Twilight of the Idols*. In *The Antichrist, Ecce Homo, Twilight of the Idols, and Other Writings*, ed. Aaron Ridley and Judith Norman, Trans. Judith Norman. Cambridge: Cambridge University Press.

———. 2006. *Thus Spoke Zarathustra*, ed. Adrian Del Caro and Robert Pippin, Trans. Adrian Del Caro. Cambridge: Cambridge University Press.

Pippin, Robert. 2008. Review of *The Affirmation of Life*, by Bernard Reginster. *Philosophy and Phenomenological Research* 77 (1): 281–291.

———. 2010. *Nietzsche, Psychology, & First Philosophy*. Chicago: University of Chicago Press.

Reginster, Bernard. 1997. Nietzsche on Ressentiment and Valuation. *Philosophy and Phenomenological Research* 57 (2): 281–305.

———. 2006. *The Affirmation of Life*. Cambridge, MA: Harvard University Press.

Richardson, John. 1996. *Nietzsche's System*. Oxford: Oxford University Press.

Schacht, Richard. 1983. *Nietzsche*. New York: Routledge.

Shaw, Tamsin. 2007. *Nietzsche's Political Skepticism*. Princeton: Princeton University Press.

Sinhababu, Neil. 2007. Vengeful Thinking and Moral Epistemology. In *Nietzsche and Morality*, ed. Brian Leiter and Neil Sinhababu, 262–280. Oxford: Oxford University Press.

Wallace, R. Jay. 2007. *Ressentiment*, Value, and Self-Vindication: Making Sense of Nietzsche's Slave Revolt. In *Nietzsche and Morality*, ed. Brian Leiter and Neil Sinhababu, 110–137. Oxford: Oxford University Press.

CHAPTER 15

Uncivil Society: Hegel, Kojève, and the Crisis of Political Legitimacy

Adam Adatto Sandel and Julius Krein

At the end of the Cold War, commentators were quick to pronounce the end of history, meaning that only one political system, liberal democracy, could be recognized as legitimate. This pronouncement drew, in a broad sense, on Hegel's view that history is the realization of freedom, and that freedom inheres in a representative state that could be described as a certain form of liberal democracy (though different from our own). Yet, since then, the many ways in which our politics seem to have moved away from Hegelian aspirations have gone unnoticed. What if, rather than moving toward some Hegelian ideal, we are actually falling away from it? What if the Soviet Union's collapse actually destabilized what had constituted, in the West at least, a more Hegelian order?

The election of Donald Trump in 2016, along with the rise of "populist" movements across Europe, raised new questions about the strength and legitimacy of the Western liberal democracies—perhaps even among their

Portions of this essay were adapted from Adam Adatto Sandel, "Putting Work in Its Place: Lessons from Hegel," *American Affairs* Volume I, Number 1 (Spring 2017): 152–62.

A. A. Sandel (✉) • J. Krein
American Affairs, Boston, MA, USA

own voters. Commentators immediately began to pronounce "the end of the end of history."[1] But what if the apparent "end of the end" is really a reaction to our society's falling away from Hegel's political vision? Perhaps his vision has insight that we overlook, or are too quick to dismiss.

HEGEL ON THE UNITY OF ECONOMY, FAMILY, AND STATE

G. W. F. Hegel's notion of modern ethical life (*Sittlichkeit*), as laid out in his *Philosophy of Right*, contains a great deal of insight into our present predicaments. It can be understood as a concrete ideal of social life that finds implicit expression in American practice, and that, at the same time, helps shed light on our social and political crisis.

The precise structure of ethical life, as Hegel envisions it, is not a perfect model for our own. The division of society into a landowning estate and a business class, each with its own house of parliament, for example, is antiquated and implausible. But the basic structure of ethical life—constituted by the family, civil society, and the state—persists today. It is within that structure, moreover, that people (at least in Western societies) realize their identity and agency. For many people, it is difficult, if not impossible, to understand themselves without reference to the roles of spouse, parent, child, sibling, producer, consumer, and citizen.

Indeed, Hegel's ethical life provides a model of the free society from which we are falling away. The balance that Hegel envisions among the three institutions, or "moments," of ethical life (the family, civil society, and the state) is teetering on the brink of collapse. Civil society is beginning to encroach on the state and the family to the detriment of all three institutions. Such encroachment is eroding the distinctive kind of freedom that pertains to each realm. Our current social and political crisis of work, and especially of blue-collar work, can be understood as a symptom of civil society gone awry.

Much has been written on the working-class anger and resentment that helped elect Donald Trump to the presidency and that has driven other "populist" movements. This anger is not simply about job loss to foreign competitors and technology, but also a growing sense that traditional blue-collar work is no longer honored as it used to be. When employees find themselves replaced as a result of automation, for example, they not only face the difficulty of having to find new work. They also face a judgment by society (and by the company that laid them off) on the kind of work they do: that their job is menial and adds little or nothing that a machine cannot accomplish at a cheaper price.

We mainly think of work as a source of income and material well-being rather than as a source of identity. And yet, paradoxically, we allow the realm of work to infiltrate nearly every aspect of our lives. Digital devices tether us to the work place in every waking hour. And we find it difficult to disentangle family life from the seemingly ubiquitous demands of our jobs.

Such anxieties concerning work are not simply individual or economic concerns. Without trivializing real economic hardship, the widespread inability to see these issues as something more than individual and economic concerns is perhaps the clearest sign that our attitude toward work has become a larger problem. As a society, we are losing the ability to conceive of the human and political aspects of work; the sense in which work constitutes a distinctive aspect of life that is integral to self-assurance and agency, and the sense in which it might contribute toward a common good.

Hegel understands civil society as a "system of needs," based on the division of labor and trade. Basic human needs —for food, shelter and clothing—can be met more easily and efficiently if people specialize in producing what they are good at and then engage in trade. As the division of labor develops, and people are able to satisfy their basic needs with relative ease, they turn to fulfilling desires that go beyond the necessities. The development of desire, in turn, leads to further divisions of labor, and thus arises a complex economy. To this extent, Hegel's account is rather familiar, deriving largely from Adam Smith. But the perspective from which Hegel views the division of labor is different from Smith's. Whereas Smith is primarily concerned with the division of labor and trade as factors that determine the wealth of a nation, Hegel is concerned with these social arrangements insofar as they pertain to freedom and recognition.

The key, for Hegel, is that in civil society, social esteem depends not on family or religious affiliation but on the ability to provide a particular good or service. To take a contemporary example: If one is talented at cutting hair or playing basketball, customers or fans will accord that person respect quite apart from the social class into which he or she was born. In modern societies, observes Hegel, members of the economy are able to choose their career paths according to their interests and talents, and to gain recognition for doing so. Recognition is reflected in the wages, or payment, for a job well done. The freedom to develop one's interests and talents is the fulfillment of individuality; it means striking out on one's own, making a name for one's self and not simply inheriting a title.

But such freedom, as Hegel sees it, is not self-subsistent. It depends for its full realization on another, contrasting realm of life in which the individual belongs simply as a member: that of the family. Unlike the economy, in which recognition is based on particular interests and abilities, the family is the sphere of "immediate unity" based on love. One attains recognition in the family "not as an individual but as a member." In a well-ordered family, members love and care for each other unconditionally, in a way unmediated by particular interests and talents. They might still appreciate each other for particular qualities and skills, but such appreciation is not the primary basis of their recognition. In this ideal, family members commit to each other and stick together regardless of their career aspirations and accomplishments. Hegel sees in such loyalty a kind of freedom that exists in contrast to the individuality of the marketplace. Unlike a producer or a consumer, who is limited by the various other professions in society, a family member enjoys, within the family, the freedom of being unlimited by anything external, or alien. In the well-ordered family, the identity of each is absorbed within the whole.

Such communal freedom provides a contrast to the individual self-direction that prevails within the economy. The special significance of civil society, of particularity and distinction, emerges only in relation to a community in which esteem is undifferentiated. The family and civil society thus, for Hegel, form a pair: Unconditional love versus recognition based on merit; immediate unity versus individual self-expression. He suggests that the full enjoyment of one depends on the other.

But this pair of institutions, and the distinctive form of recognition that prevails within each, depends, for Hegel, on a third—the state. Today we tend to think of the state as necessary to provide defense and to enforce property rights. Some would add that it should provide a safety net for the poor. Hegel recognizes all of these familiar functions. He devotes special attention to the predicament of those who lack the particular skills rewarded in civil society at any given moment. The state, he thinks, should provide for the poor so that inequalities do not grow too vast. But he thinks the state is about something more than any of these important functions. The ultimate purpose of the state is to remedy a certain deficiency in the kind of freedom that civil society provides. In civil society, individuals win distinction as parts of an elaborate system of interconnected vocations. In doing so, they achieve independence vis-a-vis the family. But vis-a-vis each other, they are bound in relationships of *dependence*.

Consider a small business owner, such as the owner of a coffee shop. His ability to win distinction as a producer of fine coffee depends on a multitude of factors not entirely within his control. He depends on the landlord from whom he rents the space, the roaster who supplies the beans, the manufacturers who make the trucks that ship the beans across country. These other members of civil society on whom the owner of the shop depends are "others" in a sense that is remote, impersonal, and even alien. (In a vast economy with a highly developed division of labor, the owner of the shop has probably never met or even spoken to many of his suppliers.) If the shop owner, and anyone in civil society, is to be fully free, fully independent, he must come to understand the impersonal others on whom he depends as equal participants in a common way of life that transcends particular needs and desires. To promote such understanding—a sense of the common good, of the identity of each with all—is the purpose of the state.

The notion of the state as embodying the common good hearkens back to Jean-Jacques Rousseau, a figure who had great influence on Hegel and whose notion of the "general will" in contrast to the particular interest finds expression in French republicanism today. But Hegel disagrees with Rousseau in one crucial respect: Whereas Rousseau believes that the common good, or general will, finds expression only when citizens set aside their particular interests, Hegel believes that such an ideal is a misguided abstraction. The common good, and the sense of patriotism that sustains it, can be achieved only by *integrating* particular interests within a body that deals with matters of common concern.

Hegel's basic point is that the concrete way in which individuals win distinction as members of the economy should be the basis for their participation in the common good. Rather than do away with all partial associations at the level of the state, Hegel's state gives them equal recognition. In contemporary terms, a system that accords a representative role to all elements of civil society—not just powerful ones such as Wall Street and big business—overcomes the problem of state capture by special interests. By acknowledging all guilds, vocations, and professions, the state encourages them to transcend their purely individual, self-interested character. By bringing representatives of each profession face to face for the purpose of deliberating on matters of public concern, they come to know and respect each other as distinctive parts of the common good. The state can thus be seen to recapture a kind of family spirit at the level of society as a whole, but in a way that preserves rather than dissolves the differences of civil society.

Taken together, the family, civil society, and the state, constitute a differentiated whole in which each part is integral to the others. The family, with its immediate unity, cannot exist without civil society and its differentiation. Each provides a distinctive kind of freedom in contrast to the other. Civil society, for its part, cannot exist without the state. Without a body that unifies civil society and gives public recognition to the various professions, they would be unable recognize each other as contributing in distinctive ways to the social whole. The state thus secures the freedom of civil society, which, in turn, promotes the freedom of the family. Together, the three institutions embody the "idea of freedom."

THE ENCROACHMENT OF CIVIL SOCIETY ON STATE AND FAMILY

The problem that we face today might be described in the following Hegelian terms: The economy, or civil society, has colonized the state on the one hand and the family on the other. By encroaching upon the very spheres of life in contrast to which it attains its distinctive dignity, the economy has itself become corrupt. Members of the economy are increasingly less able to understand themselves as providing for a family and as cultivating a particular skill that contributes to the common good. They instead understand themselves as embroiled in a competitive race to an ever-receding pinnacle of success and, at the same time, as stuck in the vicious cycle of consumption and emptiness.

The sense in which civil society has colonized the state is most evident in the influence of big money and special interests on politics. It has become evident to many American voters that the government represents a few prominent economic interests and not others. Far from the Hegelian vision, in which the state gives public recognition to all professions, thus embodying a differentiated whole, the contemporary state arguably serves some at the expense of others.

But there is a subtler sense in which civil society and the state have merged to the detriment of both; a sense reflected in the very ideology of establishment politics on the Right and Left. One could call it the ideal of meritocracy, or "fair equality of opportunity": Eliminate barriers to success, such as dire poverty, prejudices based on race, religion, and gender, and then let the free market operate unimpeded. In different forms, this has been the core message of mainstream politics on the Left and Right. Their differences are not to do with the meritocratic ideal itself but on how to achieve it. Whereas the left emphasizes a stronger safety net for the poor, the right emphasizes unfettered free enterprise. But both versions have failed to resonate with the electorate. And from Hegel's perspective we can see why. Although eliminating unfairness and overcoming bigotry are worthy goals, they are worthy for the sake of a higher purpose of the state: to embody a common good that gives public recognition to the variety of professions and their contributions. In Hegel's terms, when the state acts to regulate the economy, to mitigate inequalities, and provide for the poor, or when it acts to maximize GDP and to encourage consumption, the state acts merely as an extension of civil society.

But civil society has not only encroached upon the state. It has also permeated the family. That dire economic necessity can put pressure on family ties is well known. When mothers and fathers are working long and exhausting hours to make ends meet, they have less time to spend with their children and with each other. It should not be surprising that low-earners have more children out-of-wedlock and divorce at significantly higher rates than affluent professionals.[2]

But equally disconcerting, and less recognized, is the sense in which the family is eroding in a different way among the upper-middle class. Increasingly, the family is losing its distinctive character as a sphere of "immediate unity" in which interests, talents, and achievements are secondary to unconditional membership. Such erosion finds striking expression in "helicopter parenting," the way in which mothers and fathers anxiously hover over nearly every aspect of their children's lives, especially those pertaining to achievement in civil society. Helicopter parenting amounts to an obsession with career success, as if attaining to the prestigious heights of law, medicine, business, politics, or NGO work were the ultimate token of a life well-lived. Instead of guiding their children toward a range of career paths that will enable them to support themselves and a family of their own, while also instilling in them certain virtues of character that transcend the workplace, parents frenetically monitor their children to make sure they are poised to get into the eighth-grade math league at age ten, or ready to try out for varsity baseball as a freshman. They demand rigid practice schedules, berate their children for poor performance, and offer various incentives for achievement. Recognition in the family comes to be based on the achievement of particular tasks on the path to the Ivy Leagues.

The home, whose purpose is to provide a contrast to the economy, has become colonized by it. Upper-middle-class family life has become defined by aspirations that might be worthy *in civil society*, but which should be irrelevant to family solidarity. From the perspective of the corruption of immediate unity, it is all the same. The notions of loyalty, commitment to each other *because* we are family (quite apart from what we do for work), and devotion to children (quite apart from what they do), is giving way to the resume conception of the good spouse or child. It is perhaps little wonder, then, that increasing numbers of successful professionals are simply deciding to forgo having families, which are becoming, for them, merely another source of career and social pressure.[3]

The dissolution of immediate unity represents a corruption not only of the family but also of work. Without a secure grounding in a sphere of life in which recognition is unmediated by particular interests and abilities, the realm of work becomes all-consuming. People begin to expect everything from their job. In such an atmosphere, it is no wonder that a demand for "meaningful work" is asserted with urgent intensity. A job that may be hard, rote, and even painful, but at least supports a family, and is in that sense fulfilling, becomes meaningless and intolerable. Work must now fulfill "my life's purpose." From Hegel's perspective, such a demand of work is misplaced. Life-purpose, or universality, Hegel suggests, inheres not in one's job, which is about providing a particular good or service, but in the balance among complementary spheres of life—among the various professions that constitute the economy, and, more broadly, in the relations of the economy to the family and to the state. Work that is genuinely meaningful, according to Hegel, is so for two reasons: (1) it supports a family, and (2) it allows for the development of a particular talent that contributes to the common good, and for which one is publicly recognized.

Without the family and the state, however, a job well done loses its dignity. Members of the economy, unrelated to any institution that represents the common good, and unsheltered by the guarantee of membership within the family, find themselves awash in a complex and impersonal system of division of labor and trade, out of which they must try to gain some control. The pressures of landlords, remote suppliers, other industries, and fickle consumer preferences, threaten constantly to put people out of business. Thus arises the pressure to master one's circumstances, to grasp for an ever-receding sense of security by turning as much profit as possible, even if it means cutting costs, abusing labor, and supplying a lesser product that customers can somehow be persuaded to accept. Where the family and state are robust, the desire for profit is circumscribed, on the one hand, by the goal of supporting a family, and, on the other, by the goal of contributing to the common good. When the family and the state dissolve, the desire for profit has no bounds. What emerges in place of a society of mutual recognition is a system of competition governed by wholly utilitarian norms.

Kojève's Authority and the Sources
of Political Legitimacy

From this Hegelian perspective, it seems inevitable that civil society's colonization of the state and cannibalization of the family would provoke a crisis of legitimacy. It would open a space, in other words, for candidates who would challenge not only the prevailing policy consensus but also the prevailing, corrupt modes of political legitimation. Indeed, a society that serves nothing more than the meritocratic ideal could only be challenged by appeals to authority that the ruling regime no longer recognized, for such a lack of recognition was precisely the cause of the discontent. To better understand the purely political dimension of this crisis, it is helpful to turn to Hegel's twentieth century commentator, Alexandre Kojève.

In *The Notion of Authority* (1954), Kojève defines authority as one's ability to act on others "without these others reacting against him."[4] It is important to note that, under Kojève's definition, mere compulsion by force does not constitute authority but rather the absence of it. For Kojève, all authority must be recognized or legitimate: "As for 'authoritarian' action, it is by definition 'legal' or 'legitimate.' ... it is meaningless ... to speak of an 'illegitimate' or 'illegal' Authority.... To deny the legitimacy of Authority is not to recognize it—in other words, by this very act, to destroy it."[5] Authority in this context can therefore be used interchangeably with political legitimacy, as it is in this essay.

Kojève proceeds to identify four distinct and irreducible sources of authority: that of the father, the master, the leader, and the judge. The authority of any political regime, he argues, rests upon some combination of these, and stable or total political authority includes all four. Furthermore, this typology of authority can be used to explain the character of a regime. For example, a regime that legitimates itself based on the authority of judge, master, and leader—in that order of emphasis—would correspond to "bourgeois 'conservatism'" (Tories), while a regime of judge, leader, and master would correspond to bourgeois liberalism. The permutation of leader, master, and judge would produce Bolshevism, and so on.[6]

Although Kojève does not explicitly connect his typology with Hegel's three moments of ethical life, there is an apparent and direct correspondence. The authority of the father derives from the family. The authority of the master and leader are associated with the government or the state, strictly speaking, and the judge's authority is associated with the bourgeoisie or civil society. (It is also necessary to note that Kojève's classification of authority relates to the ways in which government is conceived of and legitimized among rulers and ruled, not to the statutory power of any particular branch or apparatus of the state or the personal qualities of its leaders.[7]) These associations will become clearer if each is examined in turn.

All authority, according to Kojève, has a temporal structure. The authority of the father is fundamentally the authority of the past or tradition. It is, therefore, the authority arising from and embodying the sphere of immediate unity. It is impossible to choose or elect one's father or creator, just as it is impossible to choose one's past or tradition. One is simply born into it as a member. Less intuitively, Kojève also asserts that what is often called the authority of the majority is ultimately the authority of the father. For the authority of the majority is simply the name given to the "general will" when the latter loses its divine or ideological character and which it loses its claim to justice or the authority of the judge. Insofar as the "general will" is the "cause of the whole," or what allows for the conception of a whole, then any authority ascribed to it is "the Authority of the ('final') 'cause'—that is to say, also that of 'tradition,' of all that contributes to the preservation of identity with itself"[8]—the father.

Kojève groups the authority of the master and the authority of the leader into the ensemble of "governmental authority."[9] As in Hegel, the authority of the master arises from the recognition of victory in competition or war. The master overcomes the animal fear of death in order to gain recognition. Hence the authority of the master is the authority of the immediate present—of the urgent or existential risks of the present. This type is represented most obviously by the military commander or, more broadly, by the "executive." The authority of the leader, meanwhile, is the authority of the future; the leader exerts authority by organizing his followers around a project or initiative. This is the authority exercised by both the parliamentarian and the revolutionary.

Finally, the judge holds authority as the embodiment of justice or equity, as one perceived to have special knowledge of a just order. This is also an authority of the present, as it is based upon the judgment of what is. The judge does not propose projects, nor is his authority based upon mere knowledge of traditional law. But unlike the master, who inhabits the kinetic present, the judge inhabits the eternal present of the Platonic forms. Justice is not arbitrary or temporary; it represents the penetration of eternity into time. The judge's equitable arbitration in the present, irrespective of a claimant's past or future, is the reason such authority is sought by and associated with the bourgeoisie or civil society. It is "the Authority of the Judge that comes closest to 'bourgeois' morality."[10]

The authority of the judge, moreover—resistant to temporalization—necessarily exists in an adversarial relationship with the other three temporal types. Indeed, the judge "has no true authority except in so far as he sets himself (if need arises) against the three other Authorities." If the others were inherently just, the judge would not represent a distinct form of authority.[11] At the same time, however, the judge relies upon the others in a way that they do not rely upon the judge. The judge at some point requires a state—more broadly, to be realized, justice must be experienced within time, within history—yet political power, even when it involves justice, "has always been accompanied by the others (Authority of the Leader, of the Master or the Father) and *dominated* by them."[12]

THE INSTABILITY OF MODERN POLITICAL AUTHORITY

Modern political regimes, according to Kojève, are differentiated from their ancient counterparts principally by their exclusion of the authority of the father. This exclusion produces a fundamental instability, creating conditions under which the remaining forms of authority undermine themselves.

The revolutions that produced modernity began as bourgeois revolutions, Kojève argues, and bourgeois revolutions are defined by the desire to suppress or amputate the authority of the father. The bourgeois, who is of lowly origins, must disown the past. For him to hold power, other forms of authority must become preeminent. The "destruction of the Authority of the Father," however, "is ... fateful to political Authority in general."[13] Absent the authority of father, the remaining forms of authority are set against each other and can no longer be integrated.[14] Without the father, "an achievement called inheritance" is no longer maintained; a stable basis for the immediate unity that creates "citizens"—the familial aspect of the political entity—is lost. Authority becomes apolitical and decays.

The primary consequence of the suppression of the authority of the father is that the regime must rely upon the authority of the leader if it is to remain political, if it is to remain "human": "the Present deprived of the Past is *human*, that is to say, historical or political, only in so far as it implies the Future (otherwise it is the Present of brutes)."[15] But the authority of the future as the sole source of political authority inevitably becomes detached from both the past and the present. Deprived of a past, political authority must always represent a revolutionary project. "Thus, the logical culmination of the 'constitutional' theory of a Montesquieu is the theory of 'permanent revolution' of a Trotsky."[16]

Nevertheless, this logical culmination is not its historical culmination. For such authority soon loses itself in utopian aspirations. It constructs a project with no ties to reality, "which subsequently fails to *come true* ... and it drags along with it in its downfall the Authority that has produced it—and, with it, the State itself."[17]

Meanwhile, when the authority of the future loses its connection to reality—thereby becoming ahistorical and apolitical—the authority of the historical present (the master) likewise collapses upon itself. The present, too, becomes apolitical and "dehumanized" when it is detached from the future (and already removed from the past). It thus degenerates into mere "administration"· "it becomes a pure 'technique' that deals only with what is, that is to say with 'raw' information."[18] The authority of the master, in other words, becomes a technocracy concerned only with the coordination of existing forces. But power that is only force, for Kojève, is not authority—it is not legitimacy. The problem is further compounded by the fact that the authority of the master, by its nature, "does not have a reality" if there is no risk of war.[19]

Thus the last remaining authority is that of the judge, but the judge's authority does not survive fully intact, either. The authority of the judge, always in a complex and partially adversarial relationship with the others, can only function as an authentically political authority when it is integrated with them—when in adjudicates between and is supported by the other political authorities, giving them stability and harmony.[20] Yet when the others have ceased to function as political authorities, the authority of the judge necessarily becomes apolitical insofar as justice itself necessarily becomes particularized. Justice becomes individual or private justice, purely "bourgeois" justice. The final result is the collapse of political— fully human—authority:

> There is no longer, strictly speaking, a State or citizens as such: there is a "Society" made up of isolated individuals ('private' persons) ... which are regulated by the ('private') judicial Authority, and the Government is nothing more than a *force*, with the responsibility of carrying out the acts of the judicial Authority.[21]

The conclusion of the bourgeois revolution, then, is the end of political authority. All spheres of life are subordinated to the apolitical and ahistorical present of civil society.

THE END OF HISTORY?

It is increasingly clear that the end of the Cold War did not result in the flowering of Hegelian mutual recognition within realized and self-conscious nation-states. Rather, it only provoked a new attempt to create a universal civil society by de-integrating the economy from the other political institutions or authorities. Although evocative of the Hegelian idiom, what the declaration of the end of history has come to mean stands in radical contradiction to Hegel's thought. In retrospect, it has become an expression for the transformation of the entire world into an unbounded and unbalanced civil society, a world in which national sovereignty and citizenship are eroded from without while the family and the state are colonized from within.

Such a world can represent the end of history in only one respect—as the elimination of the political, of the "human." Insofar as it can only be accomplished through the destruction of the political, however, such an end state can never have legitimacy; it could be maintained only by force, and its authority could never be authentically recognized. Kojève himself at times suggested that a global, homogeneous state would be the end of history. Yet if such a state is simply the universal and unconstrained civil society of our "unipolar" world—and it is difficult to conceive of it in any other way—then it is far from a society of Hegelian mutual recognition. As the foregoing analysis of Kojève's understanding of authority makes clear, such an outcome is thoroughly incompatible with political recognition. In Kojève's own words, the domination of bourgeois civil society is "simply the progressive disappearance of political reality as such—that is to say, of the Power or the Authority of the State: life is dominated by its animal aspect, by concerns related to food and sexuality."[22]

It was perhaps inevitable, then, that this erosion of the human would provoke a political reaction. Hegel would argue that it could never represent an "end of history" precisely because the elimination of the human would always provoke resistance. When the morality of civil society colonizes the state and the family, it effectively destroys all political authority and thereby deprives itself of any genuine political legitimacy as well. The "populist" movements of recent years might, at bottom, be interpreted to be revolts against this expansion of civil society and its subordination of what should be balancing institutions or authorities.

It is equally unsurprising that these movements appeal to forms of authority that have been suppressed and are no longer recognized. Perilous as it might be to analyze contemporary campaign rhetoric, it is striking how frequently Trump appealed to the themes of "father,"[23] master ("winning"—in his personal career and with respect to foreign policy) and leader ("make America great again" as a unifying project), and how little he appealed to "justice"—compared to his opponents, and vice-versa.

Those critical or fearful of Trump and "populism" generally may be right in their apprehension that these movements have little concern with (private) justice and may, to varying degrees, even be hostile to it. But such criticism, if it stops there, ignores the arguably deeper crisis of political legitimacy facing our institutions. The opponents of "populism," especially in 2016, were incapable of offering any compelling alternative because they have come to view "politics" as merely the administration of civil society—as the administration of private justice within it. They can offer competing adjudications of conflicts between, for example, professionals and workers or rural areas and metropoles, but their narrow and apolitical conceptions of authority can no longer integrate individuals within a political whole or recognize the manifold ethical "moments" within human life.

Far from building a Hegelian politics of mutual recognition, we are increasingly losing the ability to recognize authentically human work or politics. It is unclear whether today's "populism" can offer any constructive contributions toward reintegrating human and political institutions. But unless a balanced relationship between the family, civil society, and the state—past, present, and future—is restored, then today's crisis of legitimacy will continue.

NOTES

1. Shadi Hamid, "The End of the End of History," *Foreign Policy*, November 15, 2016, http://foreignpolicy.com/2016/11/15/the-end-of-the-end-of-history/.
2. See, for example, Thomas E. Trail and Benjamin R. Karney, "What's (Not) Wrong with Low-Income Marriages," *Journal of Marriage and Family* Volume 74, Issue 3 (June 2012): 413–427.
3. Various studies of this phenomenon are summarized in Sharon Lerner, "Knocked Up and Knocked Down: Why America's Widening Fertility Class Divide is a Problem," *Slate*, Sept. 26, 2011, http://www.slate.com/articles/double_x/doublex/2011/09/knocked_up_and_knocked_down.html.
4. Alexandre Kojève, *The Notion of Authority (A Brief Presentation)*, ed. Francois Terré, trans. Hager Weslati (London: Verso, 2014), 8.

5. *Ibid.*, 10–11.
6. *Ibid.*, 67–69.
7. In other words, the authority of the legislator or the judge is not necessarily related to the power of, for example, the legislative or judicial branches, or even to the biographical characteristics of the rulers. It rather concerns how the purposes of the state are conceived or the ends toward which authority is exercised and perceived to exist. For instance, if the main purposes of the state are believed to be to uphold contracts and maintain a "level playing field," that state would be said to be dominated by the authority of the judge. Likewise, a state that based its legitimacy on a new political project would be dominated by the authority of the leader; military defense or conquest, the master; and preserving social traditions, the father.
8. *Ibid.*, 41.
9. *Ibid.*, 76.
10. *Ibid.*, 91.
11. *Ibid.*, 51–52.
12. *Ibid.*, 22.
13. *Ibid.*, 70.
14. For Kojève, the liberal "separation of powers," when it constitutes a separation of authority, heralds the decline of political authority. It is beyond the scope of this essay to discuss this specific argument in detail. Cf. *Ibid.*, 63–87.
15. *Ibid.*, 64.
16. *Ibid.*, 64.
17. *Ibid.*, 75.
18. *Ibid.*, 75.
19. *Ibid.*, 77.
20. *Ibid.*, 52.
21. *Ibid.*, 75–76.
22. *Ibid.*, 65–66.
23. George Lakoff, "Understanding the Allure of Trump," *Berkeley Blog*, University of California at Berkeley, August 1, 2016, http://blogs.berkeley.edu/2016/08/01/understanding-the-allure-of-trump/.

LIST OF REFERENCES

Hamid, Shadi. 2016. The End of the End of History. *Foreign Policy*, November 15. http://foreignpolicy.com/2016/11/15/the-end-of-the-end-of-history/.
Kojève, Alexandre. 2014. *The Notion of Authority (A Brief Presentation)*, ed. Francois Terré, Trans. Hager Weslati. London: Verso.

Lakoff, George. 2016. Understanding the Allure of Trump. *Berkeley Blog*, University of California at Berkeley, August 1. http://blogs.berkeley.edu/2016/08/01/understanding-the-allure-of-trump/.

Lerner, Sharon. 2011. Knocked Up and Knocked Down: Why America's Widening Fertility Class Divide is a Problem. *Slate*, September 26. http://www.slate.com/articles/double_x/doublex/2011/09/knocked_up_and_knocked_down.html.

Trail, Thomas E., and Benjamin R. Karney. June 2012. What's (Not) Wrong with Low-Income Marriages. *Journal of Marriage and Family* 74 (3): 413–427.

CHAPTER 16

A Festival for Frustrated Egos: The Rise of Trump from an Early Frankfurt School Critical Theory Perspective

Claudia Leeb

INTRODUCTION[1]

Although the fascist agitator doubtlessly takes up certain tendencies within those he addresses, he does so as the mandatory of powerful political and economic interests. Psychological dispositions do not actually cause fascism; rather, fascism defines a psychological area which can be successfully exploited by the forces which promote it for entirely non-psychological reasons of self-interest.[2]

Scholars in the US American context in a recent *Logos* publication, edited by Chris O'Kane, have convincingly noted that the contemporary Frankfurt school, of the sort represented by Habermas, Honneth and Fraser, with its dismissal of psychoanalytic and Marxist thought, and its focus on providing critical theory with a normative foundation, does not have much, if anything, to offer when it comes to grasping the rise of Trump in the United States. To grasp the rise of Trump, they argue, we must turn our attention to the first generation of Frankfurt school thinkers, including

C. Leeb (✉)
Washington State University, Pullman, WA, USA

© The Author(s) 2018
M. B. Sable, A. J. Torres (eds.), *Trump and Political Philosophy*,
https://doi.org/10.1007/978-3-319-74427-8_16

297

Adorno, Horkheimer and Marcuse, who all drew on a combination of
Freud and Marx to grasp the rise of fascism in Europe and the proto-
fascist elements in the United States.[3]

Theodor W. Adorno, in his "Freudian Theory and the Pattern of Fascist
Propaganda" (2002), in which he analyzes the techniques by which fascist
agitators in the United States and Europe aimed to get followers, argues that
one needs to apply a psychoanalytic approach to grasp the agitators' overall
approach, which Freud delivered in his *Group Psychology and the Analysis of
the Ego* (originally published in 1922), published long before German fascism became acute. According to Adorno, Freud "clearly foresaw the rise
and nature of fascist mass movements in purely psychological categories"[4]

Curiously, none of the thinkers who draw on Adorno to analyze the rise
of Trump draw on this text, and the only one who draws on psychoanalytic insights to grasp the rise of Trump, Samir Gandesha (2017), suggests
that we must eschew Freud, which is rather surprising given their general
complaint in the aforementioned *Logos* edition that the contemporary
Frankfurt school has done away with psychoanalysis as a critical tool. This
omission seems to be a symptom of the continuing eschewal of psychoanalytic thought in the Anglo-American context in general and in political
and social theory in particular.

In this chapter I return to Freud's *Group Psychology and the Ego* to grasp
the rise of Trump in the United States. Following the tradition of the early
Frankfurt school critical theory, I combine the insights of Freud with a
Marxist analysis, to show how the socio-psychological mechanisms inter-
act with economic factors in the rise of Trump. I also draw on Adorno's as
well as Alexander and Margarete Mitscherlich's use of Freud's text to
grasp the socio-psychological aspects of the techniques of fascist agitators
in the United States and in Europe.[5] Furthermore, one cannot understand
the rise of Trump without an intersectional approach, which means that
we must not only consider class, but also gender and "race" to grasp his
appeal to the masses, which I pursue in this chapter.

However, I do not claim to give an exhaustive picture of the psychoanalytic
mechanisms that led to the rise of Trump, as that would go beyond the space
of a book chapter. Rather, I focus on some of the mechanisms that I consider
as central to grasp Trumpism.[6] In particular, I will discuss ego-ideal replacement, idealization in narcissistic love, the liberation from repressions and frustrations, and the displacement of hatred onto vulnerable groups.

The guiding aim of the analysis of fascist agitators in the United States in
the post-World War II era, to which Adorno's essay "Freudian Theory and
the Pattern of Fascist Propaganda" belongs, was to find out if European fascism can also happen in the United States. At the time of their analysis, the

answer for them was that under current conditions—a booming economy and a relatively stable welfare state—this is unlikely to happen. However, this does mean that in changed economic circumstances there is the potential that what happened in Europe can also happen in the United States. As John Abromeit (2016) convincingly points out, the economic circumstances in the United States today are much closer to those of Europe in the 30's, which is why we must pay close attention to the early Frankfurt school insights into the rise of fascism in Europe and their assessment of the proto-fascist elements in the United States.

Here it is also important to clarify the (dis-)connection between fascism and right wing populism. Here I follow the perspective of Abromeit (2016), who points out that fascism is an extreme form of right-wing populism. Such a view underlines that the two are connected, without conflating them. Such (dis-)connection also underlines the inherent dangers of Trumpism, and that political theorists must do everything to grasp what made him rise, which also includes being open to theories that political theorists (even of the early Frankfurt school kind) usually dismiss or ignore.

This chapter is composed of four sections, including this introduction. The next section, "Ego-Ideal Replacement of Frustrated Egos," shows how the frustrations of neo-liberal capitalism led to ego-ideal replacement. The middle section, "Narcissistic Love and Displaced Hate," explains some of the dangerous consequences of ego-ideal replacement which one also finds in narcissistic love, and how Trump managed to successfully displace the anger generated by capitalist exploitation upon vulnerable minority groups. The fourth section, "The Trump Festival," explains how the liberation from social and moral constraints worked to favor Trump. I conclude with a few words on how we can avoid sliding from Trumpism into fascism.

EGO-IDEAL REPLACEMENT OF FRUSTRATED EGOS

The early Frankfurt School's deployment of Freud can help us understand Trump's appeal. In particular, these thinkers draw on Freud's ideas of a libidinal tie between the leader and her followers, and ego-ideal replacement to grasp the rise of fascism in Europe and the appeal of fascist agitators in the United States. Freud's ideas allow me to avoid showing contempt for those who voted for Trump, which is readily equated with the working-class, that is the class that has always been readily blamed for fascism and continues to be blamed for the rise of right-wing populism in both Europe and the United States. After all, it was not only the working-class that supported Trump. As in all forms of populism there was cross-class support, and a large constituency of people with college and graduate degrees also voted for him.

In this chapter I am interested to find out what turned the American people into a "psychological mass",[7] in which, as Adorno explains, "modern [wo/]man revert to patterns of behavior which flagrantly contradict their own rational level and the present stage of enlightened technological civilization".[8] The answer that Freud gives to this question is the existence of a libidinal tie between the members and their leader. Libido is the energy "of those instincts which have to do with all that may be comprised under the world 'love'" with sexual union as their aim".[9] In terms of masses the libidinal instincts that have been diverted from their sexual origin, "though always preserving enough of their original nature to keep their identity recognizable (as in such features as the longing for proximity, and self-sacrifice)".[10]

Trump won the support of millions of people for aims that are largely incompatible with their own rational self-interest by synthetically producing a libidinal bond between himself and his supporters. How did he manage to do that? As with fascist leadership, Trump aims to "keep primal libidinal energy on an unconscious level to divert its manifestation in a way suitable to political ends".[11] There is too little in the content of Trump's views, though, that could be loved, and positively bond people to him.

However, as Freud puts it, "the leader or the leading idea might also, so to speak, be negative, hatred against a particular person or institution might operate in just the same unifying way, and might call up the same unifying emotional ties as positive attachment".[12] The unifying emotional ties that bind supporters to Trump and to each other implies both positive and negative attachments. Both promote open hatred and hostility against immigrants, particularly (but not only) those from Middle Eastern nations and Latin American countries. Ego-ideal replacement generates a positive attachment between the leader and her followers, which is the core psychological mechanism that allows a leader to manipulate a mass. The libidinal structure of a mass is the result of a "distinction between the ego and the ego ideal and to the double kind of tie which this makes possible—identification, and putting the object in the place of the ego ideal".[13]

To begin with, our mental existence has been "separated into a coherent ego and into an unconscious and repressed portion which is left outside it".[14]

The ego is originally purely narcissistic and enjoys full self-sufficiency. However, because it then has to contend with demands from the environment, which it cannot always meet, it splits part of itself off—the ego ideal, which represents the ideal view we have of ourselves, or what we aspire to be like. The ego ideal monitors the narcissistic ego to keep it in line with the ideal, via the functions of reality checking and moral conscience, which is why the ego ideal is often in conflict with the ego.[15] The tie between the leader and her followers is based upon the followers putting the object (the leader) in place of their ego ideal, and the tie between the followers is established via identification with each other.

Based upon Freud's analysis Adorno and the Mitscherlichs argue that the rise of fascism is based upon ego-ideal replacement. However, they also suggest that the bond between the leader and her followers is based on identification, suggesting that ego-ideal replacement implies identification.[16] Similarly, contemporary critical theorists of the early Frankfurt school tradition, such as Gandesha (2017), argue that identification is at the basis of Trumpism.

However, Freud makes clear that ego-ideal replacement is *not* the same as identification, which is a result of his distinction between *Verinnerlichung* (introjection) and identification. Introjection refers to the process whereby the followers replace their ego-ideal with the foreign object (the leader). In contrast, identification is the process that establishes tie between the followers.

In psychoanalysis identification implies the earliest expression of an emotional tie with another person.[17] When a person identifies with another person, she molds her own ego ideal after the object she has taken as her role model.[18] As a result the person has enriched herself with the properties of the model. In contrast, when one introjects an object, the ego is not enriched as in identification. Rather, the "ego is impoverished, it has surrendered itself to the object, it has substituted the object for its own most important constituent".[19]

People who voted for Trump did not identify with him, or took him as their role-model. Rather, they have "introjected" Trump into themselves, which means that they have replaced their ego ideal with him, which allowed them at the same time to identify with other Trump followers. The result is a mass of Trump supporters with impoverished egos, who have surrendered their egos to their leader. The problem with such surrender is that they substituted the leader (Trump) for their own most important constituent—their ego ideal.

Since the chief function if the ego-ideal is the testing of reality, as well as "self-observation, the moral conscience, the censorship of dreams, and the chief influence in repression", it is no surprise that there is no outcry from his followers when Trump proposes the most appalling policies and violates existing norms that hitherto had been unquestioned.[20] How has Trump managed that millions of people replaced him with their ego ideal, which allowed him to manipulate them for his own purposes? Here we must combine a psychoanalytic approach with an economic analysis.

In the United States today, particularly since the crisis of neo-liberal capitalism in 2008, but even before that, most people have experienced economic insecurity and many cannot even meet their daily basic needs, such as adequate shelter and having enough to eat.[21] People are at the same time blamed for their economic situation, since the predominating liberal capitalist ideology suggests that there are no class, gender and racial limits to economic success, and everybody can make it from dishwasher to millionaire, if you just try hard enough.

If you are still not an American "success story", well, then perhaps you just have not tried hard enough. People are not just confronted with frustrating economic conditions (which one also finds in other nations), but a liberal capitalist ideology that makes people feel personally responsible for not doing better. In such a scenario people frequently cannot live up to their ego ideal—the internalized standard of liberal capitalist society, that is economic success—which generates narcissistically wounded egos that feel devalued, and which Trump exploited for his electoral success.

Trump himself is one of the loudest proponents of the neo-liberal capitalist ideology of the success story, which we find for example in his argument that he likes to appoint billionaires to his cabinet, because they are "smart, successful" people—which implicitly tells all those people, who have not lived up to the success story, that they are losers. Insofar as Trump contributed to further insult already narcissistically wounded egos, why do they continue to support him?[22]

By replacing their own ego ideal with Trump via introjection, Trump supporters could obtain all those qualities that they have not been able to attain in their own lives, which helps to explain how they could idolize Trump even as he calls them losers. However, the leader does not need to possess any of these qualities. Rather, Trump was met by his followers half way, who invested him with the qualities of greatness, perfection and importance, because they could then obtain those qualities for themselves via ego-ideal replacement.[23]

However, as Adorno further points out, "while appearing as a superman, the leader must at the same time work the miracle of appearing as an average person, just as Hitler posed as a composite of King Kong and the suburban barber".[24] Because some minor parts of the narcissistic libido, which were not invested into the leader, remain attached to the followers' ego, the "superman" must still resemble in some aspects his followers.[25]

Here we can find a basic device of fascist propaganda—the concept of the "great little man", which refers to "a person who suggests both omnipotence and the idea that he is just one of the folks, a plain, red-blooded American, untainted by material or spiritual wealth. Psychological ambivalence helps to work a social miracle. The leader image gratifies the follower's twofold wish to submit to authority and to be the authority [her/]himself".[26]

Trump's startling failures as a past presidential candidate supported his electoral success. It was not despite such failures, but *because* of them, that he won the support of frustrated egos, who themselves suffer from feelings of failure by not being able to live up to their ego ideal. Posing as both the new King Kong of America who makes "America great again" and at the same time pretending that he is just one of them, "a plain, red-blooded American" he was the ideal subject for ego-ideal replacement.

Narcissistic Love and Displaced Hate

Another way to understand ego-ideal replacement in the masses is with Freud's distinction between mature and narcissistic love. In narcissistic love, one choses a love object not for the sake of its own merits, as in mature love, but because "the object serves as a substitute for some unattained ego ideal of our own. We love it on account of the perfections which we have striven to reach for our own ego, and which we should now like to procure in this roundabout way as a means of satisfying our narcissism".[27]

Adorno, based on Freud's insights, points out that in the formation of fascist masses, narcissistic love plays a central role, because of the characteristic modern conflict between a rational ego and the continuous failure to satisfy their ego ideal demands. Such conflict results in strong narcissistic impulses which can be satisfied only through idealization, which implies a partial transfer of the narcissistic libido to the object. As he puts it, "by making the leader [her/]his ideal [s/]he loves himself, as it were, but gets rid of the stains of frustration and discontent which mar his picture of his own empirical self".[28]

Similarly, the "love-object" Trump was chosen by his followers to satisfy their narcissism, because of the conflict between their ego and their continuous failure to satisfy their ego ideal demands. People "fell in love" with Trump, because he provided the illusion for them that they "can become great again," even if they continue to be exploited and insulted by the class to whom Trump and his cabinet belong,[29] and can barely survive. Insofar as they replaced their ego ideal with Trump, they could get rid of their stains of frustration and discontent that are the result of the injustices produced by neo-liberal capitalism.

In mature love the critical ego maintains its functions and the lover only identifies herself partially with the love-object, and she is thereby enriched with some of the love-object's qualities and undergoes a partial change using the love object as a model. In contrast, in narcissistic love the person substitutes an alien object for her own ego ideal, and as a result the ego blindly submits to the love object and the reality orientation of the old ego ideal is brushed aside.

In narcissistic love the saying that "love is blind" predominates, and "every command of the idolized object, the leader, becomes ipso facto just, lawful, and true," which means that the love object has been put in place of the ego ideal.[30] Freud explains such love-blindness with the "phenomenon of sexual overvaluation", which implies that "the loved object enjoys a certain amount of freedom from criticism, and that all its characteristics are valued more highly than those of people who are not loved".[31]

Trump also enjoys a remarkable amount of freedom from criticism from his followers. No matter what policies he pushes that are against their rational self-interest they continue to defend their love choice. Like a person in love who finds excuses for all the bleak imperfections of her love-choice, Trump supporters are always ready to defend their "great choice", even if their choice contributes to further erode their existence.[32]

The danger of narcissistic love is that the functions of the ego ideal cease to operate and "the criticism exercised by that agency is silent; everything that the object does and asks for is right and blameless. Conscience has no application to anything that is done for the sake of the object; in the blindness of love remorselessness is carried to the pitch of crime....*The object has been put in the place of the ego ideal*".[33] Such blindness of love becomes a problem, when a leader promotes inhumane policies, such as the "Muslim ban" and the erection of a wall along the US-Mexico border, which his followers seem to support without any remorse and "to the pitch of crime".[34]

Here we also encounter the short step from being in love to hypnosis, where one finds "the same humble subjection, the same compliance, the same absence of criticism, towards the hypnotist as towards the loved object".[35] In hypnosis the hypnotist has stepped into the place of the ego ideal, and as such, argues Freud it is "no wonder that the ego takes a perception for real if its reality is vouched for by the mental agency which ordinarily discharges the duty of testing the reality of things".[36]

The phenomenon of Trumpism is akin to a mass hypnosis, where Trump stands for the hypnotist who has stepped in the place of the ego ideal of his supporters. The danger of such a scenario is the full subjection of the followers to the leader and the absence of criticism of him and the policies he enacts. Furthermore, since he replaced the agency that tests reality, it is of no surprise that they (mis)take the reality he describes for them as real, such as that they will be or are already economically better off or "great again", because such reality is vouched for by the mental agency (Trump himself), which has been put, via introjection, in place of their ego ideal.

As the Mitscherlichs point out, Hitler also "fulfilled the idea of greatness for his subjects who had long been crippled by absolutism and, in turn projected his idea of greatness on the "race" which supposedly gave distinction to the German people".[37] Also the American people have long been crippled by neo-liberal capitalism, and Trump's campaign slogan to make America "great again" fulfilled the idea of greatness for his supporters, which is why he was chosen for ego-ideal replacement. The idea of "race" played a further role, since it is the idea of racially inferior people (mostly Muslims and Mexicans) which is openly promoted by Trump, and promotes the idea that the Trump mass itself belongs to a "superior race".[38]

However, as Freud outlines, "we find that behind the tender love there is a concealed hostility in the unconscious".[39] (Freud 1989b: 76). It seems that the concealed hostility against Trump, which is that of class, insofar as he belongs to a hostile class that exploits a working-class that becomes more and more feminized and racialized, but also that of gender and race, insofar as he promotes open hostility toward women and minorities, has also been repressed into the unconscious of his supporters. Psychoanalysis explains the mechanisms of such repression.

"The hostility is then shouted down, as it were, by an excessive intensification of the affection, which is expressed in solicitude and becomes compulsive, because it might otherwise be inadequate to perform its task of keeping the unconscious contrary current of feeling under repression".[40]

Trump supporters also seem to shout down their concealed hostility toward their leader though an intensification of affection, expressed in their heightened idealization of him, which is evident in Trump gatherings, where his followers fiercely express their continuing support for their object-choice, despite his obvious failures as a leader.

However, Trump and his administration also use the psychoanalytic device of *Verschiebung* (displacement) to keep such hostility repressed. In "Elements of Anti-Semitism" Adorno outlines the ways in which displacement played a central role in the specific economic reason of what the early Frankfurt school termed bourgeois anti-Semitism. He points out that "the rights of [wo/]man were designed to promise happiness even to those without power. Because the cheated masses feel that this promise in general remains a lie as long as there are still classes, their anger is aroused".[41]

Here the bourgeois fascists branded Jews as the opposing race and as wanting to have unlimited economic power, so that the masses could *verschieben* (displace) their anger against the bourgeois exploiter upon the Jews which was necessary for the bourgeoisie to conceal domination in production.[42] However, behind the branding of Jews as the opposing race, we find the ultimate target of bourgeois fascism—workers and minorities. The exploiters made sure that it remained concealed from workers and minorities that they are the ultimate target of the bourgeois racist tactics, because the displacement of their anger upon Jews secured their continuing exploitation. Without concealment, workers and minorities could have directed their anger upon the real source of their problems—their bourgeois exploiters.

Today in the United States the working-classes are angry and feel mocked because their promise of happiness remains a lie as long as they are exploited. Here Trump succeeded, by branding Muslims and Mexicans as the opposing race that takes away the jobs of workers, to introduce a new form of bourgeois racism, which allowed the working-class to displace their anger against the class of exploiters—to which Trump and his cabinet belong—onto these branded groups. Also here the ultimate target is the working-class itself, which remains concealed from them.

The branding of Muslims and Mexicans as the opposing class had also an integrating function for Trump supporters. As Freud explains, "the social feeling is based upon the reversal of what was first a hostile feeling into a positively-toned tie in the nature of an identification".[43] Class, gender, and race hostility of Trump supporters might be reduced toward fellow Trump supporters once they identify with each other via their bond to their leader. However, any such "social feeling" that identification between the mass members generates, can easily revert to hostility again, because identification easily reverts into its opposite.[44]

Once the hostility between the group members resurfaces, "aggression is projected 'outward' onto an alien group, be it another nation or a minority. It is actually a significant feature of ecstatic mass movements that within their boundaries aggression disappears, only to reappear in the persecution of scapegoats".[45] Branding Muslims and Mexicans as the opposing class had the double function of keeping the unconscious aggression of Trump followers against their leader, and the aggression among his followers in check, which at the same time keeps the libidinal tie between them intact.

The Trump Festival

To get a deeper understanding why Trump and not another leader was selected for ego-ideal replacement, it is important to understand that "the ego ideal comprises the sum of all the limitations in which the ego has to acquiesce, and for that reason the abrogation of the ideal would necessarily be a magnificent festival for the ego, which might then once again feel satisfied with itself".[46] Trump had and continues to have such an appeal for the people, because he allowed a magnificent festival for millions of frustrated egos, whom he allowed, via abrogating their own ego ideal by replacing it with himself, to feel once again satisfied with themselves.

As Freud further explains the separation between the ego and the ego ideal "cannot be borne for long either, and has to temporarily undone. In all renunciations and limitations imposed upon the ego a periodical infringement of the prohibition is the rule".[47] In festivals the split between the ego and the ego ideal is temporarily undone, and its cheerful character is a result of the release such undoing brings for the ego.

People with narcissistic wounded egos voted for Trump, because he allowed not only a periodical lifting of renunciations as we find it in festivals, but a more extended one (especially when he became president of the United States). His followers choose him as their ego-ideal replacement, and not another candidate, because he presented himself as free from limitations, such as when he claimed during the Republican primary that he could shoot someone and everyone would still vote for him, and his repeated dismissal of any conventions of how to run for president. [48] In a sense Trump himself has abrogated his ego ideal, and by introjecting him it generated an extended festival for his followers.

Insofar as the ego ideal is also "the chief influence in repression", ego-ideal replacement is also central for the success of fascism, insofar as it permitted everyone the freedom to indulge in sadistic impulses.[49] Since Trump followers could replace their ego ideal with that of the leader, the split between the ego and the ego ideal is more undone, which brings a more extended release from the pressures of ego ideal than a festival, and also explains the cheerful character of masses particularly when they gather around their leader at mass rallies.

Freud points out that when we are awake we make use of special artifices to allow what is repressed to circumvent the resistances, "and for receiving it temporarily into our ego to the increase of our pleasure. Jokes and humor, and to some extent the comic in general, may be regarded in this light".[50] It seems that Trump not only generates a festival for his supporters, but also for those who oppose him, which is evident in the never ending jokes about Trump in the press. However, the hope to hope that such jokes awaken those that are blinded by their love for him.

Here it is important to note that Trump succeeded *because* of his openly racist and sexist behavior, not despite it. He also generated a festival for his followers, which allowed him to become the president of the United States, because he lifted the moral restriction of being openly racist, sexist and classist. People, who harbored such hostilities, which they had to repress or at least could not openly voice before Trump's electoral campaign, did not have to repress them anymore and could now openly voice their own hatred toward women and the poor, as well as racial and sexual minorities.[51]

As the Mitscherlichs further explain, all are grateful for the leader, because he allows "inner liberation from stifling, pettifogging restrictions, which gives them wings to do great deeds".[52] Once one is liberated from stifling restrictions (such as not being able to voice sexist, classist and racist slurs) in the Trump festival, one gets "wings to do great deeds" and the narcissistically wounded ego is a story of the past. Here we can see how the feeling to be "great again" is the feeling of being unrestricted like this.

As Freud further points out, "there is always a feeling of triumph when something in the ego coincides with the ego ideal. And the sense of guilt (as well as the sense of inferiority) can also be understood as an expression of tension between ego and the ego ideal".[53] Trump had also an appeal to those who count as "successful" people in neo-liberal capitalist society, because he allowed *everyone* to do away with the tension between the ego and the ego-ideal, and accompanying feelings of guilt for the enjoyment one receives from succumbing to the Trump-mass, where "the individual is brought under conditions which allow [her/] him to throw off the repressions of his unconscious instinctual impulses".[54]

Trump had a particular appeal to the working-classes, because the doing away with the tension between ego and ego ideal also did away with the accompanying sense of inferiority that is the result of the neo-liberal capitalist demand that "they must make it" and if they don't it is their individual fault, and not a result of liberal capitalist structures that produce such scenarios. Trump's triumph is a result of an exploitation of such feelings of inferiority, which he allowed to vanish by making the narcissistic ego coincide with the ego ideal.

Last (but not least), as a reality TV star, Trump was and continues to be particularly successful at creating a festival for the American people. Whereas one could enjoy him on reality TV before, now one can continue to enjoy his acting on TV, in the switched (but connected) role of the president, who makes a fool of himself. You don't even need a show like Saturday Night Live to parody him, he does it himself. In a way the reality show has become real, and from one's isolation in one's private bedroom, with a click of the remote control or a tap on one's iPhone to access Twitter and Facebook, one can enjoy the "great little man" who is the enlargement of one's self, and with that feel connected to millions of other Trump supporters who watch the same spectacle.

Certainly, the task of winning the masses for aims that are contrary to their material interests cannot be accomplished by rational means, but must be oriented psychologically by mobilizing unconscious processes. "This task is facilitated by the frame of mind of all those strata of the population who suffer from senseless frustrations and therefore develop a stunted, irrational mentality. It may well be the secret of fascist propaganda that it simply takes men for what they are: the true children of today's standardized mass culture, largely robbed of autonomy and spontaneity".[55] The standardized mass culture in the United States, whose outgrowth in reality TV and social media Adorno did not predict, also created an irrational mentality, which Trump successfully exploited by mobilizing unconscious processes for his own political aims.

Conclusion

Here the crucial question remains, what can be done that Trumpism, which bears uncanny connections to fascism, does not slide into a repetition of the disaster that fascism brought onto the world stage? Adorno suggests that socialized hypnosis breeds within itself the forces which will do away with "regression through remote control, and in the end awaken those who keep their eyes shut though they are no longer asleep".[56] Although Adorno might be a bit too optimistic here, the hope is that once Trump supporters, particularly those from the exploited classes, become aware that they are still living in poverty, and that they are still exploited as workers or have no jobs at all, despite all of their love object's talk, they will be able to open their eyes (which have never been completely shut) and realize that life is not a festival after all.[57]

They then will also become aware that they are exploited by a system, which is fully maintained by their leader, which will also allow them to find the real object of their anger. At this point the repressed unconscious hatred toward Trump and his cabinet might not be held in check anymore with ever more idolizations of him and projections upon vulnerable minorities, and the Trump supporters will redirect their anger upon their leader and his cabinet, which has lost at this point all credibility for them. Then the Trump followers will step out of the mass, and become individuals with their own rationality again, which has always lurked behind the surface of their blind love. However, as with people who are in love and "fall out of love" because their love object disappoints them, the former Trump supporters will quickly forget their love-object, and make him alone responsible for the mess he created, thereby aiming to forget that it is them who voted him in and supported him, and as such they are also responsible for the disaster we are in now.

NOTES

1. I would like to thank all those that have given me excellent feedback on this chapter, which assisted to greatly strengthen it: Marc Sable, John Abromeit, Matt Stichter, Amy Allen, and Joan Braune.
2. Theodor W. Adorno, "Freudian Theory and the Pattern of Fascist Propaganda," in *The Culture Industry*, ed. Jay Bernstein (London and New York: Routledge, 2002), 150–151.
3. *Logos* 16, no. 1–2 (2017): http://logosjournal.com/.
4. Adorno, "Freudian Theory and the Pattern of Fascist Propaganda," 134.
5. The Mitscherlichs were critical and psychoanalytic theorists who revived psychoanalytic thought for social theory in Germany after World War II.
6. I use Trumpism as shorthand for the rise of Trump.
7. I will refer to "psychological mass" in short just as "mass".
8. Adorno, "Freudian Theory and the Pattern of Fascist Propaganda,"135.

9. Sigmund Freud, *Group Psychology and the Analysis of the Ego*, trans. James Strachey (London and New York: W.W. Norton & Company, 1989a), 29.

10. Freud, *Group Psychology and the Analysis of the Ego*, 29–30.

11. Adorno, "Freudian Theory and the Pattern of Fascist Propaganda," 136–137.

12. Freud, *Group Psychology and the Analysis of the Ego*, 41.

13. Freud, *Group Psychology and the Analysis of the Ego*, 79.

14. However, the ego is not as coherent and stable as we would like it to be, because the unconscious portion exposes the ego "to constant shocks", and in dreams and neuroses this portion asks "for admission at the gates, guarded though they are by resistances" (Freud, *Group Psychology and the Analysis of the Ego*, 80).

15. Whereas Freud uses in his earlier work the notion of the ego ideal, in his later work, where the idea of the super-ego predominates, the ego ideal somewhat disappears or is part of the super-ego. However, it is of no coincidence that the core text which elaborates the psychology of the masses—*Group Psychology and the Ego*—draws on this term, and that psychoanalytic thinkers of the early Frankfurt school kind (such as Adorno and the Mitscherlichs) chiefly refer to this term when elaborating the rise of fascism.

16. See Alexander and Margarete Mitscherlich, *The Inability to Mourn: Principles of Collective Behavior*, trans. B. R. Placzek (New York: Grove Press, 1975), 22–23. To be fair to Adorno, he points out that it is impossible to discuss the very subtle theoretical differentiation in Freud's psychoanalysis, particularly between identification and introjection, and that he contents himself with a few observations on the relevancy of the doctrine of identification to fascist propaganda (Adorno, "Freudian Theory and the Pattern of Fascist Propaganda," 139).

17. Freud, *Group Psychology and the Analysis of the Ego*, 46.

18. Freud, *Group Psychology and the Analysis of the Ego*, 48.

19. Freud, *Group Psychology and the Analysis of the Ego*, 57. For a vivid example of introjection see: http://www.cnn.com/videos/politics/2017/02/18/donald-trump-supporter-gene-huber-intv-nr.cnn.

20. Freud, *Group Psychology and the Analysis of the Ego*, 52. Examples include not using the office for personal enrichment while in office, respecting separation of powers, and all which goes under the header of "acting presidentially." I would like to thank Marc Sable for this insight.

21. 13–14% of the population lives in poverty in the US (43.1 million people); see https://poverty.ucdavis.edu/faq/what-current-poverty-rate-united-states. One of the central reasons for Trump's appeal is the absence of a rigorous critique on capitalism on the left in the United States, which has largely arranged itself with free market capitalism. Trump's "critique" on capitalism, however skewed, helped him earn the vote of the working-classes.

22. I would like to thank Amy Allen for pointing at this puzzle.
23. Freud, *Group Psychology and the Analysis of the Ego*, 79.
24. Adorno, "Freudian Theory and the Pattern of Fascist Propaganda," 141.
25. Adorno, "Freudian Theory and the Pattern of Fascist Propaganda," 141.
26. Adorno, "Freudian Theory and the Pattern of Fascist Propaganda," 142.
27. Freud, *Group Psychology and the Analysis of the Ego*, 56.
28. Adorno, "Freudian Theory and the Pattern of Fascist Propaganda," 140–141.
29. See Andrew Restuccia, Nancy Cook, "Trump's conservative dream team" Politico.com, 11/30/16
30. Mitscherlich, *The Inability to Mourn: Principles of Collective Behavior*, 60.
31. Freud, *Group Psychology and the Analysis of the Ego*, 56.
32. See also https://www.newyorker.com/magazine/2017/07/24/how-trump-is-transforming-rural-america.
33. Freud, *Group Psychology and the Analysis of the Ego*, 57
34. That such politics were so readily accepted is the result of the long history of suppressed racist and sexist currents in the U.S. politics—a suppression that has been lifted by Trump. See my section on the "Trump Festival" for further elaboration.
35. Freud, *Group Psychology and the Analysis of the Ego*, 58.
36. Freud, *Group Psychology and the Analysis of the Ego*, 58–59.
37. Mitscherlich, *The Inability to Mourn: Principles of Collective Behavior*, 27–28.
38. Trump often implicitly signals racism, but tries to explicitly deny it at the same time. For a full explanation of how this works see: Robin Dale Jacobson, *New Nativism Proposition 187 and Immigration Debate.* U. of Minnesota Press, 2008.
39. Sigmund Freud, *Totem and Taboo: Some Points of Agreement between the Mental Lives of Savages and Neurotics,* trans. James Strachey (London and New York: W.W. Norton & Company, 1989b), 76.
40. [1989b] Freud, *Totem and Taboo: Some Points of Agreement between the Mental Lives of Savages and Neurotics,* 62.
41. Max Horkheimer and Theodor W. Adorno, *Dialectic of Enlightenment,* trans. John Cumming (New York: Continuum Press, 2002), 172.
42. Horkheimer and Adorno, *Dialectic of Enlightenment,* 174/1.
43. Freud, *Group Psychology and the Analysis of the Ego*, 67.
44. Freud, *Group Psychology and the Analysis of the Ego*, 47.
45. Mitscherlich, *The Inability to Mourn: Principles of Collective Behavior*, 58.
46. Freud, *Group Psychology and the Analysis of the Ego*, 81.
47. Freud, *Group Psychology and the Analysis of the Ego*, 81.
48. http://www.reuters.com/article/us-usa-election-idUSMTZSAPEC1NFEQLYN.
49. Freud, *Group Psychology and the Analysis of the Ego*, 52.

50. Freud, *Group Psychology and the Analysis of the Ego*, 81.
51. That also women and racial and sexual minorities voted for Trump despite the lifting of such prohibitions can perhaps be explained that they have internalized such hatred in themselves.
52. Mitscherlich, *The Inability to Mourn: Principles of Collective Behavior*, 58.
53. Freud, *Group Psychology and the Analysis of the Ego*, 81.
54. Freud, *Group Psychology and the Analysis of the Ego*, 9.
55. Adorno, "Freudian Theory and the Pattern of Fascist Propaganda," 149–150.
56. Adorno, "Freudian Theory and the Pattern of Fascist Propaganda," 153.
57. Trump's wanting to do away with Obamacare, as an example, helped some Trump followers to wake up

BIBLIOGRAPHY

Abromeit, John. 2016. Critical Theory and the Persistence of Right Wing Populism. *Logos* 15 (2–3) http://logosjournal.com/2016/abromeit/.
———. 2017. Right-Wing Populism and the Limits of Normative Critical Theory. *Logos* 16: 1–2. http://logosjournal.com/2017/right-wing-populism-and-the-limits-of-normative-critical-theory/.
Adorno, Theodor W. 2002. Freudian Theory and the Pattern of Fascist Propaganda. In *The Culture Industry*, ed. Jay Bernstein, 132–157. London/New York: Routledge.
Freud, Sigmund. 1989a. *Group Psychology and the Analysis of the Ego*. Trans. James Strachey. London/New York: W.W. Norton & Company.
———. 1989b. *Totem and Taboo: Some Points of Agreement between the Mental Lives of Savages and Neurotics*. Trans. James Strachey. London/New York: W.W. Norton & Company.
Gandesha, Samir. 2017. The Neoliberal Personality. *Logos* 16 (1). http://logos-journal.com/2017/the-neoliberal-personality/.
Horkheimer, Max and Adorno, Theodor W. 2002. *Dialectic of Enlightenment*. Trans. John Cumming. New York: Continuum Press.
Mitscherlich, Alexander and Mitscherlich, Margarete. 1975. *The Inability to Mourn: Principles of Collective Behavior*. Trans. B. R. Placzek. New York: Grove Press.

CHAPTER 17

Nationalism, Universalism and Nihilism: Trump's Politics in Light of the Strauss-Kojève Debate

Angel Jaramillo Torres

In an article published at the website of *American Greatness* an author, under the *nom de plume* of Publius Decius Mus, argues that the Presidential election of 2016 is a re-edition of Kojève-Strauss debate on tyranny.[1] It is not entirely facetious to suggest that, according to Decius, had Strauss lived today he would have supported the Trump candidacy.

In what follows I will take my bearings from some important comments made by Leo Strauss and Alexandre Kojève during their debate on tyranny that can shed light on Trump's politics. My chief assertion may be briefly stated thus: the disagreement between Kojève and Strauss regarding the universal and homogeneous state may be less important that their agreement regarding the need for civility (and thus civil religion) in politics.

Although Strauss's judgment on Trump will remain forever in the shadows of the unknown, I would disagree with the view that, in their debate on tyranny, Kojève represented globalism and Strauss nationalism.[2] In what follows, I argue that, while Kojève and Strauss regarded the philosophical life as the best life, they engaged in a debate where at stake was consideration of

A. J. Torres (✉)
Universidad Nacional Autónoma de México, Ciudad de México, México

315

the best political regime. I further argue that neither Kojève nor Strauss, as philosophers, hold any allegiance to a particular regime. Taking due distance from conventional opinion, I show that, for Kojève the universal and homogeneous state was meant as a yardstick to judge other regimes. Kojève was agnostic as to the possibility of its realization, and perhaps knew that a world divided into empires was the most likely scenario for the world in the foreseeable future.[3] As for Strauss, while he took issue with Kojève's notion of the universal and homogeneous state, he likewise was not a defender of the modern nation-state, partly because he wanted to see whether political wisdom from the classical ancient Greek philosophy could shed some light on our political conundrums. Thus I advance the idea that Strauss would have not regarded Trump's nationalism as a way out of the dilemmas facing the American polity.

Contra Decius, I think that Strauss saw the main alternative to the philosophic life not in the political life but the ideological life.[4] I hasten to add that on this issue Kojève was in complete agreement with Strauss.[5] Their debate on politics and philosophy conceals a previous agreement on the most important issue, namely, should we live a life devoted to free inquiry, or should we live a life of obedience to an inscrutable God? Because this is not the place to discuss this most important theme, I focus only on the thematic discussion between the two philosophers on the best regime, its relation to the political life, and the tyrannical soul, using the case of Trump as the chief example.[6]

Kojève's "End of History" and Trump as the Last Man

In what follows, I will investigate whether Kojève would have been wholly opposed to Trump's candidacy or whether he might have qualified his position. Regarding the issue of globalism and nationalism, it seems, at first blush, that Kojève would have rejected Trump's nationalistic position. There are, however, suggestive comments made by Kojève that make one suspect that he was at least ambivalent regarding the virtues of globalization.

Although he was born in Russia and was forced to leave the country after the Bolshevik faction dethroned Czar Nicholas II, Kojève was educated in Germany and France. The gist of his political philosophy is contained in his *Introduction à la Lecture de Hegel*, a collection of his lectures on Hegel's *Phenomenologie des Geistes* between 1933 and 1939 that he addressed to young French intellectuals and philosophers, destined to dominate the world of letters in France throughout the twentieth century.[7]

In his interpretation of Hegel, Kojève took his bearings from the fourth chapter, section A of the *Phenomenologie,* where the dialectic of the master and the slave is discussed. According to Kojève, history takes place insofar as the slaves work and engage in great deeds. But history can end when recognition becomes universal and a state of equality of all human beings is guaranteed. The political expression of this situation is what Kojève called the universal and homogeneous state. The fateful consequences of this idea are laid out by Leo Strauss in his polemic with Kojève.

To me the category of the "universal and homogeneous state" is a kind of a regulative idea, or a hypothesis that should be probed and whose status as truth depends on the possibility of the actualization of the end of history, and ultimately on whether Being is historical or eternal.[8] Thus the first thing to point out about Kojève is that he embraced the Socratic vote of ignorance concerning the issue of the possibility of an absolute truth.[9] As a philosopher, Kojève holds no allegiance to any regime, including the universal and homogeneous state.[10]

If human beings are marked by an essential finitude (Unendlichkeit) then the end of history cannot be actualized.[11] The political consequence is the impossibility of constructing a "universal and homogeneous state" and therefore the unavoidability of the closed society. As a Socratic philosopher, Kojève ought to concede his ignorance of whether an actualization of absolute knowledge can occur.

Given the above, one can surmise that Kojève had always in mind the possible actualization of the two main alternatives: historical Being or eternal Being: He was thus open to the possibility that history would *not* end.[12] It thus logically follows that we should imagine Kojève's evaluation of the Trump candidacy in both scenarios: the end of history scenario and the scenario where history does not end or has not ended.[13]

Under the hypothesis that history has not ended, we are not living under conditions of global tyranny, but in a world mastered by empires that share power over the planet.[14] There is no global tyranny, but there are statesmen—some of whom are actual imperial tyrants—in constant competition for hegemony and prestige.[15]

If history has not ended, Trump is neither an animal nor a snob.[16] He would then be a human being who has become the leader of the greatest empire on earth. Geopolitically, Kojève conceived of a new Latin Empire, morally founded on the practice of *la dolce vita,* which would oppose philosophically both the Anglo-American way of life and the Soviet Union's attempt at political domination over the planet.[17] He might have been amused at Trump's naiveté, recklessness, or lack of prudence in believing a rapprochement between the United States and Russia was possible, at the time when Vladimir Putin has chosen the side of the Slavic Orthodox.[18] On the other hand, he might have applauded Trump's shrewdness in brokering a deal with the evangelical movement during the primaries: For Kojève a nation is ultimately defined by a common religion.[19] But, as argued below, this common religion has become secular in the United States.

When we turn from the heights of geopolitics to an examination of the soul we can ask ourselves what kind of man Trump is, according to Kojève. As the elected president of a democratic-liberal commonwealth, Trump is undoubtedly a man with a great deal of authority over a sizable part of the American electorate. On the basis of Kojève's analysis of the authority of the leader in elections, one can assert that, during the campaign, Trump possessed more authority than that which Hillary Clinton was able to have. While the rationale of most Clinton supporters was an anti-Trump sentiment, Trump was able to generate an authentic base among supporters who saw in him the incarnation of a "project".[20]

As for Trump's personal behavior and alleged baseness, Kojève's judgment would have probably been that, while Trump's lack of sexual self-control should not be a reason to reject him, Trump's workaholism and his desire to become a celebrity would render him a slave.[21] In Kojève's judgment, Trump would be closer to the slave than to the master.

Trump belongs to the individualistic world of bourgeois liberalism. In that regard, he is perhaps the ultimate bourgeois who, as such, announces the arrival of the last man at the end of history. For Kojève, Trump's chief concern with wealth, his measuring everything in money, his refusal to pay taxes and contribute to the common good, and his overriding focus on his family life renders him a non-political man. Is his presidential candidacy a way to turn him into a man with political virtue? Kojève clearly distinguished between the private or the family and the public or the state. If we judge by the importance Trump has bestowed upon his family and the centrality it occupied in his campaign, one can understand why in office Trump has contaminated the public sphere with private concerns. Trump represents the invasion of the bourgeois world (animal desire) into the world of political virtue. Being an outcast despised by the Washington political elite, Trump feels the need to govern with a new team and new people who do not have connections with the old regime. Will he keep the Republican elders as advisors or will he get rid of them? According to

Strauss, whereas Hitler orchestrated a putsch against the gentlemen, Xenophon's Hiero allowed them to live peacefully in the city. Strauss's point is not contradicted by Kojève.

What kind of president would Trump be, in Kojève's opinion? Since Trump rules with the support of a Republican Congress, an unchecked Trump would probably try to lead a revolutionary government, one whose aim is, in the words of one of his main advisors, to deconstruct the deep state. Kojève has a reason of his own to suggest that a statesman who acknowledges philosophical origins to his ideas can trigger a rapid reform of government. In his several books and multiple statements, Trump has boasted that he possesses political knowledge even though he does not.[22] From a Kojèvian perspective, there are reasons to believe that Trump's administration will not only generate a realignment of political parties but a new era in American politics. It is still too early to assess whether Trump's overhaul of the government will be successful. At the time of this writing, however, the Trump administration has not yet been able to make Congress pass any significant law, has been attacked by the mainstream media, and has been placed in a defensive position by the investigation of Special Counsel Robert Mueller.

Drawing on Hegel's suggestion made in the *Phenomenologie des Geistes*, Kojève assigned a consequential role to slander in revolutionary politics.[23] Slander is a way of desacralizing the world. For Hegel and Kojève, since the beginning of the Enlightenment, the human spirit destroys what Hobbes called the kingdom of darkness. This necessary step in human history requires terror to destroy the theological world. One can draw a parallel between the way terror, in Kojève's account, undermined the culture of the Middle Ages and the way Trump's systematic slander against his rivals subverts the culture of political correctness in America. This point has not been overlooked by shrewd observers of all political persuasions. One can say that a revolt against the genteel posture of the cultural and political elites was a hallmark of the Trump presidential campaign. The most radical supporters of such a revolt maintain that the politeness of the so-called chattering classes, or what Kojève called "the Republic of Letters," is trapping America in a kind of Weberian iron cage of extreme rationalization.[24] From this standpoint, Trump's significance lies in his being a medium through which American culture can be cured of the ills that trouble it. To many of Trump's advocates, there seems to be a connection between the culture of political correctness, which manifests itself more clearly in university campuses and the media establishment, and the increasing bureaucratization of the

American state. This is what in Europe used to be called *Kulturpessimismus*, an attitude which has been a staple of some quarters of the American Right. Drawing on ideas by James Burnham developed in *The Managerial Revolution* and *The Machiavellians*, the intellectuals supporting Trump have made the point that the United States has entered into an era of what Francis Fukuyama called political decadence.[25] The way out of this dystopia is to regain power for the people against the "managerial elite". According to this view, Trump is the unlikely leader that would energize a sizable part of the people to recover the power that the Constitution guaranteed to them in the first place. It is not necessary to disagree with this view if we agree that the most important question is whether Trump can "deliver the goods," but whether he can become a good leader.

Perhaps rather ironically, Kojève can be of some help here. In the debate on tyranny, Leo Strauss takes issue with Kojève's alleged incapacity to distinguish between good and bad tyranny. This prima facie argument, however, proved to be wrong and Strauss later admitted that, for Kojève, present-day tyranny has satisfied Xenophon's requirements for a good statesmanship.

We do not need to accept Kojève's notion of the end of history to realize that Kojève distinguishes between acceptable statesmanship and unacceptable tyranny. One of the features of an unacceptable tyranny is demagogy. For Kojève, the demagogue is a political man who adapts his conduct to the demands of the worst.[26] The statesman who is a demagogue is neither an "enlightened despot" nor is he a "pedagogical tyrant". The "enlightened despot" and the "pedagogical tyrant" are helpful to the "many" in that they educate them to be better than they are. The Lincoln of the First Inaugural Address would have said that they foster "the better angels of our nature". Whatever the virtues of Trump might be, even his surrogates in the "Republic of Letters" agree that he is not necessarily enlightening his supporters.

When it comes to discussing the scenario where history has ended, then, Trump's rise merely fulfills, secretly but undeniably, Hegel's assertion that history ended in 1806, when Napoleon was victorious in the Battle of Jena. Even though Trump is almost certainly unaware of this, he would be another brick in the wall toward setting up the universal and homogeneous state. Some of his supporters see in him a symbol of the kind of nihilistic revolt, spelled out by Strauss in his debate with Kojève, against this "darkening of the world". Trump would be the charismatic leader who will destroy the "iron cage" of the administrative state and liberate the people from their chains.

But if we are truly living at the end of history, Trump cannot be this hero. Kojève is closer to the mark when we consider an important footnote to his *Introduction à la Lecture de Hegel*. In Kojève's interpretation, at the end of history, man would be either an Americanized Japanese or a Japanized American. Either an animal that has become a snob or a snob that has become an animal: a snobbish animal.[27] Is it not true that Trump is a creature of the U.S. media? One can argue that this is the most snobbish section of American society. Just as with Woody Allen's characters in *The Purple Rose of Cairo*, so Donald Trump seems to have escaped from the TV screen and become real, all the while behaving like a Thrasymachus gone berserk.

Leo Strauss and Donald Trump: The Philosopher and the Anti-Politician

Against most commentators, I argue that Strauss did not unqualifiedly support the nation-state in his debate with Kojève. Strauss did support American republicanism, but only insofar as it is a mixed regime embedded within a modern commercial polity: one that remains inferior to the way classical political philosophy understood the mixed regime. Although the United States is afflicted by almost the same modern deficiencies as the universal and homogeneous state, it may be superior because in it there is still a space for liberty. Next I argue that, for Strauss, Trump's moral psychology cannot really be defended—from neither the standpoint of ancient political philosophy, nor from the Bible. Even if Strauss were to acknowledge that the American regime was corrupted, he would have rejected the irrational, Nietzschean solution that some have seen in the rise of Trump. I finish the section by noting that Strauss might have supported the idea of American greatness, but not necessarily in the way Trump conceives it.

Commentaries on the debate on tyranny between Strauss and Kojève tend to come to the conclusion that Leo Strauss took the side of the modern nation-state against the universal and homogeneous state.[28] Strauss, however, distinguishes between a completely open society and a closed society. According to Strauss the advantages and disadvantages of these arrangements were discussed by an array of ancient philosophers, who advised against a fully open society on several grounds.[29] Since the modern nation-state was not yet a historical reality, they only defended one kind of closed society, namely the Greek city-state. In Strauss's presentation, the nation-state may be as deficient a regime as the universal and homogeneous state. Compared to the ancient city-states which were less hostile to human nature, the globalized state and the modern nation-state are equally guilty of degrading humanity. They degrade humanity because both are a result of modern technology. Following Nietzsche on this point, Strauss saw in modern societies and particularly in America the forces of leveling and homogenization. What else is the idea of the American way of life but an attempt at leveling what is diverse?[30]

Politically speaking, for Strauss the distinction between antiquity and modernity is more meaningful than the distinction between open and closed societies. One of the reasons Strauss chose to comment on Xenophon's *Hiero* was because he wanted to compare this ancient philosopher with Machiavelli—the inaugurator of modernity.[31] *On Tyranny* can be read as one of the most thoughtful installments in the history of the quarrel between ancients and moderns. In passing, I would add that this quarrel is less meaningful for Strauss than the investigation of what the philosophical life is. But here we are merely focusing on the discussion of the political.

What divides politically Strauss and Kojève is that the former supports aristocracy as the best possible regime, while the latter advances the universal and homogeneous state as the ideal. As a political thinker, but not as a philosopher, Strauss took the side of aristocracy because he thought it might be more akin to human nature than any other regime. Since Kojève's Hegelian political-anthropological project—which he never finished—was founded on the idea that nature must be jettisoned, one could argue that the right understanding of "nature" is what separates the political projects of both thinkers. Be that as it may, insofar as present-day nation-states are not aristocracies, Strauss would take issue with them.

Those who argue that Strauss would prefer the nation-state to the universal and homogeneous state have a point. Insofar as the present-day international concert of nation-states is a system of closed societies, Strauss would prefer it to the tyrannical global state, which, in his view, would be the most pernicious and total form of closed society. However, his support for the nation-state was qualified. According to Strauss, Machiavelli resorted to patriotism to mitigate "the policy of iron and poison" or what has classically been known as tyranny. As Strauss argues in *Thoughts on Machiavelli*, all nations have their foundation in an original injustice. At their core, all patriotisms are ideologies meant to cover this primeval violence.[32]

Patriotism can be said to be justified if the nature of the regime defended is not completely tyrannical. Although Strauss leaves no doubt that a pure philosopher (cf. Socrates) could have been perfectly happy living even under tyrannical conditions, he points out that a self-respecting gentleman could not possibly live under the yoke of a tyrant.[33] The American republic is a modern incarnation of a mixed regime. But Aristotle and Polybius, to name two ancient political thinkers, never considered the possibility of a mixed regime operating within a large commercial republic. To conciliate these two was work done largely by Montesquieu in his magnum opus *De L'esprit des Lois*. One of the main purposes of the framers of the American constitution was to found a large commercial republic that would also be a liberal regime in which the division of powers could keep tyranny at bay.

But, in his conception of the "mixed regime" Strauss takes his bearings from classical political philosophy. For Strauss, the mixed regime is the "practically best regime" which "is the rule, under of law, of gentlemen". From this idea, one can say that for the "mixed regime" to exist, the rule of law is not enough; the leaders must also be gentlemen.[34] The situation in which America seems to find itself today is of a functional modern mixed regime in which the executive branch is led by a man with a tyrannical soul. Since a large number of political scientists tend to agree that in the United States the Presidency has enlarged at least from the Roosevelt administration in the 30s, a tyrannical person heading the administration poses a danger to the Republic.[35]

Strauss's discussion on Kojève's Hegelian political philosophy touches on a point that puts Trump closer to Kojève. According to Strauss, the morality promoted by the Hegelian Kojève is too lax, since it is a combination of the ancient morality of the masters and the modern slave morality. Strauss held that both the morality of the ancient political philosophers and biblical morality asked for a high degree of self-restraint and set a high standard for moral behavior.[36] Although Trump has not encouraged anyone "to oust from their positions men who do the required work as well as we could" nor has he tried to extend his "authority over all men in order to achieve universal recognition,"[37] his success has nevertheless depended not on the pursuit of excellence or virtue but rather on the cultivation of the lowest passions. He is thus the child of the Machiavellian revolution. As for the biblical standards, leaving aside that his life has certainly not been oriented by the Christian gospel (he is divorced, lies systematically, etc.), he imitates what for Strauss is the cardinal originality of Machiavelli: blasphemy.[38] But in the case of Trump such blasphemy is not directed necessarily against the scriptures but against present-day understanding of decency. Whether an all-attack on decency is necessary at this juncture is a question that remains open. However, as seen below, it's unlikely that Strauss would have thought it necessary.

Trump is the most vivid example of a man in power lacking the slightest sense of self-control. Agreeing with Kojève on this point, Strauss would have viewed Trump as a consummate bourgeois. The philosopher, in Strauss's presentation, cannot help but feel himself intensely pained by diseased or chaotic souls. Had he lived today, it is no overstatement to say that Strauss would have felt contempt for Trump: "we know how ugly or deformed a boaster's soul is; but everyone who thinks that he knows, while he really knows not, is a boaster."[39]

The issue of the tyrannical soul can be spelled out by resorting to a cursory exposition of the discussion about mercenary love and non-mercenary love in *On Tyranny*.[40] Strauss interpreted Xenophon in the *Hiero* as showing that the tyrannical ruler's purpose required disregarding non-mercenary love. Although all politicians take their bearings from non-mercenary love, they tend to conceal their pursuit of pure prestige with a rhetoric which pays lip service to decency. Trump is certainly in a league of his own when it comes to shamelessly revealing his willingness to infringe upon basic rules of decency, in both words and actions.

Strauss would certainly have recognized the tyrannical soul inhabiting Trump. The question is whether he would have seen in him the predatory being who is "dangerous, intemperate, passionate, 'tropical',"[41] and whose time has come to renovate a decadent polity.[42] The slogan "let Trump be Trump" can be read as a plea for unleashing the forces that will upset the status quo preventing America from thriving (at least for his supporters).

The Nietzschean predatory being is at once a cause and an effect of the modern condition. But this kind of tyrant seems to be the opposite of Xenophon's presentation of Cyrus, who has a cold or unerotic nature.[43] In his genealogy of modernity—with its three waves—Strauss argues that the lowering of classical standards has led to the eclipse of reason. It seems that for Strauss's understanding of the modern tyrant, as opposed to the ancient, the issue of the unleashing of irrationality comes to the fore. If Trump is truly the Nietzschean tyrant who will do away with political decay, nothing prevents him from becoming the purveyor of bad tidings. After all, as someone who came of age during the Weimar Republic, Strauss was mindful of the degree that the cure can be worse than the disease.

Strauss, however, would probably have been sympathetic to Trump's 2016 call to action, and his idea of greatness. But for Strauss greatness has to do, on the one hand, with the capacity of a regime to guarantee *libertas philosophandi* and, on the other, with the ability of a political order to foster great political actions.

Despite his endorsement of ancient aristocracy, Strauss wanted his readers and students to learn how the American regime might be defended. He taught that this defense might be successful not because the regime was "American," however understood, but because he saw affinities between modern liberal republics and the Platonic emphasis on freedom of philosophizing.[44] It is on this affinity that the "greatness" of America is founded.

As for the meaning of political actions in human affairs, one of the gravest consequences of the Kojèvian universal and homogeneous state is the impossibility of human beings engaging in great deeds.[45] This capacity for noble great actions still takes place within the horizon of what can be called, paraphrasing Charles de Gaulle, *le monde des patries*.

Although Strauss would not have thought of Trump as a gentleman neither in its ancient nor in its modern definition—he might have supported his idea of opposing globalization because of its destructive consequences for humanity. The survival of ἄνδρες (men) is a political struggle in which Trump, albeit unwittingly, may be one with Strauss.[46] During the primaries, Trump was certainly successful in presenting himself before Republican voters as a man who not only speaks truth to power, but does so in a self-reliant, vigorous manner. To what extent this exercise in manliness was an act of showmanship is a question worth asking in light of Trump's five military deferments during the 1960s. Even if Trump is not himself a paragon of masculinity, his rejection of the universal and homogeneous state might have the consequence of keeping a world of nation-states in a situation where "great deeds" are still possible. If history has ended and the universal and homogeneous state has finally conquered the globe, then meaningful political action is no longer possible.

But Strauss does not forget that the rejection of a globalized planet may be nihilistic in nature—"a negation not enlightened by a positive goal."[47] As was alluded above, many of the shrewdest apologists of Trump have argued that the main significance of his presidency is the "deconstruction" of the "deep state." In light of this fact, it could be argued that the Trump presidency is mainly an exercise in negation. "Make America Great Again" focuses on the past, which is thought of as glorious, but forgets the horizon of the future. Yet jettisoning the future is one of the traits of the nihilist.

If we continue following Strauss's argument against Kojève's notion of the universal and homogeneous state, and use it to make sense of Trumpism, we arrive at a point where Hobbes steps in. According to

Strauss, Hobbes' concept of the fear of violent death as the fundamental passion will still exist in the universal and homogeneous state: "in that state, the risk of violent death is still involved in the struggle for political leadership."[48] But this will be the privilege of "a tiny minority". Strauss asks himself whether "the last refuge of man's humanity is political assassination in the particular sordid form of the palace revolution."[49] So far the United States has been immune to the dynamics of palace revolution. This has been a blessing, and something that has set America apart from most nations. Let's hope that the denouement of the Trump administration does not trigger the temptation of the politics at the end of history

NOTES

1. He says that the election pitted "globalism versus nationalism, immigration "versus particularism, levelling similarity versus genuine diversity, the "universal and homogeneous state" versus a heterogeneous community of separate and distinct nations." "A progressive Smear against Pro-Trump Intellectuals" *American Greatness*, October 17, 2016.

2. The *locus classicus* is Leo Strauss, *On Tyranny*, Corrected and expanded edition, including *The Strauss-Kojève Correspondence*, ed. Victor Gourevitch and Michael S. Roth, (Chicago: University of Chicago Press, 2013). However, the quotations here correspond, in the case of Kojève to *Philosophy, History and Tyranny, Reexamining the Debate between Leo Strauss and Alexandre Kojève*, ed. Timothy W. Burns and Bryan-Paul Frost (Albany: State University of New York Press, 2016). This edition contains an English translation of the second printed version of Kojève's manuscript, as *Tyrannie et Sagesse*, in *De la tyrannie* (Paris: Gallimard, 1954), 215–280. As for Strauss, the quotations are taken from the fall issue, 2008, of *Interpretation* (Henceforth *Interpretation*), which contains an English translation of the more complete French version of Strauss's "Restatement" (29–78).

3. See footnote 15 of this essay.

4. Decius: "For Strauss, the political and philosophic lives are the two highest answers to the fundamental question: How should I live?" *American Greatness*, "A Progressive smear against Pro-Trump Intellectuals", October, 16, 2016. On this point I agree with Heinrich Meier that the main alternatives are the philosophical life or the theological life. Although this point cannot possibly be developed here, I refer the reader to Meier's work for further provocation. See especially *Über das Glück des philosophischen Lebens: Reflexionen zu Rousseaus Rêveries in zwei Büchern*, (München: C.H. Beck, 2011) and Heinrich Meier, *Politische Philosophie un die Herausforderung der Offenbarungsreligion*, (München, C.H. Beck, 2013).

5. Alexandre Kojève, *Introduction à la lecture de Hegel*, (Paris: Gallimard, 1947), 139. Heretofore LHI.
6. According to Kojève contemplation allows us to negate the historically given.
7. Among the attendees of Kojève's courses on Hegel were Raymond Queneau, George Bataille, Maurice Merleau-Ponty, André Breton, Jacques Lacan, Raymond Aron, among others.
8. Whoever has read Kojève's en *guise d'introduction,* to his collection of lectures on Hegel, should not overlook the tentative, hypothetical character of several of his sentences. One important example is the following: "Car si l 'histoire de l'homme est l'histoire de son travail et ce travail n'est historique, social, humain qu'à condition de s'effectuer contre l'instinct ou «l'intérêt immédiat» du travailleur, le travail doit s'effectuer au service d'un autre, et il doit être un travail forcé, stimulé par l'angoisse de la mort". ILH, 30. This sentence leaves open the possibility that the history of man may not be the history of his labor, a hypothesis which would bring Kojève's whole project into a collapse.
9. Ibid. Leo Strauss agrees with Kojève on this point. See his judgment on Friedrich Heinrich Jacobi in *Leo Strauss on Moses Mendelssohn* (Chicago: University of Chicago Press, 2012), 283.
10. Since his youth, Kojève had seen himself as a philosopher in a Socratic fashion. See *Tagebuch eines Philosophen*, Matthes & Seitz Berlin (translated from the Russian into German by Simon Missal), 2015.
11. ILH, 82.
12. ILH, 15–16. The political theologian Carl Schmitt leaves open these two possibilities in *The Concept of the Political*, 53–54.
13. Strauss and Kojève are both against historicism but admit the historical character of human thought. Kojève, *Interpretation*, 7.
14. See the correspondence between Kojève and Schmitt in *Interpretation*, Vol. 29, No. 1 (Fall 2001), 103. The key statement by Kojève is located in the letter Paris, 11/VII 55. In responding to Schmitt's objections to Kojève's assertion that history has ended, Kojève writes: "But—as I have mentioned—a philosopher, and a Hegelian in addition, may not play the prophet."
15. "À l'heure actuelle ce sont ces États-nations qui, irrésistiblement, cèdent peu à peu la place aux formations politiques qui débordent les cadres nationaux et qu'on pourrait désigner par le terme «d' Empires»". "Esquisse d'un doctrine de la politique française" paragraph 10 in *Hommage a Alexandre Kojève: Actes de la «Journée A. Kojève» du 28 janvier 2003* (Paris: Éditions de la Bibliothèque nationale de France, 2007), 86–98.
16. In a note to the second edition of his lectures on Hegel, Kojève, corrects his previous view that the end of history will be tantamount to the

re-animalization of human beings. Having spent some time in Japan, Kojève reached the conclusion that the future of the world belongs to the Japanese culture where the relation between subject and object has become totally formalized. Human beings are snobs. ILH, 436–437.

17. Ibid. Paragraph 25. Kojève refers to the term "dolce farniente".

18. Alexander Dugin, *Putin vs Putin: Vladimir Putin viewed from the Right*, (Budapest: Arktos, 2015). Although Dugin supported Putin's backing of Trump, his work can be read as a meditation of the insurmountable gulf that separates liberal America from Orthodox Slavic civilization.

19. *Extrait*, paragraph 25.

20. Alexandre Kojève, *The Notion of Authority (A brief Presentation)* Edited and introduced by François Terre and translated by Hager Weslati, Verso: 2014. For Kojève, elections do not give authority. On the contrary, someone is elected because he already possesses authority, 80.

21. ILH, 85

22. *The Art of the Deal* can be read in a serious promoting the life of pursuing leadership. In a speech in Mobile, Alabama occurring during his campaign Trump recommends that all politicians read this book to govern better. Trump's book, philosophically speaking, takes its bearings from American pragmatism. Trump, of course, never held any public office before his election.

23. ILH, 136–137.

24. Max Weber, *die Protestantische Ethik und der Geist des Kapitalismus*, Edition Holzinger. Taschenbuch, Berlin, 2016, 197.

25. James Burnham, *The Managerial Revolution*, New York, The John D. Company, Inc., 1941. James Burnham, *The Machiavellians: Defenders of Freedom*, New York, The John Day Company, Inc., 1943. Francis Fukuyama, "American Political Decay or Renewal?" *Foreign Affairs*, July/August, 2016.

26. See Kojève's retort to Strauss in their debate on tyranny.

27. This is Kojève's answer to Strauss's query on whether the universal and homogeneous state is a political framework for the rise of the last man. ILH, "Note de la Seconde Édition," 436–437.

28. See essays on the subject in *Philosophy, History and Tyranny, Reexamining the Debate between Leo Strauss and Alexandre Kojève. Op Cit.*

29. "Classical philosophy created the idea of the universal state. Modern philosophy, which is the secularized form of Christianity, created the idea of the universal and homogeneous state" *Interpretation*, 70.

30. Leo Strauss read carefully the theoreticians of "The Lonely Crowd" such as David Riesman and was aware of the nihilistic and leveling potential of American society. See Leo Strauss, *On Nietzsche's Thus spoke Zarathustra* (Chicago: The University of Chicago Press, 2017), 65.

31. "Hiero comes close to the Prince." *Interpretation*, 39.
32. "Ordinary return to the beginning means return to the terror accompanying the foundation." *Thoughts on Machiavelli*, (Chicago: The University of Chicago Press, 167.
33. *Interpretation*, 47–48.
34. "The full authority under law should therefore be given to men who, thanks to their good upbringing, are capable of "completing" the laws (Memorabilia IV 6.12) or of interpreting them equitably." *Interpretation*, 53.
35. The classic study is Arthur M. Schlesinger, Jr., *The Imperial Presidency* (New York: Houghton Mifflin Company, 1973 [2004])..
36. *Interpretation*, 50.
37. *Interpretation*, Ibid.
38. Leo Strauss, *What Is Political Philosophy* (Chicago: University of Chicago Press. 1959 [1988]), 11.
39. *Interpretation*, 63
40. *Interpretation*, 64.
41. "Note on the Plan of Nietzsche's Beyond Good and Evil" in Laurence Lampert, *Leo Strauss and Nietzsche*, (Chicago: University of Chicago Press, 1996), 197.
42. Francis Fukuyama, Ibid.
43. *Interpretation*, 64.
44. Leo Strauss, *Liberalism Ancient and Modern* (Chicago: The University of Chicago Press, (1968) 1989), 35.
45. *Interpretation*, 72.
46. "There will always be men ανδρες who will revolt against a state which is destructive of humanity or in which there is no longer a possibility of action and of great deeds." *Interpretation*, 73.
47. *Interpretation*, Ibid.
48. *Interpretation*, 74.
49. Ibid.

BIBLIOGRAPHY

Burnham, James. 1941. *The Managerial Revolution*. New York: The John Day Company, Inc.
———. 1943. *The Machiavellians: Defenders of Freedom*. New York: The John Day Company, Inc.
Burns, Timothy W., and Byan-Paul Frost, eds. 2016. *Philosophy, History and Tyranny, Reexamining the Debate Between Leo Strauss and Alexandre Kojève*. Albany: State University of New York Press.
Dugin, Alexander. 2015. *Putin vs Putin: Vladimir Putin Viewed from the Right*. Budapest: Arktos.

Fukuyama, Francis. 2016. American Political Decay or Renewal? *Foreign Affairs*, July/August.

Hommage a Alexandre Kojève: Actes de la «Journée A. Kojève» du 28 janvier 2003. Paris: Éditions de la Bibliothèque nationale de France, 2007.

Kojève, Alexandre. 1947. *Introduction à la lecture de Hegel.* Paris: Gallimard.

———. 2014. *The Notion of Authority (A Brief Presentation).* Edited and introduced by François Terré and translated by Hager Weslati. New York: Verso.

———. 2015. *Tagebuch eines Philosophen.* Trans. Simon Missal. Berlin: Matthes & Seitz.

Lampert, Laurence. 1996. *Leo Strauss and Nietzsche.* Chicago: University of Chicago Press.

Schlesinger, Arthur M., Jr. 1973(2004). *The Imperial Presidency.* New York: Houghton Mifflin Company.

Schmitt, Carl. 1976. *The Concept of the Political.* Trans. George Schwab with comments on Schmitt's Essay by Leo Strauss. New Brunswick: Rutgers University Press.

Strauss, Leo. 1958. *Thoughts on Machiavelli.* Chicago: The University of Chicago Press.

———. 1959. *What Is Political Philosophy?* Chicago: The University of Chicago Press. 1988.

———. 1961. *On Tyranny.* Corrected and expanded edition, including the Strauss-Kojève Correspondence, ed. Victor Gourevitch and Michael S. Roth. Chicago: University of Chicago Press. (2013).

———. 2008. Restatement, (edited by Emmanuel Patard). Interpretation: *A Journal of Political Philosophy*, 36: 1 (Fall), 29–78.

———. 2012. *Leo Strauss on Moses Mendelssohn.* Translated, edited, and with an interpretative essay by Martin D. Yaffe. Chicago: University of Chicago Press.

———. 2017. *On Nietzsche's Thus spoke Zarathustra.* Chicago: The University of Chicago Press.

Trump, Donald (with Tony Schwartz). 1987. *The Art of the Deal.* New York: Ballantine Books.

Weber, Max. 2016. *Die Protestantische Ethik und der Geist des Kapitalismus.* Berlin: Edition Holzinger.

CHAPTER 18

Deleuze's Politics of Faciality: Trump and American Exclusion

Maira Colín García

If we are forced to name a political phenomenon that was not predicted by the wisdom of political science it is certainly the victory of Donald Trump in the 2016 Presidential election. There are endless disquisitions that attempt to explain this electoral result. However, the main reason to write this essay is to reflect on the quality of the discourse that Trump delivers from the most important pulpit of the greatest democracy on the face of the earth.

In his discourse, *America's* president appeals to a social order in which subjects bound to a paradigm are produced, and where individuals must correspond to the American stereotype: middle class men of Caucasian origin, among other characteristics, in which the construction of a normative order exists only for those who belong or are married to that power discourse.

This essay was translated from Spanish by the editors. In some cases, citations are to Spanish language editions; these have been translated from Spanish, rather than from the original English or French. The reader will find English translations of texts by Deleuze, Guattari, Butler and Levinas in the references.

M. C. García (✉)
Universidad Iberoamericana, Mexico City, Mexico

M. B. Sable, A. J. Torres (eds.), *Trump and Political Philosophy*,
https://doi.org/10.1007/978-3-319-74427-8_18

331

In this scenario, minorities are considered threats to that social order. For the America that Trump proposes, the production of residual lives is needed, bodies stripped of legal protection and political representation.

This chapter tries to explain Trump's discourse using a fundamental concept elaborated by Gilles Deleuze and Felix Guattari: faciality. They use faciality to describe a mechanism by dint of which diversity of bodies and experiences is homogenized and normalized. I argue that faciality can be very useful for understanding Trump's America. His discourse and policies can be seen, in the view of Deleuze and Guattari, as producing mentalities and discourses, establishing limits and setting spaces which constitute "real" Americans.

The face that the Trump political regime generates is the most dangerous tool of his administration's technologies of power, since from there they seek to promote subjects even more restricted than those that already exist in the complex, contemporary capitalist society of the United States.

The faciality of this regime has created a racist, discriminatory, heteronormative imaginary, a segregated public space. This face has yet to be deciphered and its possible lines of flight generated. From Deleuze and Guattari's standpoint, Trump's political *performance* must be taken as a possible opening, as a symptom capable of generating ethical repositionings that would lead the American community to genuinely ask about its political order.

In the West, the face is the part of the body that, by antonomasia, represents subjects. The face normalizes us, classifies us, gives an account of who we are. If what we are corresponds to the stereotype, we have the power system on our side, but if not, we will be classified as an object.

I conclude the essay by proposing that the ethics of Emmanuel Levinas can help us to reconsider that the recognition of the other and its differences is precisely what constitutes us; that diversity should be our priority and that Trump's political performance offers a possibility for rescuing this ethical position in the political order.

FACE, TERRITORIALIZATION AND POLITICS

In an interview conducted by Vittorio Machetti, Deleuze and Guattari explain that the fundamental idea on which *The Anti-Oedipus* is based is that the unconscious is a producer, a factory, a kind of mechanism that produces other mechanisms: a desiring machine. The two theorists grant Freud the discovery of the unconscious, but they take issue with the founder of psychoanalysis for having turned it into a bourgeois theater, a space of representation in which it is impossible to realize that desire is produced. For the two theorists the unconscious is akin to what Nietzsche called the will to power or what Spinoza called "active affect." It is a repressive representation of a problem inscribed in the tragedy of Oedipus. From the Oedipus complex a self is constituted that organizes the flows of desire.

Desire is then the very production of desire and that production of desire is designated by the French philosophers "desiring machine." The desiring machine is located in what they call the social machine, which is the economic-political system of production. (This difference occurs only in phenomenological terms because, in reality, the two processes are integrated.)

It is important to note that Deleuze and Guattari are machinists who think that machines, broadly speaking, generate a subjectivity, but not just any kind of subjectivity, rather one in which the visible and the invisible are clearly defined by normalization's parameters in social life.

Now, in this machinic and vitalistic vision of desire it is necessary to consider the role of the body. The body is a surface of immanent inscription, a "surface that allows the inscription of certain symbolic practices."[1] The body is the battlefield, the canvas. Therefore, the body, without a doubt, also has a political dimension.

Deleuze and Guattari took from Antonin Artaud the concept of "a body without organs," which imposes a limit to the desiring machine because it is an organism not formed by that machinery. It is not a body that forms a producing subject, but rather it is the unproductive, a disarticulation of the organism. "A body without organs is made in such a way that it can only be occupied, populated by intensities. Only the intensities pass and circulate."[2]

This body without organs is opposed to the idea of hierarchizing organisms; rather, it aspires to a continuum of intensities. Rather than normalizing and hierarchizing organisms, of qualifying and quantifying the bodies, through the continuum of intensities the body is allowed to be perceived from intensive capacity. "A body is understood by its power to affect and be affected."[3]

In a body without organs there is no longer just representation (as one lives within the oedipal psychoanalytic construction, to use an example) there is no longer a Self that hierarchizes the organs that make up the bodies, but the body without organs is experienced in and from its intensive power.

We then have desire, desiring machines (which are linked with social machines) and Bodies without Organs. From there, our two French theorists provide a revisionist history of capitalism. The central theme of *The*

Anti-Oedipus is desire as production, and the purpose of it is to demonstrate that there is no system that codes and decodes desire as the political-economic order. So we enter the explanation of the three stages of the capitalistic social machine: of savages, barbarians and the civilized.

It is this archeology that allows them, some years later, to describe in the text included in the book *A Thousand Plateaus*, and that has the title Year Zero-Faciality, the relationship between the different conceptions of body and head, and the different modes of production of subjectivity in the different stages of capitalism: "The face constructs the wall that the signifier needs to rebound, constitutes the wall of the signifier, the frame or the screen. The face tills the hole that the subjectification needs to manifest itself."[4]

The face is the most important signifier of the West. It is what gives identity, what singles out. That face does not only determine the head, but extends to the whole body and its artifacts, and to everyday objects, to clothing, to the place of origin. Undoubtedly, the face is the device by which the whole body will signify.

The modes of production of the face then depend on the so-called *abstract machine of faciality*, that is, the device that generates the face, which works in two dimensions. The first dimension considers what we might call a face of reference, that is, the primary descriptions of what we call a face: Someone is a man or a woman, rich or poor, is Asian or Caucasian, et cetera. "A child, a woman, a family mother, a man, a father, a boss, a teacher, a police officer, or they speak a language in general, they speak a language whose significant features fit specific facial features."[5]

With that face of reference a selection of the supposed individualities is carried out which, when being normalized, produce what the device classifies as desirable. In that sense, individuals do not have a face, but it is the face that has them.

Now, *the abstract machinery of faciality* produces normalization, but it also breeds outcasts—it classifies them—it rejects inadequate faces, those that do not correspond to the agency of power. Thus, a social production of the face occurs which holds sway over bodies, organizes them and codifies them to produce images of that normalization. The face is thus born as a control mechanism that ensures a specific social production.

Recall that subjectivity in Deleuze is constituted through machinic processes. It is then from the power that the abstract machinery of faciality generates a subjectivity that we call the head (a feature that renders us individuals) and turns it into a face (a feature that renders us homogeneous). In this mutation, the head is deterritorialized from the body, that is, it literally abandons the territory of the body, crystallizes as a face (regulated and classified) and disregards the body's power of becoming. In Deleuze and Guattari, the body is not a receptacle of secondary importance—as Descartes enunciated—but that active power of variable intensities which allows the production of multiple experiences.

When the head becomes a face, this possibility of polyphonic production is lost: "The face is only produced when the head ceases to be part of the body, when it ceases to be encoded by the body, when it ceases to have a multidimensional polyvoid body code—when the body, including the head, is decoded and must be over-coded by something we will call face."[6]

The face is a configuration of meaning, a projection on discourse of what must be established by the dictatorship of significance. "The face constructs the wall onto which the signifier needs to rebound; it constitutes the signifier's wall, frame or screen. The face bores the hole that subjectification needs to manifest; it constitutes the black hole of subjectivity."[7]

Out of the three different states of faciality's abstract machinery, the one that Deleuze and Guattari call the Christ-face achieves the definitive separation of the head and the body. This is where the head becomes the most important part of the dissected Western body, and it is at this point that the face becomes the center of the body's grammar, in an overflow of affections that dislocates the possibility of the lines of flight in pursuit of a supposed identity: the identity of Western man.

The device of the Christ-face is the one that defines how a Caucasian Western man should look, that is, the subject of enunciation. In this regard, a normal man should resemble that Christianized face; that face pre-exists any individuality as well as any evidence that the face cannot and should not be universal, even though from the West we aspire to it.

Thus, deviations from this normality constitute an Other that threatens the order established by that technology of power. "If the face is in fact Christ, in other words, your average ordinary White Man, then the first deviances, the first divergence-types, are racial: yellow man, black man, men in the second or third category."[8]

The faces constituted are thus dictated by Trump in his speeches and actions and represent an identity scheme from which ideological attacks have as their main functions, to hierarchize and then exclude.

Trump and the Face of Exclusion

The right to which the new U.S. president belongs to positions itself with a face that demands the negation of the other. It justifies discrimination based on skin color and sexual orientation; it extols nationalism at the expense of migrants; it fosters the supremacy of those bodies it reads as male over those of women. That is to say, there is a production of subjectivity that annuls and discards those who do not conform to the face of the Great America that Trump promises. As Deleuze argues, "Or take the face: we think faces have to be made, and not all societies make faces, but some need to. In what situations does this happen, and why?"[9]

A construction of a normative order exists in which a single face is established, a correct face able to build the desired social body. That discourse of power and its repetition (in speech and acts) attempts to mold subjects who, moreover, do not realize (or believe they do not realize) this process of subjection. There is, of course, a biopolitics that delimits canons and normalities and that uses the different performativities of the body in order to justify ideological discourses and political positions.

> When people in a society desire repression, for others and for themselves, when there are people who like to harrass others, and who have the opportunity to do so, the "right" to do so, this exhibits the problem of a deep connection between libidinal desire and the social field.[10]

The faciality model that that the Trump government established completely represents its political proposals, the country-face that it wants to exalt, that face which embodies "America's" values.

The face that emerges from the Trump government has a correlate: American society cannot stop peering into that portion of the population that gave Trump victory. Faciality reflects the landscape it faces and the landscape needs a face that completes it, that transforms it into a signifier, into a reflective surface that relates and normalizes the supposed individuality of those who exist in the community.

The face's effectiveness lies in the fact that the signifier takes the character of truth: The face never deceives because its function is that it is seen—and who better than the State to show it, distribute it, order it? The face, as Deleuze and Guattari point out, is political.

> Never does the face assume a prior signifier or subject. The order is totally different: despotic and authoritarian concrete assemblage of power ➤ triggering of the abstract machine of faciality, white wall/black hole ➤

installation of the new semiotic of significance and subjectification on that holey surface. That is why we have been addressing just two problems exclusively: the relation of the face to the abstract machine that produces it, and the relation of the face to the assemblages of power that require that social production. The face is a politics.[11]

The dangerousness of the policy of faciality exercised by a government is that, in order not to make its power obvious, it participates in different discourses that have to be seen in everyday life as completely readable. So not only is there a promise to build a wall that strictly divides the border between Mexico and the United States, but there is talk of returning to a great America where consumer goods were mostly produced within American territory. It is broadcasted in all the news channels of the world how aid to Puerto Rico in the face of a natural disaster is not the same as in the case of the victims in the South after Hurricane Harvey. Likewise it tries to deny a symbolic institutional place to the figure of the first lady.

Subjectivity is a *performance*: The subject produces, again and again, a generic identity and, very importantly, a corporeal identity. The discourses of power and their repetition (in speech and acts) are capable of shaping that generic identity and, therefore, determine bodies and individuals.

The subject suffused by faciality hardly accounts for this process of subjugation, of what power discourses and their repetition do to him, and considers himself strong, sure of himself, aware of a will to power and his desires. The greatest enabler of the shaping of the subject is language.

While we all submit to the act of being defined, the process of facing undertaken by the Trump government is mediated, in large part, by violence, and that violence has, as one of its main mechanisms, language. (Think of Trump's statements on the NFL where he uses words and concepts that denigrate the players, or of speeches in which he discredits NAFTA's advantages to his country, or of the gestures he projects when Muslim countries are spoken of).

It is under *the abstract machinery of faciality* that a government like that of Trump produces, as Judith Butler argues, residual lives, abject faces that do not qualify to be protected economically, socially and legally by the State. Vulnerability is not homogenous for everyone: "Certain lives are highly protected...Other lives do not enjoy such immediate and furious support, and they will not even qualify as 'worthwhile' lives."[12]

Butler asks "what is it that constitutes the human, the properly human life, and what is not?"[13] Donald Trump believes he has certainty about what a face is and what that category excludes; he believes he summarizes in his actions, decisions and discourse the identity of the American people.

What Trump's speech fails to consider is that we are practically unable to account for ourselves if it is not through alterity. We are an incomplete, discontinued narrative. We live in an environment where recognition of otherness is impossible, ergo, there is no possibility of recognizing oneself. We are immersed in the always unfinished process of subjection. In Butler's terms:

> The encounter with another generates a transformation of the self from which there is no return. In the course of this exchange it is recognized that the self is the type of being in which permanence within itself proves impossible. One is forced to conduct oneself outside himself. One proves that the only way to be known is through a mediation that occurs outside oneself, which is external, by virtue of a convention or a rule that one has not done and in which one cannot be discerned as an author or signer of one's own construction.[14]

The constitution of a self is very weak. What is believed to be the self is subordinated to social norms that precede us and to the other that affects us.

> I do not arrive in the world separate from a set of norms that are lying in wait for me, even as a pure potential, prior to my first wail. So norms, conventions, institutional forms of power, are already acting prior to any action I may undertake, prior to being an "I" who thinks of itself from time to time as the seat or source of its own action.[15]
>
> ..."I am already affected before I can say 'I' and that I have to be affected to say 'I' at all."[16]

It is fundamental that in the pursuit of otherness—that is, of the construction of the subjectivities of the other and of oneself—that faciality be suspended. Mechanisms must be considered that unfacialize bodies, that reject the signifier of what Trump has wanted to sell as the only America that is worthwhile. These mechanisms allow for processes of subjectivation and identity that demarcate or attempt to denounce the despotic individuation of a regime like the one that today governs the United States.

Undoing the Face: Ethics and Politics in the Trump Era

As Marina Garcés points out, the political is not the institutions or social processes to which political science scholars appeal, rather the political is:

...an exceptional and discontinuous event...like a creation or a suspension, like a radical novelty or a dissent, the political—word or action—is conceived as a cut or a detour, as something irreducibly *other* in relation to the modes of work that takes place in the social sphere.[17]

It is also from this area that we can articulate ethics. Ethics is an event that breaks the process of subjectivity, breaks the solipsism of the modern self and supports care for the other, because it is from that otherness that one has the possibility of existence.

For Levinas (who also conducts an analysis of the face completely different from that articulated by Deleuze and Guattari), ethics is a relationship with the other that cannot be conducted in a premeditated way, as a disinterested metaphysics. There is an overflow of the meaning of the other, which allows one to understand the reception of the other regardless of what is looked at, its objectification, the reply and the discourse. "From the moment the other looks at me, I am responsible for him without even having to take responsibility in relation to him; Your responsibility concerns me. It is a responsibility that goes beyond what I do."[18]

The process of faciality implies the political and, according to Deleuze and Guattari, "until man has a destiny, that would be to escape the face, to undo the face and facializations."[19] We must escape the logic of faciality, the production of identifications. It is a priority to develop rebellious meanings in order to escape the signifier and subjectivation. It is a priority to deterritorialize what technologies of power have done with bodies and with the configuration of faces.

In this regard, what Deleuze and Guattari are seeking is a gaze that de-subjectivizes, that fractures meaning and lets the immanence of bodies flow, a gaze of heads. This structures must be dismantled and new forms of enunciation explored. An ungrammatical subject is looked for that, in its singularity, enunciates events more than subjective traits, that recognizes the powers in its body and in the body of the others—the multiplicities that make up what we usually call identity, marginal becomings. "If the face is a politics, undoing the face is also another politics, which leads to real futures, every one a clandestine future."[20]

In their proposal Deleuze and Guattari have come up with the figure of forager heads, which are those heads that disassemble the face; heads that return to be part of bodies; heads that are, again, part of the immanent power that Deleuze and Guattari affirm there is in a body.

340   M. C. GARCÍA

Forager heads are part of those bodies without organs that constitute a possibility to break forms of representation, to refer to flows, to the ungrammatical, to what is normalized: "Immanence is not related to any Object as a unit superior to everything or with a Subject as an act that works the synthesis of things: we can speak of a plane of immanence when immanence is not immanence of anything other than itself."[21]

Deleuze forces us to think in a different way, to trace the archeology of the biopolitical features that today constitute many discourses of current governments. His efforts nominate the possibilities of lines of flight and of interstices with organic references, so that we do not forget the devices of power that are exercised over individuals who believe they are determined subjects.

Before this scenario we must always appeal to a constant plan of flight. We must flee the pressures that force us to define what a body is, how it is identified and what body fits within the parameter of normality.

Americans must free themselves from the traits of faciality represented by Donald Trump. Many political scientists have tried to explain this through phenomena such as "authoritarianism," which leave us with the argument that the population's predispositions and ideological thinking gave victory to Trump and thus this is a spectrum of the population which needs to be studied.

Deleuze and Guattari bet on a *continuum* in the process of faciality. Any other movement that appeals to a principle and an end would not only be a Byzantine exercise, but absolutely dangerous: "[A]ny detranslation (that is, any dismantling of a device) that is too brutal runs the risk of being suicidal, or cancerous, that is, or else, it opens up to chaos, emptiness and destruction, or it closes the strata on us again, hardening even more, and even losing its degree of diversity, differentiation and mobility."[22]

Today, American society fits this description very well: "Contemporary history is increasingly being dominated by an expansion in claims of subjective singularity: linguistic contests, autonomist claims, nationalistic, national issues that, with total ambiguity, express an aspiration to national liberation, but on the other hand that are manifested in what I would call conservative reterritorializations of subjectivity."[23]

Undoing this face does not imply ignoring it but turning it into something else, combining it with other forces. Discontinuity, rupture, multiplicity. What Trump offers to the inhabitants of his country is the possibility of breaking the prison of organic, discursive stratifications that are a product of the processes of individuation and subjectivity in order to give way to an intensive body that is extensively related with other bodies.

Defacing the machinery of faciality makes room for an open and thus infinite self, in perpetual construction, and it discards the cartographies of the face and body to which we have been subjected. It goes beyond the pathological subjectivity that political regimes such as Trump's try to establish in order to make room for lines of flight that account for the vertigo that means recognizing themselves and recognizing that the other exist with which we will always be interacting and, therefore, it is a nonsense to cancel it.

Notes

1. Claudia Tornini Kruse, "Etica, estética y cosmética del cuerpo: la escritura de Diamela Eltit" (master's thesis, Universidad de Chile, Facultad de Filosofía y Humanidades, Departamento de Literatura, 2012), 2.
2. Gilles Deleuze and Félix Guattari, *El Anti-Edipo: Capitalismo y esquizofrenia*. (Barcelona: Paidós, 2015), 158.
3. Gilles Deleuze, *Spinoza: Practical Philosophy* (San Francisco: City Light Books, 1988), 124.
4. Gilles Deleuze and Félix Guattari, *Mil mesetas* (Valencia, Spain: Pre-textos, 2015), 176.
5. Deleuze and Guattari, *Mil Mesetas*, 174.
6. Deleuze and Guattari, *Mil Mesetas*, 176.
7. *Deleuze and Guattari, Mil Mesetas*, 174.
8. Deleuze and Felix Guattari. *A Thousand Plateaus: Capitalism and Schizophrenia*, (Minneapolis: University of Minnesota Press, 2005), 178.
9. Deleuze. *Negotiations 1972–1990* (New York: Columbia University Press, 1990), 26.
10. Deleuze. *Desert Island and other texts 1953–1974* (Los Angeles: Semiotext(e), 1995), 263.
11. Deleuze and Guattari. *A Thousand Plateaus*, 181.
12. Butler. *Vida precaria: el poder de la violencia y el duelo* (Buenos Aires, Paidós, 2006), 58.
13. Butler, *Vida precaria*, 35.
14. Butler, *Dar cuenta de sí mismo: violencia ética y responsabilidad,* (Buenos Aires: Amorrortu, 2009), 45.
15. Judith Butler, *Senses of the Subject* (New York: Fordham University Press, 2015), 6.
16. Butler, *Senses of the Subject*, 2.
17. Marina Garcés, *Un mundo común* (España: Bellaterra, 2013), 40.

342   M. C. GARCÍA

18. Emmanuel Levinas, *Totalidad e infinito* (Argentina, Amorrortu, 2009), 207.
19. Deleuze and Guattari, *Mil Mesetas*, 176.
20. Deleuze and Guattari, *Mil Mesetas*, 192.
21. Deleuze and Guattari, *Mil Mesetas*, 37.
22. Deleuze and Guattari, *Mil Mesetas*, 683.
23. Felix Guattari, *Caosmosis* (Buenos Aires, Manantial, 2002), 13.

BIBLIOGRAPHY

Butler, Judith. 1991. Contingent Foundations: Feminism and the Question of 'Postmodernism', *Praxis International* 11 (2): 150–165.

———. 2005. *Giving an Account of Oneself.* New York: Fordham University Press.

———. 2006a. *Precarious Life: The Powers of Mourning and Violence.* New York: Verso. http://www.wkv-stuttgart.de/uploads/media/butler-judith-precarious-life.pdf.

———. 2006b. *Vida precaria: el poder de la violencia y el duelo.* Buenos Aires: Paidós.

———. 2009. *Dar cuenta de sí mismo: violencia ética y responsabilidad.* Buenos Aires: Amorrortu.

Deleuze, Gilles. 1996. *Conversaciones (Spanish Edition).* Valencia: Pre-Textos.

———. 2004. *Desert Islands and Other Texts, 1953–1974.* Semiotext(e) Foreign Agents Series. Los Angeles: Semiotext(e).

———. 2005a. *La isla desierta y otros textos.* Valencia: Pre-textos.

———. 2005b. *Pure Immanence: Essays on a Life.* 2nd ed. Cambridge, MA: Zone Books.

———. 2007. La inmanencia, una vida…. In *Ensayos Sobre Biopolítica: Excesos de Vida,* ed. Giorgi, Gabriel, and Fermín Rodríguez. *Espacios Del Saber.* 1a. vol. 67. Buenos Aires: Paidós.

Deleuze, Gilles and Félix Guattari. 1983. *Anti-Oedipus: Capitalism and Schizophrenia.* Trans. Robert Hurley, Seem Mark, and Helen R. Lane and Preface by Michel Foucault. Minneapolis: University of Minnesota Press.

Deleuze, Gilles, and Félix Guattari. 1987. *A Thousand Plateaus: Capitalism and Schizophrenia.* Minneapolis: University of Minnesota Press.

———. 2015a. *El Anti Edipo. Capitalismo y esquizofrenia.* Barcelona: Paidós.

———. 2015b. *Mil Mesetas.* Valencia: Pre-textos.

Garcés, Marina. 2013. *Un mundo común.* España: Bellaterra.

Guattari, Félix. 1995. *Chaosmosis: An Ethico-Aesthetic Paradigm.* Bloomington: Indiana University Press.

Guattari, Felix. 2002. *Caosmosis.* Buenos Aires: Manantial.

Levinas, Emmanuel. 1974. *Humanismo del otro hombre.* México: Siglo XXI Editores.

———. 1980. *Totality and Infinity: An Essay on Exteriority.* Hingham: Springer.

————. 2005. *Humanism of the Other*. Reprint ed. Urbana: University of Illinois Press.

————. 2009. *Totalidad e infinito*. Argentina: Amorrortu.

Tornini Kruse, Claudia. 2012. Etica, estética y cosmética del cuerpo: la escritura de Diamela Eltit. Master's thesis, Universidad de Chile, Facultad de Filosofía y Humanidades, Departamento de Literatura, http://repositorio.uchile.cl/bitstream/handle/2250/111487/Tornini%20Claudia.pdf?sequence=1.

INDEX[1]

---

[1] Note: Page numbers followed by 'n' refer to notes.

Alt-right, 11, 12, 117, 194, 195,
　199–205, 207–210
　See also Never Trump; Trumpism
Ambitions, 12, 50, 74, 75, 79, 95,
　103, 110, 239, 247, 251
　compare to greatness, 110
America, 2, 17–18, 25, 43, 53–54, 61,
　73–83, 117, 131, 160, 177, 193,
　199–204, 215–231, 237, 258,
　282, 297, 300, 316, 331
American Civil War, *see* Civil War
American Founding, *see* Founding
Anger, 7, 12, 10, 51, 52, 55, 89,
　131–134, 136, 139, 140, 142,
　143, 146, 148n6, 165, 180, 194,
　248, 263, 264, 269, 270, 282,
　299, 306, 310
　See also Contempt; *Ressentiment*
Anglo-Americans, 239, 240, 249,
　298, 317
Anton, Michael (Publius Decius Mus),
　77, 86n11
Appearances, 43, 78, 243
Apprentice, The, 238
Aquinas, St. Thomas, 3, 4, 61, 66,
　68, 70
Aristocracy, 45, 52, 138, 322, 325
Aristotle, 3, 4, 9, 19, 25–40, 44, 45,
　63, 64, 66–70, 85n7, 93, 115,
　179, 323
　Nicomachean Ethics, 28, 30, 64,
　　66, 70
　Politics, 3, 25, 85n7
Arrogance, 32, 51
　compare to ambition humility, 12
　See also Ambitions; Pride
Assassinations, 55, 326
Assimilation, 240
Athens, 44
Atlantic Monthly, 148n6
Authority, 5, 6, 31, 48, 65, 75, 79,
　107, 108, 114–116, 119, 121,

　122, 184, 188, 203, 210, 261,
　262, 267, 289–294, 295n7, 303,
　318, 323, 328n20, 329n34
　of the father, 6, 289–291
　of the judge, 6, 290–292, 295n7
　of the leader, 290, 291, 295n7, 318
　　(*see also* Legitimacy)
　of the master, 289, 290, 292
　　(*see also* Tyranny; Slavery)
　See also Legitimacy
Axis (World War II), 201

B

Baby boomer generation,
　193, 199, 200
Bankruptcy, 20n2
Bannon, Stephen, 12, 62, 195–197,
　199–204, 208, 209, 210n1,
　210n2, 246
Battleground states, 216, 219, 220
Bazelon, Emily, 54, 55, 58n34, 58n36
Best regime, 316, 323
Beyond Good and Evil
　(Nietzsche), 275n5
Birtherism, 131
Blacks, *see* African-Americans
Blasphemy, 323
Blue America, 117, 160, 161,
　172, 282
　See also Democratic Party
Border wall, 133
Bourgeois, 6, 289, 291–293, 306,
　318, 324, 332
　compare middle class, 306
Bullshit
　compare to demagogy, 12, 38, 40,
　　210, 320
　compare to nihilism, 11, 139,
　　210, 261
　compare to sophistry, 196
Buon Senso, see Common sense

Made in the USA
San Bernardino, CA
24 August 2019